THE ROLE OF THE MODERN CORPORATION
IN A FREE SOCIETY

SOUNDINGS

A Series of Books on Ethics, Economics, and Business

THOMAS DONALDSON, EDITOR

THE ROLE
OF THE MODERN CORPORATION
IN A FREE SOCIETY

by
JOHN R. DANLEY

University of Notre Dame Press
Notre Dame   London

Library of Congress Cataloging-in-Publication Data

Danley, John R., 1948–
    The role of the modern corporation in a free society /
    by John R. Danley.
        p.   cm. — (Soundings ; v.)
    Includes bibliographical references and index.
    ISBN 0-268-01647-X
    1. Social responsibility of business.   2. Business ethics.
3. Corporations—Philosophy.   4. Corporations—Moral
and ethical aspects.   I. Title.   II. Series: Soundings
(Notre Dame, Ind.) ; v.
    HD60.D26   1994
    658.4′08—dc20   93-2103
                                                                        CIP

∞ The paper used in this publication meets the minimum requirements
of the American National Standard for Information Sciences—Permanence of Paper
for Printed Library Materials, ANSI Z39.48-1984.

To
MARGARET

La richesse en elle-meme n'est autre chose que la nourriture, les commodites et les agrements de la vie.

Cantillion, *Essai*

Every man is rich or poor according to the degree in which he can afford to enjoy the necessaries, conveniences, and amusements of human life.

Adam Smith, *The Wealth of Nations* (quoting Cantillon)

Contents

Preface   xiii

1. Introduction   1

   THE NATURE OF THE QUESTION   5
   IDEOLOGIES/BUSINESS PHILOSOPHIES   11
   THE "IS/OUGHT" CONFUSION   21
   PLAN OF THE STUDY   24

2. Classical Liberalism   27

   MINIMAL GOVERNMENT AND LAISSEZ-FAIRE   31
   POLITICAL ECONOMY AND MORAL THEORY   40

3. Natural Rights and Social Contracts   41

   NATURAL RIGHTS THEORY   43
   PROBLEMS   47
   THE "SOCIAL CONTRACT"   51
   ACTUAL CONTRACTS   54
   TACIT CONTRACTS   56
   HYPOTHETICAL CONTRACTS   59
   THE CORPORATION AND THE SOCIAL COMPACT   69

4. Classical Liberalism and Utilitarianism: Friedman   75

   POLESTAR: AN INITIAL FORMULATION   80
   POLESTAR AND RULE UTILITARIANISM   86
   THE IDEAL AND THE ACTUAL   93

CONVENTIONAL RULE UTILITARIANISM   98
IDEAL RULE UTILITARIANISM   104
FRIEDMAN'S POSITION   105

5. Evaluating the Utilitarian Defense of Classical
   Liberalism   107

   THE INADEQUACY OF UTILITARIANISM AS A
     THEORY OF OBLIGATION   110
   ORDINAL MEASURES OF UTILITY   114
   COLLECTIVE CHOICE PROCEDURES:
     THE IMPOSSIBILITY THEOREM   117
   PARETIAN NOTIONS   120
   FURTHER LIMITATIONS   123
   CONCLUSION   126

6. Freedom and Well-Being in the Liberal Tradition   127

   UTILITY AND PURPLE BALLOONS   130
   ADAM SMITH   131
   UTILITY AND WELL-BEING   135

7. Micro-Managerialism   141

   REVISIONIST LIBERALISM AND MANAGERIALISM   146
   THE BIG CHANGE/THE NEW AGE   154
   THE MANAGERIAL REVOLUTION   163
   MANAGERIAL PROFESSIONALISM   170

8. Evaluating Micro-Managerialism   179

   DESCRIPTIVE THESIS OF SOCIAL RESPONSIBILITY   179
   MORAL ARGUMENTS FOR SOCIAL RESPONSIBILITY   186
   MANAGERIAL DISCRETION   198

9. Macro-Managerialism   209

   SOCIAL RESPONSIBILITY: THE COMMITTEE ON
     ECONOMIC DEVELOPMENT   210
   KEYNESIANISM   222
   OLIGOPOLY, MONOPOLY, AND EXTERNALITIES   230

10. The Meaning of Corporate Responsibility in a Pluralist
Framework 235

DESCRIPTIVE PLURALISM 236
PRESCRIPTIVE PLURALISM 248
MANAGERIALISM AND PRESCRIPTIVE PLURALISM 256
CONCLUSION 266

11. Liberalism and the Corporation: The Challenge of
the Global Market 267

GLOBAL COMPETITIVE MARKETS AND THE
TRANSNATIONAL CORPORATION 271

Notes 289
Bibliography 325
Index 337

Preface

Circumstances coaxed me into the area of Business Ethics and Business and Society. In 1977–78, under some pressure from the accrediting body, the School of Business at Southern Illinois University at Edwardsburg approached our Department of Philosophy to develop a course in Business Ethics. As junior member with a background in contemporary political philosophy, it fell to me to "volunteer" for this odious task, and to begin to work with "them."

That auspicious beginning has proved a remarkable opportunity. New teaching and research interests seemed to emerge naturally. New relationships with colleagues in economics, management, accounting, and the other disciplines of the School of Business flourished. Among the faculty there I found a zealous commitment to liberal arts and humanities. I even found myself deeply and willingly involved in curriculum revision in the School of Business. As a consequence of those curricular modifications, I have the luxury of being involved in one of the interdisciplinary teams of business and liberal arts faculty (philosophy, history, political science) responsible for two innovative central core courses there.   This study is also the result of those experiences and interactions. The list of those to whom I owe a debt of gratitude is long and I can mention only those who have had the most direct relationship to this project. I am extremely grateful for the support from Southern Illinois University at Edwardsville, the Graduate School at SIUE, the School of Humanities, and the Department of Philosophical Studies. Tom Paxson, Carol Keene, Galen Pletcher, Don Elliott, Don Strickland, Norm Nordhauser, Marsha Puro, Don

McCabe, John Virgo, and George Sullivan have all provided generous encouragement and help.

I want to especially acknowledge Tom Donaldson's contribution. Without Tom's persistent faith in this project, and his gentle persuasion, the work would never have been completed. His confidence overcame my occasional self-doubts.

The staff at University of Notre Dame Press is exceptional. Jeannette Morgenroth, my editor, has been extremely helpful; she deserves special thanks.

Finally, I want to express appreciation to my wife, Margaret, who, though busy with her own career, often extended direct assistance and always contributed to a climate of support and encouragement.

The shortcomings and weaknesses, many of which I am painfully aware, are, of course, my responsibility.

1

Introduction

As Edward S. Herman notes, in the opening lines of *Corporate Control, Corporate Power*, a "central feature of economic development in the past century has been the rise of the large corporation, both nationally and internationally, to a strategically important position."[1] Not surprisingly, this emerging corporate presence has evoked an intense and wide-ranging controversy. By the close of the nineteenth century, populists and progressives, echoing deeply rooted American cultural and political sentiments against bigness and the concentration of economic power, were already railing against the ascendancy of the large corporation, the growing industrial and financial concentration, and the resultant political and economic dislocations. With only brief lulls, the controversy has continued through to the present.

Thus, the debate over the modern corporation has become a persistent component of public discourse and academic discussion in this country. At one level, the debate arises in the context of concrete issues concerning the corporate role in plant closings, in unemployment and underemployment, in poverty and urban decay, in product safety and quality, in employee safety, health, welfare, and security, in unjust discrimination, in pollution, and in the husbanding of natural resources, to name only a few. At another level, the debate revolves around issues of public policy and governmental involvement in economic and corporate activities. Many of the most divisive public policy disputes involve disagreements about not only the nature of markets but also the nature of the corporation, the alleged role of corporations in creating or solving problems, the control or lack of control of corporations, and so forth. The implications of resolving these disputes extend well beyond the borders of this nation, into the

1

lives of citizens of other countries, just as lives in the U.S. are daily touched by corporate and public policy decisions made elsewhere in the world.

In many ways, this debate is occurring in countries throughout the world, and, as global competition transforms economies and industries in nearly every country on earth, the debate will likely intensify. Each culture will, of course, confront the issue in light of its own history, traditions, and understandings, and from its own unique position of economic and political resources. Indeed, largely because of relatively singular historical and cultural circumstances, the debate has raged with special fervor and significance in the U.S. Here, although the evolution of large organizations was compatible with the penchant for the pragmatic, the development ran against the grain of the rugged individualism for which this country is also widely noted. Consequently, Americans have been especially ambivalent about the growth of the large corporation and the growth of big government; that uneasiness has moved the debate about the corporation toward the center of the political and intellectual landscape and linked the debate with the controversy over big government.

This study grew out of an attempt to make sense of and evaluate this important debate. The intent is not to provide an historical chronicle, as important and illuminating as that might be,[2] but to offer a philosophical analysis of what can be described as the *fundamental question*: WHAT IS THE APPROPRIATE ROLE OF THE MODERN CORPORATION IN A FREE SOCIETY?[3]

Because proposing a philosophical analysis may appear to be seriously misguided, if not preposterous, a clarification is in order. Having been trained in the analytic tradition of philosophy, which is concerned to understand and make intelligible language as it is actually used, I find something very natural about this kind of inquiry. As Richard E. Flathman notes in *Toward a Liberalism*, analytic "moral and political philosophers are committed to a close examination of the language actually employed in moral and political discourse."[4] Since debate over the fundamental question has played such a central role in the actual discourse in this country, attending to the use of language in that larger context is fitting. However, having said this, by "philosophical analysis," I propose nothing esoteric, mysterious, or exclusively analytic.

In the broadest sense, as understood here, philosophical analysis involves four moments. The first stage consists in the clarification of the issue and relevant concepts. In this case, the focus is upon the nature and importance of the fundamental question and related concepts.

The second moment consists in the identification and clarification of the positions taken with respect to the issue. Generally speaking, two alternative positions can be identified, representing what has been described as the Classical and the Managerial business ideologies.[5] To focus upon these is to abstract from the loud cacophony of voices in public discourse, but these competing frameworks are widely recognized, and many, if not most, participants bring to the debate the assumptions of one framework or the other. Philosophers in the field of Business Ethics, business school faculty involved in the field of Business and Society or Social Issues in Management, as well as practicing managers, social critics, commentators, and reformers all seem to function within one framework or the other. These ideological orientations provide a springboard for closer analysis. According to the Classical view, the primary responsibility of corporations is to compete economically in the context of a limited government. For many, if not most, this means that the primary responsibility is to increase profits for stockholders; true believers would claim that the *sole* responsibility is to maximize profit for stockholders. Managerialists, on the other hand, appear to deny this, charging that the Classical view embodies an obsolete set of values and presupposes a reality which no longer exists, if indeed it ever did, and as such is empirically mistaken and morally flawed. In this "enlightened" perspective, presupposed by most researchers in Business Ethics and Social Issues in Management, corporations have responsibilities to a wide variety of "stakeholders" (employees, suppliers, distributors, competitors, consumers, local communities, governmental agencies, etc.) whose interests must be weighed in making a decision. In reality, identifying only two positions is a dramatic oversimplification, but as the analysis proceeds, nuances within each framework can be developed.

The third moment consists in the identification of the arguments which are or can be employed in defense of the positions. This requires searching for the relevant missing premises, i.e., for alleged facts, empirical generalizations, models, and theories marshaled in support of a position. Since at best one usually confronts only argument fragments or enthymemes, it is more accurate to speak of *reconstructing* rather than identifying arguments. Although reconstruction often involves some degree of creativity, that creativity must be constrained by the principle of sympathy, the idea that one should seek arguments which are as strong as possible, consistent with the other beliefs of the advocate. A convenient way of initiating the study is to begin with the existing ideologies, the beliefs, values, and principles of the business community, and then move to identify the theoretical framework which can support that ideological orientation.[6] Given this material, arguments can be reconstructed. Another way of stating this point is to note that the interpretation requires placing assertions in a larger context which provides meaning and justification.

The fourth and final phase of philosophical analysis consists of the evaluation of the reconstructed arguments. Since these arguments invoke premises which make up the Classical or Managerial frameworks, the evaluation of the arguments necessarily involves an analysis and evaluation of these two business ideologies.

Philosophers are not, to say the least, any better situated than others to execute any of these tasks. On the contrary, because arguments developed in defense of these positions involve a wide range of extremely complicated empirical and theoretical claims, in most respects the legal theorist, sociologist, economist, organizational theorist, political scientist, and historian are in better positions to understand and evaluate these assertions than philosophers. Hence, philosophical analysis in the broadest sense is best not left exclusively to philosophers but is an inherently interdisciplinary enterprise. Nonetheless, there is a limited but critical role for philosophical analysis in a narrower sense.

At bottom, as I will make clearer below, the debate over the fundamental question is a normative one, a debate which involves questions of values, responsibilities, duties, and obligations. Thus, analysis in the broad sense requires a moral analysis. Moral analysis is, then, an essential component of the broader philosophical analysis and, indeed, cannot easily be separated from analysis in the broader sense. Nor should it. On the one hand, descriptive analyses often serve as Trojan horses by which policy recommendations, resting upon substantive yet uncritically endorsed normative assumptions, are covertly introduced. Moral analysis should serve to identify and evaluate these. On the other hand, there are many, including some philosophers, who pretend to be able to provide a moral analysis without addressing important and complex descriptive assumptions. Yet it is difficult, if not impossible, to engage in a discussion of values, responsibilities, duties, and obligations at a practical policy level without relying upon these important descriptive claims about the world. Consequently, descriptive assumptions are inadvertently or unreflectively smuggled into prescriptive pronouncements and judgments. These may be not only extremely controversial[7] but may seriously mislead and distort moral judgment. For this reason, there is a need for descriptive analysis *and* normative analysis, the two modes together requiring interdisciplinary understanding and communication, an elusive goal toward which this study strives.

The results of this investigation are disturbing, if not alarming. In spite of the recent revival of interest, there are compelling reasons to conclude that the Classical framework is inadequate. But there is ample evidence to confirm that the Managerial framework, which often postures as an alternative and which is widely presupposed by researchers in the areas of Business Ethics and Business and Society, is equally untenable. The soothing and seductive proposition that corporations have a responsibility to do more than merely profit maximize for stockholders obscures assumptions about the economic and political environment of the modern corporation which are empirically dubious and morally dangerous. Managerialism correctly raises reservations about the Classical view, but the stakeholder approach fails to provide an adequate alternative.

In the final chapter, I shall place the debate over the fundamental question against the contemporary background of transnational corporations competing in an increasingly global market. In that context, the weaknesses of Managerialism appear even more glaring. This new reality, however, poses serious challenges for liberalism itself. As this study will demonstrate, both the Classical and Managerial frameworks are rooted in the liberal tradition, but neither correctly appropriates what is most valuable there. However, even after identifying the strengths in that tradition, the problems posed by attempts to formulate a liberal response to the fundamental question in the context of the global economy remain formidable.

THE NATURE OF THE QUESTION

The need for a moral analysis arises from serious limitations in the literature concerning the question of the corporate role, especially in the fields of Business Ethics and Business and Society. Research has been hampered by a failure to take more seriously the renewed challenge posed by the Classical framework and an unwillingness on the part of Managerialists to explore more vigorously the presuppositions of their own framework. As I will explain, Managerialism evolved as a part of larger attack on the assumptions of Classical Liberalism shortly after the turn of the century. With the victory of the New Deal, however, Managerialists gained strategic advantages, and, by the 1960s, the Classical framework was in retreat. Managerialists were dismissing the view as "obsolete." In the 1970s, the intellectual orthodoxy of the New Deal was overturned, especially in economic theory, and the challenges of stagflation and international competition made it clear that the world was radically different. With the "Reagan revolution" in the 1980s, political realities changed as well. "Classical" free market solutions—economic competition, limiting government interference—have regained intellectual and political respectability. Even Revisionist Liberals took to market solutions. The failure of Managerialists to respond to the challenge of the new reality is serious and is rooted in part in the failure to come to grips with the nature and importance of the fundamental question. That has, in turn, yielded confusion concerning the kinds of arguments appropriate to a defense of an answer.

In particular, three important features of the question have not been consistently appreciated. First, the question is fundamental. Although I believe that a reasonably strong case can be made that the question is also historically and politically fundamental, I believe that the question is also conceptually fundamental. Basic questions of corporate strategy and corporate policy presuppose a response to the fundamental question. Responses to specific concrete issues can only be formulated in light of a commitment to a response at the general level. One cannot intelligently discuss the question of whether General Motors is acting responsibly in closing down dozens of U.S. factories, for example, without taking a position regarding the question of the role corporations ought to play in society. Further, the objectives of management training and education cannot be determined without having developed a response to the question. Only after determining the role the corporation should play can one determine how managers should be trained and the relevant knowledge acquired. Finally, one cannot determine questions of public policy with respect to the corporation and the market without having developed an answer to the fundamental question. Should we allow or require corporations to address significant social problems alone, or should government become involved? Should we keep corporations out of the business of social issues?

Second, as already suggested, the fundamental question is a normative one. Philosophers are not alone in distinguishing normative language from nonnormative language. "Nonnormative language" is *descriptive*, functioning to describe the world. This is the language of "is," as in "Snow *is* white" and "The GDP *is* down 2 percent from last year." "Normative language" functions, on the other hand, evaluatively or prescriptively. "Evaluative language"—assigning a value to things, as in "That is a *good* car," or "He is a *good* person"—is the language of value, invoking what is good, bad, or evil. "Prescriptive language" prescribes behavior, as in "One *ought* not hold a golf club that way," or "You *ought* not kill the innocent." This is the language of ought, of obligation, of duty, of what should or should not be done. Not all evaluative or prescriptive language is moral, of course; much is nonmoral. But clearly, describing the world is quite different from assigning value or prescribing. One should take care not to confuse the world of "is" with the world of "good" or "ought."

The fundamental question, then, seeks a normative response about the role that the modern corporation *should* play in a free society, about the corporation's obligations, duties, and responsibilities, if any. This is not to suggest that the nonnormative version of the question is unimportant or irrelevant. The question of what role the corporation currently plays in our society is extremely important.[8] Economists will attempt to provide descriptive answers based upon economic models. Political scientists will examine different dimensions, with different theoretical constructs. A general "descriptive theory of political economy," a theory explaining or modeling the interactions of the government and the economy, is critical in formulating a response to the fundamental question, but describing the role of the corporation in society is unmistakably a different exercise from prescribing the appropriate role. The kinds of evidence and argumentation relevant to each exercise are quite different.

The point can be illustrated simply. Any practical moral judgment (roughly, one having practical import in the world) must rely both upon descriptive premises involving assertions about states of affairs in the world and upon general normative moral judgments about what is good or evil, about what one ought or ought not do. Hence, any proposed answer to the question of corporate role must invoke not merely descriptive premises, which may involve descriptive models of the firm, the economy, and a descriptive theory of political economy, but also normative premises. Prescriptions cannot be generated from claims about facts alone. Prescriptions move beyond mere issues of the "way the world is," toward issues of the way the world should be, or toward issues of what is good or evil.

Third, and perhaps most importantly, the nature of the question is such that it involves not only ethical theory, but ethical theory writ large, i.e., "normative political philosophy" or "normative political economy."[9] That is, any answer rests upon a theory of the appropriate role of government, a theory of political philosophy. A complete theory of political philosophy incorporates a theory of political economy or political morality, i.e., a theory about the legitimate relationship between government and the economy, the extent to which government may legitimately interfere in economic transactions. Conceptually, the flip side of the fundamental question is a question about the appropriate role of government in a free society. Hence, David L. Engel is correct when he claims in "An Approach to Corporate Responsibility" that the issue of social responsibility "cannot be debated except against the background of a general political theory."[10] Any analysis of the debate over the corporate role must be sensitive to the descriptive and normative theories of political economy presupposed by participants.

Again, although the focus of this project is conceptual, analysis cannot and should not be severed from an appreciation of the political and historical realities which have shaped, and continue to shape, the debate. While throughout most of Europe, an active role for a strong central government was a well-established political reality before the twentieth century, in the U.S., industrial and financial capitalism developed largely in the absence of any strong central government. Thus, a strong private sector dominated by extremely powerful corporations antedated the growth of big government. This is not to deny that federal and state governments routinely threw in their lot with the business community for economic development in the nineteenth century, only to acknowledge that Washington, D.C., and the state capitals had relatively meager resources to offer. Depending upon one's perspective, the growth of government is to be explained either as a response to the perceived threat posed by the corporate combines, as a counterbalance to political and economic concentration in the commercial sector, or as a means for the corporate sector to exercise greater control of the markets, as market flight. In either case, the question of corporate role is historically associated with the question of what role government should play. Around the turn of the century, in the U.S. at least, these were open and living questions in a way very much unlike Europe. Through the first decades of this century, when the shape of the central government in the U.S. was still largely undetermined, the debate over corporate role was one of the most important battlefields upon which the war over the appropriate role of government was fought. And long after the establishment of the strong federal government, debate over the appropriate corporate role remains a surrogate for debate over the appropriate role of government.

The important function of a theory of political economy is evident in one of the most notable defenses of the idea that the sole responsibility of a corporation is to profit maximize. Milton Friedman defends the thesis in his widely read "The Social Responsibility of Business Is to Increase Profits."[11] In this view, the role of government should be minimal, and very little interference in the market is thereby condoned. The vision is defended by appeal to the wonderful workings of "the system," which provides freedom and other great material benefits. This defense, like other Classical defenses, rests upon one version of a familiar theory of political economy known as Classical Liberalism, refurbished with a more sophisticated contemporary economic theory. Friedman's defense of profit maximization cannot be abstracted from this larger context. Moreover, Friedman would agree that profit maximization may lead to perverse outcomes unless the conditions of the competitive market are satisfied.

According to the Managerial framework, the role of the corporation is to do more than maximize profit. The Managerialists never clearly spell out what this might involve, but many speak of the importance of the corporation being a good citizen, thereby suggesting noneconomic civic and political duties. Corporate managers on this view become something like "statesmen" or "stateswomen." One challenge of this study is to reconstruct the theory of political economy which is being presupposed. It is clear, however, that Managerialists reject the theory of Classical Liberalism and accept as legitimate a much more extensive and active role for government, with some of the activities of economic control tolerated or even encouraged. Thus, theories of political economy play an especially important role in the debate over the fundamental question, a role which is too often ignored.

These obvious and elementary points about the nature of the fundamental question would not need emphasis except that they are so frequently ignored. Indeed, the most serious limitations in the fields of Business Ethics and Business and Society (Social Issues in Management) arise largely from overlooking them. Those limitations have not only hampered the development of important lines of research but create impediments to the kinds of interdisciplinary understanding and communication which is required.

In some respects, researchers in Business and Society have moved closer than philosophers toward a philosophical analysis in the broader sense, and even toward the kind of moral analysis required. For one thing, writers in the area of Business and Society have grasped the significance of the fundamental question. In one representative text, for instance, *Business and Society: A Managerial Approach,*[12] Frederick D. Sturdivant claims that his purpose is to provide students "with a thoughtful and systematic treatment of the role of business in American society." The first chapter notes that the "role of business in American society has long been the subject of debate" and proceeds to develop the theme of the rise of the. large modern corporation, citing the complexity of the relationships in which the modern corporation is involved and claiming that each of these relationships raises important issues. What, for example, is the responsibility of the corporation to stockholders, former employees, present employees, to the community, to the environment, and so forth? Sturdivant then writes:

> At the heart of these issues is the underlying question of the appropriate role of business in a free society. The definition of this role is incredibly complicated and is, in itself, an incomplete answer to the problem. The other half of the challenge is to devise means by which executives, having arrived at a reasonable definition of their appropriate role, can do an effective job of *managing* this aspect of their business. (9)

The passage reflects the recognition that the question of the corporate role is fundamental to the more specific issues, and an understanding that this general issue must be addressed before the relevant skills and objectives of management can be determined.[13]

Ironically, too many philosophers in Business Ethics have largely ignored the question, or have treated the problem of "corporate responsibility" as one problem among others, in abstraction from the background questions of political economy. Philosophers have been

quick to fix upon specific problems, and there is no shortage of pene-
trating analysis and argumentation. But analysis too often remains at
this level. Articles are written debating whether McDonnell Douglas
was morally liable or morally responsible for the Paris crash of the DC–
10; whether corporations have an obligation to keep inefficient plants
open and/or negotiate plant closings with the local community; on
the responsibilities for honest advertising, etc. These important issues
are often treated intelligently and sensitively. However, an analysis
of the more general issues, such as those raised by the fundamental
question, are left largely untouched. The result is a failure to understand more clearly some of the underlying normative and empirical
presuppositions which shape the analysis of concrete issues.

This same point can be made in slightly different terms. Richard
De George identifies three levels within the field of Business Ethics.[14]
At the macrolevel, the field is concerned with issues of political phi-
losophy/political economy, with "possible justifications of economic
systems" or with proposals for alternative systems or modifications. A
second level is characterized by the study of business within the "free
enterprise system." De George claims that since corporations "are the
dominant feature of this system, they have attracted the most attention." At the third level attention is focused upon individuals within
corporations and business. Most of the work in the field remains at the
third level, insensitive to the important role played by assumptions at
the first and the second levels.[15] But these assumptions are not, after
all, idle appendages to judgments made at the lower levels. One's
judgments at the intermediate or individual levels are influenced
by descriptive and normative presumptions about the free enterprise
system and government; one's judgments about the particular issues
at the third level is mediated by descriptive and normative theories of
political economy and the justifications employed there. By avoiding
the fundamental question, the philosophical analyses are incomplete
and in some instances misguided. The underlying assumptions of
analyses at the practical level must be exposed.

IDEOLOGIES/BUSINESS PHILOSOPHIES

An approach which is often found in the field of Business and
Society is preferable to the track taken in the field of Business Ethics
in yet another way. A once-common strategy in Business and Society

is to discuss competing "ideologies" or "business philosophies," usually in connection with the discussion of the debate over corporate
responsibility. Philosophers generally eschew this approach. To some
extent this is understandable in light of the tendency to avoid coming to grips with the fundamental question. If the question is not
perceived as important, there is little interest in exploring answers.
Moreover, many philosophers, especially in the analytic tradition,
are revulsed by a methodology which employs ideological constructs,
believing the idea to be "too sociological," or too vague to be of
use in analysis, or both. Nonetheless, participating in this debate by
examining competing ideological frameworks can have philosophical
merit if correctly pursued. Attention to these constructs can provide
an *initial step* in an attempt to clarify the positions being asserted and
in reconstructing arguments in defense of those positions. Moreover,
on closer inspection, the ideologies identified can also be recognized
for what they are, namely, appeals to a theory of political economy
employed to defend a response to the fundamental question. That is,
the ideological frameworks are vague expressions of a theory of political economy, or a number of similar theories of political economy.
Thus, philosophers have missed a promising strategy for approaching
the fundamental question.

Unfortunately, the potential to pursue and explore the broader
descriptive and normative theories of political economy which are
embedded in these ideologies has not been actualized by researchers in
the area of Business and Society either. This is apparent by examining
some representative treatments. One of the earlier texts in the field,
still valuable, is Joseph W. McGuire's *Business and Society*.[16] After
discussing the foundations of capitalism and tracing the growth of
business institutions in the U.S., McGuire turns to the competing
ideologies or "business philosophies." The Classical tradition is out-
lined first, with brief descriptions of the ideas of Adam Smith, David
Ricardo, Jeremy Bentham, and the Social Darwinists. The treatment
of alternatives to the Classical tradition includes discussions of John
Dewey's pragmatism, Frederick Taylor's scientific management (also
presented as pragmatism), Elton Mayo's views on social responsibility,
and John M. Keynes's "new economics." While brief, the exposition
clearly represents as an alternative to the Classical tradition what
others would call the Managerial ideology, or the Managerial framework. McGuire stresses the continuity between the two. In his view,
the Classical tradition is incorporated into the Managerial but has

been "humanized," and by taking into account the developments in the economy and society in the twentieth century, the Managerial perspective on the economy is more realistic. Taylor and Mayo are "noteworthy" because they represent a way which permits business persons to "strive for profits more efficiently and humanely." Keynes is characterized as maintaining the profit incentive while applying the important insights of the Classical economists to a changed world in which government must play a more active role.

Not only does this anticipate later discussions of competing ideologies in Business and Society, but McGuire also reflects the confusions and weaknesses in the treatment of ideology. For the most part, McGuire proceeds as if he were merely *describing* the business philosophies. But there is a quiet tendency to assume the Managerial perspective, with little or no argument. The Classical framework is assumed to be basically sound, as modified by Keynes. The closest McGuire comes to argument is to suggest that the new business philosophy is "more humane" and "realistic." In later chapters, when it makes a difference, this new business philosophy is merely presupposed. When McGuire turns to discuss the question of corporate responsibility, for instance, the Managerial position is assumed, but there is no explicit treatment of the normative dimensions of the problem. McGuire appears to believe that these two models are not incompatible because he apparently believes that profit maximization requires acting more humanely and realistically. He ignores the very realistic possibilities that economic competition may force a choice between humane treatment (whatever that means) and profitability.

Later texts follow McGuire's strategy of coming to the subject through competing business philosophies or ideologies, but in important respects the discussions are even less satisfactory than McGuire's. This may be attributable, in part, to how the business philosophies were treated. A favorite source in later works is *The American Business Creed*, by Francis X. Sutton et al.[17] Based on a review of speeches, articles, and books written by business leaders and representatives of important business institutions, such as the National Association of Manufacturers, the authors attempt to identify the major beliefs and values of the American business community. Accordingly, there is one "creed," with two versions, called the Classical and Managerial business ideologies. The work is valuable as an attempt to provide an authoritative description of the beliefs, values, and ideals which are, in fact, operative in the American business community. The work is also suggestive insofar as the authors tend to believe that behind the vague phrases and beliefs of individuals espousing an ideology, one can identify the theoretical frameworks which give rise to those be-liefs. Behind the Classical business ideology, for example, the authors believe one can easily detect the ideas of Classical Liberalism and the Classical tradition of economic theory.Beyond this, however, the analysis is even more troublesome than McGuire's. While McGuire sketches different theories and fails to identify carefully the relation-ship between the Classical and Managerial, merely stressing an alleged continuity, Sutton et al. introduce the puzzling idea that the two ideologies are asserted to be different versions of the same creed. This too is probably an attempt to highlight continuity and commonality between the Classical and the Managerial, but the authors nowhere define the relationship between an ideology and a creed, nor do they bother even to define a creed, let alone describe its content. This is quite an oversight for a work titled *The American Business Creed.* One would be hard pressed to find even a sentence devoted to these critical issues. This has the effect of further blurring the relationship between the two frameworks. At times the authors come close to identifying the creed with the Classical business ideology and the ideas of Classical Liberalism. It never occurs to them that the creed may well be the broader intellectual tradition of liberalism, and that these two ideologies presuppose different versions of liberalism, Classical and Revisionist.

Contributing further to confusion is the fact that the characteriza-tion of the Managerial ideology is extremely diffuse, unfocused, and sketchy. At points the authors suggest that the Managerial ideology is distinct from the Classical, at other times they suggest that it is merely a matter of differing emphases. Given this lack of clarity, it is not surprising that the theoretical core behind the Managerial ideology is never identified in the way Classical Liberalism is found to lie behind the Classical ideology. Nor does this even appear to be an important concern. McGuire's attention to the ideas of Keynes, Mayo, and others is entirely lost, and nothing takes its place.

Other texts in Business and Society generally share these limita-tions.[18] When the two ideologies are presented, the implications for the debate over corporate responsibility are usually traced, but there is little attempt to go beyond the ideological level to identify the theoretical frameworks which might give more rigorous expression to the ideas and which might serve as the basis for the construction of arguments to defend those views. Instead of developing an argument, they routinely assume the Managerial framework.

This unwillingness or inability to reason about the frameworks is not, I believe, a function of the limitations associated with writing a textbook rather than a more research-oriented monograph. George C. Lodge's *The New American Ideology*,[19] for example, contrasts the old ideology of individualism, property rights, competition, limited state, and scientific specialization with the "new" ideology of communitarianism, rights and duties of membership, community need, an active state, and holism/independence. The old ideology is the Classical business ideology; the new ideology is the Managerial ideology. But Lodge never develops a clear line of argumentation to suggest why the new values are more adequate than the old ones. Or, consider Gerald F. Cavanagh's *American Business Values in Transition*.[20] Cavanagh provides one of the most extensive and thorough discussions of ideology in the Business and Society literature. Chapter 1, "Values and Ideology in American Life," offers a brief historical sketch of the dominant constituents of American values and ideology, describes the important functions of ideology, and argues that an ideology is necessary even for business. Chapter 2 continues in this vein and concludes with a discussion of the "American Business Creed," an allusion to the work of Sutton et al. After contrasting the Classical and Managerial frameworks, Cavanagh makes it apparent that the Managerial views are morally preferable. Yet nowhere is any argument provided to defend this presumption. Both Lodge and Cavanagh could be interpreted as suggesting that since the new ideas are in fact becoming accepted, they are the correct ideas. Or, the theory might be that whatever society generally accepts should be accepted (by business and everyone else?). In Cavanagh's most recent work, *Ethical Dilemmas in the Modern Corporation*,[21] coauthored with Arthur F. McGovern, ideology plays a much more subdued role, the emphasis being on ethical dilemmas confronting the manager. The contrast there between the "Traditional Business Values" of freedom, individual responsibility, and growth, and the newer "social values" of dignity of the human person, community (common good), and justice (equity), echoes the earlier work, as well as the contrast between the Classical and Managerial views. Again, however, there is no explicit defense of these views.[22]

There is, in principle, nothing unphilosophical about an approach to the fundamental question which begins by examining the ideology of a group, i.e., the beliefs, values, and principles of a group. Nor is there anything in this approach which precludes developing a reasoned defense of a framework. Not only can this approach facilitate accurate and sympathetic reconstruction of arguments, but the method can be characterized in part as dialectical in the Aristotelian sense—the art of eliciting truth by beginning with prevailing opinion. Aristotle launched his investigation into the nature of justice by inquiring "What do citizens say is just?" He began, in other words, by surveying the opinions, beliefs, and theories of contemporaries. Analogously, many in Business and Society appear to begin with the question "What role do people say that corporations ought to play?" By examining patterns in these answers, one discovers the ideological orientations. But this can serve only as an initial step. The question is how to resolve an issue when there are significant disagreements, as in this case.

Neither is the unwillingness or inability to provide a reasoned defense of a framework a function of the fact that researchers fail to recognize the normative component of an ideology, either. Cavanagh's treatment is reflective of the approach taken by many in Business and Society. Generally, "ideology" is used nonpejoratively. An ideology is understood as a cognitive/normative/emotive schema according to which the rich data of the world is organized and individuals provided orientation. An ideology is compared to a web of beliefs or a pair of glasses. Ideological schemata filter inputs, give meaning and significance to some, disregard others. And, as in a web, cognitions and values are woven together. The image of the web also captures the extent to which there is a hierarchy of important cognitions and values within an ideology. Core beliefs and values are in the center of the web while less essential ones are located at the extremities. But is there an assumption here that one cannot reason about or evaluate values and principles?

In "The Connection between Ethics and Ideology,"[23] Lodge not only recognizes the normative function of an ideology but comes close to making that function central. Although the work of a nonphilosopher, this article appears in the first volume of the *Journal of Business Ethics*. The piece recalls many of the points of Lodge's *The New American Ideology*, and constitutes a plea to philosophers to take more seriously the importance of ideology. As Lodge puts it, ideologies are frameworks of ideas which a community uses to define values and to make them explicit. Ideology is the source of legitimacy of institutions, and the justification for the authority of those who manage them. Ideology can be conveniently seen as a bridge which a community uses to get from timeless, universal non-controversial notions such as survival, justice, economy, self-fulfillment and self-respect to the application of these notions in the real world. (86)

Here is an awareness of the normative function of an ideology, and Lodge recognizes that the normative issues extend beyond the microissues of individuals in organizations, De George's third level, toward macroissues. What is at stake is the legitimacy of institutions and authority, and these institutions include corporations and government.

Cavanagh's *American Business Values in Transition* reveals the same understanding. After identifying the ideology of the society and of business culture, Cavanagh turns to "Personal Values in the Organization" (chapter 3). In chapters 4 and 5, Cavanagh returns to the macroissues, the question of political economy as it were. Chapter 4 discusses "Marx's Challenge to Free Enterprise," and chapter 5 surveys "New Challenges to Free Enterprise and Its Values." Only then does Cavanagh return to values within the corporation. In short, the strategy is to understand specific issues which confront the corporation or issues which confront individuals within the corporation in the context of a larger macroframework of beliefs, values, and principles which these writers describe as an ideology.

Having identified the important normative function of ideology, however, researchers seem incapable of providing an argument to defend one framework over the other. Thus, although the approach taken by many of those operating in the field of Business and Society is on the right track, there is a serious failure to pursue this path to the next logical step. The step involves an analysis and evaluation of the frameworks involved.

Philosophers, on the other hand, have too often ignored Lodge's call. That call involves an appeal to understand the extent to which very general descriptive and normative assumptions about the nature of important institutions in society, corporations, and government affect judgments of specific issues. Kenneth E. Goodpaster is one of the few philosophically trained scholars to note its importance in the field of Business Ethics. Goodpaster describes, in "Business Ethics, Ideology, and the Naturalistic Fallacy,"[24] the plight of many with philosophical training in ethics as they approach the area of applied ethics. Good-paster notes how ethicists have turned to the study of important and relevant contemporary issues, such as those involving the corporation in society, where the issues "seem compelling" and "people care" about the answers. The philosopher then turns to ethical theory, the "history of philosophical debate over the appropriate frameworks or principles for deriving duties, obligations, rights and virtues." After attempting to determine which of these is most defensible, he turns again to the practical. At this point, Goodpaster notes, the philosopher begins to "feel uncomfortable."

> There seems to be a persistent and nagging "theoreticality" about these philosophical frameworks that poisons their practicality. They seem so distant from active, daily decision making, especially the decision making of corporations and other key institutional "actors" on the human stage. They seem colorless and too general, like high-level major premises in search not only of minor premises but of whole substrata of minor arguments. The magnitude of the "gap" between principle and practice seems overwhelming. Too many unknown facts are missing. Too many assumptions have to be made before anything like *prescription* seems possible, let alone warranted. (228)

The "philosophical frameworks" to which Goodpaster refers are different ethical theories. For many philosophers, normative philosophy consists in reviewing the history of different ethical frameworks, such as utilitarianism, Kantianism, Aristotelianism, and so forth, or in developing a new variation of one of these and then determining which is most adequate. Adequacy is often judged without testing the compatibility of the theory with a larger political philosophy or political economy. Having determined which theory is most adequate, the approach is then to apply that theory directly to issues concerning individuals in large organizations or to the organizations themselves.

As Goodpaster suggests, that approach is indefensible. The attempt to apply the ethical theories is unmediated by other theories and assumptions. This is the gap to which he refers. His solution is to turn away from these narrow frameworks of ethical theory and to "work backwards" toward the ideological assumptions of the main institutional actors. This approach involves examining public discourse and attempting to identify the ideological frameworks of the disputants, exactly what is proposed here. The point is that in applied ethics one must necessarily fill in the middle-level premises with assumptions involving complicated questions about the nature of individuals, corporations, markets, government, and so forth, in order to address specific issues. These assumptions can be characterized as constituting an ideology or a framework. The only choice is between introducing these unconsciously and/or surreptitiously, or introducing these only after having unearthed and held up the assumptions to critical reflection. Moreover, by focusing exclusively upon ethical frameworks at the expense of the ideological frameworks, philosophers have tended to ignore the importance of normative questions of political economy.

By ignoring ideology, much of the work in the field of Business Ethics appears to lack an appreciation of its own Managerial framework. The important role of ideology is missed entirely by Tibor R. Machan and Douglas J. Den Uyl who complain bitterly, in "Recent Work in Business Ethics: A Survey and Critique,"[25] that Business Ethics texts fail to distinguish carefully between several branches of normative philosophy—ethics, social ethics, public policy, law, and political theory. For Machan and Uyl this alleged failure creates a number of negative consequences. They are alarmed by what they characterize as an "excessive" focus upon public policy issues, a focus which "has turned the field into little more than a vehicle for ideological expression—almost all left of center."

> Unlike medical ethics which seems able to generate ethical issues that are not directly related to public policy questions, business ethics is still in search for an identity distinct from political ideology. (120)

Machan and Uyl claim that this failure has the effect of misrepresenting the content of the course to students. In their view, students expect a course like medical ethics where they are "given an idea of how they ought to conduct themselves in their chosen profession."

Machan and Uyl correctly detect that much work in Business Ethics presupposes a Managerial framework, one which is "left of center." It is left of center, of course, only if one assumes that the center is represented by Classical Liberalism or libertarianism. The criticism, however, is misdirected. It assumes that because one can distinguish between the branches of ethics, social ethics, public policy, law, and political philosophy that these are somehow hermetically sealed from one another. Are we to suppose that one's position with respect to the moral limits of law and one's political philosophy will have no significant impact upon public policy, social ethics, and ethics? On the contrary, the different spheres and different levels are intimately connected. Historically, ethical theories have generally been associated with the attempt to defend a particular normative theory of political economy. This is as true of utilitarianism as it was of Plato and Aristotle. Even if one were to hold the view that one can develop an adequate ethical theory prior to turning to the other areas of philosophy, how would it be possible to confront concrete issues, even in medicine, without middle-level premises involving political philosophy and other descriptive assumptions? Machan and Uyl lament that the attention to public policy issues generates nothing much more than political ideology, but if discussions of public policy are nothing more than political ideology, why are discussions of ethics, social ethics, law, or political philosophy anything more than expressions of ideology?

The underlying presumption that ethical analysis should focus primarily upon individual cases while ignoring the larger institutional frameworks—social philosophy, law, public policy, and political philosophy—is a standard ploy. This presumption is not surprising given the assumptions of the Classical Liberal tradition which attempts to reduce any phenomenon to individual transactions. This obscures the extent to which our intuitions about individualistic ethical judgments are shaped by our views about broader issues of economics, social theory, law, and political philosophy. It assumes that our initial individualistic opinions should not be reviewed in light of the larger macrolevel issues.

If there is a problem with much of the research in Business Ethics, it is not that the focus upon public policy issues turns the field into a vehicle for ideological expression. The weakness is that more attention has not been paid to the larger ideological framework itself, or to critical reflection on the assumptions involved. What is needed is, not exclusive attention to individual decision, but a careful examination of the Classical and the Managerial ideologies. More precisely, what is required is to discover the theoretical frameworks of the Classical and Managerial views. There are some discussions in Business Ethics of the Classical framework; there are virtually no critical discussions of the Managerial except by the few opponents from the Classical.

THE "IS"/"OUGHT" CONFUSION

Thus, although the Business and Society literature reveals a sensitivity to the centrality of the fundamental question and the important role of ideology, the implications of those insights have been ignored. There are few attempts to draw out the theoretical frameworks upon which the ideologies rest (or could rest), or to provide reasoned defenses for the positions taken. The recognition of the normative importance of ideologies reveals an intuitive understanding of the normative significance of the fundamental question of the appropriate role of the modern corporation in a free society, but there is a serious confusion over the nature of normative argumentation.

There is no shortage of examples of the confusion. Consider, for example, *Corporate Social Responsiveness: The Modern Dilemma*, by Robert W. Ackerman and Raymond A. Bauer.[26] In the preface, Ackerman and Bauer attempt to explain their position by referring to two texts which they claim come closest to theirs. One is the once very widely used *Up against the Corporate Wall*, a book of cases by S. Prakash Sethi.[27] According to Sethi, the objective of his book is *purely descriptive*, to make students sensitive to social issues, aware of the "complexity of the motives of various parties," and familiar "with the success and failure of their strategies and tactics"(p. x.). This is to be achieved by examining cases which merely *describe* actors, actions, and strategies, and thus merely relate the way the world *is*. Sethi explains that the purpose is not to praise or condemn any actors or "successful" or "unsuccessful" strategies, not to prescribe courses of actions or strategies, and not to recommend what one *ought* to do. The other work is *Corporate Social Responsibility* by Richard N. Farmer and W. Dickerson Jogue.[28] According to Farmer and Jogue, it is "not enough to decide that a certain course of action is required." One must "justify this action ethically, socially, and financially."[29] But how can the book by Ackerman and Bauer be similar to two books so radically different in purpose? Sethi's cases *describe*; Farmer and Jogue are interested in *ethical* justification and discussions of what one *ought* to do. Morally defending a course of action is quite different from describing one.

Having claimed that their book is close to these two other books, Ackerman and Bauer claim to be engaged only in description. Citing "The Apologetics of 'Managerialism'" by Edward S. Mason,[30] Ackerman and Bauer claim that the Classical rationale for the corporation is no longer valid but that "no new rationale has been developed to take its place"(14). They deny that they are opting for the Managerial rationale. Ackerman and Bauer argue that many, including social philosophers, legal scholars, and economic and political theorists, continue to search for a new rationale, but there is an "absence of consensus." "Hence," they claim, they favor a more "empirical approach" (15). "Basically, we are proposing a sociological rather than legal or philosophical definition of the role of the corporation" (16). The approach, in other words, is not normative but purely descriptive. Their hope is that this might facilitate a new rationale. The importance of the idea that a rationale must be grounded in an adequate understanding of the world cannot be overemphasized. However, this does not itself provide ethical justification.

Yet, in spite of the disclaimer, the text adopts the familiar Managerial view that corporations have obligations to stakeholders and ought to act in ways other than those which merely maximize profit for shareholders. The text discusses the nature of the Social Audit, explains why social policy should be consistent with corporate strategy, and suggests ways to implement social responsibility. In short, the claim that the purpose of the text is only descriptive/sociological appears more like an excuse for failing to defend this rationale than a genuine attempt to describe.[31]

In *Business and Society: A Managerial Approach*, for example, Sturdivant reflects the same confusion.[32] After identifying the fundamental question and sketching the Classical and Managerial alternatives, Sturdivant proceeds as if he is merely describing these alternatives, as if he is merely describing the role played by the corporation in society. At critical moments, however, it is clear that he has opted for the Managerial position and is advocating a course of action for managers based on an answer to the fundamental question without ever having argued against the Classical view or having provided arguments in favor of the Managerial.

Philosophers have given this particular kind of confusion a name, the "naturalistic fallacy." David Hume is usually mentioned as the first to have clearly expressed the fallacy. In his *Treatise* he complains that in reading various books the authors will

> proceed for some time in the ordinary way of reasoning and establish the being of a God, or make observations concerning human affairs; when of a sudden I am surpriz'd to find that instead of the usual copulations

of propositions, *is*, and *is not*, I meet with no proposition that is not connected with an *ought* or an *ought not*. This change is imperceptible; but is, however, of the last consequence. For as this *ought*, or *ought not*, expresses some new relation or affirmation, 'tis necessary that it shou'd be observ'd and explain'd; and at the same time that a reason shou'd be given, for what seems altogether inconceivable, how this new relation can be a deduction from others, which are entirely different from it. (Book III, part I, section I, 469)

An avid reader (and writer) of history and political theory, Hume is puzzled by the frequent shifts. In the midst of accounts which purport merely to describe, and which therefore involve the verb "is," there suddenly appear prescriptions, with the telltale language of "ought." Similarly, one reads Business and Society texts which often purport to deal only with issues of what "is" the role of the corporation in contemporary society, only suddenly to find claims involving the issue of what role the corporations "ought" to play. Hume wishes to understand how authors deduce an "ought" from an "is"; he wants to know about the license which allows authors to move from describing the world to prescribing. There is a confusion between "is" and "ought." It is one thing to describe an ideology; it is another to provide a moral defense of it. There is nothing illegitimate or illicit about advocacy. Yet it is not unreasonable to inquire about the reasons for the adoption of the prescriptive mode. Why is one ideology better than another? No defense is given.

In "Business Ethics, Ideology and the Naturalistic Fallacy," Kenneth Goodpaster cites other instances.[33] Goodpaster writes:

And whether the categories be [George] Lodge's "New American Ideology," [Michael] Novak's call for a new defense of "democratic capitalism." [Robert] Heilbroner's talk of the decline of the "business civilization," [Christopher] Stone's remarks about the need for a shift in "corporate culture," [Thomas] Petit's talk of a "moral crisis in management," or [Michael] Maccoby's reflections on a new business "psychostructure," the underlying challenge remains: How can we achieve a *philosophically* clear understanding of the normative status or force of this middle-level phenomenon we are calling ideology? (230)

Goodpaster's point is stated delicately. To ask How can "we achieve a philosophically clear understanding of the normative status" of an ideology? is politely to call attention to the "is"/"ought" confusion, to the lack of defense for positions espoused by these authors which involve substantive normative claims.[34] All of the authors cited reject the Classical framework and adopt Managerial assumptions, yet there is a conspicuous absence of reasoned defenses. There is often the suggestion that the studies are merely descriptive, but normative claims arise repeatedly. To put it less delicately, normative premises are smuggled into the account.

Thus, in spite of the philosophically promising approach which begins by identifying the competing ideologies as attempts to respond to the fundamental question of corporate role, proceeds to identify the theoretical core as a means of reconstructing arguments, and then finally assesses the arguments, too many studies founder after identifying the competing ideologies. Rather than analysis and argumentation, there is confusion and obfuscation. The normative component of the ideology is recognized, but there is no attempt to offer a moral defense.

PLAN OF THE STUDY

The need for this study arises from these limitations. The plan for proceeding is dictated by the four moments of philosophical analysis. This chapter has brought into focus the nature of the issue, the normative nature of the fundamental question. The major tasks are reconstructing and analyzing the arguments in defense of the positions involved. Chapters 2–6 provide an analysis of the Classical position; chapters 7–10 focus upon the Managerial. Chapter 11 examines the challenges confronting liberalism in the context of the global market.

Chapter 2 sketches the intellectual core of the Classical framework, the theory of political economy known as Classical Liberalism. That will provide an opportunity to outline the liberal tradition in general, and to frame the issue between Classical Liberals and Revisionist Liberals. Classical Liberalism advocates the minimal state with laissez-faire capitalism. Although a number of different ethical theories have been invoked in an attempt to provide moral legitimacy for the tenets of Classical Liberalism, three deserve special attention, the natural rights theory, social contract theory, and Utilitarianism.

The natural rights and social contract defenses of Classical Liberalism will be examined in chapter 3, where the theories of John Locke and Robert Nozick will be examined. As I shall demonstrate, both natural rights and contractarian defenses fail. The implications reach well beyond the question of the defensibility of Classical Liberalism. Contractarian thought now constitutes one of the most important alternatives to utilitarianism or natural rights theory and has been employed in attempts to defend the more than minimal state of Revisionist Liberalism. In A *Theory of Justice*, for instance, one of the most widely read and discussed contractarian theories of this century, John Rawls defends something like a welfare state which would clearly involve rather substantial interference into the operation of the free market. The methodological difficulties which afflict and ultimately undermine Nozick's theory, however, strike with equal force against any hypothetical arguments, including Rawls's. If Managerialists wish to find solace in a moral defense of the more than minimal state, they must look elsewhere.

Historically and theoretically, utilitarianism plays an extremely important role in attempts to justify the basic tenets of Classical Liberalism. Because of its great diversity, the discussion of utilitarianism continues through chapters 4, 5, and 6.

Chapter 4 examines the position of Milton Friedman as a contemporary defender of Classical Liberalism and the idea that corporations should do nothing other than profit maximize. I shall argue that his theory is best understood as a utilitarian defense, and while there are good reasons for rejecting utilitarianism as an inadequate moral theory, utilitarian defenses should not be rejected out of hand. The problem with utilitarianism is not that optimizing utility or efficiency is not important; it is that there are other considerations which are also morally relevant. Thus, if it can be shown that Classical Liberalism optimizes utility, that will count as a strong reason in its favor. However, by exploring other problems in the attempt to defend Classical Liberalism, it becomes clear that these arguments are extraordinarily weak.

One important problem concerns the definition and measurement of utility. Chapter 5 examines difficulties in the attempts to measure utility and demonstrates the limitations of Paretian arguments for free enterprise. Finally, the moral force of any argument which attempts to legitimize laissez-faire capitalism on the grounds that this system is optimally efficient or utile depends upon the understanding of efficiency or utility which is involved.

Chapter 6 examines the problems in the theory of value which further erode these defenses of Classical Liberalism. Chapter 6 will also provide the basis for understanding Revisionist Liberalism.

In chapter 7, attention is redirected to the Managerial framework, where I argue that the predominant version of Managerialism is Micro-Managerialism, a perspective narrowly confined to theses about the nature of the modern corporation and their alleged moral significance.

I argue, in chapter 8, that Micro-Managerialism is inadequate because it fails to address questions concerning the nature of the system of which the modern corporation is only a part. Insofar as Micro-Managerialism presupposes a particular understanding of the system, that understanding appears obsolete.

Macro-Managerialism addresses the broader questions concerning the system. Chapter 9 outlines this more adequate version and identifies the underlying theory of political economy as New Deal Liberalism, a particular variety of Revisionist Liberalism with two important components. First is the economic component, a set of economic theses the significance of which allegedly supports a more active role for government in regulating the market. Roughly speaking, this component can be described as Keynesian. Chapter 9 argues that this framework provides little meaning for social responsibility.

The other component of Revisionist Liberalism is pluralism. Chapter 10 argues that Managerialists tend to rely upon a pluralistic model in an effort to understand society, and they rely upon prescriptive pluralism in an effort to legitimize certain developments, namely, the mixed economy with a welfare state. That attempt, I argue, fails.

In chapter 11, I shall return to the theme of the internationalization of the modern corporation. I review these ideologies in light of this emerging new reality.

2

Classical Liberalism

Although *The American Business Creed*[1] was published in 1956, the core ideas of the Classical business ideology appear to have changed very little since then. A virtually identical description of the Classical ideology could have been constructed by sifting through more recent pronouncements of the National Association of Manufacturers, the group whose literature provided much of the basis for *The American Business Creed*, or by creating a collage from speeches of conservative politicians or representatives of the business community. With the ascendancy of the "Chicago school" of economic theory, Classical ideas have regained credibility. By means of more popular writers, such as the supply-siders, the ideas have also begun to find more widespread acceptance. The so-called Reagan revolution moved the rhetoric of the contemporary scene even closer to this conservative perspective identified in the period 1900–1949 by the authors of *The American Business Creed*.

As many have recognized, including the authors of the *The American Business Creed*, the basic ideas of the Classical ideology are essentially those of Classical Liberalism. While this outlook is often described as "conservative," the philosophical ideas have long been recognized and designated as those characteristic of the liberal tradition. These are liberal in contrast to the traditions of Marxism/socialism, fascism, or monarchism. Classical Liberalism is conservative in contrast to the more "liberal" liberalism of Revisionist Liberalism, which represents the theoretical core of the Managerial framework.

That the Classical and Managerial frameworks are both grounded in the liberal tradition should come as no surprise. Lionel Trilling

27

was close to the mark when he quipped that in America, liberalism is not merely the dominant political orientation, it is the only one.[2] Monarchists or royalists do not exist. Those sympathetic to communism, socialism, or fascism are considered by most as radicals and exist only at the fringe of political existence. The strongest antiliberal force in America is probably theocratic and can be found among religious groups seeking to identify the U.S. principles of state and society with the Bible. In spite of the rhetoric about cultural diversity, the homogeneity of political values in the U.S. contrasts sharply with some Western European countries, where there has been, until quite recently, less cultural diversity but greater political heterogeneity. In France, for instance, a few monarchists coexist with a larger number of Marxists and socialists, and with an even larger number of liberals of both the Revisionist and Classical variety. The story is the same in other countries.

Characterizing this diffuse liberal tradition is difficult. In *Toward a Liberalism*, Richard E. Flathman notes[3] that "liberalism has never been a closely integrated or firmly fixed doctrine; its proponents have held to a considerable and frequently changing variety of views and its historians and critics have regularly disagreed concerning its main ideas and tendencies."

In *Liberalism*,[4] however, John Gray attempts to formulate the tradition's basic tenets. According to Gray, it is a "definite conception, distinctively modern in character, of man and society." This conception

> is *individualist*, in that it asserts the moral primacy of the person against the claims of any social collectivity; *egalitarian*, inasmuch as it confers on all [humans] the same moral status and denies the relevance to legal or political order of difference in moral worth among human beings; *universalist*, affirming the moral unity of the human species and according a secondary importance to specific historic associations and cultural forms; and *meliorist* in its affirmation of the corrigibility and improvability of all social institutions and political arrangements. (x)

The roots of this conception, in Gray's view, reach back to ancient Greece and Rome, and the sources are as diverse as Stoicism, Epicureanism, and Christianity. Further, Gray contends that liberalism has taken on a "different flavor" in different national cultures as French, German, and English nationalism each developed distinctive characteristics. American liberalism, "though much indebted to English and French thought and practice, soon acquired novel features of its own." However, this liberal conception is not to be identified with any particular moral, national, ethnic, or religious tradition.

There are family resemblances within the liberal tradition as well as significant differences among representatives.[5] All liberals stress political egalitarianism, one reason that the position was radical or revolutionary. In contrast to those who hold that political power is rightfully held as the function of birth or intelligence, liberals claim that political rights should be distributed equally among all citizens. Historically, of course, those to be considered as citizens with the right to participate in the political process has slowly expanded. Originally only white males with substantial property holdings were franchised. One by one, very gradually, the requirements of being white, being male, and possessing substantial property were discarded. Liberals also share a commitment to free market capitalism and limitations upon government power. Liberals are concerned with liberty, freedom from political interference. However, there are enormous disagreements within the liberal tradition concerning the appropriate range of free- dom, over the form government should take, and about the legitimate scope of government, especially the extent to which government may interfere in, supplement, or even replace the market in some spheres. In debates within liberalism over the appropriate scope of government, Classical Liberals take the most minimalist positions and are especially opposed to much regulation of the economy.

Gray's brief sketch, however, fails to do justice to one of the central values of liberalism, i.e., the value of freedom or liberty. "Liberty" can be understood as particular kind of "freedom," namely, freedom from political coercion, but the two words are often used synonymously. Because freedom is highly prized, liberals seek liberty from political coercion and urge limitations upon governmental power. But this focus upon the importance of freedom and liberty should not obscure the deeper underlying liberal commitment. Few liberals see freedom as a thing to be valued in itself. Freedom is valuable because of a deeper value commitment. As William Kymlicka writes in *Liberalism, Community, and Culture*,[6] liberalism begins with some "basic claims about our interests."[7] According to Kymlicka, for liberals our "essential interest is in leading a good life, in having those things which a good life contains."[8] Although this claim may appear obvious, even banal, important consequences follow. For instance, the interest in leading a good life provides an interest in having freedom to reflect, to think, and to reevaluate one's conception of the good life. One also has an interest in being able to live one's self-chosen life plans without undue interference. Moreover, reflection may cause one to abandon one life plan in favor of another. In short, the basic interest in pursuit of the good life entails an interest in the freedoms of belief, association, action, and so forth. The dispute among liberals, then, primarily revolves around what will count as undue interference. What right does the government have in interfering with the freedom of individuals? This is a critical question in liberal thought, and one which divides Classical and Revisionist Liberals.

The Classical American business ideology is rooted, then, in the mainstream of the liberal political morality but represents a particular variety of the liberal tradition known as Classical Liberalism. "Classical Liberalism," as the term is employed here, refers to a theory of political economy which is closely identified with ideas of the late eighteenth-century and nineteenth-century English liberals such as Adam Smith, Jeremy Bentham, John Stuart Mill, and Herbert Spencer, although similar conceptions can be found in other thinkers such as John Locke in the late seventeenth century, or Immanuel Kant in the eighteenth.[9] Smith's impact needs little explanation, but Mill's contribution is less widely appreciated today. His *Principles of Political Economy*[10] was published in 1848 and, as Donald Winch notes, "had no equal in terms of scope and stature."

> Considered simply as an economics textbook, it enjoyed a longer active life than any comparable work either before or since. Unlike its successors, including the work which replaced it as the bible of English economics, Alfred Marshall's *Principle of Economics*, published in 1890, it was read by the serious minded public as well as by dedicated students and those who merely wished to pass exams. Indeed, it was the last work of its kind to combine broad appeal with authoritative exposition. (11)

Mill's nineteenth-century England exemplifies, as Gray notes, "the historical paradigm of a liberal civilization"(26), and many other writers have seen there the "golden age of liberal theory and practice" (26). For the most part, the golden age was the age of Classical Liberalism.

The influence of English liberalism, especially Classical Liberalism, on American liberalism has even deeper roots. Locke's imprint on Americans such as Thomas Jefferson or Benjamin Franklin is unmistakable. Without doubt, however, the most significant influence on American thought occurred during the heyday of English Classical Liberalism, and the late nineteenth century and early twentieth century also constituted the heyday of Classical Liberal ideas in the U.S. Although thinkers such as Locke, Adam Smith, and John Stuart Mill represent the Classical Liberal tradition, the form of Classical Liberalism which became most popular in this country rested on simple and crude caricatures of the tradition. Its views came to be known and understood through advocates of Social Darwinism, such as Spencer. Only those aspects of Smith or Mill which reinforced the stereotypes were highlighted. John M. Keynes cites the enormous influence of these rather corrupted ideas,[11] as Classical Liberalism was reduced to the simplistic doctrine of "laissez-faire," associated with the sanctity of liberty from government interference and private property, and preached from the pulpits of England and the U.S., taught through primers, and disseminated to an even wider audience through the popular press.

MINIMAL GOVERNMENT AND LAISSEZ-FAIRE

As a theory of political economy, Classical Liberalism is a theory of politics, economics, and the relationship between the political and the economic. Quite simply, Classical Liberalism urges, *advocates*, minimal or limited government, a free market capitalist economy, and a laissez-faire government policy toward the economy. Although often purporting to be little more than a descriptive theory about how government and the economy work, this is clearly a prescriptive normative theory. The emphasis upon the descriptive components functions to provide rationales for prescription. Theories of the way free markets work, however, only supply the basis for their desirability; if a free market yields maximal social welfare or efficiency, for example, that will be used as a reason for urging laissez-faire. Held among Classical Liberals are widely divergent theories to explain why the free market is best, but they all converge in a general policy of laissez-faire.

"Laissez-faire," of course, comes from the French physiocrats who were advocating that the French monarchy restrain from attempts at economic regulation. Laissez-faire means literally "leave alone to make" or "leave alone to produce." "Laissez" is the imperative form of the verb, the form demanding that someone leave the market alone. Adam Smith agreed with the policy of the physiocrats but did not follow them in measuring the wealth of the economy in terms of the production of agricultural goods. While the term seems to originate with the physiocrats there is a much longer history in England that government should stay out of the economy in order to allow for greater productivity.

At the core of liberal theory, whether Classical or Revisionist, are the ideas that the individual person is valued and that freedom, especially liberty from interference by government, is essential for the growth and well-being of the individual.[12] Many liberals follow Mill and speak of liberty as a necessary condition for the achievement of human happiness. For Mill and most liberals, freedom is not good in itself; freedom is valuable extrinsically, not intrinsically. It is valuable as a means, perhaps even a necessary means, of achieving what is most valuable: happiness or the good life. In the general line of argument from Mill, even though freedom can be misused and abused, its value on the possessor is immediate and generally good. Consequently, many liberals believe that this idea suggests that a *presumptive case* exists for freedom. Given that the effects of freedom on the possessor are generally good (the possessor is free to pursue his or her own conception of the good life and therefore grow in knowledge and experience in that pursuit), the burden of proof should be upon anyone who wishes to interfere in this freedom.

The importance of liberty leads Classical Liberals toward a theory of the political which is reflected in many of the jingoistic phrases still used today. Government should be minimal or very limited. "A good government is one which governs the least." Some have described it as the "nightwatchman" form of government, the notion being that government serves little function other than the protection of basic interests like property. To capture how minimal the state should be, others have described this form of government as "anarchy with a constable." The centrality of liberty also lends support to laissez-faire capitalism, a system which allows individuals the liberty to produce and exchange goods and services on the basis of mutually acceptable terms.

Behind the slogans, the important questions, of course, remain: To what extent can government legitimately interfere in individual freedom? To what extent can government legitimately interfere in economic transactions? Where is the line to be drawn? How minimal is minimal? That is, while there is agreement that interference in the liberty of individuals is usually illegitimate, a bad thing, are there any good reasons to override the presumption in favor of liberty? If there are good reasons, what are they?

Except for anarchists, nearly everyone would agree that it is permissible to interfere in the freedom of an individual for the sake of preventing an individual from harming another.[13] Thus, this constitutes one possible ground or reason for using coercion against another, i.e., for interfering in liberty. This idea has been called the "harm principle." What distinguishes Classical Liberals from others is that they come very close to claiming that the harm principle is *only* legitimate reason for interfering in the liberty of an autonomous mentally competent adult.[14]

One may wish to claim that offending someone is harming, but this kind of harm, if it is really a harm, is of such a trivial and minor sort that theorists generally distinguish between the harm principle and the "offense principle." The offense principle expresses the idea that it is legitimate to interfere in the freedom of another in order to prevent that individual from offending another. Some Classical Liberals are willing to accept a *limited* offense principle. That is, Classical Liberals do not wish to see the state become involved in interfering in liberty by *prohibiting* behavior merely because it offends others. It is, for one thing, difficult both to define "offense" and to determine what will offend different individuals. Rather than being enjoined, however, potentially offensive behavior could be *regulated.* For example, public sexual activity or nudity may be offensive to some, and Classical Liberals will usually support attempts to regulate such behavior in a fashion which is as minimally disruptive to all parties as possible. For example, nudity may be banned in some public places but allowed in others where those who might be offended can easily avoid the offense; signs could be posted warning those likely to be offended to stay clear of an area. Aside from this minor exception, Classical Liberals attempt to draw the line between illegitimate and legitimate interference in liberty by appealing to the unsupplemented harm principle. The harm principle has become the cherished principle of the Classical Liberal view of minimal government.

For Classical Liberals, prevention of harm is alleged to be the *sole* legitimate function of government. This is to say, indirectly, that there are many reasons which do *not* count as good reasons for interfering in liberty.[15] Classical Liberals reject the principle of "legal moralism," the idea that government may legitimately intervene in freedom on the grounds of acting to prevent someone from doing something immoral. The function of government is not, at least directly, to make individuals behave morally. As more contemporary liberals are fond of saying, the function of law is to prevent crime, not sin. This is not to say that the liberal theory avoids appealing to morality; it does not. A moral defense of the harm principle or any other proposed liberty-limiting principle must be given. But Classical Liberals, as well as most other liberals, deny that the function of government should be to enforce morality per se. Classical Liberals also reject the principle of "Paternalism."[16] That is, they claim, the government should not be in the business of protecting people from making bad choices which might harm themselves. A root idea is the autonomous individual, capable of making his/her own choices. The autonomy of the individual, liberty, is highly valued. Paternalism is an affront to autonomy. Moreover, Classical Liberals reject the welfare principle, the idea that the immediate function of government is to promote the social welfare or the greatest happiness, to force some individuals to help others.[17] Individual autonomy cannot be violated for the sake of helping others or improving the general welfare. The minimal state then, stands in sharp contrast to the state which attempts to enforce morality (legal moralism), to protect people from harming themselves (paternalism), or to force individuals to benefit others (the welfare principle).

For Classical Liberals, the minimal state is a civil libertarian state. The function of the state is to prevent harm to another, and, for the most part, if one consents to an act, one cannot complain of being harmed. Thus, there is no room for so-called "morals offenses" here. What adults consent to in private is of no concern to the state. There should probably be no laws against prostitution, homosexual relations, distribution of pornographic or obscene materials, and so forth. In fact, some liberals supported this kind of legislation, but the grounds appear to be not so much a matter of principle as of political expediency in a Christian culture where many find these activities repulsive. Not only is the state not concerned with making people moral, it is non-paternalistic. The function of the state is not to prevent people from injuring themselves. Strictly speaking, suicide should not be a concern of government, provided there is care to insure that the choice is autonomous, i.e., that the individual is an adult and is capable of rational thought. (Of course, if the suicide would constitute harm to another—e.g., break a contract—then it could be prevented.) Drug use, even drug addiction, should not be the concern of the state except at the point at which harm to another is threatened. And the minimal state is clearly not a welfare state as we have come to know it; taxing individuals for the sake of helping others would constitute an illegitimate incursion into the liberty of autonomous individuals. Some Classical Liberals would claim that individuals have moral or religious obligations to help the poor, the "unfortunate," those handicapped and unable to compete, but government has no right to force individuals to be moral. Government has no right to direct individuals about how to fulfill those obligations, even if they do exist.

Many "conservatives" do not adhere consistently to the Classical Liberal framework today. Within the business community, and within the country as a whole, there are often attempts to argue that government has no right to interfere in economic freedom, no right to regulate contracts, wages, health, safety, and so forth. But this is occasionally accompanied by calls for governmental regulation into other areas which are entirely private. These would include many "morals offenses," private behavior between consenting adults. "Liberals," today, Revisionist Liberals, while vigorously defending civil liberties against "conservative" attacks, often claim that government interference into economic decisions is legitimate.

Since the harm principle is the key to the Classical Liberal position, and since debate with those advocating a more than minimal state will to a great extent revolve around this principle, a great deal rests upon the notion of harm involved.[18] Classical Liberals did not devote much attention to explaining or defending the concept, but "harm" was interpreted extremely narrowly. More than likely, they relied upon the narrow interpretations as reflected in the common law tradition. The basic idea can be expressed as follows:

In contemporary coinage, to harm another is to invade another's protected interest. Certain interests which are taken to be so important that they require protection are life, health, liberty, contract, property, possessions, reputation, and freedom from seriously disturbing mental states, for example. A moral defense for this selection can be sketched. Liberals are generally reticent to say that they have knowledge of what is truly good for all persons. They believe that individuals will disagree over conceptions of the good, over particular life goals and life plans. Therefore, they continue, it is important that each person have the liberty to determine her own life plan and to live out that life plan (so long as it harms no one else). Moreover, liberals believe that there are some interests which should be protected as essential to living one's life plan, regardless of which particular life plan one chooses to follow. Hence, the short list of interests—in life, health, property, and so forth—represents an attempt to determine what would be required to live a good life regardless of the particular conception of a good life one happens to develop (within certain limits).

The sole function of government, then, should be to protect individuals from being harmed, i.e., to prevent individuals from killing, injuring, taking away another's freedom, violating contracts, robbing or in some other way seizing another's property, or injuring another's reputation. Aside from this, individuals are left at liberty to pursue their own vision of the good. For this purpose, the government enforces law. Certain harms are made criminal, others civil. In an ideal world, no person would knowingly harm another and there may be no need for a justice system in the minimal state. However, in the real world, the government provides a justice system which serves to determine whether indeed an individual has been harmed by another. If an individual is determined to have been harmed, the state (the court) determines the appropriate compensation and insures that compensation is paid. In some cases, namely those involving criminal harms, the minimal state will punish. In short, the minimal state offers very limited services. Because the function of the state is to protect against harm, a police force is established to protect citizens from other citizens; a military is required to protect citizens from foreign threats; a judiciary is established to judge whether harms have occurred to citizens and, if so, what compensation will be necessary; a penal system will punish offenders.

There is another important distinction which must be addressed. If it is legitimate to interfere in an individual's liberty in order to prevent harm to another, it must be possible to distinguish harming another from merely failing to benefit another. If I fail to provide food for a starving neighbor and that neighbor dies, have I harmed him or have I merely failed to benefit him? If I fail to throw a life jacket to a drowning child near the beach where I read, have I harmed or merely failed to benefit her? Where does one draw the line between harming and failing to benefit? This line is important because it will determine the extent to which the state can tax citizens for the sake of preventing harm. Taxation for Classical Liberals is legitimate, provided revenues are for the purpose of necessary functions of government. If the only legitimate reason for interfering in liberty is to prevent harm, then one must determine where to draw the line between harming and failing to benefit. Does the state have a responsibility to attend to the needs of the poor, the physically handicapped, the mentally incompetent? Do Classical Liberals support a "safety net"? Does the state have a right to tax citizens for the sake of attending to the needs of these "less fortunate" ones?[19] During the nineteenth century and much of the twentieth, there was no doubt: Classical Liberals often argued that not only does government have no responsibility to administer to the needs of the poor, the physically handicapped, or the mentally incompetent, but to tax for this sake is morally illegitimate. This argument rests on a particular construal of the harm/nonbenefit distinction. According to Classical Liberals, allowing someone to starve is not to harm them. Being in a situation of starvation is a harmful condition, but unless I have brought it about that others are in this situation, I have not harmed them. If I am passing along the lake and find someone drowning, I am not harming her by not assisting, I am merely failing to benefit her. Had I pushed her in the lake and she drowned, I would have harmed her. But I did not act. I am omitting to act by not offering assistance, even though I could offer assistance without any great cost to myself. The distinction is construed along the lines of acting/omitting-to-act. Acting to place someone in a harmful condition is, generally speaking, to harm them. Merely omitting to act to remove someone from such a condition is not a harm.

While there is good reason for believing that this distinction is suspect, it was reflected in common law and remains a central component of the legal system in the U.S. Thus, if the state is restricted to preventing harm, and if no one is harming fellow citizens by merely watching them starve, then the state cannot tax citizens in order to provide a safety net for citizens.

The position of Classical Liberals is not as cold as it might at first sight appear. Although allowing a poor person to die as the result of starvation or exposure is not to harm that person, some would argue that to allow such a person to die would be immoral because one has an obligation of charity, or beneficence. Violating a duty of charity is immoral. Citizens ought to help. But to violate a duty of charity is not the same as violating a duty of not harming. By failing to feed the starving, one could argue, an individual is not harming, but one is violating a duty of charity. According to the Classical Liberal, the state has no right to enforce morality and force citizens to discharge the duty of charity, even assuming that such a duty exists.[20]

One further qualification must be noted. Most in the Classical Liberal tradition understand the unsupplemented harm principle to incorporate not only what can be called the private harm principle but the public harm principle as well. The foregoing discussion involved the private harm principle, which claims that interference in liberty is justified on the grounds that one is preventing an individual from harming *another specific individual*. Thus, if I am about to shoot Jones, Smith might interfere in my liberty and justify his coercive action by appealing to the private harm principle, i.e., that he was preventing harm to a private, particular individual. Most would accept the idea that in some regards there is also a public interest or a public good which must be protected (not promoted, but protected). By not paying his taxes, Jones may not threaten harm to any particular individual; however, this kind of behavior is a threat to the public good, and, consequently, Jones's liberty may be intruded upon in some cases on grounds that the public good is threatened. Without this principle, it is difficult, for example, to see how in the minimal state one could justify laws against tax evasion. Crimes, of course, are considered invasions of the interests of the state, and justification of criminal sanctions would require appeal to the *public harm principle*. Murder is, after all, not only a civil wrong but a crime against "the people" of the state.

The public harm principle is dangerous for Classical Liberals. The principle does not justify interference to promote the public good (the welfare principle), only to protect the public good. But, since it is usually much more difficult to determine what might constitute a clear and present danger to the public interest than it is with respect to individual private interests, this principle could open the door for a rather extensive state. This principle may be invoked to attempt to justify taxation for an infrastructure, for example; one could argue that without bridges and roads in repair the public interest is threatened. The public harm principle also constitutes the basis for the claim that the state has a right to coin money and to provide a monetary framework. Further, those who attempt to argue that the minimal state has a right to prevent monopoly in the economic sphere will also need to appeal to the public harm principle as a way of protecting the public good as well as individuals. That Classical Liberals generally assume some version of the public harm principle also helps explain why there is such a wide range of disagreement among Classical Liberals themselves on the scope of governmental activity. Nonetheless, the principles remain intact. The state is minimal, concerned only with harm and, then, primarily only with private harm.

From this interpretation of property, liberty, and contract, Classical Liberalism guarantees and provides protection for the capitalist market. Capitalism can be roughly defined as a social economic system in which there is private ownership of the means of production. A market system is one in which things like price, quantity of production, things produced, quality of goods, and so forth are determined by the market (i.e., free transactions between individuals), not by some central authority.

By defending a particular interpretation of property, liberty, and contract, Classical Liberalism created the market as a private sphere to be protected by the minimal government but not regulated by government (except to determine claims of violation of contract or property, etc). The state will protect private property and possessions. The state has no right to interfere in the liberty of consenting adults, including the liberty to exchange goods and services or to contract, provided no one is harmed. Violating a contract is a harm. Fraud or deceit constitutes harm. Thus, the state will enforce contracts and punish fraud and deceit in contracts and exchanges.

Apart from this kind of involvement in the market, Classical Liberals support the policy of laissez-faire, the idea that government should leave the market alone.[21] The function of government becomes little more than protecting the requisites a free market. Classical Liberalism proposed fairly radical changes in the status quo; those who advocate the position today also propose radical changes in the status quo. The contemporary nation state bears little resemblance to the minimal or limited state of Classical Liberal theory. As with any radical reform proposals, not only must the promised benefits be great, but also the reform must be clothed with some kind of moral legitimacy. Why, for instance, should the sole purpose of government be to protect against harm? Why should government not regulate the economic sphere? One of the great tragedies of the contemporary scene is that even the proponents for minimal or limited government and laissez-faire capitalism have either lost touch with the moral arguments which have been used to buttress this view, or else proponents choose to ignore those arguments.

POLITICAL ECONOMY AND MORAL THEORY

As Gray indicates, in an attempt to morally legitimize their views, liberal theorists have appealed to a wide and diverse variety of normative theories. This underscores the extremely important point that theories of political economy take priority in formulating practical policy positions. Moral theory underdetermines, as it were, one's views in these areas. The search for the theory of political economy embedded in an ideology or framework is much more useful as a means of understanding the views of advocates than an initial search for ethical theories. Admittedly, the nuances of one's theory of political economy, whether Classical or Revisionist Liberalism, will vary according to the nature of the moral defense which is invoked. Yet those are differences at the margins and occur within the context of a more basic agreement. This also suggests that the disagreements between Classical and Revisionist Liberalism may rest as much upon descriptive disagreements as normative ones. Some utilitarians have been led to support Classical Liberalism, while others have been led to support Revisionist Liberalism, for example.

Nonetheless, a theory of political economy requires a normative defense, and any analysis must be sensitive to the different kinds of moral theories which have been invoked, insofar as they may make a significant difference in the arguments which can be developed. In the midst of the variety, Gray identifies two major moral traditions which have contributed most to the development of liberal thought, particularly Classical Liberalism, namely, utilitarianism and natural rights theory:[22] "Liberal moral and political claims have been grounded in theories of the natural rights of man as often as they have been defended by appeal to a utilitarian theory of conduct, and they have sought support from both science and religion" (x).

Actually, three traditions should be identified. Although traditionally associated with natural rights theories, social contract theories constitute another distinct and significant approach to political and moral philosophy, as I will soon explain. Hence, all three merit attention. Chapter 3 focuses upon natural rights and social contract theories. Chapters 4 and 5 will examine utilitarian defenses of Classical Liberalism.

3

Natural Rights and Social Contracts

John Locke's *Two Treatises of Government*[1] appeared over three hundred years ago. Following decades of political upheaval, the treatises were both a sign of the times and significant contributors to subsequent developments. The language of natural rights and social contract infused the rhetoric of the relatively conservative English revolutionaries of the Lockean variety, as well as the more radical. Those ideas echoed throughout the English colonies in North America during the American Revolution some eighty years later.[2] And, with the eruption of the French Revolution in 1789, *The Rights of Man* captured the emerging classes' aspirations, which were expressed in the belief in certain basic natural rights existing independently of the positive law of any nation. As remote and distant as these events may now appear, the tradition of natural rights and social contracts continues to influence contemporary thinkers. In the U.S., that tradition is often invoked in an attempt to defend the ideas of Classical Liberalism, the minimal state, and the free market.

This chapter will probe and evaluate that defense. The investigation should be of considerable interest to Managerialists as well, and not merely because the analysis will undermine one defense of the Classical framework. Recognizing that utilitarianism and the natural rights theory represent important and influential approaches to moral reasoning, some Managerialists have attempted to incorporate both into a normative decision-making process for managers. In *Business and Society: Corporate Strategy, Public Policy, Ethics*, for example, William C. Frederick, Keith Davis, and James E. Post reject the Classical view that the manager's sole responsibility is to maximize profit, and they develop instead an "analytical approach to ethical

41

problems."[3] Alternatives are analyzed in three steps. The first involves the application of utilitarian theory, natural rights theory, and then questions of justice and fairness to each alternative under consideration; each alternative is to be evaluated in light of each ethical consideration. Step two compares the results of step one. Here, a unanimity rule is invoked: If an alternative would be wrong according to a utilitarian account, a natural rights account, and in light of considerations of justice, then, the authors claim, that alternative is likely immoral. If, on the other hand, an alternative is judged to be morally right in light of each moral perspective, the alternative is likely to be moral. If the unanimity rule is inapplicable and the comparison yields mixed results—for example, if an alternative is right from the perspective of one or two theories; wrong, according to another— then the manager must prioritize the considerations. Regardless of the merits of this approach, if taken seriously it rests, at least in part, upon a theory of natural rights. Consequently, if the theory is found to be seriously wanting, grave reservations can be raised with respect to the approach, regardless of which ideology it is used to defend.

Two important factors entail that the focus of the chapter, however, cannot be restricted to natural rights theory. First, natural rights defenses of Classical Liberalism necessarily involve social contract theory, so any analysis of the natural rights defense must analyze the theory of the social contract. Second, other compelling reasons extend the inquiry into the area of social contract theory.

Social contract theory cannot and should not be identified exclusively with natural rights theories. Within the last thirty years, philosophers and political philosophers have come increasingly to believe that utilitarianism is not a viable moral theory in itself. Some have returned, therefore, to natural rights theories in a quest for an adequate alternative. Because the problems with those theories themselves are, as I will demonstrate, so severe, most have looked elsewhere. Many believe that social contract theories not grounded in natural rights provide the solution. Consequently, contractarian theories have proliferated.

The revival of contractarian thought began with the publication of John Rawls's A Theory of Justice[4] in 1971. Robert Nozick's Anarchy, State, and Utopia[5] followed shortly thereafter. More recently, David Gauthier's Morals by Agreement[6] has appeared. Each book is extremely important and widely discussed. But as they illustrate, social contract theory is neither exclusively associated with natural rights theory nor exclusively employed to defend the minimal state. Rawls develops a contract argument in an attempt to defend his two principles of justice, principles which entail something like a welfare state. Rawls's two principles are described in A *Theory of Justice* as follows:

> *First Principle.* Each person is to have an equal right to the most extensive total system of equal basic liberties compatible with a similar system of liberty for all. *Second Principle.* Social and economic inequalities are to be arranged so that they are both: (a) to the greatest benefit of the least advantaged, consistent with the savings principle, and (b) attached to offices and positions open to all under conditions of fair equality of opportunity. (302)

Clearly, the basic liberties are not limited to those necessary to protect individuals from being harmed by another. Moreover, the distribution of economic and social goods is determined not by market forces but by a principle which forbids unequal distributions unless they work to make the least well off better off. Reflecting this trend, social contract arguments have proliferated in applied ethics also, especially in the fields of Business Ethics and Business and Society, where they have been utilized by those attempting to defend the Managerial idea that corporate responsibility goes beyond profit maximization for stockholders. Hence, again, a discussion of contract theory will be of more than idle concern to Managerialists. First, natural rights theory itself must be addressed.

NATURAL RIGHTS THEORY

Most theories of morality will claim that there are moral rights, on the one hand, and moral duties, obligations, and responsibilities, on the other. Theories are distinguished, in part, by how these moral rights and moral duties are defended. Utilitarianism would defend moral rights and duties on the grounds that their observance promotes net utility for all. Natural rights theorists disagree and argue that certain moral rights are fundamental entitlements, irreducible to considerations of general social utility. In their view, any moral right either is itself a natural right or is derived from a natural right. These rights are understood to be possessed by virtue of some characteristic, often reason. Since modern liberal theorists generally believe that all humans possess this capacity (either actually or potentially), natural rights are held to be distributed equally. In this sense, natural rights theory and the liberalism which flows therefrom are individualistic and egalitarian. Moreover, natural rights are entitlements which, it is claimed, exist independently of whatever rights happen to be recognized legally or institutionally at any particular time or place. Those theorists, like Locke or Nozick, who adopt a very short list of natural rights have tended to support Classical Liberalism.

Locke's defense of a liberal state is found in the second of the *Two Treatises of Government*. Here Locke develops a natural rights theory, endeavoring to legitimize a limited parliamentary form of government. Contemporary Lockeans employ the argument as a weapon against what is often perceived to be overzealous democratic governments which act on behalf of "the people" to infringe the liberty of some.

The Lockean view is unmistakably liberal: one of the highest ideals is liberty, or freedom, of the individual. For Locke, humans are autonomous agents who should be at liberty to do with their person, property, or possessions anything whatsoever, "within the bounds of the laws of nature." This amounts to saying that a person is free to dispose of her person,[7] property, or possessions so long as she does not violate the rights of another. The right of liberty, then, is a right which cannot be understood without specific reference to these other rights. For Locke, it is safe to say that one is free to do anything so long as one does not harm another in her person, property, or possessions. If one overreaches, going beyond "the bounds of the laws of nature" to harm another, then two other natural rights are relevant. A human harmed by another possesses the right to be compensated for the harm. Further, a human possesses the right to punish those responsible for harming another, at least in some cases;[8] the punishment must be in some sense suitable to the harm and such that it would deter others from harming. Hence, three of the most important rights are those of liberty, compensation, and punishment.[9]

Until the "bounds of the laws of nature" are delineated, until "harm" is explicated, the limits of liberty are unclear and the appropriateness of compensation and/or punishment remains indeterminate.[10] One way of interpreting the notion of harm is to understand harm, as I have suggested in chapter 2, as an invasion of interest. According to this line, humans have certain enduring interests which persist behind fleeting, transitory, conscious desires. Included among these enduring interests are those in life, health, liberty, property, possessions, reputation, and contract, as well as freedom from seriously disturbing psychological states that are induced by threats to those interests. With this basic list of interests, content can be provided to the notion of harm. To harm someone is to invade one of these protected interests. Stealing, robbery, burglary, taking property or possessions without consent of the owner are morally wrong because they invade an interest in property and possession. Killing is wrong (except in self-defense or for punishment) because killing overruns an interest in life. Beating or injuring is wrong because they violate an interest in health. Kidnapping, restraining another's legitimate freedom of action, is wrong because it disregards an interest in, or right of, liberty. Slanderous and libelous claims are wrong because they go against an interest in reputation. Breaking contracts is wrong since it negates an interest humans have in keeping contracts. Also included in the list of interests or rights is the interest of living free of seriously disturbing psychological states. For example, being threatened with murder, robbery, or injury induce a state of fear. Many believe that humans have a right not to be disturbed in these ways. Only the more serious disturbances would count as harms; other actions which disturb would be considered only as offenses or nuisances.

This list of harms touches upon nearly all of the major constraints on liberty; the outlines of the basic moral theory is complete. The theory is one of permissibility, the only duty being the duty not to harm; anything else is permissible. Moral obligations are minimal. Morality amounts to little more than avoiding traditional common-law crimes.

Through all this, Locke says virtually nothing about corporations, which existed even in his time, of course. Labor guilds, municipalities, ecclesiastical organizations, and trading companies, including joint partnerships, were familiar entities. All of them functioned under a charter granted by the crown. Often the charters granted monopolies of trade and/or production and were specially crafted to suit the purposes deemed appropriate by the throne. Under the mercantile polices of the state, the corporation became a tool of state polices. A trading company might hold the only license in London or all of England to make soap, or the only license to produce and sell playing cards abroad. The East India Bay Company, which employed later liberals like James Mill and his son, John Stuart Mill, was such a company with rights to trade with India. A similar practice was originally followed by state legislatures in the U.S. Special incorporation charters contained provisions restricting where the corporation could be located, capitalization, debt structures, etc. General incorporation charters became predominant only after the Civil War and evolved to the point where corporations were chartered with virtually no constraints except to follow the law.

The corporation as we know it today can be situated in a Lockean natural rights framework, however, by viewing it as an artificial person, a collective of natural persons joined together contractually with common interests. Within that framework, the appropriate role of a corporation is no different from that of any other natural person. The corporation as artificial person is free to do anything so long as it harms no one. If it harms, then it is obligated to compensate, or may be subjected to punishment, or both. Within this framework there is no moral obligation to maximize one's own self-interest, but there is generally an assumption that humans will be naturally inclined to promote their own good. Morality provides the guidelines within which self-interest should operate. Acting in one's self-interest is not immoral.

An obligation to maximize profit must be generated by additional considerations. For instance, if individuals in a collectivity such as a corporation contract among themselves or contract with someone else (e.g., board of directors, the CEO) to maximize profit, then an obligation to maximize profit is created. This obligation would exist by virtue of the promise or contract.

The real debate concerns the extent to which government can interfere in the liberty of individuals, artificial or natural. If extensive government interference is legitimate, the government might have a right to limit the nature of contracting so that the corporate charter would entail social responsibilities other than profit maximization. Or, extensive government interference might allow free contracting for the creation of corporations but virtually do away with a free market. The Classical Liberal is bent upon limiting the role of government in order to maximize freedom. The basic objection is that government interference constitutes a violation of some natural right. For a government to limit prices or set rates through a regulatory agency, for example, could be viewed as appropriating property from the corporation. To fix minimal wages or to regulate working conditions could be viewed as an interference in the right of two parties to join in contract. Some would even argue that the government has no right even to require that corporations be chartered by the state, on the grounds that the requirement of chartering constitutes an interference in the right of contract.

But these questions cannot yet be addressed. Natural rights theory begins with the rights that individuals have in the state of nature. Discussions proceed on the assumption that governments do not exist. In reality, humans today live in political organizations such as nation states. For instance, Locke claims that we have a right to compensation and punishment: Why, then, do states prohibit individuals from taking the law into their own hands, extracting by force, if necessary, compensation for an automobile accident, or locking up an offender in one's basement for life as punishment for murder? How do governments fit into this scheme? If no state is morally legitimate, then it is clear that no state has a right to interfere in one's freedom. Hence, to address the important question of the appropriate role of a corporation within a free society, the discussion must turn to social contract theory. Before engaging in such an analysis, however, problems with natural rights theory itself can be identified.

PROBLEMS

An examination of merely a few of the serious problems associated with natural rights theory will explain why the theory is largely discredited. As John Gray writes in his book on *Liberalism*, the "difficulties involved in constructing a plausible theory of natural rights today are formidable and in all likelihood insuperable."[11] This is not to say that there is serious doubt about whether humans possess moral rights not to be harmed in their important interests, all things being equal. This is not to take exception to the idea of the importance of freedom and liberty from interference. The question is whether natural rights theories can provide a forceful and coherent explanation of these intuitions. Analysis demonstrates the impossibility of that endeavor.

The problems concern the list of natural rights provided and the failure to address adequately three important questions. First, what reasons can be offered for believing that humans possess natural rights? This is not necessarily the same question as whether one agrees that harming another is immoral, all things being equal. The question is whether appealing to natural rights offers any plausible account of why harming is immoral, all things being equal. Second, supposing that humans do possess natural rights, how can we know that the list provided by Locke, Nozick, or any other theorist contains all and only those rights? That is, by what criterion or set of criteria are natural rights identified? This question is related to the first. A theory which

purports to explain why humans have natural rights may simultaneously explain why we have some rights and not others. Third, how
is any particular mention of a natural right to be interpreted? I have,
for instance, suggested the outline of an exposition for "harm." There
are numerous other key concepts which must be explicated. How will
"contract" be understood? What will count as a contract? What will
count as property? Philosophers, lawyers, and jurists have engaged,
and continue to engage, in long and protracted debate over each of
these issues. Very different theories follow upon varying exegeses of
these central concepts.

The importance of these questions should be evident. If the moral
legitimacy of the minimal state and of free market capitalism is said
to rest upon natural rights, this defense will be ineffective unless
natural rights themselves have some credibility and unless the list of
natural rights is accepted. If no compelling reasons for the existence
of natural rights can be given, then one's defense of the minimal state
and market capitalism will be useless against anyone who does not
accept those premises. Some might attempt to ground these natural
rights in some divine decree, i.e., God bestowed inalienable rights,
but Classical Liberals tend to eschew this appeal. Even if one accepts
that there are such things as natural rights,[12] the force of the second
question remains. How can one determine whether those natural
rights mentioned by Locke are the correct ones? Perhaps Locke's list
is too long. Perhaps it is too short.

Locke, for his part, does nothing more than to supply a list. He
provides neither an argument purporting to demonstrate the existence
of natural rights nor an argument defending his particular set. In
other words, Locke merely assumes that this is the correct moral
theory and then proceeds to develop a political philosophy based
upon it. This weakness, too, has serious implications for the defense
of the minimal state and market capitalism. If any one of the items
on the list of natural rights is not included, that defense collapses.
Suppose, for instance, that it turns out that Locke's belief in the
right of private property is specious. The moral props would then be
kicked from under one of the critical notions of capitalism. Or, conversely, if Locke's list is too short, and other rights should be added,
the defense of the minimal state and market capitalism might also
vanish. Many have argued that the list of natural or human rights is
much longer. The United Nations Declaration of Human Rights, for
instance, includes things like the right to employment, the right to

sufficient food, and so forth. If those in the Classical tradition wish to reject these candidates, what reason can be given? If these are included, then the government may be responsible for much more than protecting humans from harm. Government would then have some responsibility for providing jobs, food, shelter, and so forth. Thus, if a longer list of natural rights is assumed, a more than minimal state is probably legitimate.

The interpretation of particular natural rights is also critical. For instance, when a poverty-stricken worker "agrees" to sell his/her labor to another, is this really a contract? Some argue that an "agreement" in situations like this is not sufficient to establish a contract because of "duress," "exploitation," "inequalities," etc. Depending upon how "contract" is construed, even a minimal government may wish to forbid exchanges which are exchanges made under duress, or as a result of exploitation, or even when one party is greatly disadvantaged in the bargaining. Government might interfere to prevent harm to an individual by having minimum wage laws, for example.

Contemporary proponents of the Lockean minimal state such as Nozick have done nothing more to provide a response to any of these elementary questions. Like Locke, Nozick merely assumes in *Anarchy, State, and Utopia* the existence of a narrow list of natural rights. This prompted Thomas Nagel to title his review of Nozick's work "Libertarianism without Foundations."[13] Moreover, Nozick provides little reason for believing that the list of natural rights is not much longer. Such a theory takes on the complexion of seriously begging the question, i.e., assuming these particular natural rights only because they provide a defense for what one seeks to defend.[14]

A longer list would have important ramifications for corporate persons as well as natural persons. If there are obligations to help others under certain circumstances, these cannot be ignored when natural individuals associate and form corporations. Corporate persons may also have much wider obligations, obligations which extend beyond, or conflict with, self-interest or profit maximizing. The role of the corporation would be radically upset if the defense of the minimal state and free market capitalism were altered. A longer list of natural rights might well entail an elimination of the free market.

There is one other comment about the short list. Many cultures, including our own, have a commonsense understanding that humans have certain obligations or duties to others. These duties may be slight, but they are generally recognized. For instance, many cultures would recognize a moral duty to offer assistance to another who is in great need, when one can do so without any great cost or danger to oneself or others. In some cultures, the Inuit or Bedouin, something like this is reflected in the duties of hospitality. Many recognize the obligation to warn others of impending danger. In the view of Locke and Nozick, these obligations are non-existent. This conflicts with our commonsense judgments. Now, a theory may cause us to reevaluate our commonsense judgments. But a short list of natural rights offers no explanation of why we should discount these other rights in particular. Indeed, Locke and others have sought to admit the existence of these duties but to explain them away as *religious* obligations.

Thus, the fragility of the natural rights theory, and the associated idea that the corporation has no obligation except to avoid harming another, is apparent. This defense does not even do justice to the liberal tradition itself. The only passage in which Nozick even suggests something like a defense of the existence of natural rights is revealing. He refers to natural rights as "side constraints" upon our actions and is clearly concerned to protect individuals from utilitarian considerations which would require the sacrifice of individuals for the sake of the common good under certain conditions.

> The moral side constraints upon what we may do, I claim, reflect the fact of our separate existences. They reflect the fact that no moral balancing act can take place among us; there is no moral outweighing of one of our lives by others so as to lead to a greater overall *social* good. There is no justified sacrifice of some of us for others. This root idea, namely, that there are different individuals with separate lives and so no one may be sacrificed for others, underlies the existence of side moral constraints . . . (33)

The reasoning here, if any, is extremely murky. The idea that there are "different individuals with separate lives" is unobjectionable, except that for Nozick this is taken to mean that humans are not connected in morally significant ways to other human beings, that humans have no duty whatsoever to other individuals except to leave them alone. Most everyone would agree that humans ought to live "separate lives" in the sense that partners in important and intimate relationships, such as relationships between spouses, friends, siblings, and parent and a child, should not allow identities and interests to become totally submerged. Most, however, would claim that these relationships create moral duties, obligations, and responsibilities. The moral relevance of human relationships is totally excluded from this minimalist perspective.

Furthermore, even given this distorted idea of the importance of "separate" persons, it does not follow that any sacrifice for another individual or the social good is always morally objectionable. The widely recognized problem with utilitarianism, one which is developed in later chapters, is the fanatical conviction that the social good is the only morally relevant consideration. Utilitarianism, too, ignores the fabric of human relationships and reduces all relationships to considerations of social welfare. The status of the minimalist natural right theorists is equally fanatical in denying the moral relevance of anything except not harming another. This view excludes, not only considerations of social good, but any other goods as well.

This sterile and barren conception cuts itself off from the genuine roots of liberalism. By failing to address the most obvious and important questions, the view remains superficial. Why is autonomy important? Why is living "different and separate" lives important? Why are freedom and liberty important? For liberals, freedom is important as a means to some other end, namely, the flourishing of human potentiality. That flourishing is, or is necessary for, human happiness or well-being. In that context the significance of living different and separate lives makes sense. Yet the emphasis on separateness should not ignore the background of relatedness. Flourishing involves other humans, mixing one's own interests, happiness, and well-being with those of others. The liberal emphasis on individualism need not lead toward isolationism. Making human flourishing paramount could generate a list of rules or guidelines for flourishing. Liberals have generally included freedom as an important component. Very likely, however, the list would be much longer than the one proposed by Nozick. Human flourishing might well involve the actualization of obligations beyond merely avoiding harm to others. And human flourishing might best be accomplished outside the narrow confines of the minimal state.

THE "SOCIAL CONTRACT"

Even if the short list of natural rights were acceptable, the defense of the minimal state would remain incomplete. Proponents of the Classical framework need to demonstrate, in Nozick's phrase, *that a minimal state and nothing more extensive is morally legitimate.* On the one hand, the more than minimal state must be shown to be illegitimate. If something more than a minimal state is legitimate, then that state might well be morally permitted to interfere in market transactions in ways which would disrupt the free market and impose on corporations duties beyond those of avoiding harm. The battle with the Revisionist Liberals is waged on this flank. Classical Liberals must also protect their other flank against the threat of anarchism. Thus, on the other hand, the legitimacy of the minimal state itself must be demonstrated. It is not sufficient to demonstrate that according to the short list of natural rights the meddling welfare state is morally unjust. Perhaps no state is legitimate.

In short, natural rights theorists must venture into political philosophy. For them, that involves the theory of the social contract. In the liberal tradition, political philosophy revolves primarily around four related questions. Given the importance bestowed upon the value of individual freedom, the first is whether any government is morally legitimate. As Nozick puts it, "Why not anarchism?" By what moral right can anyone interfere in freedom? Second, supposing that some governments are morally legitimate, what is the scope of the coercive powers which government may wield? What are the limits, if any, of legitimate governmental interference in the liberty of citizens? Third, what obligations are owed the state by citizens? Do citizens have a duty to conform to unjust laws? Under what conditions, if any, are civil disobedience, rebellion, and revolution justified? Finally, there is the question of the extent to which governments may punish offenders of law.

That natural rights theory relies upon contract theory to fashion responses to these questions is more than historical accident.[15] Natural rights are grounded in individual natural persons. If other entities, collectivities of natural persons such as a corporation or a government, have rights, those rights are ultimately derived from the rights of natural persons. The minimalist conception of the natural rights tradition, as represented by Locke and Nozick, offers only scant resources for constructing a morally legitimate state. About the only available resource is the freedom of individuals to contract together, thereby creating larger collectivities with derivative rights and duties. In this view, the state is the unnatural artifact of consenting adults.

While this sounds simple enough, closer inspection reveals serious difficulties with contract arguments. These difficulties come into sharper focus by identifying the nature or logic of contract theory. Unfortunately, the literature is generally bereft of careful discussion of this important matter. Classical texts, J. W. Gough's *The Social*

Contract[16] and Otto Gierke's *Natural Law and the Theory of Society*[17] never address the issue. Recent advocates do little more than refer to the earlier sources. Critics usually attack a particular contract theory and then hastily generalize. Therefore, let me suggest a model.

Contract arguments can best be understood as instances of a process argument.[18] Actual and hypothetical process arguments can be distinguished. In an "actual process argument," an outcome O is morally justified if and only if it can be shown that O *has arisen* from an initial situation S by a process P, and that S and P are morally defensible. Rawls's idea of pure procedural justice exemplifies an actual process argument. His discussion of a poker game illustrates the important features. Suppose a number of players voluntarily come together to play poker. Each has come by her money legitimately. Each understands the rules. This can be described as an initial situation S. By virtue of this description, we can accept that S is morally legitimate. Now the game begins. The game can be considered as a morally defensible process P for reaching an outcome O, a distribution of money. The process can be described as morally legitimate because the betting is voluntary, the rules are understood and accepted by all, and the rules are followed scrupulously. At an agreed-upon time, the game is finished. An outcome O, a distribution of money, has arisen. Is the outcome morally legitimate? According to an actual process argument, O is morally legitimate because O has arisen from S by P, and S and P are themselves morally legitimate.

"Hypothetical process arguments," on the other hand, claim that an outcome O is legitimate if and only if O *would arise* from an initial situation S by a process P, and S and P are morally legitimate. Actual process arguments are grounded in history and morality. One must demonstrate that an outcome actually arose by an actual process from an initial situation which actually existed. In hypothetical process arguments, one need not demonstrate that the initial situation actually existed or that the process actually occurred. Moral defenses of S and P are required, but beyond this the argument will consist of logic, not history. Hypothetical process arguments must demonstrate that an outcome O *would* arise, not that it has.

Contract arguments are process arguments in which the process invoked as morally defensible is a process of contracting, i.e., giving consent, compacting, choosing, giving one's word, promising, etc. Actual contract arguments require that an outcome O arose from an initial situation S, often called a state of nature, by a process P, contracting, and that S and P are morally legitimate. The attractiveness of contract arguments rests upon the general consensus that, all things being equal, if mentally competent mature adults contract with one another, the contract has moral force. The intuitiveness of the contract notion is complicated by the fact that contract arguments do not rely exclusively upon actual contracts. They variously rely upon one or another of a number of different kinds of contracts, the most important of which are actual, tacit, dispositional, or hypothetical. Because there are different kinds of contracts, there are very different kinds of contract arguments. Which, if any, of these arguments will support the claims of the Classical Liberals? Indeed, will these arguments support any claims at all? By carefully examining each of the different kinds of contract argument, I will demonstrate that this approach is nothing more than a blind alley.[19]

ACTUAL CONTRACTS

Actual contract theories claim those and only those governments which arose as a result of an actual contract are legitimate. Strictly speaking, an "actual" or "express contract" consists of an offer, an acceptance of the offer, and what the law calls a consideration. Some party must offer terms to another party, the terms must be relatively clear and intelligible, the parties must understand and accept the offer, and something must be exchanged. Valid contracts require, among other things, that the parties enter into the agreement voluntarily.[20] Thus, actual contract theories require that the relevant parties (e.g., "the people" and "the queen") actually contract together, satisfying these conditions. In the words of the Declaration of Independence, legitimate government rests upon the consent of the governed.

To explain "Why not anarchy?" contract theorists begin by placing individuals in a nonstate or prestate anarchistic situation, generally referred to as the state of nature. For actual contract theorists this is understood historically. Indeed, Locke appears to believe (sometimes) that humans did in fact live in a state of nature and only later came together through a contract to form a society and a government. His is really a two-contract theory. First, parties contract to form a society, and then a contract is struck to create a government for the people. For Locke, a vivid image of the contract between the people and the government would be the coronation of the new king, or perhaps the Bill of Rights being signed by William and Mary after the Glorious Revolution.

Legitimacy rests exclusively upon the showing that an actual contract was negotiated. Theorists attempt to make this plausible by explaining that individuals had (and continue to have) a motive to move from a state of nature to form civil society and a government. The explanations are based upon the purported instability, or what Locke calls the inconveniences, of the state of nature. Market forces, it can be argued, operate to push individuals together. There are economies of scale. Moreover, in the state of nature strife would be a constant. Individuals would be hesitant to commit themselves to any agreements without an agency which would enforce contracts. And even well-meaning and considerate individuals would confront serious obstacles to peace and security. Disputes over whether an individual in fact had been harmed by another would erupt frequently, given that each individual would be left on her own to judge her own case. Any dispute over property rights, over damage to property, over injury, over compensation for damages or injury carries the potential for escalating to violence. Ultimately, disagreements could be resolved only by force or threat of force.

On this view, then, the state is morally legitimate since it is nothing more than the result of a contract in which individuals freely and knowingly consent to *transfer* certain rights in exchange for benefits.[21] Specifically, Locke believes that although each individual retains the right of self-defense, the rights to determine whether a person has been harmed, the amount of compensation due, and the appropriate punishment, if any, are transferred to the state. Thus, taking over these functions, the state provides a penal and judicial system. Further, the state provides protection against harm. The laws should be publicly known and police retained to prevent anyone from harming another. A military force provides protection against harm from foreign invaders and from insurrection. Since people have contracted for these services, taxation amounts to little more than paying for contracted services. Citizens purportedly have no moral complaint because the obligations are the result of self-imposed contractual obligations.

This is a compelling story. Actual contracts are morally important considerations which carry much force. Too much force in fact, because the story is fictitious.[22] It is highly unlikely that any society or government arose from a state of nature by a primordial contract. The idea of a state of nature and an actual contract is a myth. Consequently, if a government does not rest upon an actual contract with the people, according to this theory, that government is not legitimate. Thus, *actual contract arguments establish requirements which*

are sufficiently high to render illegitimate virtually every existing state.
Actual contract theory proves unworkable because it immediately
yields these anarchistic consequences. And actual contract theory is
no kinder or gentler to Classical Liberals in this regard than to others.
This anarchistic consequence follows even if one could find the ideal
minimal government with a perfectly free market existing somewhere
on earth. Unless a historical event occurred in which citizens contracted together for this state, it has no claim to moral legitimacy.

There is another problem. Even if one could discover an existing
state which arose as a result of individuals contracting together, there
is no guarantee that it would be a minimal state. Actual contract
theories can as readily legitimize a welfare state as a minimal state.
One can imagine situations in which individuals contracted together
for a welfare state. Humans have been known to act in all sorts of
bizarre ways. Thus, if the defender of the minimal state wishes to
employ the actual contract argument as a defense, there is no longer
any basis for criticizing the more than minimal state in principle
as immoral. The debate turns on historical reality, on what actually
happened or did not happen. No abstract argument can establish
either the legitimacy of the minimal state or the illegitimacy of the
more than minimal state.[23]

Finally, actual contract theory is itself unstable. Consider the first-
born of the original contracting parties. Suppose there is ratification
by all members of a state (minimal or more than minimal). What
happens with the next generation? What happens when a child born
into this state reaches adulthood? Anarchism again threatens. Unless
the contemporary population agrees to a contract, the state loses
legitimacy. In those situations, the free-rider problem is great. The
incentive in the next generation is to enjoy the benefits of governmental services while refusing to enter the contract. Governments do
not, of course, allow this choice. The opportunity for free-riding would
quickly destroy the status of the state's moral legitimacy and lead to
deteriorating services with the subsequent collapse of the state itself.
Actual contract theory offers few resources to handle this problem.

TACIT CONTRACTS

Faced with the threat of anarchism, the threat that actual contract
arguments do not guarantee a particular outcome, and the threat posed
by the second generation, contract theorists tend to slink quietly away

from a reliance on the notion of an actual contract. Locke, for example, shifts from the requirement that actual consent be given toward the idea that only tacit consent is necessary. The tacit contract notion is often introduced to solve the problem of the second generation. Reaching the age of maturity and not leaving the state, it is argued, constitutes tacit consent to the government. For each generation, then, not leaving the state renews the contract. Those who do not wish to contract may leave. One of Plato's early dialogues, the *Crito*, presents this kind of an argument.

That tacit or implicit contracts carry moral force is reflected by their recognition in law. In some circumstances, the law sees fit to characterize transactions as contractual when the conditions necessary for an express contract are not satisfied. If I enter a cab and say to the driver, "Take me to the airport," I have made a tacit legal contract. I did not explicitly negotiate with the driver. I did not explicitly offer to pay the amount of money on the meter. In fact, I did not even offer to pay for the ride at all. The driver did not say that he expected to be paid and would drive me only if I agreed to pay. In short, strictly speaking, there was no offer and no acceptance. The law, however, appears to believe that this was all *tacitly* understood in this situation. Flagging a cab and uttering the words "Take me to the airport" count as an offer with the terms as posted in the cab. Starting the meter counts as accepting the terms.

Tacit contracts carry moral force as well, but as in law only in very restricted circumstances. In a tacit contract both parties must understand (or could easily come to understand, or should understand) the conditions which are implicit. Entering a cab has a certain meaning in our culture. Individuals in that culture either understand or should understand (could easily come to understand) the conditions involved. On the other hand, in situations where the conditions are not widely understood, the notion of a tacit contract makes little sense and carries little force. If I stop and pick up a hitchhiker and drop him off at the airport, then I am in no position to complain that I am owed money because of any tacit contract which exists. There is no generally understood set of conditions which suggest that hitchhikers owe drivers anything.

The notion of a tacit contract must be severely restricted because extending the idea beyond narrowly circumscribed areas would permit scenarios in which individuals would be unwittingly or involuntarily entering into contracts. Obligations could be fabricated in all sorts of relations. What is to count as tacit consent? Consider the problem in one particularly sensitive area. Does cohabitation over a period of years (absent express contracting or marriage vows) create contractual obligations analogous to those created in legally recognized marriage? Is a long-time lover to be entitled to death benefits analogous to those of a surviving spouse? After a cohabitative arrangement ceases, can one party sue for continuing support, as a spouse may sue in divorce? These issues hinge upon whether a tacit contract has been involved. In this case, our intuitions are often conflicting, especially given that homosexuals, for instance, are forbidden to marry legally. Our moral intuitions may coax us into accepting some relationships as involving legal tacit consent in order to correct what we may view as injustices in other areas of law. The point, however, is that in this area whether a tacit contract is involved is extremely controversial because the social meanings involved are not clear.

The suggestion that failure to leave the place of one's birth con-stitutes a tacit contract with the ruling government is, I would argue, even more controversial. If cohabitation is a borderline case, this case is beyond the line. In the case of cohabitation, both parties voluntarily agree to take up residence together. Residence could have been taken up with another party, or with no one. But one is born into a country; one does not decide to take up residence there. Further, if one is forced to choose between giving consent to the existing government and leaving the country, this is not a free, voluntary decision but a decision under duress. Leaving a cohabitative arrangement may involve some degree of hardship, but it is usually not of the same magnitude of hardship as leaving a country. Emigration involves enormous sacrifice. As Hume pointed out, one cannot honestly say of a poor shopkeeper that he voluntarily decides to remain in England when the alternative is abandoning the sole means of support for himself and his family, abandoning a network of friends and relatives, abandoning everything which is dear. When the mob approaches a shopkeeper with those terms, society usually describes the situation as extortion. There is also the point that in today's world one must find a country to which to immigrate. In breaking off a relationship with another person within one's own country, one is generally able to move to another apartment, street, county, city, state, or region. For many, immigration is not possible. Who will accept the peasant from Nicaragua or Salvador?

This last thought invites another objection. Consider a dictatorship in which the peasants, too poor to move, too weak to revolt, perhaps too uneducated even to understand fully their own plight, remain and continue to be exploited by the government. According to tacit contract theory, by remaining they offer tacit consent to the government. By the same token, this will legitimize less drastic situations, such as the welfare state. They could, indeed, lend legitimacy to a minimal government (if one could ever be found). Thus, by distorting the notion of tacit contract to include the "decision" to remain in a country, tacit contract theory avoids the anarchism of actual contract theory. The cost for this security is high. Virtually any government is rendered legitimate, a mimal government, a welfare state, or a totalitarian regime.

HYPOTHETICAL CONTRACTS

Contract theorists have recently sought refuge by moving even farther from the idea of actual contract toward dispositional and hypothetical contract arguments. Before turning to hypothetical contract arguments proper, i.e., nondispositional hypothetical contract arguments, a few comments about dispositional theories are in order.

"Hypothetical contract arguments" are a particular instance of process argument which allege that an outcome O (e.g., a state) is morally legitimate if and only if O *would arise* (or would have arisen) from an initial situation S by a process P, where S and P are morally legitimate. "Dispositional theories" rely, not upon a process involving actual or tacit consent, but upon the idea that consent would be given if the people were asked. This is a particular kind of counterfactual or hypothetical contract. These theories search for actual evidence, "dispositions" of the people, to determine whether individuals would consent, if asked. Like tacit contract theories, dispositional theories have roots in the actual world but do not rely upon actual contracts or actual consent. There is no claim that certain behavior constitutes tacit consent, only that certain behavior provides evidence of a disposition to contract or consent. Recognizing that behavior which is invoked as evidence of a tacit contract, such as the failure to leave a country, is too weak to support the claim that a tacit contract exists, dispositional theories move to the position that although no actual or tacit contract exists, one would exist if the parties were provided the opportunity to consent.

Dispositional theories are, nonetheless, as implausible as tacit theories, and for the same reasons. Dispositional theories afford no special comfort to defenders of the minimal state. The more than minimal state can be as readily legitimized as the minimal one. Many populations clearly have the disposition to accept welfare or more than minimal states. Worse, not only can socialists and welfare capitalists claim that the masses would consent, if asked, but the most despotic tyrannical regimes can make similar claims. Just as with tacit theories, virtually any political situation in which the population is not on the verge of rebellion or revolution will count as legitimate. In many instances, the claim that the population would consent if asked is well grounded. Because of extreme poverty, enforced ignorance, weakness, or perceived impotency it may well be true that *if asked* the people would consent.

This objection notwithstanding, there remains no good reason why the legitimacy of an outcome should rest upon the fact that consent would be given, if the relevant parties were given the opportunity to respond. Severing the link with actual contracts severs the connection with the moral grounding in consent. Although there may be some special circumstances within which one might accept a disposition to consent as having some moral force, these are extremely rare, and the force is slight. Medical emergencies constitute a clear case. There are situations which demand immediate action, because the consequences of a failure to act are severe and irreversible, but consent from the endangered party (say, Jones herself) or a surrogate (next of kin) cannot be obtained. How should medical personnel respond? One plausible response is to determine the course of action to which the victim would have consented, if she would have been asked. Whatever the force of this kind of reasoning, it is not clear that the plausibility of this response rests entirely, if at all, on the disposition of the victim to consent. Perhaps many believe it would be permissible to proceed, based upon some moral obligation to help in absence of clear evidence that the victim would object. That is different from a policy which would forbid acting unless there is clear evidence that the victim would consent. And even if the moral force does rest upon the victim's disposition to give consent, this kind of case is not at all like situations involving the moral legitimacy of political structures. The citizens of a tyrannical regime are not in a position analogous to that of Jones. These citizens may not die immediately unless some intervention is taken. More importantly, citizens are alive and capable of responding to questions about whether they consent to the political structure. If the citizens would agree, then why should we not ask them? Dispositional theories offer no advantages over tacit contract theories and all the disadvantages. What of nondispositional theories?

"Nondispositional" theories, which I shall refer to simply as "hypothetical contract theories," claim, not that actual individuals would consent or contract if given the opportunity, but that hypothetical individuals, in a hypothetical situation, would give hypothetical consent to (would contract for) an outcome. These represent one of the most influential kinds of argument in contemporary ethical and social-political theory. Rawls's *A Theory of Justice* rests upon a hypothetical contract argument, as does Nozick's *Anarchy, State, and Utopia*. The fashionableness of these arguments has tended to obscure their inherent weaknesses and limitations, but there are indications that philosophers are becoming increasingly skeptical of this approach. Indeed, Rawls himself, as I will suggest below, appears to have joined the retreat.

Attending carefully to the nature of hypothetical contract arguments reveals their emptiness and irrelevance. Four major premises are involved:

Hypothetical Process (Contract) Arguments
1.   Any outcome O *is legitimate* (justified, just) if and only if
     a.   O would arise from an initial situation S by a process P,
     b.   S is morally defensible (legitimate, justified,etc.),
     c.   P is morally defensible (legitimate, justified, etc.).
2.   S would arise from an initial situation S.
3.   S is morally defensible (legitimate, justified, etc.).
4.   P is morally defensible (legitimate, justified, etc.).
C.   Therefore, O *is legitimate* (justified, just, etc.).

This basic form captures the logic of all hypothetical process/hypothetical contract arguments. Unlike other process/contract arguments, the key components here are hypothetical. The parties making the choice, or giving consent, or entering into a contract are hypothetical parties; the initial situation, S, is hypothetical; and the contracting process itself is hypothetical. Following traditional contract theorists, Nozick refers to the initial situation as a state of nature. Rawls refers to the initial situation as the original position. Rawls's argument is that the two principles of justice are just (fair, morally legitimate) because they would be chosen in the original position. That is, the two principles are just (fair, morally legitimate) because they would arise from an initial situation S (the original position) by a process P (the parties freely choose), Premise 2, because the description of the original position is philosophically favored (morally legitimate), Premise 3, and because the process of free, rational choice is morally legitimate (this is a fair procedure), Premise 4. Nozick's claim is that the minimal state and nothing more extensive is morally legitimate because the minimal state and nothing more extensive would arise from a state of nature by a process violating no rights. In other words, the outcome O, the minimal state and nothing more extensive, is morally legitimate because O would arise from a state of nature S by a process P (Premise 2) because the description of the state of nature is morally legitimate (Premise 3) and because the process violates no rights (Premise 4).

Hypothetical contract arguments offer one major strategic advantage over competitors. The outcome of the process in other arguments depends upon an actual process involving actual persons. History is notoriously unreliable and unpredictable. There is no guarantee that one's favorite outcome and only that outcome will in fact be legitimized. By escaping history, theorists obtain control over the outcome. Premise 2, for example, requires demonstrating that a particular outcome would arise. Other contract arguments require searching reality to discover in fact which contracts exist, whether these are actual, tacit, or dispositional. Hypothetical theories solve the problem of uncertain outcomes by transforming the problem into one of deduction. Once the assumptions which describe the initial situation are accepted, the question of whether a particular outcome would arise is wholly a question of logical inference. In A Theory of Justice, for example, Rawls holds out as an ideal the deduction of the two principles of justice from the original position. "What these individuals will do is then derived by strictly deductive reasoning from these assumptions about their beliefs and interests, their situation and the options open to them."[24] In arguments such as Nozick's, the problem is also one of logical inference, not empirical reality. Of course, neither the argument in Rawls nor in Nozick in fact approaches the rigor of a strictly deductive argument, but that is the model.

Consequently, a good portion of the literature on contract theories revolves around the question of whether a process P would generate O, given the description of the initial situation assumed by the theorist. Critics continue to allege that the two principles would not be chosen by parties in the original position, for example, or that Nozick's minimal state would not arise by a process violating no rights. In principle, a hypothetical theorist could defend the truth of Premise 2 as a logical truth, and a computer suitably programmed with inference rules could readily check the deduction. When theorists succeed in establishing this rigor, we will then be saved from the task of having to read about one-third of this literature.

Attention moves, therefore, from Premise 2 to Premises 3 and 4. The real debate swirls around the issue of which assumptions to allow in the description of the initial situation and in the process. Is the description of the initial situation morally defensible? Is the process invoked morally defensible? The problems here are overwhelming.

The problems go beyond the immediate, normative ones. A critical issue involves the question of the empirical realism of the assumptions. If a hypothetical situation is to be described, then how many false assumptions are we to allow? Should we assume that the parties are altruistic, indifferent to their own welfare and others', equally interested in everyone's welfare, or interested only in their own welfare? Should we assume scarcity, moderate scarcity, moderate abundance, or abundance? The "empirical" assumptions will be pivotal in determining which particular outcome can be deduced. Having abandoned reality, how far should we travel? In constructing empirical models, theorists have defended assumptions which are generally recognized to be false on the grounds that they function as a part of an overall theory which has more explanatory power than alternatives. But when one is constructing a model to function normatively, the conditions according to which we should allow assumptions which are known to be false are no longer clear. The appropriate test is lacking.

The problems associated with the issue of empirical realism complicate the moral questions exponentially. How should we determine whether a hypothetical initial situation is morally defensible, legitimate, or fair? Even the most reasonable person is left without adequate intuitions when confronted with the task of choosing a set of hypothetical empirical assumptions while at the same time choosing morally defensible principles to apply. The question is not which moral principles or moral judgments apply in our world, but which moral principles or moral judgments are relevant to some hypothetical world. These are two quite different matters. Two individuals may be in close agreement on correct moral principles in this world, and their application, but disagree about how to handle the hypothetical case. And even this simplifies the real problem. The choice of principles adopted will also have an impact on which descriptive assumptions to make.

One way of testing our intuitions about the construction of the initial situation is to trace outcomes which would arise given a particular construction. Whether one accepts a particular description of the initial situation, then, depends upon whether the assumptions involved in the description will generate the desired outcome. If one seeks to defend the minimal state, then assumptions which generate the minimal state and nothing more extensive are chosen. Disagreements over outcomes are immediately translated into disagreements over descriptions of the initial situation, and debates over the initial situation depend upon the kinds of outcomes which are desired. Hypothetical arguments are, therefore, essentially question begging. If one agrees with an outcome, one will agree with the description of the initial situation which generates that outcome. If one disagrees, then one will disagree with the description. This is a classic *petitio*. If there are disagreements over whether this or that political structure is morally legitimate, whether the minimal state or the welfare state is morally legitimate, they cannot be resolved by developing a hypothetical contract argument.

In *A Theory of Justice*, there are tensions which suggest that Rawls is struggling to find a response to this objection. To be fair, one might argue that the original position should be neutral between differing outcomes. But if it is genuinely neutral, then no particular outcome would arise. We would not know whether the two principles or some other conception is justified. On the other hand, Rawls wants to claim that the initial situation is not neutral, but the biases can be defended on moral grounds which do not beg the question against other moral theories. This he fails to do. The struggle is reflected in another tension. There are, in *A Theory of Justice*, competing conceptions of the contract argument itself. At one level, Rawls describes using contract arguments as heuristic exploratory devices. Rawls believes that different ethical and political conceptions can be associated with different conceptions of the original position. By constructing a description of the original position which would logically entail the principles for utilitarianism, for example, one could learn a great deal about utilitarianism. At a different level, Rawls conceives of contract arguments as a device within the process of reflective equilibrium. Tentatively, our moral intuitions would be reflected in the particular assumptions embedded in the original position. These can be tested by deducing the outcome which would follow. If the outcome conforms to other of our intuitions, this provides additional warrant for our intuitions. If the outcome does not, then we must alter some of our intuitions. By repeatedly using this process, Rawls expresses the hope in A *Theory of Justice* that our views would come to cohere, that we would reach a point of reflective equilibrium. At this point, Rawls suggests, we have stumbled upon the philosophically favored description of the original position. We can assume that the assumptions embodied in the description of the initial situation are justified because they generate the desired outcome and conform to other judgments. Having established that the original position is morally defensible, then the contract argument could be employed in still a different way, as a contract argument per se, as a justificatory device. In this sense, the two principles are alleged to be just because they would arise by choice from the original position.

But does the contract function only as a device within the method of reflective equilibrium, or independently as a justificatory device, a contract argument in its own right? That is, are the two principles defended on the grounds that they are the result of a process of reflective equilibrium, i.e., they cohere with our other considered opinions? Or, are they justified because they would be chosen in the original position? The first alternative involves abandoning contract theory for a coherence theory of morality. The second involves a commitment to contract theory.

The problem with the second alternative is that unless hypothetical contract theorists can develop a means of demonstrating the legitimacy of the description of the initial situation independent of the idea that these assumptions yield the outcomes desired, then it is difficult to see how the charge of question begging can be avoided. Neither Rawls, nor Nozick, nor any other contract theorist has yet proposed a means for doing this.

Perhaps the most attractive alternative is merely to abandon the charade of contract theory. Unable to address satisfactorily this issue in A *Theory of Justice* or subsequently, Rawls has apparently conceded. In his later work, there is no longer the pretense that the description of the original position is neutral in anything but a very weak sense. Contract arguments are understood in the first two of the three senses described above. They are cast as useful devices to illuminate the different assumptions embodied in competing traditions, and as devices which assist in unearthing the principles which "we" accept, which are latent in "our" views. The contract device functions to bring our intuitions and principles into reflective equilibrium.[25] At bottom, then, the defense marshaled for the two principles rests upon coherence theory, not contract theory. In a later article, reflecting this shift, Rawls speaks of the notion of justice as "political" not "metaphysical." The principles are legitimate because they provide the best fit with "our" considered moral and political judgments.[26]

This gambit opens a different set of strategic difficulties. How, for example are "we" to demonstrate to "them" that "our" views are correct? If "they" are Classical Liberals, and "we" are Revisionist Liberals, then how shall we proceed? In this theory, the only way to proceed is to demonstrate to the Classical Liberal that some of her own judgments lead to positions beyond the minimal state, that some of her convictions are internally inconsistent, or that, on reflection, some of those assumptions should be altered.[27] I do not by any means wish to discount the coherence theory. It is, perhaps, the correct one. It lends theoretical support to the practical importance of dialogue and an exchange of views between differing parties. The point, however, is that this is a much different kind of approach to justification than the contract approach, and should not be confused with it.

Rawls's apparent abandonment of the hypothetical contract argument as a justificatory device is also precipitated by an even deeper and much more disturbing problem—irrelevance. The problem of irrelevance stalks all hypothetical contract theorists. The fundamental assumption of hypothetical contract arguments, expressed by Premise 1, is that an outcome will have moral legitimacy just in case that outcome would arise from an initial situation by a process, provided both the initial situation and the process are morally defensible. No argument is ever offered in defense of this premise. On reflection, it is extremely counterintuitive. The fundamental assumption of actual contract theory, that if mentally competent and mature adults contract together, then the outcome is morally legitimate, is plausible. That a person actually entered into a contract with another person is morally relevant in determining the duties and responsibilities of the parties.

This is reflected in Rawls's discussion of pure procedural justice, an example of an actual contract argument. As I indicated earlier, when discussing the nature of pure procedural justice, Rawls uses the example of the poker game.[28] The outcome, the distribution of the money, is alleged to be legitimate (if and) only if the game actually takes place. As Rawls himself claims, the parties must actually play the game, and they must play the game fairly (violate no rules). Why then does Rawls claim that the hypothetical contract argument is one of pure procedural justice?[29] A hypothetical contract is not an instance of pure procedural justice. A hypothetical poker game is not a poker game. The counterintuitiveness of the fundamental assumption of a hypothetical contract argument should be apparent. Accepting that assumption would be tantamount to claiming that the legitimate distribution of the money in a poker game can be determined before shuffling the cards, without actually playing the game. Of what relevance is a hypothetical contract?

Speaking bluntly, Ronald Dworkin goes to the heart of the issue: "A hypothetical contract is not simply a pale form of an actual contract; it is no contract at all."[30] To wit, hypothetical contracts carry none of the moral force of actual contracts. The relevance of an actual contract is apparent. The relevance of a hypothetical contract is not. When told that the two principles would be chosen by individuals in the philosophically favored original position, our response may well be "So what?" When told that a minimal state and nothing more extensive would arise from a state of nature by a process violating no rights, our response may well be "So what?" What is the relevance of a hypothetical contract? The fundamental assumption seeks to tie together hypothetical states of affairs and events with the actual world, but how are they relevant?

Irrelevance is illustrated by examining a simple case. Assume for the moment that ethical egoism is the correct moral theory, that one's obligation is to act according to rules which will promote one's own interest. A contract theorist now approaches and suggests that the ethical egoist determine the morally legitimate rules of the political order by considering what self-interested hypothetical parties would do in some hypothetical choice situation. The egoist agrees that those individuals would choose outcome O. Outcome O would, indeed, be in the self-interest of the individuals in that hypothetical situation. The problem, however, is that this provides no reason for the ethical egoist to assume that she should accept O, because in the real world O may not be in her self-interest. Indeed, is there any guarantee that O would be in the self-interest of anyone?

There is a moral gap between the hypothetical world and the actual one. And this moral gap appears regardless of the moral assumptions one wishes to assume. It is not a function of the particular moral presuppositions (e.g., ethical egoism) which are packed into the description of the initial situation. What one ought to do in some ideal world is certainly not necessarily what one ought to do in this world.

In a chapter discussing "The Logical Status of Rawls's Argument" in *Understanding Rawls*,[31] Robert Paul Wolff states the problem succinctly.

> And finally, there remains the residual question, so what? Even if a satisfactory characterization of formal rationality can be fielded, and the two principles can be established as the solution, in a suitably strong sense, of a problem in collective choice, why should that fact persuade us to adopt the two principles as the fundamental criteria for the evaluation or correction of our social institutions? (184)

This same point can and should be raised with regard to Nozick's argument. Indeed, the point is pertinent to any hypothetical contract argument.

Building a theory upon a hypothetical contract guarantees conflicts with reality. The clash is most intense when hypothetical contracts confront real ones. Are actual, historical contracts to be ignored, trumped, and nullified by fictious, hypothetical contracts? Consider in more detail a scenario sketched above. Suppose that Nozick's individuals with the liberty to do with their person, property, and possessions whatever they desire, so long as they do not harm another, compact together to create a welfare state. If contract theory is accepted and actual contracts are morally valid, then there is nothing to guarantee that the welfare state would not be morally legitimate in some circumstances. It all depends upon what kind of contract the parties agreed upon. The defender of the hypothetical contract argument must claim that the outcome of contracting by actual individuals is now irrelevant, and that the only relevant contract is the hypothetical one of hypothetical individuals. There may be many legitimate moral reasons to intrude into the contracting process. Appealing to hypothetical contracts hardly appears to be one of them. If in some actual instance, individuals acted altruistically to create a welfare state, is Nozick suggesting that we should ignore their actual commitments and proceed only to accept commitments which would have been made if they had acted purely from self-interest? Is the autonomy of an actual human, an autonomy which Nozick claims to value highly, to be ignored on the grounds that some autonomous, hypothetical individual would not contract for the more than minimal state?

Further counterexamples can be generated, but they would only reinforce a point which should be already clear. Hypothetical contract arguments will provide no foundation for moral legitimacy. In light of their irrelevance, it is no surprise that Rawls has abandoned the enterprise as well.

THE CORPORATION AND THE SOCIAL COMPACT

This journey through social contract theory has only apparently wandered from the issue of the role of the corporation in a free society. The excursion was necessary in order to explore and evaluate the natural rights/social contract defense of Classical Liberalism. The implications of the results extend beyond the defense of Classical Liberalism. Problems confronting contract arguments, especially hypothetical contract arguments, undermine attempts by Revisionist Liberals as well. Thus, Managerialists who seek legitimation for a more than minimal state will find no support in contract arguments for a Revisionist Liberal welfare state.

The results also illuminate weaknesses in many other arguments invoked in applied and professional ethics. For purposes of illustration, two can be addressed.

Toward the end of *Of Acceptable Risk*,[32] for instance, William W. Lowrance turns to the issue of social responsibility. Lowrance's work is a classic in the literature of risk analysis and the concept of safety. It is important and influential. But when Lowrance turns to the issue of social responsibility, his analysis falters. In contrast to those who claim that the primary or sole responsibility is to the client/employer, Lowrance holds that in addition to a number of readily agreed-upon social responsibilities, scientists and others in the technical community have

> obligations to frame risk and safety issues in proper relation to factors of equity, cost, efficacy, and so on, and obligations to interpret new findings for the lay public. There are also attitudinal and procedural responsibilities such as defending against suppression, misinterpretation, and falsification of data, and preserving the distinction between factual and valuation decisions. (122)

One would have thought Lowrance's list of obligations could be defended easily and directly by appealing to a few rather noncontroversial moral truisms. The obligation to avoid misinterpretation and falsification of data, for example, would appear to be an instance of a responsibility not to commit fraud, to lie, etc. The responsibility to warn the public, for example, would appear to rest on nothing more than the moral idea that humans have a responsibility to warn or assist others in need when one can do so without any great cost or risk to oneself.[33] But Lowrance cannot resist the cultural fascination with contract arguments. Rather than resting his defense on the noncontroversial and immediate, he claims that over the years a "tacit but nonetheless real compact has developed."[34] The parties involved are alleged to be the profession and society. The consideration in the "contract" is supposedly the investment through subsidization in training scientists and other technical people, and the powers and privileges accorded the profession for self-regulation, etc. In exchange for this, the argument continues, the profession "agrees" to assume responsibilities to serve and protect the interests of society.[35]

What is to count as a tacit contract? Who has actually agreed? The argument's sentimentality could be ignored except that it is potentially dangerous. If the evidence Lowrance offers to support his claim of the existence of a tacit contract is accepted as sufficient, then virtually any relationship between society and a group of individuals will suffice. Just as tacit contract theory in political theory will work to legitimize virtually any arrangement, including tyrannical despots, so also would tacit contract theory in professional ethics legitimize the status quo ante regardless of the ethical texture of the arrangements.[36] If the arrangement between society and the profession involved the exclusion of Jews and females, would we be willing to accept that professionals had a responsibility not to employ members of these groups on the grounds that this is a part of the tacit contract? Similar objections press against any attempt to establish social responsibilities for corporations based on a tacit contract.

In *Corporations and Morality*, Thomas Donaldson offers one of the more well-developed attempts to ground the social responsibilities of business in a social contract.[37] The title of chapter 3, in which the argument is presented, "Constructing a Social Contract for Business," itself reflects one of the key difficulties. That is, the enterprise involves "constructing" a contract, not identifying one.

Like most, this analysis fails to identify the logical structure of contract arguments and, consequently, tends to blur important moral and logical distinctions. This in turn makes it difficult to determine whether Donaldson intends to develop a contract argument which rests upon the notion of an implied (tacit) contract, or a hypothetical contract. Either approach fails.

Much of what Donaldson says supports the interpretation that his argument rests upon the notion of a tacit contract. In that sense, the argument would be very similar in form to Lowrance's. Surveying the history of the contract tradition, Donaldson makes three claims. First that the tradition of the social contract is a tradition of social change and reform. Second, that two forms of contract can be distinguished, actual and implied. Third, that the tradition emphasizes the consent of the parties. Apparently, Donaldson sees himself as relying upon implied consent and associates this tradition with reform. The reform is morally defensible because it is allegedly grounded in the consent of the parties.

Clearly, the tradition has emphasized consent or contract, but, as the analysis of this chapter has demonstrated, the moral force of that notion is tied to actual consent and actual contract. Those who venture from actual contract arguments leave behind the moral force associated with them. As one moves toward tacit contracts, dispositional, or hypothetical contracts, it is difficult to understand how the moral force of actual contracts any longer has relevance.

This is related to Donaldson's second claim. There are not merely two kinds of social contract arguments, actual and implied, but at least four: actual, tacit (implied), dispositional, and hypothetical. An implied contract, i.e., a tacit contract, is closely connected to actual contracts, but the areas within which one can legitimately claim that tacit contracts exist are extremely limited. It is one thing to claim that by entering a taxi cab on a New York City street, I have contracted with the driver. It is quite another to say that "business" has contracted with "society," ignoring the fact that it is quite senseless to speak of parties in this case. The same problem afflicts Lowrance's argument.

Among the more threatening problems with the implied contract approach is that it undermines Donaldson's first claim. While there is good historical evidence that the contract tradition has been associated with reform, this may be as much a result of the association with the natural rights approach as the contract approach. The tradition can be, and has been, associated with nothing more than the purported justification of the oppressive status quo. As such, the method involves describing the current power arrangements, then claiming that the "parties" have consented to these, and then reading into the "contract" the latent responsibilities. Indeed, this appears to be Donaldson's move in "Applying the Contract to Business," the section of his chapter 3 where the responsibilities of business are allegedly identified. The claim is that there have been exchanges with associated responsibilities and expectations.

But, by what right can one describe the status quo as involving consent between parties? No one claims that actual consent has been given, but by what right can one assert that the arrangements reflect implied consent. Even if one were allowed to describe the parties as "business" and "society," how does the *fact* that certain arrangements (distributions of power, control, resources, etc.) pertain in this society lead to the conclusion that this arrangement is the result of an implied contract? If this counts as a contract, then everything can be counted as a contract. If every historical development is to be described as a contract, then we should be careful to distinguish illicit from licit contracts. Therefore, what defense is there that the arrangement in our society between business and society is the result of a *legitimate* implied contract. Are these parties equal? Have they both been informed? This is an especially odd way of describing the historical reality in this country, where powerful large corporations developed much earlier than a strong federal government, where large corporations and financial interests overwhelmed the ability of state governments to regulate.

Moreover, even if one granted that these arrangements could be described as contractual, there is little reason to believe that the content of the contract involves the kinds of responsibilities suggested by Donaldson. The kinds of responsibilities one can read into these implied contracts is limited only by imagination. According to Donaldson, corporations have a responsibility to work to benefit employees, consumers, etc., based on the contract. However, one might argue that a careful reading of history over the past few decades reveals a much different contract. One might argue that the society has agreed to high levels of pollution, unemployment, minimum protections for workers, poor health care for all but those associated with large corporations, poor education for a substantial proportion of the population, provided that corporations treat the already well off well.

Or, one might argue that "society" speaks through a political system which is itself dominated by business interests. Are we to accept and legitimize the status quo as the result of a contract when the interests of "society" were largely determined by the party with whom "society" was to make a contract?

These obvious problems with the notion of implied contracts suggest that Donaldson must really be engaged in developing a hypothetical contract argument. There is some textual support for this as well. In the first paragraph of the chapter Donaldson describes the argument as a "metaphysical abstraction." Shortly thereafter he describes the method in political theory as a "theoretical means" for justifying the state. Donaldson describes the process as one of "constructing" the social contract. Most importantly, however, when Donaldson is articulating the content of the implied contract, his approach is not to identify evidence from history, or to focus upon social structures and arrangements. Rather, he proceeds more along the lines of someone who identifies what the interests of the parties should be, and then claims that given these interests, this is the kind of contract which would follow.

The interpretation of the argument as a hypothetical contract is of little solace, however. While a hypothetical contract argument might conveniently avoid many of the pitfalls associated with tacit contracts, these arguments are themselves indefensible.[38]

4

Classical Liberalism and Utilitarianism: Friedman

While Milton Friedman is widely regarded as one of the most articulate spokespersons for the Classical view that the appropriate role of the corporation in a democratic society is to adhere to the principle of profit maximization, and while his essay, "The Sole Responsibility of Business Is to Increase Profits,"[1] is widely reprinted and analyzed, there is little agreement over the nature of his argument. The difficulties in interpretation are apparent in Christopher Stone's *Where the Law Ends*.[2] In chapter 8, "What Exactly Are the 'Antis' Against?"— often used as a companion piece to Friedman—Stone attempts to reconstruct Friedman's arguments. Four are identified. The first three are easily stated. According to Stone, Friedman believes that corporate managers have a responsibility to profit maximize because they promised the stockholders, because they are agents of the stockholders, and because it is a part of the role of managers to maximize profit. Once these arguments are reconstructed and examined carefully, the weaknesses become evident.[3]

Consider the "promissory argument," frequently used by other apologists. According to this argument, management has a responsibility to maximize profit for stockholders because management (or the board) has promised the stockholders as much. In more standard form, the argument looks like this.

Promissory Argument
1. One ought always keep one's promise.
2. Management (bd. of directors) has promised stockholders to maximize profit.

75

3.   Therefore, management ought to maximize profit for stockholders.

Clearly, as Stone notes, this argument suffers from both empirical
and normative difficulties. Empirically, it is simply false to claim that
management or the directors have promised stockholders to maximize
profit. Nor do they promise to increase profit. Nor do they promise
even to try to increase profit. Management and directors promise little,
if anything. Stocks are not issued with any such promises, written,
verbal, explicit, or implicit. Legally, managers must be quite careful
not to promise anything very substantial because should the future economic picture turn cloudy, any assertions about future earnings could
count as fraud or deceit. Stockholders do not receive any promises
from management upon purchase of stock, nor are any promises made
during the course of a normal annual stockholders meeting. The
promissory argument flies in the face of reality. Normatively, the
argument is also problematic. Even if one assumes that a promise
had been given, it would not follow that management always had an
obligation to keep that promise. Few, if any, would accept Premise 1.
There are many situations which might arise in which another moral
duty overrides one's duty to keep promises. Thus, even if management
made a promise, which it has not, that promise would be binding only
sometimes in some cases.

Friedman can also be interpreted as developing an "agency argument." According to this argument, management has an obligation
to act only to increase or maximize profit for stockholders because it
is the agent of the stockholders. This argument can be reconstructed
as follows.

Agency Argument
1.   Agents ought always to act only to maximize the interests of
the principal.
2.   Management is an agent of the principals, the stockholders.
3.   Therefore, management ought always to act only to maximize
the interests of stockholders.

This argument also suffers factual and normative problems. First
of all, it is incorrect, as a point of law, to claim that management
is an agent of the stockholders. At law, management is considered
either as an agent of the corporation, which is not to be confused
with stockholders, or management decisions are identified with the

decisions of the corporation itself. In neither case is management an agent of the stockholders. The legal and political reality of the past century has, in fact, been the story of an erosion of the influence of stockholders in corporate decisions. Second, the argument confronts normative difficulties similar to those in the promissory argument. Legally, it is not true to say that the agent is obligated always only to maximize the interest of the principal. There are a number of things an agent must not do in spite of the fact that it is in the interest of the principal. Most would agree that this reflects our moral intuitions. Morally, an agent may have a duty to regard the interests of the principal as primary in most cases, but often conflicting duties will override that duty, and morality will require some other course of action. Analogously, even if management was the agent of the stockholders, which it is not, it might have *other* obligations which might occasionally (in extreme circumstances) override the duty to the principals.

The third argument is the "role argument." This argument suggests that management ought to maximize profit because this is a duty of the role. This argument looks something like this.

Role Argument
1. One ought always to perform the duties of one's role.
2. One of the duties of management's role is to maximize profit.
3. Therefore, management ought always maximize profit for stockholders.

Premise 2 of this argument is difficult to evaluate. As a matter of fact, it is difficult to discern the duties of a position. For most upper-level management positions there are probably few job descriptions written, and without something like a job description it would be difficult to arrive at a clear picture of what a particular manager's role is.

Even if one were to grant that maximizing profit was one of the duties of a role, Premise 1 is suspect. First, it is not at all clear that one has a moral duty to perform the duties of a role. Some have argued that accepting a position is like promising or contracting to perform the duties of a role, but this flies in the face of the conventionally accepted doctrines of being free to terminate employment at will. If one had promised or contracted to perform a set of duties, why should it be possible to quit a job and take another merely because the new position offered better benefits? That difficulty aside, Premise 1 is untenable because even if one normally has an obligation to perform the duties of role, there are surely cases in which other duties override that duty. Those who claim that managers have obligations other than to maximize profit need only establish that in some cases these other duties are stronger. Few would accept the view, as indicated in Premise 1, that one must always perform the duties of role. Most importantly, this argument is an excellent illustration of begging the question. The critical question is to determine the appropriate role of the corporation, or the appropriate role of the corporate manager, in the liberal society. One cannot answer the question with an argument which utilizes the conclusion as a premise.

After noting the serious factual, legal, and normative errors involved in these arguments, Stone turns to what he considers Friedman's strongest and most important argument, the "Polestar argument." Unfortunately, Stone's treatment of this important argument leaves it shrouded in mystery. He offers the idea that under the influence of positivism many became suspicious of appealing to moral values or principles. In the midst of this moral skepticism the principle of profit maximization is seized upon, for some reason, in order to provide some guidance in this world of moral uncertainty. This argument is called a Polestar argument because for Stone the principle serves as a point of reference, a Polestar, a point with which to orient oneself. The analogy between profit maximization and the Polestar is left obscure. In what way is that principle like a Polestar? It is easy to understand why we might navigate by the North Star, but why the principle of profit maximization? Needless to say, if this is the argument, it is hardly worthy of serious attention and it is difficult to understand how Stone can refer to this as the strongest argument. Further, there is nothing like a Polestar argument in Friedman's article or in his *Capitalism and Freedom*.[4]

Stone's attempt to interpret the Polestar argument suffers from two serious problems. First, the interpretation fails to take seriously the importance of Friedman's theory of political economy. "The Social Responsibility of Business Is to Increase Profits" is too often read without sufficient attention to the author's *Capitalism and Freedom* from which the article is abstracted. In the book his sketch of a theory of political economy, Classical Liberalism, in chapters 1 and 2 is unmistakable. That discussion provides a context for the remainder of the book in which more specific issues are treated. Second, the interpretation fails to explore the deeper normative structure of Friedman's theory. Stone's attempt to reconstruct the Polestar argument does not even make sense of Friedman's comments acknowledging that the principle of profit maximization is connected somehow with doing what is "best for all." Reference to what is best for all suggests, obviously, an appeal to utilitarianism.

In what follows, I shall develop an interpretation which accords Friedman's theory of political economy the position of central importance it deserves. I shall also argue that Friedman is to be interpreted as developing a utilitarian argument.

Consistent with his economic approach, it is most natural that it should be interpreted as a preference-based rule utilitarianism in which "utility" is understood ordinarily in terms of actual preferences. The moral skepticism to which Stone is sensitive is real, but the locus is misplaced. Those adopting a theory of value which is based on actual preferences usually believe themselves to be avoiding substantive commitments to a theory of value. Even if that belief were correct, which it is not, it ignores the basic normative structure of the argument. One cannot be a normative skeptic at the same time that one prescribes policies on the grounds that they produce what is best for all. By appealing to actual preferences, a theorist is merely clarifying how "best" is to be understood. That is only a part of the normative debate. To claim that we ought to do what is best for all is to appeal to utilitarian considerations.

Although some, especially economists, might object to characterizing Friedman this way, it will become apparent that his efficiency arguments will carry force only to the extent to which he links his argument with utilitarian considerations. For others, the interpretation of his position as utilitarian should not be surprising. What is surprising is the complexity of what appears on the surface to be a very simple utilitarian defense. No less than four distinct utilitarian arguments are involved in his view. Thus, although Friedman enjoys posturing as a moral skeptic who wishes to defend little more than individual freedom against others who would violate freedom in the name of having authoritative moral knowledge about what is good and right, his position rests not only upon abstract descriptive models whose applicability is often suspect but also upon contentious and implausible normative assumptions.

The analysis will run through this and the next two chapters. In this chapter, the basic normative structure of the position can be exposed. In the next two chapters, the position can be evaluated. The utilitarian defense merits this kind of serious attention. Friedman's position represents one of the most credible and influential defenses of this view. Moreover, in the process, not only can the complexity of Friedman's views be carefully examined, but alternative utilitarian lines of defense can be explored. This examination will also help establish a foundation for evaluating the Managerial framework in the following chapters and for going beyond Managerialism in the final chapter.

POLESTAR: AN INITIAL FORMULATION

When one turns to *Capitalism and Freedom* in search of the argument which might offer support for Friedman's claim that corporations ought to maximize profit, one is struck by lack of clear argumentation. Although there is a near-moralistic fervor and tone throughout, Friedman rarely tips his hand about his moral presuppositions. Indeed, Friedman presents himself, for the most part, as merely describing the world, rather than prescribing. Friedman postures as developing a theory which avoids moral assumptions, and those who disagree are characterized as attempting to impose questionable value judgments. Chapter 2, for instance, concerns "The Role of Government in a Free Society." It is, of course, a presentation of what Friedman takes to be the appropriate role, of what he believes the role of government *should* be. Friedman does place himself in the liberal tradition, although he recognizes that the sense of "liberal" has changed such that his views are now called "conservative."

The major theme, as reflected in the title, is about the relationship between capitalism and freedom. Indeed, for liberals of any stripe, Classical or Revisionist, individual freedom and liberty are crucial.

In the introduction, Friedman sketches three arguments in defense of competitive capitalism and limited government, i.e., Classical Liberalism. Two arguments are described as "protective reasons" for these. Protecting individual freedom requires limiting government and decentralizing power. The claim is that the free competitive market has an important role in providing for this protection. There is also a "constructive reason," namely, that "the great advances of civilization, whether in architecture or painting, in science or literature, in industry or agriculture, have never come from centralized government" (3). Though this latter claim is patently false, the sentiment is probably that a free society is the best guarantee for "great advances." Thus

Friedman's major avowed thesis: the important relationship between democracy and capitalism, between political freedom and economic freedom, is that capitalism is a necessary, although not sufficient, condition for democracy—political freedom requires economic freedom. For example, the exercise of free speech through a free press would be useless if government controlled the means of accumulating the economic wherewithal to exercise free speech.

On its surface, Friedman's defense does not rest upon the virtues of the productive capacities of capitalism and hence does not appear to rest upon utilitarian considerations. The only hint of that theme comes from the preface to the 1982 edition of the 1962 work. There he explains that the book was based upon lectures given during the mid-1950s when he and a small number of other fellow travelers were largely ignored because they were viewed as eccentrics. These eccentrics were "deeply concerned about the danger to freedom and prosperity from the growth of government, from the triumph of the welfare state and Keynesian ideas." In the book, there is virtually no explicit reference to the comparative productive capacities of capitalism. Instead, Friedman argues from the position of the debater who identifies a point of commonality and then attempts to demonstrate to his opponent that this point of commonality supports his views, not the opponent's. That point of commonality is the value of political liberty or political freedom. If Friedman can demonstrate that free market capitalism is a necessary condition for political freedom, then he believes that he will have undermined those who seek to destroy the operation of the free market. This rhetorical device relieves Friedman from having to explain why political freedom is a good thing, for example.

In chapter 2, where Friedman turns to address "The Role of Government in a Free Society," he merely asserts what he takes to be the appropriate role of government in a free society; there is no explicit argument. What is offered is the familiar description of the Classical Liberal state.

A government which maintained law and order, defined property rights, served as a means whereby we could modify property rights and other rules of the economic game, adjudicated disputes about the interpretation of the rules, enforced contracts, promoted competition, provided a monetary framework, engaged in activities to counter technical monopolies and to overcome neighborhood effects widely regarded as sufficiently important to justify governmental intervention, and which supplemented private charity and the private family in protecting the irresponsible, whether madman or child—such a government would clearly have important functions to perform. The consistent liberal is not an anarchist. (34)

The final sentence is revealing. Friedman is aware that his ideal state is sufficiently minimal to warrant a disclaimer that it is not anarchistic. Indeed, Friedman's state is not, strictly speaking, the minimal state but the limited state of Classical Liberalism.[5] In another place, he makes clear that he does accept that government may legitimately act to alleviate poverty. There is a safety net here, albeit a very limited one. He merely objects to the way in which many welfare programs have been developed. He prefers, of course, direct cash payments and a negative income tax. Friedman refers to "law and order" and "property rights," but never spells out in any detail what they might mean. It is clear, however, that he follows the Classical Liberals in opposing legal moralism, paternalism, and the welfare principle.[6] Unstated is the reliance upon the private harm principle. The function of government is to prevent harm. To harm an individual is to invade an interest in life, liberty, health, property, possessions, contract, and reputation, for example. Basically, the function of government protects the requisites for a system of free enterprise and civil liberties.

Friedman relies upon the public harm principle as well. If he were forced to defend the legitimacy of the government's regulation of the money supply, the existence of antitrust laws, or the right to interfere in cases of neighborhood effects, he would most likely appeal to the protection of the public good, the public harm principle. This can be illustrated by considering the problem of neighborhood effects, or externalities. Although there are positive externalities, of most concern are negative externalities. A "negative externality" is the externalization of costs, the imposition of costs upon neighbors. Pollution constitutes a familiar example. If a coke plant, steel mill, or power plant burns fuel which significantly pollutes the air, there will be costs borne by neighbors of the facilities. Not only will housing values decline, the paint on automobiles and homes deteriorate more readily, and windows need extra care, but also respiratory diseases and deaths will increase. These costs, including, sometimes, increased risk of death, are real, but they are not completely shouldered by the producers or buyers of the products. The prices of the products do not reflect the true costs. Friedman recognizes a role for government in these areas. To legitimize a role, however, Friedman would likely need to appeal to the public harm principle.

Like Plato's *Republic*, Friedman's ideal state is an ideal. The existing state is much more extensive. At the end of chapter 2, Friedman provides a long list of reforms. He opposes parity price support programs for agriculture, tariffs or restrictions on exports, government control of output (e.g., farm programs or prorationing of oil), rent control, minimum wage laws, "detailed" regulation of industries, the social security program, licensure provisions, public housing, the draft, national parks, the legal prohibition on carrying mail for profit, and publicly owned and operated toll roads. Friedman is also in favor of turning back the legal clock which allows retained earnings. He advocates forcing corporations to return all dividends to stockholders rather than keeping some for reinvestment. He proposes the elimination of the corporate income tax. He opposes the inheritance tax and progressive income taxes, if their object is redistribution. In addition to the argument that things like minimum wage laws and licensure provisions interfere unduly in the liberty of individuals to contract, Friedman complains that government does not accomplish what it seeks to do in any case. The idea is that the market performs many functions better.

Friedman's aversion to exposing the mediate (e.g., private and public harm principles) or ultimate (utilitarian) normative foundations is a characteristic of other chapters as well. Even in the chapter concerning distribution of income he attempts to sidestep the issue. His argument against an inheritance tax with a redistributive function goes like this.[7] The physical and mental endowments of an individual are partly responsible for one's current status in distribution of income and wealth. No one wishes to redistribute because of differences in income which result from differences in physical or mental endowments. Being born into a wealthy family, inheriting wealth, is not significantly different than being born with a set of genes which contribute to economic success. Therefore, for consistency's sake, there should be no inheritance tax as a means of economic redistribution. Friedman also resorts to a fable to attack the idea. Suppose three Robinson Crusoes settle upon three very different islands. One is an island which provides the inhabitant with luxury. The others must struggle to survive. One day they all learn of each other's existence. Friedman claims that the two who are less well off have no right to a redistribution. This story is supposed to confirm our intuitions. The story, of course, will provide no response to someone who claims that, indeed, the two struggling Crusoes do have a right to some sort of assistance. The problem is that Friedman, as is typical, provides no argument for his views.

Friedman's hesitancy to elaborate on his underlying moral presuppositions may well reflect, as Stone suggests, a positivistic fear that moral discourse is meaningless. If that were true, however, there is no rational way of criticizing or defending different views. This approach has some short-term rhetorical advantage. Friedman is attempting to convince an opponent that the opponent's views are mistaken given a value which they both share. Unfortunately, Friedman's arguments are not compelling without an explanation of the reasons which stand behind the agreement about the value of political freedom. Just as Thomas Nagel noted that Robert Nozick holds a libertarianism without foundation, so too has Friedman developed a theory of political economy without foundations. At least Nozick began by assuming a set of natural rights, demonstrating some of the moral assumptions involved in his political theory. Friedman merely asserts a political theory.

Or, more precisely, Friedman's theory has a foundation, a foundation in the utilitarian tradition of Classical Liberalism, but he dutifully avoids disclosing it. The evidence in support of this hypothesis is textual and contextual. The closest Friedman comes to identifying with utilitarianism is the passage in which he identifies with some of the descendants of Bentham and the Philosophical Radicals. The descendants are liberal theorists such as Ludwig von Mises and Friedrich von Hayek[8] who support a minimal or limited state. According to Friedman, the Philosophical Radicals—James Mill, Jeremy Bentham, and John Stuart Mill—saw a connection between economic freedom and political freedom. The Radicals believed that political freedom would bring economic freedom, i.e., laissez-faire was in the interest of the voters and they would vote to support not only laissez-faire policies. What concerns Friedman and other "descendants" of this tradition is that many of these Radicals, especially Bentham, supported not only laissez-faire but also interventionist policies. In fact, the Philosophical Radicals saw a much more important role for government in regulating the economy than Friedman and contemporary Classical Liberals and did not tend to see most economic regulation as a significant intrusion into freedom. Friedman's economic background itself would suggest a proclivity toward utilitarian calculation.

Friedman must ultimately ground the discussion of freedom. Is freedom valued in itself? Or, is freedom extrinsically valuable, that is, valuable as a means to some other good? Friedman's case echoes the utilitarian argument of earlier Classical Liberals, especially John Stuart Mill's in On Liberty. Ultimately, the value of freedom rests in its connection with utility/efficiency. Freedom is valuable not in itself but only because it generates efficiencies. Interference in freedom of contract, for instance, is immoral in the final analysis only because of costs in the efficiency of the market, because that sort of interference does not optimize utility for all.

This is revealed, briefly, in Friedman's "constructive reason" for his position. The tenets of Classical Liberalism are defended, not only as protections against unwarranted intrusions into one's freedom, but also for the constructive reasons that these arrangements produce positive benefits, the "great advances" of civilization, "progress" in art, science, industry, agriculture, and so forth. In short, the importance of protecting freedom lies in the consequences. And if one takes the further step, the step of inquiring why those great advances are good, the answer is probably that they contribute to the welfare of all, promote the goodness of society, lead to the greatest happiness. In short, freedom is valuable, in combination with a particular political-economic arrangement, because freedom maximizes net utility for all.

Freedom is alleged to be instrumentally valuable because freedom, as a component of a system of competitive capitalism with limited government, produces what is "best for all." A government which seeks to regulate the market, to restrict economic freedom or political liberty, therefore, is alleged to be immoral not merely because this arrangement is contrary to the value of freedom, but because there is only one thing intrinsically good, utility, and restrictions on liberty would allegedly entail a reduction in the aggregate utility for all.

We have, then, a rough sketch of Friedman's argument. A number of important questions remain. On what grounds, for example, does Friedman believe that competitive capitalism with limited government maximizes net utility for all? Or, what is meant by "utility"? Discussion of these points must be postponed until after the structure of the utilitarian argument is developed in more detail.

A tentative reconstruction of Friedman's argument would seem to be this:

1. One ought always act to do what is best for all.

2.   If management acts to maximize profit, then this will be best for all.

3.   Therefore, management ought always act to maximize profit.

Roughly, Premise 1 asserts some version of utilitarianism, and Premise 2 relies upon some theorem in economic theory. The argument as formulated still requires a great deal of revision. For example, no one would argue for Premise 2 as stated. Profit maximization yields optimal social outcomes only under certain specific conditions. Unless these conditions can be incorporated, the premise is too vague to understand or defend. Moreover, Premise 1 also needs clarification. As stated it expresses a variety of utilitarianism known as "act utilitarianism." This kind of utilitarianism is generally considered to be seriously defective. Moreover, act utilitarianism would not provide a moral defense of Classical Liberalism. Hence, a modification of this tentative formulation is necessary.

POLESTAR AND RULE UTILITARIANISM

Utilitarianism contends that morality consists of adherence to a single principle of morality, the principle of utility (PU). This principle asserts that ultimately an agent has but one fundamental duty, and that is the duty to maximize net utility for all. An action, policy, rule, or set of rules is morally right if and only if that action, policy, rule, or set of rules maximizes net utility (goodness, welfare, happiness) for everyone.[9] In recent years, philosophers have come to distinguish two very different versions of utilitarianism depending upon how the principle of utility is applied. According to "act utilitarianism" (AU), one must apply the principle of utility directly to each proposed act. The morally obligatory action is, therefore, the act which will produce at least as great an amount of net utility (goodness) for all as any alternative action. AU has been rejected by most because it leads to extraordinarily counterintuitive consequences. Contemporary utilitarians, therefore, have developed different versions of "rule utilitarianism" (RU) in which the principle of utility is not applied directly to a particular action but is applied only indirectly to actions through rules.[10]

The basic idea of RU is simple, although it will become readily apparent that there are dramatically different versions of this theory.

According to RU, roughly, one is obligated to follow that policy, rule, or set of rules which produces at least as great an amount of net utility for all as any alternative policy, rule, or set of rules. Since an organization, institution, or system can be viewed as a complicated set of rules, RU provides a decision-making procedure for determining the moral legitimacy of organizations, institutions, and systems. There is some uncertainty whether the traditional utilitarians such as Bentham and John Stuart Mill were clear about the distinction between act and rule utilitarianism, but insofar as they were interested in testing the morality of public policies, particular institutions, and systems, they were presupposing some version of RU.

Rule utilitarians approach moral decision making differently from act utilitarians. Consider the situation in which I am considering whether to vote on a particularly miserable, cold Tuesday in November. I know that the turnout will be heavy. I consider two alternative acts. One is to vote and the other is not to vote. I know that the consequences on others in the world will be negligible in either case. My action will not affect whether others vote, my action will not affect the outcome, etc. The action will affect one specific part of the world, i.e., me. I shall be cold and miserable if I stand in line in the early morning, I shall be late, I shall be in a bad mood, I shall be sour with others, etc. Utilitarianism considers each individual affected, including myself. It is not egoistic, but it is not exclusively altruistic. As the utilitarians are fond of saying, each person counts as one and no one counts as more than one. Thus, I count as one. So, considering the consequences of each action, the world would be a much better place if I do not vote. No particular amount of good will be brought into the world if I vote; a little bit of bad (my discomfort) will be brought into the world if I do vote. Consequently, this moral theory would not only excuse me from voting but creates a moral obligation not to vote. To say the least, this is a peculiar outcome for a moral theory. It bestows on relatively minor inconveniences moral significance. This is difficult to square with our intuitions, with our serious reflective judgments. One might be willing to admit that I have no very strong obligation to vote in these circumstances, but AU makes it a moral duty not to vote. Countless examples like this can be manufactured.

RU approaches the situation quite differently. Consider two alternative rules. Rule 1 (R1) might be the rule that citizens have a duty to vote except when voting imposes fairly significant burdens on themselves or others. Rule 2 (R2) might be the rule that citizens have a duty to vote except when it is even slightly inconvenient. The rule utilitarian would probably argue that general conformity to R1 by citizens in the society would produce that greatest net goodness for everyone. Therefore, R1 is the morally defensible rule (provided there would be general conformity to it). I should act in accordance with the rule which would produce the greatest net utility for everyone. Thus, I have an obligation to vote in situations in which there are no greater obstacles than inconveniences.

Rule utilitarianism involves considering the utility associated with rules, not with single actions. As indicated above, it is also useful because it can be used as a test for sets of rules, i.e., organizations, institutions, and systems. Furthermore, within an institution or system, rule utilitarianism also provides a decision-making procedure for choosing the morally superior policy. The best policy is that one which maximizes net, aggregate utility.

This is more or less the defense marshaled by the Classical Liberals in support of the basic tenets of their position. Friedman's underlying argument follows this same line. Consider the utilitarian answers to the central questions of political philosophy. One question is whether any government is morally legitimate. That is, why not anarchy? A second is, if a government is morally legitimate, what is the scope of coercion which can be legitimately employed? Schematically, the rule utilitarian would approach the question in this manner. Consider alternative sets of rules, R1, R2, R3, . . . Rn. Each set of rules corresponds to a different form of government, R1 being no government/anarchism. The rule utilitarian would consider the consequences here and now if rules under R1 were adopted. Then, the consequences here and now if rules under R2 were adopted. After running such an exhaustive cost-benefit analysis, considering the impact on all affected parties, the utilitarians claim that that form of government which produces the greatest net goodness, the greatest net utility, is the morally legitimate one. In this way, the Classical Liberals defended the minimal government which did nothing more than protect against harm. Any form of government, then and there, which did more than protect against harm, they argued, would produce less utility for all. In the same way, the laissez-faire economic system could be defended. Various alternative economic systems should be compared and the one which produces the greatest net utility for all is claimed to be the laissez-faire. Thus, this one should be chosen.

This kind of defense is indeed quite different from that provided by natural rights. A proponent of natural rights would claim that there is a natural right of liberty and government cannot interfere except to prevent harm. For the utilitarian there is no natural right of liberty. The Classical utilitarians, however, defended the harm principle, i.e., the idea that government has no right to interfere in liberty except to prevent harm, on the grounds that the adoption of this principle generated maximal net utility. Yet, and this is a very important point, if the utilitarian cost-benefit analysis demonstrated that greater social utility could be generated by a paternalistic state or a welfare state, then the utilitarian would consistently argue that such a state and not the minimal state should be adopted. For the utilitarian, it all depends upon the facts of the situation. The question of moral legitimacy is determined in light of the situation at hand.

In the early nineteenth century, the Classical Liberals were convinced that the facts supported laissez-faire and minimal government. The scope of government should be limited to the prevention of harm. In John Stuart Mill's On Liberty, the Classical Liberal position vis-à-vis civil liberties is stated perhaps more clearly than anywhere. Citizens should be free to do whatever they please so long as they do not harm another. That is, government should be restricted to preventing individuals from harming others. Many liberals have also understood this to mean that government is allowed to prevent individuals from harming others in the collective sense, from harming the public good. The moral defense of the position is that the adoption of the harm principle produces maximal happiness. Rule utilitarianism can also be used to generate the other features of the Classical Liberal position, especially laissez-faire capitalism. Bentham was especially interested in reform of the penal system. Law and the punishments associated with violation of the law should be constructed for social utility. In order for the punishment to fit the crime, one should calculate which punishment created the desired results. There is no reason to punish except for the socially beneficial results which might follow. Since humans seek pleasure and avoid pain, undesirable behavior will be reduced by threat of punishment. Law should be designed to deter.

Nonetheless, for a rule utilitarian, the position on any topic depends upon the facts. This kind of argument does not confuse descriptive and prescriptive statements. Utilitarianism as a prescriptive theory claims that the morally justified system of rules is the one which maximizes net utility for all. That prescriptive theory will also presuppose a theory of value which involves defining "utility." Given this, however, the challenge for the utilitarian is to examine the empirical world to discover which set of rules would in fact generate optimal net outcomes. This requires utilitarianism to be forward looking. The past will be valuable as a source for making predictions about the consequences of adopting alternative sets of rules. Determining causal relationships between key variables is essential in accurately predicting which system of rules will in fact bring about which consequences.,

Thus, there is no inconsistency in the position of the Classical Liberals in advocating representative democracy for the people of England, while at the same time taking a paternalistic stance toward the people of India. Many Classical Liberals believed that the people of India were incapable of democratic rule, and that only by a period of colonization could the people be educated sufficiently to take over their own nation. For the utilitarians, the debate over colonization was a debate over the facts. What would the consequences be if England was not paternalistic, etc.? Again, the consequences on all affected parties should be considered, English, Indian, and so forth. Utilitarians also realize that over time, although one form of government may be morally legitimate for a period, as the circumstances change, a different form of government may be morally required. Hence, utilitarians need not deny that paternalistic enlightened monarchy at one time was morally correct for the English. Perhaps at an earlier time that form of government did create the greatest net utility for all. Nor is there any guarantee that in the future minimal government will always be morally defensible. There is nothing in principle in utilitarianism to rule out the possibility that a welfare state with state-controlled markets and public ownership of the means of production would be the morally legitimate form of government.

Within a representative democracy, utilitarians believed that representatives should vote consistent with the utilitarian test as well. That is, legislators should not vote according to the narrow self-interest of constituency but should seek to rise above such parochial interests and vote in the best interests of all. Those laws and policies which promote the greatest social utility should be advanced.

Utilitarianism also provides the apologist of capitalism with a simultaneous defense against "liberal" reformers who would meddle with smooth functioning of the system, as well as a defense against systematic attacks from socialists or communists. Increasing the size of government or interfering in any facet of the system, by intruding upon strict private property rights, or the right of contract, will destroy the smooth operation of the system and create less welfare for all, the argument continues. Self-interest, the desire for wealth, and profit-maximizing behavior are then bestowed with moral significance. If one assumes the arguments about the utility of laissez-faire capitalism, and if one assumes that the conditions which define that system exist, then it becomes a moral obligation to maximize profit, since by doing so one creates the greatest happiness for the greatest number of people. Social utility results from the individualistic pursuit of profit.

The structure of the utilitarian argument employed by Friedman and others might better be understood as involving a two-tiered argument. The first tier involves the moral justification for the minimal or limited state of Classical Liberalism. Let us refer to the conditions (set of rules) describing the Classical Liberal state, including the laissez-faire capitalist market, as conditions C.

Polestar I: Utilitarian Argument for Classical Liberalism

I.1.   An institution (such as the Classical Liberal state) is morally legitimate if and only if it maximizes net utility for all in comparison with alternative arrangements. (RU)

I.2.   Conditions C describing the Classical Liberal state) produce maximal net utility for all.

II.3. Therefore, conditions C (describing the Classical Liberal state) are morally legitimate.

This defense of Classical Liberalism does not explicitly legitimize profit maximization. If the assumption of profit maximization by firms is included as one of the conditions C, then this argument would legitimize profit maximization. If the profit-maximizing rule is included explicitly in conditions C, then the following Polestar argument can be constructed:

Polestar II: Argument Defending Profit Maximization

II.1. One ought always to act according to that rule which maximizes net utility for all. (RU)

II.2. Under conditions C, the rule of profit maximizing by management maximizes net utility for all. (Economic Premise)

II.3. Conditions C exist. (Existence Premise)

II.4. Therefore, management ought to maximize profit.

Friedman's other arguments should probably be recast in light of this argument. That is, Friedman should probably be interpreted as arguing that if managers acted as if they had promised stockholders, or were agents of stockholders, or had a role duty to maximize profit, then this would be best for all. In that light, Friedman would not be guilty of being insensitive to reality. Promises may not have been made by management, but management should act as if they had.

Polestar II illustrates how economic theories, moral principles, and beliefs about existing reality function together within this version of the Classical framework in an attempt to legitimize profit-maximizing behavior. Premise II.1 expresses an adherence to some version of RU. Premise II.2, the Economic Premise, expresses some economic theory or theorem. This premise, it is important to emphasize, is itself a descriptive statement. That is, once the key concept of "best for all" or "utility," is defined, Premise II.2 purports to describe what as a matter of fact would occur under conditions C. Premise II.3, the Existence Premise, is also a descriptive premise. This premise asserts that conditions C obtain. Premise II.3 reflects the important role that beliefs about facts play. Even if, for instance, Premise II.1 and Premise II.2 were accepted, the argument requires the Existence Premise. Suppose that under conditions of a free market, suitably defined, profit maximization yields results which are maximally utile. Suppose further that the correct theory of morality is one which requires only that utility, as defined in the Economic Premise, be maximized. This would not establish that any corporation or corporate manager had an obligation to maximize profit *unless* it could also be shown that conditions C, or a situation very close to C, obtains. Obviously, without competition in something like a free market situation, there is no guarantee that self-interested, profit-maximizing behavior will generate socially beneficial outcomes. On the contrary, conspiracies and restraint of trade, for example, may represent profit-maximizing behavior, but they are not likely to result in consequences which are "best for all." Hence, unless there are assurances that conditions C obtain, there is little reason to believe in the social utility of profit maximization.

The basic structure of this argument also suggests the different general lines of attack which can be directed against the argument. First, one might attack the utilitarianism which undergirds Premise I.1 or II.1, while granting Premises I.2, II.2, and II.3. Or, one might attack Premise I.2 or II.2, the economic theory. An attack upon the Economic Premise involves a dispute over economic theory. For instance, if Keynes argues that the laissez-faire market of classical economics does not always produce the greatest goodness (or is not maximally efficient) because the market can reach equilibrium at points of high unemployment, this is an attack upon one interpretation of Premise I.2 or Premise II.2. That is an economic claim with significant consequences for the moral obligation of corporate managers. Premise II.3 is also a descriptive statement. Thus, debates over the Existence Premise are not themselves moral debates either, but understandings about the world have momentous moral significance. For example, one could grant that the laissez-faire capitalist market produces what is best for all (Economic Premise), and grant the adequacy of utilitarian theory, but claim that since the free market does not in fact exist, the argument does not follow. In fact, profit maximization in a situation in which the free market does not exist may produce something like a worst case for the society. Thus, while economic debates and debates over whether certain market conditions actually pertain are not themselves moral debates, the outcome of the debates is often extremely important in determining the moral obligations of managers (or anyone else, for that matter).

These points are significant in understanding the contest between the Classical and Revisionist/Managerial frameworks. Revisionist Liberalism, upon which Managerialism rests, is not necessarily an attack upon any opposing set of ultimate values but more often is an attack upon certain economic doctrines central to the Classical framework and/or a challenge to the Existence Premise. The debate is not necessarily over the adequacy of utilitarianism, over which moral principles are relevant, or over the interpretation of moral concepts. The debate is more often over whether the free market, even if it did exist, would guarantee socially beneficial outcomes without government interference.

THE IDEAL AND THE ACTUAL

The debate is actually much more complicated. Although the attack on the Existence Premise is on the mark against the Polestar II argument as reconstructed, this rule utilitarian version of the Polestar argument does not yet do justice to the position of contemporary Classical Liberals such as Friedman. In a very real sense, Friedman and other Classical Liberals today would admit to the falsity of the Existence Premise. They are in the uncomfortable position of reformers. Consider again the conditions C involved in the argument. Friedman's ideal state was described above. This ideal state would

a. protect individuals against harms (police, system of justice, penal system, military)
b. protect the free market (probably the same as "a", e.g., protect property rights, enforce contracts, etc.)
c. enforce antitrust legislation
d. provide a monetary framework
e. engage in activities to overcome neighborhood effects
f. supplement private charity and private family in protecting the irresponsible (children and madmen).

There is virtually nothing more that Friedman would accept as a part of the ideal state. This ideal state then, roughly speaking, would constitute conditions C. These conditions would also contain more specific conditions defining the free market which can be ignored for the present. Friedman's argument is that these arrangements should be established because they would, if adopted, produce the greatest net utility for all (greatest efficiency). Given conditions C, profit maximization by corporations would, according to the economic theory Friedman invokes, generate what is most efficient. But Friedman admits that conditions C do not obtain.

What exists is not the ideal state but the mixed capitalistic welfare state. Call these conditions CC. Consider the variety of conditions beyond the ideal state which could be added to the description of the ideal state. Friedman mentions these as components of the contemporary state which he seeks to eliminate:

g. retained earnings (all earnings would be paid out in dividends)
h. corporate income tax
i. deductions for charitable contributions
j. parity price programs for agriculture
k. tariffs on imports or restrictions on exports
l. government control of output (e.g. farm program)
m. rent control
n. legal minimum wages
o. detailed regulation of industries
p. regulation of free speech by FCC
q. social security programs

r. licensure provisions
s. public housing
t. conscription
u. national parks
v. legal prohibition on the carrying of the mail for profit
w. legal prohibition on private ownership and operation of toll roads.

To this list, one might also add other functions of the more than limited state, such as

x. fiscal policy
y. cross-industry regulation (OSHA, EPA).

Critics, including the Managerialists, are correct in focusing upon the Existence Premise as an especially vulnerable point. Let conditions C be understood as describing Friedman's ideal state, a–e. Let conditions CC describe a–y, a set of conditions which comes closer to describing the current reality.

The problem with Polestar I and II is that they do not directly address our reality. They do not address the issue of whether the current situation is morally legitimate. Does it follow, for example, that since conditions CC do not correspond to conditions C, that the present government is morally illegitimate? If it is morally illegitimate, is Friedman advocating revolution, rebellion, resistance, or gradual reform? Are citizens, including corporations, morally permitted to disobey the laws of this unjust society? If so, should they violate laws in a way so as to profit maximize or in a way so as to do what is best for all? Or, should citizens and corporations act so as to bring about the reforms necessary to instantiate the Classical Liberal state? If the current situation is morally legitimate, then what are we to make of the argument for the minimal state?

These are not entirely theoretical or idle questions. In the nonideal world, to what extent should corporations take advantage of rules/laws which are from Friedman's point of view morally objectionable? If corporations can maximize profit by taking advantage of these inefficient rules, are they morally obligated to do so, or should they act as if these corrupt rules did not exist? Friedman is opposed to retained earnings. Is he advocating that the corporations in the real world resist the temptation to retain earnings even though it is legal and even though it may lead to profit maximization? Or, should corporations become involved in political campaigns as a means of bringing about the kinds of political change Friedman believes to be desirable? This is an especially sticky question, since lobbying for a more competitive market will probably entail a reduction in profitability for many firms. Is Friedman advocating that corporations lobby against profit maximization in the real world? If corporations should become politically active in some way, should they do so while not retaining earnings? If they do not retain earnings, how are they to finance the political campaigns necessary to arm the warriors fighting the battle for a just society?

Ideally, it is clear that Friedman wishes to see a situation in which corporations would be unable to get involved politically because there would be no retained earnings, no corporate income tax, no deductions for charitable contributions, no contributions to political action committees. In the ideal world, Friedman envisions every bit of revenue beyond costs of production returned to stockholders. If Friedman opposes allowing managers to use retained earnings to make investment decisions, it would appear that he would oppose allowing managers to use retained earnings for political contributions. This situation is complicated by the real possibility that by utilizing existing legal tools, such as using retained earnings for purposes of advocacy advertising or political contributions, the corporations make it more difficult for public policy to move toward the ideal. Or what of legal charitable contributions? Are corporations morally obligated not to spend anything on charitable contributions even if they can deduct it on the corporate income tax merely because in the ideal world it would be most efficient if it were not allowed? Should managers in the real world abstain from debt financing merely because the system would be more efficient if this were not allowed? In other words, there remains room for serious disagreement within the Classical camp about how believers should act before the Kingdom comes to earth.

Apparently Friedman believes it should be a matter of public policy to dismantle the welfare state and to create the ideal. Friedman needs an argument to the effect that as a matter of public policy, society ought to adopt rules which would instantiate conditions C. This would require an argument that in the long run, the costs associated with moving the situation described by conditions CC to a situation described by C, the ideal, will be outweighed by the greater efficiencies under C. Let us refer to this argument as Polestar I*, since it deals with public policy of the actual state, while Polestar I deals with the ideal. It is difficult to express this argument precisely, but this comes as close as is necessary for our purposes.

Polestar I*:

I*.1. Public policy should be such as to create (ideal) conditions in which net utility for all would be maximized. (Moral premise)

I*.2. Conditions C are such that they would produce maximal net utility for all. (Economic Premise)

I*.3. Therefore, public policy should be such as to create conditions C.

In the process of defending this argument, Friedman will also need to develop an argument to establish that conditions C are stable. That is, what assurance is there that the ideal state will remain the ideal state? He will need to explain why nothing like the ideal state has ever existed. If it has never existed, what guarantee can be provided that once the ideal state is developed, the situation will not quickly evolve back toward the mixed economy of the welfare capitalist state? Why is it that Japan and West Germany, two states esteemed as the capitalistic success stories of the past three decades, more closely resemble CC than Friedman's ideal state? If the ideal state is not stable, then any argument demonstrating the costs associated with the transition to the ideal state will be difficult, since in the long run, conditions CC will return.

There is another problem with Polestar I*. Who has the responsibility to make the sacrifices necessary to work toward the ideal? Is it immoral for individuals and groups, even politicians, to act rationally in the current reality and maximize their own utility? Maximizing one's own utility will likely prevent working toward Friedman's ideal. This issue is related to the issue of Polestar II. Even if managers/corporations ought to maximize profit under conditions C, what ought they do under conditions CC? There is no guidance provided. As stated, if conditions CC actually describe the contemporary situation, then the RU version of the Polestar II argument actually looks like this:

Polestar II: Alternate Version

II.1. One ought to act according to that rule (or set of rules) which maximizes net utility for all. (RU)

II.2. Under conditions C, the rule of profit maximizing by management maximizes net utility for all. (Economic Premise)

II.3. Conditions CC exist.

II.4. Therefore, management ought to maximize profit.

Obviously, this is invalid. Friedman's ideal state is not actual. Polestar II needs to be refined or supplemented as well. There is a serious problem of ambiguity in Premise II.1, the moral premise. That ambiguity concerns how the relevant conditions are to be treated in assessments of utility. Does morality require acting according to rules which if generally accepted would maximize net utility, even though in the real world a much different set of rules is being followed? This is a difficult issue for all sensitive individuals and groups, and one about which honest and reasonable persons are likely to disagree. Utilitarians, too, are of different minds. Consequently, there are different versions of rule utilitarianism, each reflecting a different way of dealing with the problem of the gap between the ideal and the actual, and it is not clear which is being employed by Friedman. To oversimplify slightly, consider three alternative versions of RU, "conventional rule utilitarianism" (CRU), "ideal rule utilitarianism" (IRU), or "realistic rule utilitarianism" (RRU). These three forms of RU reflect three different modes of thinking about the manner in which aggregate utility is relevant to moral reasoning. Friedman must make a choice, for he cannot employ Polestar II while at the same time admitting that Premise II.3 is false.

CONVENTIONAL RULE UTILITARIANISM

"Conventional rule utilitarianism" (CRU), sometimes referred to as "actual rule utilitarianism" (ARU), claims that agents should adhere to the conventional or actual norms of society. This theory provides a useful defense for the status quo and was associated with defenses of Classical Liberalism when reality bore a much closer resemblance to the ideal than now. Friedman cannot use this theory because he is concerned to legitimize the ideal society, not the actual one. Consequently, he must opt for either ideal rule utilitarianism or realistic rule utilitarianism.

Before leaving conventional rule utilitarianism, however, it is worth exploring. For one thing, an understanding of this theory will help to clarify the nature of the alternatives. For another, CRU has been an extremely influential theory and one often associated with defenses of Classical Liberalism.

The idea that history is evolving toward ever-higher planes has long been associated with liberalism. In *Liberalism: Concepts in Social Thought*, John Gray refers to the meliorist idea as one of the distinctive features of liberalism.[11] The idea is probably un-Christian. New Testament eschatolgoical teaching appears to reflect the view that history is the scene of a struggle between the forces of light and darkness, and that forces of darkness are getting the upper hand. Humans must choose to align themselves with one side or the other, but basically, their choice will have no impact on the final outcome. The final outcome, the eschaton, the end of time, is fast arriving. Soon God will break decisively into history, and this final battle will result in the final judgment. Those who have chosen the side of light will be rewarded; those who have chosen wrongly will be punished. The Kingdom of God will be established.

The eschatological teaching was embarrassing for the Church and gradually this theology was submerged. The Church came close to understanding itself as the Kingdom on Earth, or the Kingdom was understood to be within those who were already "saved." As Christianity spread, this seemed to suggest that the world was actually getting better, that humans may indeed have had some control over history (God willing, as it were). Liberal Christian theologians in the Enlightenment were convinced of the moral progress of western civilization. By the late eighteenth century, the idea that history represented the unfolding of some plan was common. The philosopher Hegel developed his entire philosophy around the conviction that the idea of freedom was progressively unfolding through history. Marx may have turned Hegel on his head, but the Communists were convinced that they had discovered the true logic of history. The idea is also apparent in Mill and Auguste Comte. The publication of Charles Darwin's *On the Origin of the Species* is another example of evolutionary thinking, this time without all the metaphysical presuppositions.

In short, apologists for many causes invoke evolution in support of their views. Herbert Spencer was only one of many who employed evolutionary ideas in a defense of the central ideals of Classical Liberalism.[12] Evolutionary defenses continue to surface through the present. Dozens of different kinds of arguments have been developed, and I shall make no attempt here to survey the varied assortment. One argument is of particular interest, however, because it represents an attempt to incorporate evolutionary ideas into utilitarian theory. This move is suggested by G. E. Moore's *Principia Ethica*.[13] The influence of this kind of approach has been significant. The structure of Moore's theory anticipates later attempts in the twentieth century to provide a moral legitimation for capitalism such as that of F. A. Hayek.[14]

According to Moore, the theoretically correct moral theory is act utilitarianism. Each individual should, according to Moore, act in each situation so as to produce the greatest good for the greatest number of people. Moore worried little, if at all, about the problems involved in recognizing or measuring value and focused instead upon difficulties involved in predicting the consequences of actions. The problem, Moore suggests, is not so much the assignment of values to consequences, but in determining the consequences. This caveat leads Moore to disavow act utilitarianism. Although Moore believes AU to be the correct moral theory, he argues that it is not the theory which we should adopt to guide our behavior in the actual world because, given the problem of prediction, it is virtually impossible to apply. Act utilitarianism would require each individual to weigh the consequences of each alternative course of action. Should I tell the truth here and now, or should I tell a particular untruth? Action x or action y? To determine this requires (1) knowing the consequences of x and y, through a distant future, and (2) being able to assign a value to (to quantify) the consequences. Once the costs and benefits of the alternative courses of actions were calculated, act utilitarianism required choosing that course of action which produced the greatest net utility for all. Moore argued that act utilitarianism should not be adopted because even if it were possible to quantify precisely, our uncertainty about the future makes it impossible to predict the consequences of our actions even in the near future. To quote Lenin (Moore certainly would not)—history is tricky.

A good literary example of the contingency of history is Jean-Paul Sartre's short story "The Wall."[15] In the story a resistance fighter is taken captive by the Nazis. During interrogation the fighter is told that if he provides information about the whereabouts of one of the resistance leaders, he will be set free. The man understands quite well that even if he cooperates, he will be killed. Thus, to have the last laugh, the captured man sends the Nazis on a wild goose chase, providing information he knows to be false. Although he is certain that the resistance leader will not be at the location he names, the Nazis believe him and go there. They return having found the resistance leader at exactly that location. They release the first prisoner.

Forecasting the future is truly risky business. This skeptical argument about the limitations of the human capacity to predict the future can be described as the "antirationalist argument." Moore pushes this point hard and claims that since predicting the future is so difficult, humans cannot be trusted to choose the correct act. They will generate scenarios about the consequences of their actions which will merely legitimize the course of action they really desire to pursue. Ironically, the argument against AU is that the adoption of the correct moral theory would generate antiutilitarian consequences. Moore is opposed to those who believe that reason can provide a shining beacon with which to peer into the future. Thus, for Moore, some version of rule utilitarianism should be adopted.

This raises another set of problems. Which rules should be selected? According to Moore, society's *established conventional norms* should be the relevant moral rules adopted to guide conduct. The rules which actually describe and guide behavior, not some set of reform rules, are relevant. When Moore wrote, during the early twentieth century in England, the adoption of this theory might well have legitimized Classical Liberalism. However, an argument against AU does not constitute a defense of conventional rule utilitarianism, IRU, or RRU. Moore needs an argument to demonstrate why conventional rules are morally significant rather than some set of reform rules.

Moore offered an argument in defense of conventional rules which makes use of the antirationalist argument. Suppose, for example, a group proposes some rule or set of rules different from the accepted rule or rules. Suppose, for example, that someone proposes equal legal rights for women or blacks in a society in which women or blacks are denied the right to vote. The reformers, filled with utilitarian zeal, argue that it would be best for society if women were allowed to vote. To make this claim, the reformers must determine the consequences which would follow upon the adoption of the new rule, and the consequences of following the current rule. Second, value must be assigned to the consequences of each alternative. The reformers claim that having performed this exercise, allowing women to vote would be most utile. Moore responds with the antirationalist argument. He argues that even if one can quantify and assign value to the respective consequences, one cannot predict with any minimal degree of confidence what will result when a change is initiated. Moore accused those who believed that they understood the nature of society well enough to make such predictions of being rationalists. According to this kind of argument, the rationalists assume that society is like a machine insofar as parts can be altered or replaced, the design modified, without affecting the operation of the whole machine in unforetold ways. For Moore, society is as delicate and mysterious as an organism. One cannot modify merely a part of the organism without significant repercussions for the organism, and, Moore contends, we are largely incapable of knowing with any degree probability what those repercussions will be. The slightest alteration in one organ might destroy or seriously jeopardize the entire organism.

The antirationalist argument is a favorite for many conservatives opposing governmental interference. It has been labeled by Hayek as the "constructivist fallacy."[16] Those who commit this "fallacy" believe that "social institutions can be the subject of successful rational redesign."[17] It is not clear why this is called a "fallacy." A fallacy is a mistake in logic. Those who believe that institutions can be understood with sufficient thoroughness to allow predictions about the consequences of proposed changes may be mistaken, but they are not guilty of any fallacy. Hayek and more contemporary Classical Liberals are uncomfortable with Bentham and Mill precisely because they believe the classical utilitarians fell victim to this "fallacy."

But even if one grants the force of the antirationalist argument or the point of the charge of the constructivist fallacy, this does not provide an argument in defense of conventional rule utilitarianism. The argument might show that we cannot know that the proposed reform will provide more utility than the existing arrangement, but it also shows that we do not know that the proposed reform will not. The argument undermines our ability to assess the utility of the current rules as well as of the reform rules. How then should one decide? Why not experimentation rather than the status quo? At this point, a theorist can introduce an "evolutionary argument." According to many, there is very good reason to presume that the existing mode of organization of society is utile. Namely, that society has survived provides some reason for believing in the utility of the existing norms. Society is viewed as an organism which has evolved over the centuries, slowly and gradually changing to adapt to the environment. Survival, in this view, should provide evidence for utility, the efficiency of the current arrangements.

This theory is virtually identical to ethical conventionalism. Both claim that the morally binding rules are those rules which are currently accepted in society. The difference is that CRU claims social utility for the conventional rules. Ethical conventionalism usually relies upon some other defense of the conventional norms. Like ethical conventionalism, CRU is relativistic. What counts as moral at one time or place may not be moral at another time or place. As a normative theory of obligation, the theory is inadequate. If adopted, it would yield a number of jarring implications. For one thing, virtually any reform attempt is counted as immoral. For another, if an immoral reformer is successful in altering the norms of society, those new norms become moral; the previous behavior remains immoral since the norms were different, but in the new society the behavior is moral.

In Moore's time, the conventional rule utilitarian position might have provided legitimation for the stern doctrines of laissez-faire capitalism and minimal government because those doctrines were widely accepted and had become incorporated into law. There were, of course, other tendencies in England and the U.S. as well, but the ideology of laissez-faire was firmly entrenched. Through the first years of the Great Depression in the United States the theory might also legitimize a status quo not far from the kind of minimal government desired by the Classical Liberals. However, once major changes are made in the structure of government and the economy, once the New Deal policies of the 1930s, the Supreme Court decisions of the Warren court, or the social legislation of the 1960s significantly change that structure, creating something like a capitalist welfare state, then CRU would obligingly legitimize this new order. CRU legitimizes any existing order.

Consequently, conservatives like Hayek cannot rest content in CRU but must adopt ad hoc arguments to attack the "creeping socialism" of the age.[18] Antirationalist arguments continue to be employed, but now they need to be employed against the status quo. The status quo now represents, not the process of evolutionary struggle, but an "unnatural" intervention into the "natural" evolutionary process. The natural evolutionary process, they claim, would yield a free market with a minimal state. The "conservatives" are placed in the role of reformers who seek to turn back the clock. At this point, these arguments degenerate into scholastic arguments about the "natural" as opposed to the "unnatural." Like those scholastic arguments, "natural" is a convenient disguise for some other submerged argument. What Hayek and others apparently mean is that these recent "socialist" developments should be avoided because they are unnatural, i.e., not maximally efficient.

At this point, the entire argument collapses. Both the antirationalist and evolutionary arguments have evaporated. The antirationalist argument is premised upon the claim that it is impossible to calculate the consequences of reforming society. Now these conservatives are placed in the position of arguing that they know that the result of reform away from the welfare state would produce greater utility. The evolutionary argument is no comfort because evolution has lead away from what is best for all.

IDEAL RULE UTILITARIANISM

Friedman must, therefore, appeal to some other form of rule utilitarianism. Ideal rule utilitarianism claims that agents have a moral responsibility to act according to those rules which if adopted would maximize net utility for all, even if there is not general conformity to those rules. It is possible to make Polestar II a valid argument by understanding Premise II.1 as IRU. That the ideal conditions, C, do not currently obtain is of no concern for the ideal rule utilitarian.

Indeed, the flaw in IRU is this utopian insensitivity to the actual world. The utopian counterintuitiveness of IRU is easily demonstrated. Acting according to ideal rules which would maximize net utility if they were generally adopted will often lead to dangerous *antiutilitarian* consequences. That is, acting according to ideal rules in a situation in which there is not general conformity will often make the world a worse place. Consider the ideal rules of pacifism. Ideally, if everyone acted according to rules of pacifism, the world would be a marvelous place. Does this mean that I should act here and now according to those ideal rules? Not necessarily. Ideal rule utilitarianism ignores reality. Ignoring reality may be, not only antiutile, but suicidal. Consider a corporation in a noncompetitive industry. Should a corporation act according to the rules which would define a competitive market merely because if this ideal situation existed, it would produce what is best for all?· Ignoring reality may also be suicidal in that situation. Ideal rule utilitarianism does not constitute a defensible theory. Consequently, to reconstruct the Polestar argument most sympathetically requires seeking an alternative version of utilitarianism, one more sensitive to existence. The reform-oriented version of rule utilitarianism which has been incorporated into Polestar makes a set of rules binding only if there would be general conformity to the rules.

Instead of adopting CRU or IRU, the alternative is to rely upon some version of what can be called "realistic rule utilitarianism" which claims that one ought to act according to that set of rules which maximizes net utility for all provided that there is general conformity to those rules. I will not take the time to formulate RRU in more detail, but the contrast with CRU and IRU should make the point of the theory clear. By understanding the theory in this way, this kind of argument can be formulated:

Polestar II*: Profit Maximization in the Actual World:

II*.1. One ought to act according to that rule which would produce the greatest net utility for all (provided there would be general conformance to the rule).

II*.2. Under conditions CC, profit maximization would produce the greatest net utility for all.

II*.3. Conditions CC obtain.

II*.4. Therefore, one ought to act according to the rule of profit maximization.

FRIEDMAN'S POSITION

This analysis has demonstrated the complicated nature of Friedman's position. All of these four arguments work together, and ignoring any of them would fail to capture his view. Polestar II* attempts to establish that under the current conditions, there is a moral obligation to maximize profit because this will maximize net utility for all. Interpreting Friedman's position only in this way, however, without reference to the other arguments would seriously distort his position. Polestar II* could be read as if he were content with the status quo. Polestar II* must be read in light of Polestar I*. And Polestar I* should be read in light of Polestar I and Polestar II, because the central claim is that only by reaching the ideal state of Classical Liberalism will social utility be maximized. In that situation, the ideal, profit maximization, will surely lead to what is best for all.

Having now exhumed this position, the next chapters will be devoted to evaluating this kind of defense. Ironically, one of the weakest links in Friedman's argument is Polestar II*. While formal economic theorems can establish that profit maximization in ideal competitive markets generate what is best for all, it would be very difficult to generate a formal proof that profit maximizing in the contemporary environment does what is best for all.

5

Evaluating the Utilitarian Defense of Classical Liberalism

Having reconstructed an argument purporting to legitimize the Classical response, the next task is to evaluate its strength. As the last chapter revealed, the structure of that defense is quite complicated, weaving together a number of different descriptive and normative strands. Among the descriptive threads involved is the claim that a set of conditions, call them C, define the Classical Liberal ideal of the minimal government with the competitive free market, the claim that conditions C maximize net utility for all in comparison with relevant alternative arrangements, and the claim that acting according to the rule of profit maximization when conditions C are satisfied will maximize net utility for all. However, since defenders of the Classical position are quite aware that conditions C are not satisfied, they are also committed to the claim that acting according to the rule of profit maximization under conditions CC, a description of the contemporary situation, will maximize net utility for all in comparison with alternative rules.

Both evaluative and prescriptive normative claims are involved as well. The former, pertaining to claims about what is good, involves a theory of value. The latter, pertaining to claims about what one ought to do, involves a theory of obligation. This defense includes the appeal to some version of rule utilitarianism, what I have characterized as realistic rule utilitarianism, which functions in an attempt to legitimize the Classical Liberal vision of the ideal political economy, in the defense of profit maximization under C or CC, and in the defense of public policy which would move the contemporary conditions more toward the ideal of conditions C.

In utilitarianism, economic claims can play a critical role. Indeed, if one adopts utilitarianism, moral reasoning consists entirely in the evaluation of claims like these. Their role can be appreciated by examining more carefully the nature of utilitarianism. *Utilitarianism is a theory of obligation.* Theories of obligation purport to capture the fundamental criterion or set of criteria according to which one can determine what an agent ought or ought not do. Philosophers generally distinguish two distinct types of theories of obligation, teleological and deontological. According to a teleological theory what is morally right depends solely upon the value actualized by conduct. Since value is probably actualized only through the consequences of our actions, teleological theories are often characterized as *consequentialist* theories. Ethical egoism is a familiar teleological/consequentialist theory which claims that one's sole obligation is to maximize net goodness for oneself. Utilitarianism, of course, differs by claiming that (ultimately or fundamentally) one's sole obligation is to maximize net utility (goodness) *for all.*

According to deontological theories, in contrast, right is not determined solely according to value actualized by conduct. In natural rights theory, for instance, an action is morally right just in case no natural rights are violated. In other deontological theories, that an action, rule, or policy produces value in the world may be relevant but is not the sole factor in reaching a final moral determination.

Because utilitarianism is a teleological/consequentialist theory according to which moral obligation is determined exclusively by the net value/utility of the consequences for all, claims such as those expressed in the economic premises are decisive.

Moreover, a second type of normative claim is involved. *All teleological theories presuppose a theory of value.* One cannot determine one's obligation without determining what is meant by "value" or "utility." Hence, a utilitarian defense of the Classical Liberal position necessarily rests upon a theory of utility or value. Very different theories of utilitarianism can be developed, depending upon the theory of value/utility employed. Two realistic rule utilitarians, for example, may come to dramatically different conclusions about which rules are morally legitimate, because very different understandings of utility are involved. Or, two rule utilitarians may even agree on a definition of utility but arrive at different conclusions because of a disagreement about how best to measure this understanding.

Herein lies a cautionary tale. If utilitarianism is to rely upon economic claims, then the definition and measurement of utility employed must be the same as those employed in the economic claims. One may wish to assume that there are no substantive normative constraints, as such, upon the understanding of utility in economic theory. One may claim that economists are free to adopt any theory of utility at all, within the constraints of that discipline. If, however, economists or utilitarians wish to marshal these economic claims in a general moral argument, as in the defense of the tenets of Classical Liberalism, then the definition of utility must correspond to the one used in the theory of utilitarianism.

The adoption of a theory of utility in utilitarianism is not arbitrary. Not any definition or understanding of value will do. As I will explain in more detail later, there are at least two sets of constraints, formal and substantive. The formal constraints flow from the requirements imposed by the nature of utilitarianism. Not only must a theorist develop an understanding of value which can be measured or quantified, but, since the theory requires that one adopt the rule which maximizes net value for all, it must also be possible to measure the value which would be produced by each alternative, and to compare the amount of value which would be produced by each alternative in order to be able to choose the one which maximizes net value. That entails that the value produced for each individual under a scenario be measured and somehow combined so as to arrive at a determination of the net utility for all under this scenario. Having aggregated the net utility for each scenario, these must be compared. Hence, the measurement must have the characteristics of commensurability and comparability. Second, the theory of value itself must be able to withstand substantive analysis. We would readily disregard a utilitarian argument resting upon a theory of value in which "utility" meant nothing more than "widgets." Widgets have little connection with human welfare, with what is valuable or utile for human existence and enjoyment.

Thus, the utilitarian defense involves very different sorts of claims, normative and descriptive. Each requires very different kinds of evidence for support. In the next section, I shall demonstrate the inadequacy of utilitarianism as a theory of obligation, using familiar counterexamples. The remainder of the chapter will demonstrate the limitations of the economic claims. The next chapter will explore the weaknesses of the theory of value invoked in the defense.

THE INADEQUACY OF UTILITARIANISM
AS A THEORY OF OBLIGATION

Assume for the moment that we understand clearly what "utility" means, that this understanding constitutes an adequate theory of value, and that we have good reason to believe that the descriptive claims (including the economic) are true. In short, assume that it can be shown that a situation of laissez-faire capitalism with a minimal state and nothing more extensive would maximize net utility for all. Does this constitute an adequate moral defense?

From the utilitarian perspective, the optimization of net, aggregate utility is the *only* morally relevant consideration. Whether this kind of a defense is adequate depends upon whether there is more to morality than maximizing utility. Critics have long objected that there is much more to morality than this. Based upon familiar objections, it is relatively easy to illustrate the weaknesses. Critics need not claim that utility is irrelevant to moral considerations, only that *utility is not the sole morally relevant factor.*

Consider the following situation in a three-person society (or suppose that each person is a representative person of three different classes) in which two different policies are being considered for implementation.[1] Suppose that the utilities which would be produced under each program are represented in the table below.

Weighing the Utility of Two Policies

	Policy A	Policy B
Citizen 1	31	10
Citizen 2	1	10
Citizen 3	−1	10
Total utility	31	30

According to utilitarianism, policy A should be chosen because that policy maximizes net utility in society for all. Many find this outcome objectionable because it ignores other considerations.[2] To put it crudely, utilitarianism considers nothing but the bottom line. Any disaggregated characteristic is morally irrelevant. By adopting policy A, for instance, utilitarianism gives no consideration to the fact that Citizen 3 is a loser, while Citizen 1 receives over 30 times as much benefit. A critic would note that the insignificant increase in social utility which would be achieved by adopting A does not merit the skewed distribution. One need not argue that equality should outweigh any considerations of social utility in every or even most situations. But in this case equality could be achieved at almost no loss of social utility. Equal distribution may not be the only or even the most important consideration, but it can be argued plausibly that considerations of distribution carry *some* moral weight.

Or suppose that Citizens 2 and 3 are among the least well-off members of society, and that the distribution which maximized aggregate utility left many important *needs* unmet. Citizens 2 and 3 could not afford adequate medical treatment under policy A but could afford it under policy B. Citizen 1 will be able to afford medical treatment under either scenario. There would appear to be no good reason under this scenario to adopt policy A over policy B. Maximizing aggregate welfare is a desirable policy goal, but utilitarianism would ignore any other factor, including need. That is extremely implausible.

One possible response to these criticisms can be dismissed out of hand. Apologists often attempt to deflect the force of this line of criticism by rejecting these other factors as too subjective or too controversial to carry force in a pluralistic society. Yet it is no less subjective to claim that the only relevant moral consideration is maximization of aggregate utility. The claim that concerns like need, distribution, or equality are relevant is not to admit claims which are any more highly controversial or subjective than the claim that utility is singularly relevant. Indeed, given our ordinary understanding of morality, the burden of proof would appear to be upon utilitarians to explain why our intuitions are incorrect. In fact, the agreement over the relevance of these factors is sufficiently widespread that moral theorists from quite different perspectives attempt to make room for them.

Long-standing objections that capitalism is stacked against some individuals provide other, more concrete examples of the claim that maximizing efficiency or utility is not the only morally relevant consideration. Capitalism may well be the most efficient system, may produce the greatest goodness in the aggregate sense, but may do so by sacrificing some individuals for the sake of the whole. Is this unfair? Adam Smith argues, for example, that one flaw of the system is that in the struggle between worker and capitalist, the interests of the capitalist will nearly always prevail.[3] Workers will attempt to combine in order to raise wages, and capitalists will combine in order to lower wages. In this contest, for a number of reasons explained by Smith, workers will lose; we would today posit additional reasons.[4] Workers face the organizational disadvantage of having greater numbers, which makes collective action more difficult. Communication among capitalists is better. Workers usually cannot afford not to work, so while withholding labor until a higher wage is offered may be in the long-term interests of the working class in general, and the individual worker in particular, a sufficient number of workers are always desperate for work at nearly any wage and make collective action nearly impossible.

Workers suffer in another way. According to Smith, the division of labor partly explains the efficiency of capitalism, but the workers are transformed by the division of labor. Repetitious work distorts the worker physically and, more importantly, dulls his or her mental capabilities.[5] These effects are traced in more detail by the Marxist analyst Harry Braverman in *Labor and Monopoly Capitalism*,[6] an analysis with which Adam Smith likely would have had deep sympathy. Braverman points out that the division of labor takes knowledge of production out of the hands of workers and into the hands of management. When automobiles were produced by teams of craftsmen, for instance, each gained skill in a number of areas and acquired the knowledge necessary to fabricate an automobile. The assembly line not only creates narrow, repetitious work but also moves the knowledge of the production away from the worker. Or, new sales terminals in places like fast-food restaurants and other retail outlets make it unnecessary for workers to acquire simple arithmetic skills which would have once been learned largely on the job. These skills are then not reinforced and often lost. Thus, individuals may be sacrificed for the sake of the whole in the capitalist system, as Smith realized, and this raises the question of whether such sacrifice is always morally justified, even if utile in the aggregate sense.

Furthermore, Classical economists after Smith claimed that the wage situation was bleak for workers.[7] Ricardo's iron-clad law of wages postulates that wages will tend toward subsistency in the free market.[8] As workers get wages above subsistence, more will survive. More infants of the workers will survive as well. Shortly, therefore, the supply of labor will increase, driving the wages down. This spiral downward will not be reversed until, as a result of below-subsistence wages, workers and their children begin to die, thereby lowering the supply of labor. At that point, of course, wages will begin to increase. Since workers can rarely be expected to save sufficiently during those periods when wages rise above subsistency, the outlook for the working class is dim. In a truly free market the workers face the prospect of subsistence wages. This is justified because it produces the best for all, even though most of the benefits of the efficient system are allocated to others.

These scenarios are morally relevant if one believes that something other than aggregate goodness is morally relevant. If distribution is irrelevant, then it does not matter from the moral point of view that workers sacrifice for the benefit of others, or that the income distribution is skewed against the workers.

A final point is worth mentioning. In the Classical Liberal framework, freedom is defended upon the grounds that adoption of this policy maximizes utility. The freedom to contract with another (provided no one else is harmed), for example, is a central tenet. Government intrusion through establishment of minimum wage, fit working conditions, etc., is morally illegitimate because it constitutes a reduction in aggregate utility. But if other considerations are relevant, then there may be morally good reasons to interfere in this extensive freedom of contract, to reduce the scope of freedom to some degree. In short, there may be very good moral reasons to go beyond the minimal Classical Liberal state even if that arrangement optimizes net utility for all.

Not surprisingly, during the past three decades, something like a consensus of opinion has developed that utilitarianism is not an adequate theory of obligation. Theorists have struggled to develop an adequate alternative. However, it is important not to draw the wrong conclusion. Even if utilitarianism does not constitute the most adequate theory, I would argue that it does capture an important component of morality and moral reasoning. The mistake consists in the claim that ultimately our *only* moral obligation is the maximization of net utility for all. Even if this is not our only moral obligation, it must surely count as one morally relevant consideration. Few would deny that there is a moral obligation to take into consideration the impact of a rule, policy, or institution on the overall welfare.

Hence, it is important to know whether the minimal or limited state with the free market is a better guarantor of social welfare than alternatives, even if that is not always decisive in determining the moral legitimacy of these arrangements. Defense of the minimal state and the free market should not be dismissed out of hand merely because utilitarianism is flawed. Given that utilitarian considerations are not exclusively relevant, it is important to determine the strength of the claims that the minimal state and the free market maximize net utility, that profit maximization under the conditions of the free market or under current conditions maximize net, aggregate utility, and so forth.

The strength of such a modified defense, however, will continue to rest upon the sorts of claims indicated earlier. Thus, the question is whether there is good reason to believe that the economic claims are true, and whether the theory of utility/value is adequate.

ORDINAL MEASURES OF UTILITY

As indicated above, the choice of a theory of utility in utilitarianism or in economic theory is circumscribed by a number of constraints. The formal constraints arise from the requirements of quantification. It must be possible to measure the utility for each individual under a scenario, combine the utilities of distinct individuals and sum them, and then compare the net utility for each scenario. In comparing alternative rules or alternative sets of rules (systems), it will not suffice to measure one in terms of apples and another in terms of oranges, so to speak, unless there is some way to relate meaningfully apples and oranges (e.g., 2 apples = 1 orange).

In addition, the theory of value adopted must be defensible on *substantive* grounds. For a utilitarian defense to have force, it must be shown that a particular definition of utility adopted is not merely workable and allows comparisons over different alternatives, but must also capture what is important for human well-being, human welfare, what some have called happiness. Since there may be disagreement over this issue in a pluralistic context, the quest for a substantively adequate theory of value has lead to the attempt to find a theory of good or well-being which is widely acceptable. That is, are there characteristics of a good life or of intrinsic value which are shared even by radically competing visions?

Classical Utilitarians, Bentham and Mill believed to have found an understanding of utility which satisfied both sets of constraints: pleasure. Both assumed this could be measured cardinally. Bentham defended this definition on substantive grounds, claiming that pleasure alone was intrinsically valuable, that hedonism is the best theory of value. In Bentham's "quantitative hedonism," all pleasure was of equal value; pushpin was as good as poetry. The important consideration was the quantity of net pleasure involved. The crude hedonic calculus was supposedly a device to quantify pleasure. Critics attacked Bentham's hedonism on both fronts. Substantively, quantitative hedonism was criticized as a pig philosophy which failed to capture adequately the most important aspects of human well-being. Formally, the hedonic calculus was challenged as a worthless device for measuring pleasure, even in situations in which one is dealing only with one's own pleasure. Mill's modification consisted of developing a qualitative hedonism, emphasizing the importance of qualitative "mental" pleasures. Ironically, by moving toward a more adequate theory of value, Mill moved away from the ability to quantify and measure utility. There is little sensitivity in Mill's writings to the problems of quantification.

Many economists, philosophers, and social scientists have become convinced that the cardinal approach is a dead end.[9] Ordinal measures offer a way of measuring utility which appears to satisfy the formal constraints while maintaining a connection to the hedonistic base of Classical utilitarianism. The bankruptcy of the cardinal approach is widely (although perhaps mistakenly) accepted as orthodox wisdom.

The basic idea in the ordinal approach is that individual preference orderings can be measured or elicited. This strategy is the intuitive core of preference utilitarianism, microeconomic theory, welfare theory, and collective choice theory, and the strategy is used in many other branches of philosophy and social science as well.[10] The satisfaction of preferences is taken to represent or to produce utility, where utility is understood as value, e.g., even pleasure. The conveniences of the ordinal approach are considerable. Significantly, individual preference orderings can be expressed mathematically, then manipulated. For any two alternatives, for example, Jones either prefers a to b, or b to a, or is indifferent between a and b. All rankings can be ordered this way. If, for example, we know that Jones prefers a to b to c, then by satisfying a, we know that Jones receives more utility than if b or c were satisfied. Alternatively, satisfying c yields less utility for Jones than if a or b were satisfied. Jones would be better off, as it were, if alternative a were to be satisfied than if alternative b were satisfied.

Although ordinal rankings lend themselves to formal manipulation, they contain minimal information relative to what might be captured by cardinal measures. For instance, knowing that Jones prefers apples to berries provides some good information, but does not measure how much more Jones prefers apples to berries. Nor can one determine whether Jones prefers apples to berries more than she prefers berries to chocolate. If one could cardinally measure, then perhaps one would find that having an apple would bring Jones 10 units of utility, having a pint of berries would bring Jones 9 units, and a chocolate bar only 2. Or consider the limitations when one moves to more than one-person cases. Suppose that Doe's preferences are identical to Jones's, but that if they could be measured cardinally we would find that having an apple would bring Doe 12 units of utility, a pint of berries would bring 2, and a chocolate bar only 1. If the cardinal utilitarian wished to maximize utility in this situation and had only one apple, then different distributions could be compared to determine that one (there may not be merely one) which would maximize aggregate utility. Given the cardinal measures above, Doe should get the apple. Given the ordinal measures, it is unclear who should get the apple.

Although ordinal measures provide less information, defenders cast this as a benefit, claiming that cardinal measures involve questionable substantive assumptions. For instance, cardinal measures assume that Jones's and Doe's pleasure can be measured and mapped on the same scale. It assumes that Jones's 10 units can be measured on the same scale as Doe's 12. Ordinal measures, it is claimed, do not assume any such interpersonal comparability.

Even having decided to rely upon preference orderings, one must then determine which preferences to incorporate into the formal calculus. Because actual preferences or revealed preferences are subject to a number of substantive and formal difficulties, some have moved toward ideal preferences. "Ideal preferences" might be construed, for instance, as the preferences which an individual would have if that individual were rational and had adequate information. Theories of ideal preferences, however, invite criticisms analogous to those of paternalism.[11]

Generally speaking, in economic theory, actual or revealed preferences are employed. "Revealed preferences" are those which are shown by observing humans making choices between competing goods in a market situation. There are a number of reasons for this. As James Griffen writes in *Well-Being*:[12]

> Economists have been drawn to it because actual desires are often revealed in choices and "revealed preferences" are observable and hence a respectable subject for empirical science. Also the same account of utility can then do service in both moral theory and theory of action; explanation of action has to appeal to what we in fact want rather than to such ideal

notions of what we ought to want or would want if well-informed. And both philosophers and social scientists have been powerfully drawn to it because it leaves no room for paternalism; if actual desires determine distributions, consumers are sovereign and agents autonomous. (10)

Appealing to individual preference orderings does appear to solve many of the problems associated with quantification. Reliance upon actual preferences, then, promises an understanding of utility which will satisfy the formal constraints. The question is whether the theory can be defended substantively.

It is important to stress that the appeal to actual preferences does not mean that theorists have thereby avoided any commitment to a theory of value. When Christopher Stone attempted to interpret Friedman's Polestar argument he noted that one motivation for adopting the argument might be the positivistic suspicion of discourse about morality. Positivism did lead many to move toward actual preference theory. By resting utility or efficiency upon actual preferences, advocates of this approach often pose as having avoided all substantive normative commitments. This is not true.[13] The theory of utility at the basis is, indeed, individualistic, subjectivistic, and relativistic. According to this theory, "x is good" means something like "I prefer x to other alternatives at this time." Whatever one prefers is good (for that person).[14] This is a substantive theory of value and is as much in need of defense as any competing theory.

Before turning to address this crucial issue, it is worth exploring the strength of the defense which can be mounted if one grants that theory of value/utility. If the criticism of the Classical defense turned solely upon the kind of theory of value involved, there would be a tendency to regard the dispute as an interminable philosophical debate over value. The following analysis will reveal, however, that even given this understanding of value/utility, the arguments which can be generated to defend the critical premises in the defense of the minimal state with a free market are extremely tenuous.[15]

COLLECTIVE CHOICE PROCEDURES:
THE IMPOSSIBILITY THEOREM

Any preference-based theory which purports to make judgments about aggregate utility requires that individual preferences be combined in some fashion. The challenge is to make sense of, and assign value to, collectivities of individual preferences. If one wishes to speak about doing what is most efficient in terms of these individual preferences, or of optimizing net utility (doing what is best for all), it must be possible to move from individual preference orderings to collective judgments and collective choices. This entails the adoption of rules for combining individual orderings. *Choice of a particular set of rules by which to combine individual orderings is not value neutral.* The choice of rules or functions for combining individual preferences is tantamount to the adoption of a definition or theory of social welfare or the social good. Thus, in a sense, questions of which theory of value or which theory of obligation to adopt again arise.[16] This definition of social good may well rest upon subjectivistic individual notions of the good (preference orderings), but this theory cannot itself be subjectivistic. And like the theory of good at the individual level, this theory cannot not avoid scrutiny. It is a theory involving important substantive commitments and as such stands in need of defense. Consequently, theorists have aspired to identify a set of rules for combining individual orderings which would be minimally controversial.

For illustrative purposes, consider one possible rule for combining individual orderings, the dictator rule. According to this rule, a collective choice is preferable to alternatives (is best) if and only if one individual, say, David the dictator, prefers that choice to all alternatives. Should we adopt a procedure which suggests that the best choice is one which satisfies the preferences of David? Few have been so inclined. This is objectionable not on formal grounds but on substantive, normative grounds. This proposed rule violates our democratic sensitivities, our intuitions about how to determine the social welfare or aggregate utility. Earlier utilitarians claimed that each person counts for one and no one counts for more than one. This is a normative idea; the claim that each individual's preferences should be taken into consideration is a substantive claim, not a formal one.

In this century, a substantial amount of research has been devoted to the investigation of the logic of different rules for combining individual preference orderings for the sake of determining a collective preference, and the challenge has proved much greater than anyone imagined. One of the most startling findings earned Kenneth Arrow the Nobel Prize. In 1951, Arrow published a monograph, *Social Choice and Individual Values*,[17] in which he presented his impossibility theorem. It was previously assumed that any procedure for combining individual preferences worthy of being called a rational procedure must satisfy four (originally five) conditions. Separately, these conditions appear to be so weak as to be entirely uncontroversial, even though substantive. In the second edition of his monograph Arrow identifies these as U, P, D, and I:

1. U. *Unrestricted scope*. Any acceptable procedure must be capable of processing any logically coherent set of individual preference orderings of any number of choice alternatives.
2. P. *Pareto principle*. Any acceptable procedure must be such that when every individual prefers X to Y, the procedure must rank X to Y in its social orderings.
3. D. *Non-dictatorship*. Any acceptable procedure must be such that the social choice is not determined by the preferences of a single individual, regardless of all other individuals.
4. I. *Independence of Irrelevant Alternatives*. Any acceptable procedure must be such that the social ordering of a set of alternatives depends only on the individuals' preference orderings of those alternatives.

These conditions appear quite reasonable.[18] However, in the impossibility theorem, Arrow proves that *together these conditions are logically inconsistent*. At first blush, this is an extraordinary and unsettling discovery. Most defenders of democracy, for example, believe that democracy is a collective choice procedure for combining individual preferences which is rational. If by "rational" one means a procedure which satisfies these four minimal conditions, then democratic procedures cannot be rational.

To escape logical inconsistency, at least one of these four goals must be forfeited, but which? Subsequent to this discovery, many have attempted to make more palatable the abandonment of one or the other of these assumptions. No real democracy, for example, ever satisfies U. In voting, a limited number of candidates or policies are voted upon. The alternatives are quite restricted.

Although theorists are divided over the significance of this finding, it does indicate that reliance upon preference orderings generates unexpected consequences as one attempts to combine the orderings in some way which would allow for making judgments about collectivities and social welfare. Moreover, it is also quite clear, though not widely appreciated, that the limitations of this approach drastically

restrict the kinds of comparative judgments which can be made about
competing alternative systems.

PARETIAN NOTIONS

With this brief background as an introduction, the key argument
for a free market can be addressed. For the most part, economists and
philosophers have gravitated toward the notions of Pareto optimality
and Pareto superiority as a way of determining what is "best for all."[19]
Vilfredo Pareto was an economist who pioneered in the attempt
to rely on preferences in determining social welfare.[20] A state of a
given system is defined as "Pareto optimal" if and only if there is
no feasible alternative state of that system in which at least one
person is better off and no one is worse off. Similarly, a state S^1
is "Pareto superior" to another state S^2 if and only if there is at
least one person who is better off in S^1 than in S^2 and no one is
worse off in S^1 than in S^2. These notions can be formulated more
narrowly to refer to distributional states of systems (distribution of
consumer goods, allocations of resources for producing goods), but
the broader formulation appears to capture more accurately at least
a part of our intuitions about efficiency and welfare. Whether an
individual is better off is determined, of course, in terms of whether
that individual's preferences are satisfied. Being worse off means that
an individual's preference has been violated.

These notions are extremely simple. Imagine two states of a system,
S^1 and S^2, with 3 individuals, A, B, and C. Suppose A prefers apples to
oranges, B prefers apples to oranges, and C prefers oranges to apples.
Suppose, however, that in S^1, A has an orange, B has an apple, and
C has an apple. If the system allows free trade, then likely A will
trade with C, and in S^2, A will have an apple, B an apple, and C an
orange. There is little difficulty in saying that in S^2 the individuals are
better off than they are in the original state, since their preferences are
satisfied. A and C get what they prefer, and no one has her preferences
violated. S^2 is Pareto superior to S^1 because there is at least one person
in S^2 (there are actually two persons, A and C) better off in S^2 than
in S^1, and no one is worse off. S^2 is also Pareto optimal, since there
is no other feasible arrangement which would make anyone better off
while not making someone worse off. Here, in fact, each person is
getting what she prefers.

For many, the attractiveness of the Pareto notions lies not merely in the avoidance of the problems of quantification inherent in cardinal definitions, but also in the apparent avoidance of assumptions about interpersonal comparisons. The Paretian principles, in particular, apparently avoid interpersonal utility comparisons because "better off" is understood only relative to an individual's own former condition. In the example above, A is better off than before *relative to the former condition* in which she had no apple. The system is in a better state at S^2 because some individual is better off.

These two Paretian principles are often seen as second-best alternatives to a more robust utilitarianism, that is, one employing cardinal measures. Given the problems with that variety of utilitarianism, this is perceived as the only alternative. The important question to be answered, however, is whether these principles will support the kinds of claims relevant to comparative judgments of existing economic, political, and social practices and institutions.

Paretian notions are often taken to lend support to limited government and free markets by providing rigorous demonstration of what I have characterized in the previous chapter as the Economic Premise. As Allen Buchanan points out in *Ethics, Efficiency, and the Market*,[21] the attempt to defend the free market by incorporating the Pareto notions rests on two main claims.[22] The first claim is a theoretical statement that exchanges in the ideal free market reach an equilibrium state that is Pareto optimal. This is referred to as the "First Fundamental Theorem of Welfare Economics."[23] The second claim is an assumption that actual, real-world markets, if left free, sufficiently resemble the ideal market such that it is reasonable to assume that they too will reach equilibrium at something approximating Pareto optimality.

The second claim creates a significant obstacle. The proof for the First Fundamental Theorem of Welfare Economics assumes conditions which are extremely unrealistic.[24] Buchanan briefly summarizes the description of the conditions which define an ideal market:

1. Full information is available about the performance and quality of goods and services and the costs of all alternative ways of producing them, and the cost of this information is zero.
2. Costs of enforcing contracts and property rights are zero, and property rights, including rights to the means of production, are established and stable.

3. Individuals are rational in this sense: their preferences are organized in a transitive ordering (such that if an individual prefers A to B and B to C, he also prefers A to C) and they are capable of selecting appropriate means toward their ends.

4. (a) Transaction costs are zero (transaction costs include costs of bringing goods and services together for an exchange, and costs of reaching agreements for exchange, for example costs of formulating mutually acceptable contracts, and costs of information about potential offers to buy and sell) or (b) there is perfect competition (that is, no buyer or seller can influence prices by his own independent actions and there is complete freedom to enter and exit the market) and no externalities are present. . . .

5. Products offered in the market are undifferentiated—buyers cannot distinguish between the products offered by various sellers, and vice versa. (14–15)

These conditions can be expressed formally, and the statement that such a market reaches an equilibrium that is Pareto optimal can be demonstrated rigorously. It is the rigor of the demonstration for the First Fundamental Theorem of Welfare Economics that inspires confidence in apologists for the free market.

Yet, as Amartya Sen remarks, in *Ethics and Economics*,[25] despite "its general importance, the ethical content of this welfare economic result is, however, rather modest." One very serious handicap is that since markets in the actual world never satisfy the stringent conditions of the proof, there is a serious question whether proof is relevant to real-world situations. It is clearly not enough to say that these conditions are approximated. The appeal of a logically valid deductive proof consists in its rigor. If conditions 1–5 yield the theorem, there is absolutely no logical reason to believe that conditions which only resemble 1–5 should provide a proof for the same theorem.[26] Hence, there is absolutely no reason to believe that near-perfect markets will reach equilibrium at a point which is Pareto optimal. Indeed, these conditions are sufficiently stringent that no actual market would ever come close to satisfying them. Even in markets which approach perfect competition, there are substantial information costs and never full information. Costs of enforcing contracts and property rights is far from zero.

Hence, these difficulties undermine the force of the utilitarian argument that public policy should be formulated to bring about the

the ideal world of minimal government and the free market. If even the most ideal, actual world fails to satisfy these conditions, then it cannot legitimately be claimed that this market would reach an equilibrium that is Pareto optimal. This also undermines a fortiori the argument that profit maximization in the contemporary situation would maximize utility for all. Friedman needs an argument to establish that given the conditions of the actual world, conditions CC, profit maximization in the actual market produces what is best for all (as compared with acting according to some other rule). Even a greater leap of faith is required to assert that conditions CC are sufficiently similar to those assumed in the First Fundamental Theorem of Welfare Economics to assure that equilibrium will be reached at Pareto optimality than that leap involved in believing that under the most ideal, actual conditions, C, the proof is relevant. There is no good reason for believing that either situation will reach an equilibrium that is Pareto optimal.

FURTHER LIMITATIONS

Nor is the irrelevance exclusively a function of the unrealistic assumptions. Even ignoring the ideality, the nature of this approach insures irrelevance because "best for all" in the Pareto optimal sense *has meaning only of movements within a given system.* Three severe limitations follow from this. First, because Pareto principles apply only to movements from one state of a system to another state, judgments about the initial state of the system itself are irrelevant. And clearly, our judgment of a distribution is, or should be, affected by factors influencing the initial state. Second, Pareto optimality is irrelevant to situations in which by making a few worse off, many more can be made better off. "Best for all" cannot be applied to situations in which one wishes to consider coercion. Third, because the principles apply only to movements from one state in a system to another state, the principles are incapable of yielding intersystemic judgments.

Consider the first limitation. A system is Pareto optimal or superior only relative to a preexistent state of the system. Hence, the notion of Pareto optimality or superiority is radically indifferent to the history of how the original state of the system came about, and indifferent to judgments about whether the original system (distribution) is good, bad, just, unjust, etc. The original state of a system, the property rights and distributions of property, might have arisen as a result of conquest by Atilla the Hun, for example. Or, they may have arisen as the result of the force employed by a colonial power which stripped most of the natives of their land and allowed a few of the indigenous peoples to take over plantations on which the others could work as laborers. To argue that by allowing free trade, a country would reach equilibrium at Pareto optimality ignores extremely relevant considerations. Attempts to redistribute would be opposed, of course, on grounds that this violates freedom, upsets stable property rights, and creates inefficiency. What we mean by "best for all" should in some way take into consideration the historical past and should also consider other factors of the states within the system. How one would go about this is quite another story. Justice might call for a certain amount of coercion to redistribute.

As I write, historically significant illustrations of this limitation are unfolding in the People's Republic of China and in the lands of Eastern Europe and the former Soviet Union, where market principles are being applied. Claiming that in these situations the market will reflect increased efficiency (relative to the earlier distribution) or that a situation of Pareto optimality or Pareto superiority will be reached is to say little of significance in terms of the distribution which will arise. Given that substantial capital resources were held almost exclusively by the communist parties, communist party members, and the "mob" (which accumulated capital in the underground markets), the claim that the new distributions are Pareto superior to the previous ones has little force.

This, however, leads naturally to a discussion of the second limitation. Notions of Pareto optimality are irrelevant in situations in which there is not unanimity and coercion is employed. It is widely believed that, at least in some circumstances, the coercion of some individuals produces what is best for all. For that purpose, governmental bodies retain the right of eminent domain. Cities often determine that it is best for all if a new expressway is built through a residential neighborhood in which many of the residents refuse to sell. Or, there are countless cases in which it is claimed that it would be best for all if a shopping mall (or mass transit, or a pipeline, or a building, etc.) could be built on the property of individuals who refuse to sell. In the former Soviet Union, for instance, perhaps it makes sense to redistribute forcefully some of the capital acquired "illegitimately" during the years of the former regime. Few deny that it makes sense, in principle, to speak of the welfare or interests of the community. Representatives of the business community are especially fond of this kind of language and enjoy using the rhetoric of economic development, progress, and wealth. By law, individuals forfeiting property are to be compensated "fairly." But in this familiar scenario, preferences are ignored. Some are made "worse off" because preferences have been overridden. In Paretian terms, no forced exchange ever produces what is best for all. If "best for all" means nothing more than "Pareto optimal," then it is impossible to make judgments about what is best for all here. Thus, Pareto optimality is irrelevant to the most interesting and the most important decisions in which the general welfare needs to be determined, in the ordinary situations in which there is not unanimous agreement. That is to say, these notions have little relevance to normal, real-life situations.[27]

Finally, and perhaps most seriously, there is a third limitation. Apologists for free market capitalism, including Friedman, like to claim that this system is more efficient, produces more social utility, than other systems, such as socialism or a mixed system with government interference. Classical ideologists persist in attempting to explain the success of the American "experiment" in terms of the marvelous system, suggesting that Americans would be worse off had a different system evolved. However, *it is impossible to compare systems using notions of Pareto optimality or superiority*. The most that one might show is that system A is Pareto optimal and that system B is not. Suppose that system A is something like a Classical Liberal state and that system B is something like the more than minimal welfare state. Within system A, state A2 could be described as Pareto superior to state A1. However, it is impossible to infer that either A1 or A2 are superior, inferior, or of equal value to any state in B. Pareto optimal and Pareto superior are words with meanings *only* in the context of discussing alternative arrangements within a given system. Intersystemic judgments are impossible. One could argue that if in B the welfare state were dismantled and free trade allowed, then that latter state would be Pareto superior to a former. But one could not compare this state to any in A. There is no way, given these concepts, to compare the efficiency or welfare in one system with the other.

CONCLUSION

The utilitarian defense of the major tenets of Classical Liberalism, with the associated defense of profit maximization, is extremely frail. Utilitarianism itself is inadequate as a theory of obligation because of the failure to take into consideration any factor except aggregate social utility. Even granting that aggregate social welfare is morally relevant, there are a number of other considerations which are relevant, and which may, at least occasionally, carry more weight than social utility.

The problems, however, reach much deeper. Economic theory holds the promise of a rigorous demonstration that a free market produces what is best for all, namely, given certain extremely idealistic assumptions about conditions obtaining in a free market, the First Fundamental Theorem of Welfare Economics can be demonstrated. According to the theorem, a free market will reach equilibrium at a point which is Pareto optimal. This is understood to mean "best for all." Preference utilitarians employ these claims in an attempt to morally legitimize markets free from any government interference. Unfortunately, the ideality of the conditions renders the theorem irrelevant to real markets. Moreover, even if the conditions could be satisfied, there are other limitations which entail irrelevance.

All things considered, this line of defense is without much plausibility. And the criticisms developed were independent of any problems surrounding the actual desired account of utility. When the difficulties surrounding that account are identified, the defense is weakened even further. In the next chapter, this issue can be explored.

6

Freedom and Well-Being
in the Liberal Tradition

Although freedom and the liberty of the individual are central values in the liberal tradition, they are not ultimate or intrinsic values. Freedom and liberty are essential values in this tradition because of their connection to what is most important: individual human happiness or well-being, often construed as the self-actualization and exercise of certain important human potentialities.[1] In this respect, the liberal perspective is firmly grounded in the classical philosophies of ancient Greece and Rome, and the primary ethical concern is to discover and provide the conditions within which humans may flourish. Classical Liberals, whether in the utilitarian or natural rights tradition, have lost sight of this connection and extol freedom and liberty at the expense of human well-being.

While recognizing that freedom and liberty are instruments for human welfare, utilitarianism after John Stuart Mill has distorted and cheapened this insight by trivializing utility.[2] In Mill, especially in *On Liberty*, the connection between liberty and human well-being is paramount, and the conception of human happiness is robust and rich. As utilitarianism became more self-conscious and consistent, however, the connection with what is most important has been largely abandoned. This is a consequence of attempting to satisfy the requirements imposed on a theory of utility by the nature of a theory of obligation. The formal constraints, as I have indicated, require the capacity to measure and quantify the utility associated with nearly every imaginable experience, to find the net for each individual, to sum the utilities of each individual upon some common scale, and

127

then to compare the results for each alternative. These requirements pose hurdles which are extremely taxing. The search for a solution has been the driving force in choosing a theory of utility, with little regard for whether the theory is substantively plausible. One of the major reasons for the current fashionability of the reliance upon actual preferences, in fact, appears to be little more than the promise of meeting these formal requirements.

Teleological theories of obligation, especially utilitarian theories, confront a dilemma. Conceptions of value which stand the best chance of satisfying the formal constraints tend to have only the most tenuous association with what is widely agreed to involve human welfare. On the other hand, conceptions of utility which appear to come closest to capturing our intuitions of what is most valuable for human well-being will not satisfy all of the formal constraints for wide ranges of experiences.[3]

Contemporary economic theory and the associated preference utilitarianism succumb to the first horn of the dilemma. Actual preference theory equates the satisfaction of preferences or desires with human well-being. This theory is, even on its surface, preposterous. If human well-being consisted in nothing but satisfaction of actual preferences, then whatever a human did would, by definition, be in his or her own best interest. But humans are often mistaken, frequently irrational in satisfying preferences, and customarily satisfy preferences which are contrary to their own best interests. I may prefer one drug to another, based on misinformation. As a result, I may suffer a serious illness which would have been avoided if I had chosen the better treatment. I satisfied my actual preference but that satisfaction did not lead to what was in my best interest because my preference was based on inadequate information. As James Griffen writes in *Well-Being*:[4]

> Yet, notoriously we mistake our own interests. It is depressingly common that when some of our strongest and most central desires are fulfilled, we are no better, even worse, off. . . . The objection to the actual–desire account is overwhelming. (10)

Thus, the idea that utility, human well-being, consists in nothing but the satisfaction of actual preferences is clearly inadequate.

The implications for the defense of the free market based on claims concerning net utility maximization are considerable. For instance, consider three alternative systems. One system represents Friedman's

ideal limited state with laissez-faire market, another system corresponds to a liberal constitutional welfare state with a mixed market,
and another system corresponds to a socialist state with a centrally
controlled market. Suppose further that one can measure the utility
of each system in terms of actual preference satisfaction. Finally,
suppose that Friedman's system clearly optimizes utility thus defined.
What weight should be accorded this finding? That a system satisfies actual preferences should probably be considered as *one factor*
in evaluating systems. Recognizing, however, that there is more to
human welfare than satisfying preferences, there may yet be good
reason to claim that one of the alternatives generates greater human
welfare. It is not unreasonable to believe that even if Friedman's ideal
Classical Liberal state would maximize actual preference satisfaction,
there may be alternatives which promote greater well-being in the
broader sense.

Some of the more appropriate measures of human well-being might
be simple: infant mortality rates, life expectancy, and literacy rates.
These do not, of course, capture entirely what is involved in human
welfare, but they should probably be included as important indicators.
Mortality rates and life expectancy, for instance, are good indicators
of medical support, nutrition available, sanitation, and so forth, and
may also reflect to some extent whether the population is adequately
housed and clothed[5].

In absence of other important indicators, maximizing utility or
efficiency defined in terms of actual preferences is only a small part of
what is important in assessing human well-being. This suggests that,
in themselves, appeals to utility or efficiency thus defined are not very
significant. By limiting government and by allowing the free market
to make most decisions about resource allocations, we may have
an "efficient" society, measuring efficiency/utility in terms of actual
preference satisfaction. The question of whether that arrangement is
adequately providing for human well-being in any meaningful sense,
however, is ignored.

The problem is that the attempt to include these other, perhaps
more important, aspects of well-being may not satisfy the formal
constraints in a sufficiently wide range of cases to function in a strictly
utilitarian/economic defense. But given that utilitarianism itself is suspect, why should we abandon intuitive measures of well-being for the
sake of conforming to the rigid requirements of a flawed moral theory?

UTILITY AND PURPLE BALLOONS

The defender of the actual preference theory has at least two alternatives. The most plausible is to admit that actual preference satisfaction does not constitute human well-being but continue to claim that actual preference satisfaction is at least an important component of human well-being. This alternative may assume a more or a less modest form, depending upon just how important the satisfaction of actual preferences is taken to be in human well-being. By taking this alternative, one would admit that a number of other factors can and should bear upon our judgment of whether distribution is promoting social welfare. Even this very modest claim, however, is further restricted by the problems involved in attempting to apply Paretian notions to real-world situations, as indicated in the last chapter.

The other alternative is to deny that economic theory must satisfy the substantive constraints, leaving preference utilitarianism adrift to find a means of measuring utility which satisfies both substantive and formal constraints. That is, why should we be concerned that the economic claims fail to satisfy the substantive constraints? Some will object that economists are not engaged in moral theorizing, that the concepts developed in economic theory cannot or should not be employed in a utilitarian argument such as I have suggested. According to this objection, the concept of utility involved in utilitarianism is apparently distinct from that employed in economic theory, and any argument which attempts to relate them in this manner is invalid because it involves an equivocation. Economists often speak in terms of "efficiency" and offer very specific definitions. These definitions, it is sometimes urged, have nothing to do with ordinary notions of efficiency. Further, they may have little relevance to older discussions of human welfare or utility which dominated the economic thought of an earlier age and continue to be important in contemporary discussions of public policy and in moral philosophy.

While economists are quite free to ignore substantive concerns, this freedom is purchased at a very high price: irrelevance. If "efficiency" is a term based on an understanding of utility which has little or no relevance to discussions of human welfare, then it can play no important role in moral or political argument. If the economic terms have little relevance to human welfare, then it is difficult to see why they should have any relationship to important public policy discussions. Discussions based on economic theory could be safely excluded from public policy or moral discussions as irrelevant.

Consider the following illustration. Suppose utility is measured in terms of purple balloons. Theorists might generate an elaborate argument demonstrating that by adopting certain conditions, those of the free market, a system would be maximally utile, i.e., would produce more net purple balloons than under any other conditions. If someone then urged society to adopt a free market because under these conditions society would be maximally utile, meaning nothing more than society would produce more purple balloons than under an alternative arrangement, the argument would be rightly ignored. If someone complained that by interfering in individual freedom, government is reducing the number of purple balloons which might otherwise be produced, that complaint would be considered silly and irrelevant. Purple balloons are not in any important way a measure of what is most important.

If Friedman and others are relying upon esoteric notions of utility or efficiency, then they can be safely ignored. The real concern is whether public policy and free markets are related to central human concerns, not to purple balloons. Hence, if economic theory does not address the issue of conditions which lead to optimizing human welfare, then an economic theory will need to be reconstructed which does.

ADAM SMITH

The importance of an adequate theory of value in the liberal tradition and economic theory can be no better illustrated than by recalling Adam Smith's quest. The title of Smith's work, An Inquiry into the Nature and Causes of the Wealth of Nations,[6] reflects Smith's sensitivity to this issue. Smith was involved in two distinct kinds of inquiry. One inquiry concerns the nature of wealth; the other concerns the cause of wealth, i.e., how to promote it. These are two quite different kinds of inquiry. The former is logically prior to the latter. One must determine the nature of wealth before it is possible to discuss what causes wealth. And one cannot discover the true nature of wealth as one might discover the New World. The question of the nature of wealth is minimally a question about the foundations of economic theory. Depending upon what is chosen as wealth, different causes will likely be uncovered. But by what criterion is a definition of wealth to be chosen? One could measure the wealth of a nation merely by counting the population, considering total square miles, or total arable land, or even purple balloons. Or, one could choose gold or other precious metals. Smith focused upon a definition of wealth which revolved around goods and services produced.

The decision concerning which definition of wealth to adopt is a metatheoretical or metaeconomic one. More to the point, this is a decision about what to count as value, what Smith referred to as utility. At this point, the economist has a choice. On the one hand, the economist can argue that metatheoretical, definitional decisions such as this one have little or nothing to do with morality. "Wealth" or "efficiency" can be defined in some readily measurable way, such as "purple balloons," and a theory generated which has explanatory and perhaps predictive power. To say that one system is more efficient than another or that one system is more productive of wealth than another is merely a descriptive judgment, given the theoretical definitions employed. This is certainly true. On the other hand, however, unless the definitions incorporated into the economic theory have some relationship to things valued by humans, the claim that one system is more efficient than another will be of no interest. For instance, Adam Smith's inquiry into the causes of wealth would be of interest only insofar as the notion of wealth involved was consistent with human welfare as it was broadly conceived at the time. For Smith, goods and services provided a measure of wealth, and they were morally significant because they are the kinds of things intimately connected with human welfare. Smith understood the importance of philosophical ethics and attempted to defend a particular theory of value which was not only useful to economic theory but also morally relevant.

This is apparent in Smith's critique of mercantilism. In mercantilism, a nation is viewed as analogous to an individual firm. One simple form of mercantilism is bullionism, which measures wealth in terms of precious metals. There is some sense to this, since, as a medium of exchange, bullion provides a relatively secure claim on desired goods or services; food, clothing, shelter, armies, or art could be purchased. Economic and political policy is then dictated by the need to acquire the precious metal. One direct method was conquest of lands rich in gold or silver, hence the push toward the New World. Another popular and widely used method was piracy.

Governments employed pirates to scavenge the seas. The start-up costs for piracy were considerably lower than those associated with the actual mining process itself and was thus an extremely attractive alternative. Sir Francis Drake managed to rake off enough gold and silver from the Spanish to provide a 4,700 percent return on the English investment. Queen Elizabeth used her part of the take to pay off England's foreign debt entirely and then invest 42,000 pounds in the Levant Company. From the profits from Levant, the East India Bay Company was formed, the base for much of England's other foreign investments. This caused John Keynes to quip that the booty from Drake's *Golden Hind* "may fairly be considered the fountain and origin of British foreign investment."[7] Regulated monopolies were another instrument of national economic policy. Precious metals could also be acquired through favorable trade balances, and to insure close regulation England chartered monopolies to act as virtual extensions of the government. The East India Bay Company was England in India. But does gold really capture what is most important in measuring the wealth of the nation? The existence of gold and silver does not guarantee the well-being of the country. Gold is valuable only if it can and does purchase needed food and clothing. Food is more important in a famine than gold.[8]

Thus, Smith's complaint, in large part, is that the mercantilists had failed to identify the genuine nature of wealth. One desires precious metals in the economic sense only for what they can purchase. The real wealth of a nation is not whether there is a plenitude of precious metal, but whether there are plentiful goods and services. Unfortunately, Smith did not develop this line of inquiry far enough, in spite of clear indications that he was sensitive to its importance.

For Smith, there are two kinds of value.

> The word VALUE, it is to be observed, has two different meanings, and sometimes expresses the utility of some particular object, and sometimes the power of purchasing other goods which the possession of that object conveys. The one may be called "value in use"; the other, "value in exchange." (Bk. 1, chapter 4, 32)

Smith went on to note that things which have the greatest use-value frequently have little or no exchange-value, and that things with great exchange-value often have little use. As an example of use-value Smith gives water (which he assumes to be in plentiful supply); he gives as an example of exchange-value a diamond. Given this starting point, the task for the economist following Smith is to define carefully the two senses of value in a way which is quantifiable and then attempt to discover the laws which determine use-value and exchange-value, as well as attempt to explain the relationship between them. Smith, of course, claimed that the real price of anything, the real exchange-value, was determined by the amount of labor which goes into the production of the good. This labor theory of value is fraught with well-known difficulties, not the least of which is that it is extremely difficult to measure the labor that goes into an object. Moreover, how is one to explain differences in the kinds of labor involved in the production of objects. Is the value of one hour of a dentist's labor equivalent to one hour of a person who rakes leaves? Smith himself realized the difficulties and consequently leaned heavily on the other aspect of his theory to explain prices/exchange-value. The law of supply and demand, for example, may constitute a much better explanation of exchange-value than measures of labor. Water has a low price because the supply is great (given Smith's assumption). Diamonds are expensive because the supply is limited and the demand fairly strong. Yet, to say that individuals are willing to pay $2.40/bushel for corn, or so much for water or diamonds, and to indicate that the price moves in some relationship according to the variables of availability and demand for corn, does not explain very much. To explain why individuals are willing to pay $2.40 for corn requires appeal to the use-value of corn. The demand for something appears to be tied to its use-value, its utility, its value.

In short, the discussion of exchange-value returns to use-value, or utility. Smith never moved beyond a tentative sketch of the labor theory of value and his discussion of utility was even briefer. But the idea is simple. To be utile is to be useful, practical, for humans. This idea, still rather unrefined, served important but limited purposes. For example, it could be employed as a part of an attack upon mercantilism.

To be useful is to have extrinsic value, to be instrumental as a means in achieving some other goal. Hence, usefulness is not something which is intrinsically good, but extrinsically good. Everyone may agree that usefulness is good, but this leaves open the question whether there is something else which is good intrinsically, desired for its own sake, good in itself. Money is also only extrinsically valuable, an instrument for acquiring goods and services. Even most goods and services would appear to be only extrinsically valuable. Take a bulky overcoat. No one would desire a bulky overcoat unless it were useful or good for achieving some end. Smith was never very clear about this point. Later utilitarians and economists developed utility theory by attempting to answer adequately the question of intrinsic value. For Bentham, it was pleasure. For contemporary economists, it is the satisfaction of actual preferences. Smith would likely have agreed that preference theorists have missed the mark.

UTILITY AND WELL-BEING

The second horn of the dilemma is that the closer one moves toward an adequate notion of human well-being, the less likely that notion will satisfy the formal constraints arising from utilitarianism. What, however, would an adequate theory of human well-being look like? One can be sketched by returning to the discussion of the concept of harm. For Classical Liberals, the function of the state should be restricted to the prevention of harm (private or public), adjudication of cases in which harm has been alleged, compensation and perhaps punishment in which a case of harm has been determined. To have a notion of harm, however, requires at least the rudiments of a notion of well-being. To harm another is to damage or injure that person's well-being in important respects.

Following Joel Feinberg,[9] harm is to be understood as an invasion of particular, important human interests. The delineation of which interests to protect requires a normative conception of what is truly good for a human, of human happiness or well-being. In the liberal tradition, well-being consists in the actualization of certain human potentialities. Mill's argument for freedom is that a necessary condition for human growth and development is freedom of thought and freedom of action (provided it is self-regarding and harms no one else). Such an argument establishes an interest in freedom by demonstrating a relationship with what is truly good. In the same way, Feinberg and others can generate a list of other interests which should be protected: property, person, possession, contract, liberty, reputation and freedom from fear.

This basic sketch can be elaborated in some detail. A human can be viewed as a network of interests. At one level there are what can be considered "ulterior interests" or "focal aims." I may have an interest in producing good articles in philosophy, running fast marathons, or successfully raising a family, or all of these. These are focal aims in the sense that they organize other interests and wants according to their relative importance and relevance. This is what some writers appear to mean by an interest in a life plan. Liberal theorists need not assume that any one of these life plans is superior to any other, although many, if not most, do make that assumption. For instance, collecting baseball cards[10] is a particular focal aim. That focal aim may consume nearly the entire life spirit of an individual. Collecting requires certain intellectual traits, knowing the history of different players, knowing the demand for particular cards, understanding the supply, perhaps understanding the patterns of trading in the card market, etc. These involve the actualization of capacities which are profoundly human, i.e., self-realization. But there is something shallow about a life devoted entirely to baseball cards. A richer and fuller life, it would seem, could be enjoyed by developing a broader portfolio of interests. A portfolio with different kinds of interests would also appear to be a more prudent investment. If one builds one's entire life plan around collecting baseball cards, and if the baseball card market collapses (Sony buys up all the outstanding cards and refuses to trade), one must begin anew, as it were, to reconstruct another life plan. This does not entail that liberals seek to force individuals to select a particular plan of life. On the contrary, Mill's argument for freedom is primarily an argument that individuals should be free to develop life plans and experiment.

"Welfare interests," on the other hand, are those interests which are necessary means to these more ultimate goals. As Feinberg puts it:

> In this category are the interest in the continuance for a foreseeable interval of one's life, and the interests in one's own physical health and vigor, the integrity and normal functioning of one's body, the absence of absorbing pain and suffering or grotesque disfigurement, minimal intellectual acuity, emotional stability, the absence of groundless anxieties and resentments, the capacity to engage normally in social intercourse and to enjoy and maintain friendships, at least minimal income and financial security, a tolerable social and physical environment, and a certain amount of freedom from interference and coercion. (37)

In one sense, as Feinberg notes, these welfare interests are relatively trivial. They are necessary for well-being but "grossly insufficient" for a good life. As Nicholas Rescher puts it, in *Welfare: The Social Issue in Philosophical Perspective*,[11] these are "the basic requisites" of a person's well-being. On the other hand, these interests are crucial, since without their fulfillment it is impossible to achieve many, if not all, of the more ultimate goals of one's life. For this reason, welfare interests tend to coincide with those which have been given legal protection.

This conceptual framework explains why an interest cannot be construed as the "object of a desire" or the "satisfaction of an actual preference" or "want fulfillment." There are many instances in which satisfaction of an immediate desire is contrary to both welfare interests and life plan of an individual. The immediate desire to drink alcoholic beverages just prior to piloting an aircraft (even soloing) is only one of hundreds of simple examples which can be offered. Or, alternatively, the satisfaction of other immediate wants may neither assist, nor detract from, the fulfillment of what is in one's interest. Having a candy bar to satisfy a craving before piloting is probably irrelevant to either my welfare interests or my life plan.

Hence, any theory which reduces human well-being to satisfaction of actual desires has only the loosest connection with what is most important for human beings. This is not to say that satisfaction of desires or wants is entirely irrelevant. Those wants which Feinberg characterizes as "instrumental wants"[12] are tied to ulterior interests. If I want to exercise vigorously this evening, it is not because I find the prospect particularly inviting or pleasant (though it may become so while exercising), but because this is tied to a larger, more ultimate goal (health). I may stay late at the office because I desire promotion despite an immediate desire to relax with a glass of wine. A focal aim may require, as it were, that I have certain desires, that I act on instrumental wants, not immediate wants.

If something like this conception is fairly close to capturing the idea of human well-being, it is apparent that quantification of well-being is extremely difficult. Determining that an individual has been harmed in a protected welfare interest is relatively easy by contrast. But even determining compensation for a harm is much more difficult because it requires determining the level of well-being which would have been attained had the individual not been wrongfully harmed. When one moves to consider the problems arising from the attempt to compare the impact of alternative policies on the well-being of Jones and Smith, however, the obstacles are insurmountable in many instances. It is clear that in many situations we must settle for surrogate measures or markers of well-being, most of which remain a good distance from the important dimensions of well-being.

As suggested above, actual preferences and economic measures might serve as a surrogate measure, but the limitations of these surrogates are obvious. At the very least, they should be considered in light of other important surrogates, such as life expectancy, literacy, health, etc. Economic arguments concerning efficiency, even if they were relevant to actual markets, can only capture a part of our concern with the well-being of humans in the economy.

Given the liberal commitment to individual human well-being, the central problem is the creation of conditions within which humans may flourish. Against this background, the implausibility of the case for Classical Liberalism can be summed up in the following example. Assume for the moment, with the Classical Liberal, that some form of government is morally legitimate. Suppose that by imposing a small progressive income tax, one could provide for the needy. Classical Liberals contend that this is immoral because the state should function only to prevent harm. But the only reason for limiting the state to the prevention of harm in the liberal tradition is because the limitation is believed to be the means by which human well-being can be insured. With a carefully crafted tax, however, it is difficult to see how forcing the wealthy to contribute a small proportion of income in any way significantly affects their well-being, even if some actual desires (for caviar and champagne) are unfulfilled. On the other hand, the transfer would have significant impact on improving the well-being of the poor, by providing for some of their welfare interests. If one is concerned with human well-being, there is no good reason within the liberal framework to restrict the state to the prevention of harm.

The argument I am suggesting is "utilitarianlike," but not utilitarian. It is arguable that no means of measuring well-being can be developed which will satisfy the requirements of utilitarianism. Utilitarian arguments for the minimal state or the more than minimal state, therefore, remain dubious at best. This is not to deny, however, that in many situations it is relatively easy to make judgments that one policy will produce more social welfare or well-being than another. The transfer of wealth from the wealthy to the poor is a case in point. Utilitarianism, strictly speaking, requires quantification across the board, not just in isolated patches of our lives.

In all likelihood, John Stuart Mill was not a strict utilitarian either. His notion of well-being is very close to the one sketched here. Thus,

Mill is not a very good example of a Classical Liberal. In On Liberty, where Mill develops his famous argument for liberty and diversity, his concern was with political liberties, what we would call civil liberties. This is not an argument for economic freedom in the radical sense that government has no right to interfere with any economic transaction, as Classical Liberals claim. Classical Liberals are quite aware that Mill was not a reliable ally. In Liberalism, John Gray portrays Mill as a "watershed thinker."[13] According to Gray, Mill created a system of thought "which legitimated the interventionist and statist tendencies." This is to say that in spite of Mill's general commitment to laissez-faire and civil liberties, he developed a system which legitimized the more than minimal state of the Revisionist Liberals.

As the Revisionist Liberals claimed in the latter half of the nineteenth century, humans cannot be genuinely free without adequate resources to develop. The Revisionist Liberals recognized that protection of welfare interests does not promote human welfare if these "basic requisites" do not exist. By providing for these interests, where possible, the state can spur individual well-being, thereby increasing the social good. The liberal state does not attempt to force humans to be one kind of a person, or to adopt one particular kind of life plan. The liberal state merely aims to provide a context within which welfare interests, necessary for pursuing any life plan, can be nurtured.

These comments are pertinent to natural rights theory as well. I have criticized natural rights theories as foundationless in the sense that major theorists usually assume a particular list of natural rights. Few arguments are offered in support of the position that natural rights exist, or in support of one list as opposed to another. One plausible line of defense, however, might be that natural rights are those protections which would provide the general conditions within which humans would flourish, regardless of the particular society or historical period. But the focus upon natural rights too easily distracts attention from the important question of the critical conditions necessary for human development here and now. With changing contexts, those conditions might change. There is no need to assume some everlasting list of natural rights which can be determined without heeding the specific context, including the available resources.

The implication of these insights for the legitimacy of the state, the nature of the corporation, and the appropriate role of the corporation in a free society will be developed in the following chapters.

7

Micro-Managerialism

Within the Managerial framework, the answer to the fundamental question of the appropriate role of the corporation within a free society is, at least on its surface, strikingly different from what is proposed by the Classical framework. According to the Managerialists, management of the large modern corporation (or the corporation itself) has a responsibility to be a "good citizen," to act in a "socially responsible" manner, leaving the initial impression that there is a distinction to be drawn between profit maximizing behavior and actions which are socially responsible. Still, at other times, there are intimations of a belief that acting in ways which are socially responsible is merely a means of insuring longer-term profit maximization. Too often, there is a studious avoidance of any detailed discussions of the kinds of obvious questions to which this kind of talk gives rise, reinforcing the conceptual amorphousness for which this discourse is widely known. Complicating matters further, although Managerial pronouncements are usually imbued with high moral tone, there is a suspicious lack of moral argumentation offered in support of Managerial claims.

Thus, formidable challenges are posed by clarifying and analyzing the meaning and significance of the claim that corporations ought to act in a socially responsible manner, and by identifying, reconstructing, and evaluating the moral arguments which can be offered in support of that position. The most promising strategy is to situate these ideas within the larger Managerial ideology and to identify the theoretical core of ideas from which Managerialism derives its credibility.

This is, however, not nearly as straightforward a task as identifying Classical Liberalism as the heart of the Classical business ideology.

141

There is a tendency among many analysts to discount the Managerial ideology, a tendency apparent in Robert Jackall's otherwise perceptive and valuable *Moral Mazes: The World of Corporate Managers*.[1] In spite of its many strengths, Jackall's approach to this important topic is misguided. Reflecting this dismissive approach, the Classical and Managerial business ideologies are discussed in a chapter titled "The Magic Lantern," which is devoted to the development of the public relations profession.

Jackall provides an interesting account of how these ideas were promoted by corporate interests. With respect to the Classical business ideology he notes that key business leaders, threatened by the growing success of the labor movement, New Deal policies, and apparent rise of leftist radicalism, launched "a massive public relations counterattack" in the 1950s through the National Association of Manufacturers. Indeed, one of the major sources for *The American Business Creed*[2] is the publications of the NAM which grew out of that campaign. Describing events in the 1950s, Jackall writes:

> The espousal of the classical business creed was not restricted to the NAM campaign. Individual corporations, particularly giants like General Motors, U.S. Steel, Dupont, and Ford, expanded their own internal public relations staffs and launched their own campaigns reiterating or echoing the same kind of message. The extent and range of all of these efforts were impressive. They included extensive institutional advertising campaigns extolling in various ways free opportunity, initiative, and competition; a massive advertising campaign entitled "Prosperity Reigns Where Harmony Dwells"; special editions of in-house magazines designed for public distri-bution; the placement of probusiness editorials in small dailies across the country; the syndication for several hundred papers of a cartoon series with a probusiness stance; the sponsorship of radio programs of every variety complete with probusiness homilies; and the massive production of short motion pictures telling the story of one or another industry for distribution as trailers to movie theaters or to educational or recreational organizations. (168)

During and after World War II, Jackall claims, "more liberal busi-ness voices," identified with "segments of managerial capitalism that appreciated the great economic opportunities presented by the adop-tion of Keynesian economic policies," began to express their views through the public relations campaigns of the Committee for Eco-nomic Development (CED).[3] (Jackall mentions that the NAM campaign was ridiculed by William H. Whyte, editor of *Fortune* magazine[4] but fails to mention that the publication of *The Permanent Revolution*[5] by the editors of *Fortune* is not only one of the best popular expressions of the Managerial perspective but also a primary source for *The American Business Creed*.) In Jackall's view, "ideological splits" between different wings of the business elite "centered on the proper role of government in economic affairs," and similar clashes have occurred more recently over the issue of the corporate responsibility of business.

Although informative as background, Jackall's work tends to treat these ideologies on the one hand as if they were little more than the ideas conceived on Madison Avenue, on a par with ideas used to push toothpaste. On the other hand, the discussion of the ideological split and the issue of the proper role of government in economic affairs suggests an insight into the centrality of the debate between the two ideologies over theories of political philosophy and political economy, and into the large role played in the Managerial perspective by the new economics of the Keynesians. Unfortunately, Jackall's approach prevents developing these points. In fact, they are barely intelligible, since Jackall does not sketch any of the basic ideas which supposedly constitute this public relations campaign, does not discuss how the ideology incorporates the Keynesian ideas, does not explain the debate with the other representatives of the business community over the appropriate role of government, and does little more than refer to *The American Business Creed* as a source. The approach fails to address the question of the origin or source of the ideas and ignores the issues of whether the ideas of either perspective have a basis in reality.

The authors of *The American Business Creed* themselves bred skepticism that the Managerial ideology has a distinct theoretical core. The Classical and Managerial ideologies are treated as merely different versions or strands of the same "creed." Instead of clarifying matters, this only confuses the situation, since the authors never explain the nature of this creed and never offer much in the way of specifics by which to contrast the Classical with the Managerial. With the same kind of reasoning, one might argue that Protestantism does not constitute a framework independent from Catholicism because they are both Christian, or that Lutheranism is indistinct from the beliefs of Southern Baptists, because both are Protestant. The position appears to be that the Classical ideology is the creed, and the Managerial version an abortive attempt to develop an alternative. The analogy with religion through use of the talk of the business creed also invites the inference that disagreements over values and principles in this area are as resistant to resolution as the metaphysical claims involved in religion.

This is evident in the context of the defense of the analysis of the business ideology in terms of the "strain theory," in contrast to institutional or self-interest theories. While developing that defense, the Classical and Managerial views of major topics are discussed.[6] The authors claim that the Managerial "strand must be considered a variant of the more basic classical theme of the ideology rather than a parallel alternative."[7] Although a "principal reason for the emergence of the Managerial strand . . . is precisely the discrepancy between the classical model of small and weak business proprietorships and the real world of great corporate enterprises," the authors claim that the Managerial view is "logically" incomplete.[8]

The charge of logical incompleteness rests upon a comparison of the two strands. At least seven different possible points of comparison are identified: (1) profit and ethics; (2) extent and legitimacy of business power and discretion; (3) relationship of business and consumer; (4) legitimacy of high status; (5) competition; (6) hostility toward government; and (7) attitude toward social change. The claim for incompleteness is that only one significant point of disagreement can be identified, and, it is alleged, the apparent alternative proposed by the Managerial strand is not ultimately viable.

The significant point of contrast is claimed to exist with respect to the issue of profit and ethics. The authors argue that possibly "the most fundamental source of strain in the business role is an inconsistency in the ethical norms by which American society expects business behavior to be governed."[9] Law tolerates, and social mores generally approve of, self-interested behavior; yet, self-interest "is considered to be an unworthy goal of action which conflicts with ethical norms to which society attaches great importance."[10] According to *The American Business Creed*, the Classical and Managerial versions provide answers which "stand at opposite poles."

On closer inspection, however, the alternative evaporates in its own vagueness. Because the vagueness is intolerable to individual business persons, the authors argue that it is no wonder that the classical doctrine "persists."

The managerial definition of business responsibility leaves the business-man at sea without a compass. The moral responsibilities toward others which the managerial view would have him [or her] assume are numerous, conflicting, and incommensurable. By what standards shall he [she] weigh competing moral obligations in making. . . [his or her] decisions? It is not accidental that the codes of managerial behavior which appear in ideology are extremely vague, studded with operationally meaningless concepts as "fair wages," and the like. To accept this revision of the definition of the business role is to undertake a burden with more potential for anxiety for many businessmen than to cling to the alternative ethical norms which support orientation to profit. (358)

Whatever the merits of this argument for explaining psychologically why business persons may feel more comfortable with the Classical ideology, it addresses the issue at hand only obliquely. Namely, is the Managerial version logically incomplete because the alternative requires balancing competing responsibilities? While one must have great sympathy with the charge of vagueness, which I will develop in more detail later, the larger question is whether the dispute over profit and ethics is the only significant disagreement.

With respect to the question of the extent and legitimacy of business power and discretion, the Classical view suggests that business persons are agents and victims of impersonal market forces, that power and discretion are severely limited by competition. According to *The American Business Creed*, Managerialists have relatively little to say about power or discretion. They note that the discussion of responsibility presupposes a fairly wide range of discretion, but although the Managerialists appear to reject the Classical market model, they have little to put in its place. In short, they claim, ideology "ignores" the implications of power.[11]

On the other five points of comparison, the analysis in *The American Business Creed* is largely silent with respect to differences between the Classical and Managerial views. This is extremely unfortunate and misleading. Important points have been omitted. In the discussion of competition, for example, the analysis does not return to the idea that the Managerialists believe that the world no longer resembles the model of individual competition as conceived in the Classical view. In the discussion of hostility toward government, the Managerial acceptance of New Deal policies, which implies a significant shift from Classical Liberalism, is not noted.

It is, I believe, a serious mistake both to fail to recognize the existence of a distinct Managerial ideology and to avoid coming to grips with the important ideas of the theoretical core upon which it rests. Perhaps the distinctness was overlooked by the authors of the *The American Business Creed* because of their emphasis upon popular literature and pronouncement of business leaders. In any case, the Managerial business ideology is a set of beliefs, values, and principles held by a substantial number of representatives of the business community, especially those associated with very large corporations, which arose in self-conscious opposition to some of the central ideas and the policy implications of the Classical ideology. My claim is that the distinct theoretical core is some version of Revisionist Liberalism. Not surprisingly, this functions in an attempt to legitimize the relevant institutions and authorities, to provide a normative, conceptual orientation, and to offer practical guidance.

REVISIONIST LIBERALISM AND MANAGERIALISM

The central themes in the Managerial ideology concern the alleged social, political, legal, and moral significance of purported revolutionary changes in the corporation and in twentieth-century American capitalism. According to the Managerialists, both the structure of the corporation and the political-economic system of which it is a part have been radically transformed. With growing size, power, and influence, the corporation has come to play an increasingly important role in the society. And, importantly, Managerialists claim that there has been a dramatic change in values and actions as management has been professionalized.

The ideology is "Managerial" in at least three senses. First, a central claim associated with changes in the corporation involves the thesis of a Managerial revolution, the idea that control of these important corporations has passed from owners to managers. Second, the focus of attention is primarily upon the implications of these changes for management; issues are generally translated into issues of management and corporate policy, and only rarely into public policy issues. Third, the theoretical core of the ideology consists of theses, theories, and claims developed by and appropriated from economists, social scientists, legal theorists, social critics, and political philosophers working in a loosely assembled tradition which can be described as Managerial. Intellectually, these theorists were concerned and continue to be concerned, if not alarmed, by the implications of the rise of the large modern corporation and the Managerial revolution.

The latter sense of "Managerial" as an intellectual tradition is reflected, for example, in the title of Edward S. Mason's 1958 "The Apologetics of 'Managerialism.'"[12] Although appearing in *The Journal of Business*, the essay by the then dean of the Graduate School of Public Administration of Harvard University is concerned with theses purporting to describe structural changes not only within the large managerial corporations but also within the economy as a whole. Mason explicitly identifies a number of familiar texts as sources, including A. A. Berle's *The Twentieth-Century Capitalist Revolution1*,[13] Gardiner C. Means's *The Corporate Revolution in America*,[14] Morris Adelman's, "The Measurement of Industrial Concentration,"[15] and John Kenneth Galbraith's, *American Capitalism: The Concept of Countervailing Power*.[16] Mason could as easily have mentioned what is perhaps the most important text for Managerialists, *The Modern Corporation and Private Property*, by Berle and Means.

These liberal thinkers are not concerned to prevent the growth of government in order to institute a laissez-faire market with minimal government. In general, there is a concern with the lack of competition as it is defined in the Classical model and with the growth of the economic and political power of the large corporation. All, in one way or another, conceive of the appropriate role for government and the corporation much differently from the Classical model, with the government playing a much more active role in economic matters. The tenets of some version of a Revisionist Liberalism—ideas which attempted to provide legitimation to many of the New Deal programs—are exposed. If one wishes to speak of these ideologies as having a common creed, that common creed, therefore, is liberalism.

The focus upon the corporation made these ideas attractive for incorporation into the Managerial ideology.[17] Politically, business persons and institutions espousing the Managerial business ideology gradually came to welcome and encourage the growth of a strong federal government. Thus, ironically, many of the most important ideas in the Managerial ideology were bred in a culture which was largely antagonistic, if not overtly hostile, to management and the business culture, but these ideas were imported and to a large extent anesthetized.

The immediate roots of Revisionist Liberalism, like those of socialism and Marxism, lie in the nineteenth century, a response in large part to the problems of industrialization, urbanization, and modernization, and in staunch opposition to the tenets of the Classical Liberals and the minimal state. Virtually every major European intellectual tradition spawned Revisionist Liberal theories, making generalizations dangerous, but all were extremely critical of corporate practices, expressed reservations about corporate power and the abuses and problems of capitalism, and called for government to play an active role in addressing the needs of the citizens. There was a general consensus that market failures could not be tolerated and there was an important function for government to play in ameliorating the problems associated with the development of capitalism, especially industrial capitalism.

In England, the empiricist philosophical tradition has held enormous sway. To some extent, as a result of historical and culture commonalities, empiricism has been a dominant force in the United States as well. That tradition stresses that the source of all knowledge (except perhaps of knowledge such as mathematical knowledge) is based upon the senses. This epistemological stance provided an important weapon for attacking the political claims of the divine right of kings by undermining the claims of revelation, and cleared the way for an allegiance to science, reason, and progress. The liberalism of John Locke, Adam Smith, and John Stuart Mill is grounded there. Economic theory and utilitarianism are closely allied with the same tradition.

Although usually identified with Classical Liberalism, economists and political philosophers in the liberal empirical tradition were clearly not doctrinaire. There are good reasons to believe that even Adam Smith's theory, for example, can readily support a more than minimal state.[18] For Smith, the key issue appears to be whether social needs are best met by the market, by the public sector, or perhaps by a combination of both.

The dispute, however, hinges primarily upon the facts, i.e., as a matter of *fact* which is the most efficient way to address the concerns? Moreover, as I have already indicted, Mill is widely recognized as a pivotal, watershed figure. Although the author of On Liberty argued on utilitarian grounds for the value of freedom from governmental interference in self-regarding actions and defended the harm principle as limiting the scope of governmental interference into other-regarding actions, the principle seems to have been understood primarily as a basis for civil rights. Governmental taxation, economic regulation, licensing, and so forth were not considered by Mill to be unwarranted interference in the freedom of individuals in principle; government could regulate for the common good. Mill did not believe that these governmental activities were extremely coercive. The state which

Mill advocated was far from the minimal state of the Classical Liberal conception. And, in principle, utilitarianism could always lend support for any form of government provided that form produced maximal net social utility. Indeed, utilitarians with many compatriots in the economic profession came increasingly to favor Revisionist Liberal programs.

Other traditions moved simultaneously toward analogous conclusions. By the close of the nineteenth century, idealists in Britain, France, and Germany, often under the influence of Hegel or Kant, were providing theoretical defenses of the tenets of Revisionist Liberalism. T. H. Green[19] and Bernard Bosanquet,[20] for instance, following a Hegelian line, argued against the "negative conception" of freedom in the Classical view. They claimed that freedom in the Classical position was viewed as the mere absence of an external constraint. In that view, if government did not interfere in the liberty of individuals, and government kept others from interfering in the liberty of individuals, then individuals were free. Green and Bosanquet argued that freedom from external constraint is not genuine freedom. A citizen without adequate economic, social, and cultural resources is not free to develop. Freedom requires certain resources. The poor are not free. In the name of freedom, Revisionist Liberals argued that government should take steps to make its citizens free. These steps might necessarily involve interference into the economic transactions of citizens for the sake of making more citizens free.

In 1911, L. T. Hobhouse published *Liberalism*,[21] an attempt to synthesize the philosophies of Mill and Green and the two traditions they represent. This work was reprinted eight times before it was allowed to go out of print. It was reissued in 1964 and was reprinted again in 1979.[22] *Liberalism* is often taken to represent the most systematic statement of Revisionary Liberalism. Alan P. Grimes, who wrote an introduction for the 1964 edition, quotes C. Wright Mills in *The Marxists* as claiming that *Liberalism* was "the best twentieth-century statement of liberal ideals I know."[23] The brevity of the work, together with the fact that it was relatively easy to read, probably helped contribute to its wide influence. In any case, there was growing consensus among a large portion of the population in many of the industrial capitalist countries that government should take an active role in regulating the economy and providing for the needy. As John Gray[24] writes:

It may be said that, with Hobhouse, the new revisionist liberalism, in which ideals of distributive justice and social harmony supplant the older conceptions of a system of natural liberties, had come in England altogether to dominate progressive opinion where it was not avowedly socialist. (32)

In the U.S., the roots of Revisionist Liberalism were as diverse as the immigrants who flooded the shores in the late nineteenth century and early twentieth century. English utilitarianism and empiricism, English idealism, German idealism and neo-Kantianism each produced Revisionist theories. Moreover, pragmatism developed as an indigenous philosophy and flourished. Associated with names like C. S. Pierce, William James, and John Dewey, pragmatists became severe critics both of earlier traditions and of growing positivistic influences, even though the theory had in many ways a close affinity for the earlier empiricism, valuing highly science, rationality, democracy, and individual liberty, and even though the theory aligned itself with "progressive" causes.

While Revisionist Liberalisms continued to develop here, only echoes of ideas found political manifestation until the Great Depression and the New Deal. In this respect, the situation in the U.S. was very different from European countries. As David Vogel and many others have pointed out, strong central governments existed in most European countries prior to the development of industrial capitalism.[25] Consequently, those countries had long traditions of government regulation of economic activity, of bending economic activity to conform to national interests. In the U.S., democratization preceded industrialization, while in England and on the continent, industrialization preceded democratization. Outside the U.S., Classical Liberals battled already existing strong central governments in an attempt to prevent interference in the development of industrial capitalism and to push the government toward democratic principles. In the U.S., on the other hand, although there was a political democracy much earlier, industrial capitalism produced extremely powerful political and economical interests prior to the development of a strong national government. Throughout most of the nineteenth century, the U.S. federal government was strong enough to provide tariff protection from foreign competition, substantial subsidies (e.g., 10 percent of the land mass of the U.S. to the railroads), and protection from state governments attempting to regulate corporate activity, but demonstrated little interest in much more. In this sense, the limited government served business interests quite well. Only in the closing decade of the nineteenth century does one find the federal government attempting to play a more positive role in regulating the economy and expanding services. This historical peculiarity helps explain the intensity of the debate over the legitimacy of a more than minimal state in the U.S., and the slowness with which a politically viable Revisionist Liberal platform developed. The plea for a more active government arose from the perception of significant social, political, and economic changes creating new circumstances which demanded attention by government. Theoretically, at least, the debate revolved around the basic tenets of the Classical/neo-Classical economic theories, not around altered fundamental values or principles. Economically, the Revisionist or New Deal Liberals have been and remain "Keynesians" in the sense that they have abandoned the notion that markets are self-regulating and self-correcting, and that they have let go of the related notion that government should not in any way interfere in markets. In their view, domestic markets in the U.S. were not competitive in the Classical sense. Oligopolistic and monopolistic tendencies were apparent in every major industry by the turn of the century. In each, a few huge corporations dominated, although there is some disagreement about the significance of this. Some argue that vigorous competition of a different sort has come to replace competition in the classical sense and continues to regulate corporations rather handily. Others argue that most industries have suffered from prices administered by a few corporations and that competition, if it exists at all, is in areas other than price. Most also stress market failures of various kinds. There is the claim that serious needs are left unmet by the market. Externalities mean that prices did not reflect the actual social costs for the production of goods and services, and that those costs were being unfairly shouldered by individuals and groups not benefiting from the production.

For these reasons, the argument goes, government must take a more active role to counterbalance the growth of the large corporation, to deal with noncompetitive markets and market failures. New Deal Liberalism also usually relies upon a pluralist model to understand how a society does and should function. In this understanding, the key players, economically and politically, are large institutions, organized groups of individuals, not particular individuals. Large corporations are among the most important of these players. And, New Deal Liberals were concerned with the Managerial revolution, even if they disagreed about its implications.

Through the politics of the New Deal, many of these precepts found political expression in the 1930s. The New Deal Revisionist Liberals not only provided the intellectual rationale for the more than minimal state, but were recruited to design, staff, and administer the governmental agencies resulting from the implementation of those ideas. And those ideas continued to fuel public policy through the New Frontier and Great Society programs of the 1960s, and to some extent through the early 1970s.

The ideas of Revisionist Liberalism were appropriated by representatives of the American business community and were integrated into the emerging Managerial ideology. There should be little serious doubt that these represent a framework quite independent of the Classical one. In the throes of the Great Depression, the Revisionist Liberal attempt to forge a program which protected individual freedom and the capitalist market economy from the extremes of fascism, socialism, and Marxism became particularly salient. The policies of Classical Liberalism, by ignoring needs of the people, would, it was feared, fuel a situation in which "radical" ideas would lead to a violent revolution, with a concomitant loss of civil liberty and market freedom. The solution was to increase the size, scope, and importance of government, to provide government an important role in the economy. The crisis in the 1930s created a split in the business community as well. Managerialists agreed with and adopted the arguments of the New Deal Liberals and welcomed to a large extent the growth of government.

While serving a number of useful purposes, the incorporation of many of the theses and theories of Revisionist Liberalism into the corporate sector is not, however, without problems. Significant tensions are, on closer inspection, readily apparent. The implications of Classical/neo-Classical economic theory and Classical Liberalism for public and corporate policy were immediate and clear. Whether one took the perspective of the corporate manager or of the government mattered little: either way, corporations should seek profit, and the government should protect against harm. The Managerial ideology constitutes an analogous attempt to derive the implications for strategic corporate policy from a version of Revisionist Liberalism. The continuing refrain is social responsibility, that the modern corporation has an important role to play in solving serious social problems. This refrain, however, is discordant when played against the background of ideas and theories which were introduced from the disciplines of economics and political science. There the assumption is that corporations, like other organized groups, are self-interested entities seeking either to maximize profit, power, or both. From this perspective, solutions derive from the initiative of the public sector, and the major concern is to fabricate public policy to solve problems (e.g., externalities, needs unmet by the market, unemployment) without relying too greatly, if at all, upon corporate good will and altruism. A solution may involve regulation for the purpose of eliminating externalities between competing corporations, for instance, or the creation of market incentives to induce profit-seeking behavior which will result in the satisfaction of politically desirable ends, but there is little room for corporate do-goodism, corporate citizenship, the implementation of corporate morality, and so forth.

This tension between the implications for public and corporate good which seem to flow naturally from Revisionist Liberalism (government regulation, corporate profit maximizing), and the implications which Managerialists attempt to draw (self-regulation, social responsibility) may explain why there are two identifiable strands within the Managerial ideology. The dominant strand is the refrain of the Managerial revolution, emphasizing social responsibility. Because of the almost exclusive attention to theses concerned with the firm and the role of management, I refer to this strand as "Micro-Managerialism." This is the kind of Managerialism upon which *The American Business Creed* focuses. The task of the remainder of this chapter is to explore the Micro-Managerial perspective and to identify the major theses involved. In the next chapter, those theses will be evaluated.

The following analysis will demonstrate that by focusing only on the corporation, Micro-Managerialism remains vague, abstract, incomplete, and irrelevant. Too often, the perspective degenerates into innocuous, but hollow, homilies. Without an understanding of the system within which the modern corporation functions, many of the central claims, including claims about corporate responsibility, border on vacuousness and unintelligibility. Without attention to the larger system, there is no way to delineate the constraints upon management, to trace the limitations of corporate responsibility, or to evaluate the claims about the impact on the larger social good. There should be little wonder that critics perceive the rhetoric as a thinly disguised ruse.

The other strand of the Managerial framework, which I call "Macro-Manageralism," locates the discussion of corporate policy within the broader context of changes within the capitalistic system itself, incorporating many of the theses of New Deal Liberalism.[26] Against this richer background, the rhetoric of social responsibility takes on a much different hue. That, however, is the subject of a latter chapter.

THE BIG CHANGE/THE NEW AGE

Perhaps the dominant theme among the Managerialists is that the system, the capitalist, free enterprise system has undergone a "big change," a "great transformation." The more popular literature, reflecting the Micro-Managerial perspective, is hesitant to describe the specifics of the change in the system. Details of alleged changes in the structure of the large corporation are often more forthcoming, but generally the scope of concern is even narrower, with attention being devoted to alleged changes in the values, attitudes, and actions of management. This focus tends to trivialize the structural changes, reducing them to little more than moral conversions, to changes of heart of business leaders. In this respect, the big change is described as a change from a situation in which business robber barons acted without concern for the public good to a situation in which corporate managers now act as socially conscious and morally sensitive professionals, deeply concerned not only with public relations but also with being good citizens.

The authors of *The American Business Creed* are sensitive to the centrality in the Managerial literature of the theme of a big change and of the tendency to ignore the important structural changes. Pursuing the analogy with religion, they claim that the "creation myth" of the Classical ideology is the idea that the free enterprise system with limited government preexisted in the minds of the Founding Fathers as they crafted the original documents. The idea of the big change or the great transformation is, on the other hand, considered as the "managerial version of the creation myth."[27] "The transition from irresponsible tycoon to principled manager is," they write, "the product of a moral effort by businessmen, made in response to a

perceived need, not the result of a complex social evolution."[28] There
is no doubt that the popular sources exploited by Sutton et al., such
as USA, the Permanent Revolution, undoubtedly stress the important
role of the choice of the individual business person or manager and
blur over discussions of the "complex social evolution" of corporate
structures or of the larger system. By restricting themselves only to
popular Micro-Managerial sources, Sutton et al. fail to understand the
extent to which these changes can be and are interpreted by some
Managerialists as part of "complex social evolution."[29]

Echoing the genre of religious or moral conversion and redemption,
the voluntaristic refrain of Micro-Managerialism is quite apparent in
numerous accounts in 1950s. In one widely read book titled The Big
Change,[30] Frederick Allen, for example, claims that by 1950 a big
change had occurred, and he points in particular to two developments: alleged growth within the business community of a sense of
responsibility for society which goes beyond the corporate boundary,
and a growing recognition of the importance of public relations. For
Allen, the notorious William H. Vanderbilt captures the earlier view.
In 1882, after a reporter asked Vanderbilt to explain why he had taken
a mail train off the New York–Chicago run, Vanderbilt replied with
the now-immortal line, "The public be damned!" thereby indicating
that the public interest and public perception were of little concern.
A similarly motivated remark by Mark Hanna in the late 1890s is also
illustrative. Writing a letter to a Republican attorney general who had
undertaken antitrust action against the Standard Oil Trust, Hanna
claimed that there "is no greater mistake for a man in or out of public
place to make—than to assume that he owes any duty to the public."[31]

Managerialists like to associate these attitudes with the Classical
ideology. Corporate managers are now, they claim, much different.
They are very aware of public image and go to great pains to assure
the public that its interest is of primary concern. Why a shift in
managerial sensitivity to public image and the consequent attention to
public relations should count as evidence for a big change is not clear.
Is this merely a change in the attitude of many important corporate
leaders? Have there been changes in the system? Perhaps the change is
rather small, and management has learned that profits are substantially
higher by attempting to convince the public that the decisions are
being made in its interest, rather than in the interests of stockholders.
Or, perhaps it is in the best interest of stockholders if management is
careful in the cultivation of an image of a public-spirited corporation.

Good public relations is good business. An emphasis merely on public relations is consistent with profit maximization. As such, a Managerial attack upon the Classical perspective might be little more than an argument that to maximize profit many of the *tactics* utilized in the Classical framework are outmoded. That is, perhaps managers ought to pretend not to be in the business of maximizing profit if they wish to maximize profit really. If the big change amounts to nothing more than this, a battle over appropriate tactics for profit maximization, then the claim that the Managerial perspective does not represent a distinct framework is understandable.

As evidence for a big change in the area of social responsibility, increasing concern among the business community for government service, international peace, civil liberties, and labor, is also cited by Allen. Executives had begun to enter government service in increasing numbers, and in ways which required dealing with difficult problems of an industrial and international society. Edward Stettinius of U.S. Steel accepted the job of secretary of state at the end of World War II. Paul Hoffman, of Studebaker, administrated the Marshal Plan in Europe and later headed the UN Special Fund for Technical Assistance in underdeveloped countries.

This general view is evident in a number of later, more academically oriented works as well. In *American Enterprise: Free and Not So Free*,[32] for example, Clarence Cramer not only accepts the thesis of the big change but, in discussing Allen's book, marshals further evidence. Cramer notes how Sol Linowitz, chairman of the board of Xerox Corporation, took the position as coordinator for the Alliance for Progress in Latin America. Linowitz was strongly committed to world peace and progress and argued successfully for Xerox's support for a TV program which favorably represented the UN. In spite of strong right-wing opposition, especially from the John Birch Society, Xerox put $4 million into the program and received sixty-one thousand letters of protest. The right-wing attack on Xerox, even threats of boycotts, probably led to a substantial amount of sympathetic response from other sectors as many editorials supported Xerox's stand. For some, including Cramer, this seemed an illustration of the point that strong social commitments actually "paid." Linowitz was also deeply involved in the fight against McCarthyism in the 1950s. Cramer also finds evidence for a big change in the area of labor relations. This comes partly from a comparison of the policies of Henry Ford I and Henry Ford II toward labor unions.[33]

This voluntaristic interpretation of a great transformation arising from some kind of a moral conversion is deeply ingrained and also appears in discussions of management philosophies toward workers. The older, "unenlightened" management ideas of Frederick Winslow Taylor are associated with the Classical ideology and contrasted with the "enlightened" views of Elton Mayo.

The author of the *The Principles of Scientific Management*,[34] published in 1911, Taylor is known as the "Father of Scientific Management." The central idea is to increase production by rationalizing it. Rationalization of production required analysis of worker and work. All humans, according to Taylor, are naturally lazy and instinctively inclined toward systematic soldiering, i.e., working at as slow a pace as possible. They are generally stupid and work only for the rewards, i.e., money. These "findings" framed the problem of work. From them it seemed evident that in order to increase production, a firm must give workers an incentive to produce more, a thought which led directly to piece-work wages. Since workers were stupid, it also followed that more rational minds should investigate the work, analyze the basic components, and discover the most efficient manner of doing the job through stopwatch studies, etc. Workers could not be trusted to find the most efficient methods since not only are they dull but the tendency toward soldiering constitutes a severe obstacle toward rationalizing work. One important principle in designing the work, for Taylor, was to implement vigorously the principle of specialization and division of labor. Breaking tasks into smaller and smaller units and then assigning the subtasks to separate individuals made intelligence unnecessary in the production process, thereby circumventing the problem of human stupidity. Finally, Taylor argued for close and authoritarian supervision of workers as necessary in order to prevent lazy, stupid, and soldiering workers from resorting to "irrational" productive techniques. Taylor's view is represented as a logical consequence of the basic ideas of the economic views associated with the Classical perspective. This is, of course, only partially true, but such an identification serves as a means of undermining the credibility of the Classical ideology.

For many Managerialists, Elton Mayo, a professor at the Harvard Business School, is taken to have conclusively demonstrated the falsity of ideas like Taylor's in the now famous Hawthorne Experiments. The Western Electric Company invited Mayo to examine morale and productivity at the Hawthorne Works in Chicago. The conclusions

reached by Mayo were startling. At first, Mayo improved working conditions, added amenities, and shortened hours. Production improved.
Then, Mayo convinced the treatment group to give up the changes
and return to the conditions existing prior to the beginning of the experiment. Production improved again. This suggested that conditions
themselves were not a significant factor in production, but that the
increased productivity was the result of worker's enhanced feelings
of dignity, worth, and importance. This conclusion was supported by
the fact that Mayo had thoroughly discussed the experiment with the
workers, who participated in advance in decisions concerning every
proposed change. Hence, experimental data pointed toward the idea
that the significant variable in production is a perception of dignity
and worth. This notion was popularized by the phrase that production
could be increased by *humanizing it.*

In the 1960s Abraham Maslow's psychological views[35] supplemented these and became the basis for humanizing the workplace
through Douglas McGregor's *The Human Side of the Enterprise.*[36] As
fashions change, under the influence of certain Japanese models, some
Managerialists advocate Theory Z as the latest truly enlightened *and*
productive approach.[37]

All this "evidence" is at best ambiguous. Does the flow of corporate
executives into government positions testify to a sense of social responsibility or does it witness to a recognition that profit maximization
now requires more subtle use of governmental power? One can find
numerous cases of tycoons influencing government decisions in the
nineteenth century. Has there really been a change? Moreover, is humanizing workers done on behalf of workers or as a more efficient way
of production? Many have drawn from the Hawthorne experiments a
rather cynical moral: working conditions are relatively unimportant
in themselves so long as workers can be duped into believing that
they are respected as humans. "Humanizing" is vulnerable to merely
propagandizing or manipulating workers. Much the same can be said
of the recent emphasis upon quality circles and team approaches.
Public relations may again win the day over concern with real working conditions. Even in the more theoretical treatments of some of
these issues there is a tendency both to ignore the possibility of real
conflict between profit maximization and other responsibilities which
Managerialists claim exist, and to proceed continually as if by fulfilling
those responsibilities profit will be maximized.

More importantly, what structural features of the economy and
political life of the nation have fostered these kinds of changes? The

context is ignored. To discuss only changing attitudes, public relations gestures, increased participation by corporate leaders in government, or a changed stance vis-à-vis organized labor and workforce is to fail to identify the assumptions/theories about the structural changes in capitalism which help explain and understand these other changes. Micro-Managerialism dodges discussion of those theories except insofar as they can be utilized to reinforce the theme of the importance of managerial decision making.

The discussions of the new ideology represent a more contemporary variation of the theme of the big change. Because the new age of the new ideology is only beginning to break into the existing order, there is a futuristic tone throughout this genre. There is also evidence of the pervasive confusion between description and prescription.[38] In *American Business Values in Transition*,[39] for instance, Gerald F. Cavanagh provides a historical introduction to the values and beliefs of the "traditional" business ideology, considers the role of personal values in the organization, and then treats of challenges to "free enterprise." One chapter deals with the Marxian challenge, and the other deals with contemporary domestic challenges to corporate legitimacy. The final chapter concerns "Corporate Values for the Future." Cavanagh claims that it is a "straightforward task to chart the past development of American business and economic values," but it is "more difficult and perhaps presumptuous to try to indicate the direction of future change." Assuming the role of a futurist, a social scientist, or a market researcher, Cavanagh attempts only "to point out the direction of change in future business values and goals." Reflecting a pervasive problem in this literature, the message here, obliquely stated, is that these values *should* be accepted, although virtually no reason is offered. Cavanagh is not hesitant to criticize the "inadequacies" of the Classical business ideology:[40]

1. Acquisitive materialism is encouraged by a system that provides a rationalization for self-interest and selfishness.
2. Freedom and productivity are dominant values, with less attention paid to how this freedom and productivity will be used.
3. Because of large organizations and the division of labor, individuals seldom feel a sense of human participation.
4. Traditional unbounded faith in scientific, technological, and industrial progress is increasingly questioned.
5. There is an inequality in the distribution of income and wealth, domestically and internationally.

6. Individual decisions based on self-interest increasingly fail to add up to acceptable and humane policy for society as a whole.

7. The cumbersome machinery of majority rule may not leave us sufficient time to solve the serious problems that face us.

To judge something inadequate requires a standard of adequacy. From a list of inadequacies, it is possible to collect some impression of the values which precipitate the judgments, but not a precise understanding of principles being employed. They are never stated. Thus, although Cavanagh does not shirk from judging values inadequate, he is quite resistant to the temptation to defend or even state the standards motivating the judgment. If those standards are sufficient to condemn the old ideology, would they not also be sufficient to infuse the new? The old ideology is attacked as inconsistent, and conventional wisdom is said to be crumbling in our hands.

In another place, there is a list of the new values. The major values which will likely occur after the "Second American Revolution" are[41]

1. Central role of the person
2. Participation in the decision making
3. Corporation as a servant of society
4. New measures of business success
5. Harmony with environment
6. Necessity of new legitimacy for the corporation
7. Interdependence of people, institutions, and nations
8. Vision and hope
9. Concern for others

Although Cavanagh expands and develops each of these in turn, the list constitutes merely a prediction of what the future holds. The question of whether these values, too, might be inadequate is almost entirely ignored. It is as if whatever values come into existence are adequate. Are the old values ultimately inadequate because they are being rejected by society? That is, is the distribution of income and wealth inadequate merely because society is coming to view it as unacceptable?

> It is necessary to clarify goals and to construct legislative and cultural inducements so that individual activities may better contribute to producing a more humane society. (208)

The shift reflected in this sentence should not be overlooked. In this quiet phrase, Cavanagh has stepped beyond the role of predicting the future into the role of soliciting support for these values. Cavanagh introduces a call for creating the new values through legislative and cultural inducements, not a prediction that these will, in fact, occur. Either there is a serious confusion over the distinction between descriptive and prescriptive/evaluative judgments, and Cavanagh believes that whatever is accepted should be accepted, or else this is an unconscious or surreptitious attempt to shift from descriptive predictions to advocacy. Yet the advocacy is frail. No defense is offered except that the items listed are more "humane." Still, the point I wish to make here is that for Cavanagh, the new age is arriving.

The New American Ideology,[42] by George C. Lodge, develops the same theme. Not only in his book but also in numerous articles and speeches, Lodge contrasts the ideas of the old, traditional (Classical) ideology, with those of the new (Managerial). The traditional idea is characterized as resting upon five basic ideas, the Lockean Five, which "found fertile soil in the vast, underpopulated wilderness of America and served us well for a hundred years or so."[43]

1. *Individualism.* The basic assumption is atomistic individualism. The economy and society are composed of little more than the sum of discrete individuals. Closely tied to this are the ideas of contract and equal opportunity. Individuals are allowed equal opportunity to pursue their own conception of the good in a lonely struggle. Contracts, freely entered, constitute the bonds of the economy, society, and government.

2. *Property Rights.* This is one of the key individual rights. Property rights protect the individual in his or her pursuit of the good life from others and from the government and constitute an important part of individual liberty.

3. *Competition-consumer desire.* Under this idea Lodge refers to the idea of the economic system, regulated by competing individuals each in control of his or her own property and each in search of his or her own best interests.

4. *Limited State.* The function of government should be restricted to that of protecting against harm. Lodge claims that the traditional ideology generates interest-group pluralism.

5. *Scientific specialization and fragmentation.* Lodge claims that in the traditional ideology there is a focus by specialists and experts upon the parts, with the belief that the whole will take care of itself. Here Lodge refers to the idea in the Classical

ideology of the way the decentralized system works. There is no need for centralized planning since the system ensures that individual decisions motivated by self-interest yield what is best for the whole.

This is a succinct summary of the Classical ideology, peculiar only in that it neatly avoids a direct description of *the system* as a whole, focusing instead on its more notable and important attributes.

In place of these ideas, Lodge finds a new set of ideas being accepted. The ideas represented in the Lockean Five are already, in Lodge's words, in an "advanced state of erosion." The traditional ideology is purported to be inconsistent with the real world and, specifically, the "great institutions" of America and the western world have already departed from them. These new ideas are[44]

1. *Communitarianism*. According to Lodge the spirit of individualism is being replaced with a new sense of community. The community is recognized as having needs and the survival and respect of individuals depend upon the recognition of those needs.
2. *Rights and duties of membership*. Private property has "stopped being very important." Consistent with much of the work of Berle and Means, Lodge argues that the line is blurred between private and public. The significant question is not who owns something, but who controls or enjoys the benefits of property. With the split between stockholders and management, it makes little sense to speak of stockholders as owners of private property. Rights do not emanate from contract. Rights of membership in pluralistic interest groups such as labor unions or professional or trade organizations, not property rights, guarantee security and freedom. Lodge refers to these as "communitarian rights."
3. *Community need*. Community need is supposedly replacing competition and individual self-interest as a regulator of society's economic and political decisions.
4. *Active, planning state*. The government's role in the economy is much broader than prevention of harm and laissez-faire with respect to the economy. The government's role in defining national goals, setting public priorities, and generating major programs is now widely accepted.
5. *Holism-interdependence*. Thinking in terms of the whole system, a recognition of the interrelatedness of things is replacing the narrow specializations.

At least two things are remarkable about the treatment of the new ideology. First, although many of the key elements in the Managerial view have been identified, the list provides virtually no concrete guidance. No criteria for guiding specific decisions of managers are offered except that they should accept the legitimacy of the more than minimal state, rights of members in a pluralistic society (e.g., labor union members), the regulation of property by governmental agencies in the name of community need, and so forth. This is hardly more than an exhortation to abandon the Classical ideology and to become socially responsible. The same holds true of the list provided by Cavanagh. Second, Lodge, like Cavanagh, is never very clear why these values should be accepted. Certain passages suggest an uneasiness over providing an argument in defense of a set of values. There is a tendency, prevalent throughout this literature, of confusing prediction with justification. Even if someone is correct in predicting that a particular set of values will come into existence, that is hardly a good reason for believing that these values are morally legitimate. Both of these points merit the careful attention which will be given to them later. Here, however, we must more clearly bring into focus the theses which make up the Managerial ideology.

THE MANAGERIAL REVOLUTION

Insofar as the Micro-Managerialists transcend the rhetoric of voluntarism and moral conversion involved in discussions of the big change and the new ideology, the focus is upon structural changes within the firm. Micro-Managerialists stress the revolutionary changes which have allegedly restructured the modern corporation in the twentieth century and the moral implications which purportedly follow. The model of the firm in the Classical view as a strictly legal-economic entity, is contrasted unfavorably with the model of the firm in the Micro-Managerial view, which has recently come to be known as the "stakeholder model" of the firm. In this model, the firm is alleged to be a social-political reality, not merely a legal or economic entity. The reality of the modern corporation is of a nexus of interdependent interests: stockholders, bondholders, employees (past, present, and potential ones), competitors, customers, local communities, the general public, and, perhaps, the environment. In many texts, this nexus is described as an "interactive system." The firm, management, is usually pictorially represented at the center of a diagram, encircled by other primary and secondary constituencies. The primary constituencies are those directly involved in production and distribution of goods and/or services: employees, stockholders, creditors, suppliers, customers, competitors, and wholesalers/retailers. Among the secondary constituencies are local communities, governments, foreign governments, social activist groups, media, business support groups, and public opinion.

In the words of Lee E. Preston, this stakeholder model presents management "as a process of achieving a satisfactory mix of outcomes for the benefit of a diverse collection of constituents."[45] Preston argues that this model is "the *central organizing concept*" in the field of Social Issues of Management, or Business and Society, and the model allegedly distinguishes the field of Social Issues in Management from other fields. As a matter of fact, the Classical model does not deny relationships with these constituencies, but the Managerialists interpret them differently. Perhaps most importantly, responsibilities which go beyond the economic-contractual are alleged to rest upon these relationships. These responsibilities are variously and vaguely grounded but often involve an appeal to the economic power and scope of influence of the large modern corporation. Given that corporate decisions have wide scope and significant impact on certain groups, the claim is made that the corporation has a responsibility to take those interests into consideration in the decision-making process in a fashion which is not captured by the purely economic and legal model. The unspoken assumption is the claim that management has the liberty and power to adjudicate between the competing claims of stakeholders. Apparently, the claim is that a decision *should not be based solely on the principle of profit maximization for stockholders*, although it is difficult to tell.

These claims fly in the face of assumptions in the Classical model, where it is believed that all decisions will be made according to the principle of profit maximization. In the Classical framework, this principle is bolstered by appeal to the functioning of the system, which would allegedly eliminate firms which do not act to maximize profit (or do so inefficiently), and by the idea that stockholders controlling management decisions through the board of directors would replace management which acted otherwise. Hence, in the Classical model, management does not have the liberty to deviate from the principle of profit maximization, and, since adherence to the principle is crucial for the efficient functioning of the system; this is best for all. Thus, to accept the idea that the firm is a constellation of interests with management in control and at liberty to decide to deviate from profit maximization strikes at the root of the Classical system.

Neither the stakeholder model nor the moral arguments premised upon it are new, nor do writers fail to acknowledge, to some extent, their debt to earlier scholars. One frequently cited source is, not surprisingly, *The Meaning of Modern Business* by Richard S. Eells,[46] who developed these themes in the early 1960s. But these views are actually much older. In *The Social Responsibilities of Business*,[47] Morrell Heald demonstrates that discussions of social responsibility and the related model of management which is currently known as the stakeholder model can be found in the discussions of the idea of "trusteeship" in the 1920s.

> In their shifting relations with stockholders and with employees, as well as with other groups outside the bounds of the corporation itself, managers were beginning to see themselves and their responsibilities in a new light. Instead of being mere agents for the owners, they had become coordinators, standing between and reconciling the claims of a variety of assorted interests. A new conception of managerial powers and responsibilities was inherent in this view. Formulated as the idea of the trusteeship of management. . . , it was put forward by a small group of business leaders for the first time in the 1920s. (61)

Heald also claims that although the business literature of the 1950s was filled with discussions of management's responsibilities for dealing with social problems, "in principle there was little that went beyond the trusteeship concept enunciated nearly a quarter of a century earlier," even though the concept was elaborated upon and applied in new areas.[48] The same point can be made about the more recent interest in corporate responsibility.

The idea of the trusteeship of management itself appears to have been developed within the context of the growing ideology of professionalism. In 1914, for example, Louis D. Brandeis published an article titled "Business, the New Profession," in *Business—A Profession*.[49] Later a Supreme Court justice, Brandeis was hardly a friend of big business. He had tangled with the Morgan banking interests while exposing their mishandling of the New York, New Haven, and Hartford Railroad properties, which prompted him to write *Other People's Money and How the Bankers Use It*. Brandeis believed that bigness was

166 MICRO-MANAGERIALISM

often the result of manipulation, not competition, and argued vigorously for antitrust cases. Brandeis's article claimed that the changing character of business, the growth of large complex organizations in a complex environment, requires the development of professionals whose practice is based on a body of knowledge and who embody an ethic of service to society rather than self-interest.[50] The idea of trusteeship of management came readily to fit in with this ideal of the professional as one dedicated to the good of the society, not to narrow self-interest. As business education was formalized and higher degree programs in business became accepted in the 1920s, this way of thinking could be institutionalized. Little seems to have changed since then.

By the 1930s, as the Great Depression deepened, these ideas found expression in what has become a classic text. In Heald's words:

> The publication in 1932 of *The Modern Corporation and Private Property* by two Columbia University faculty members, A. A. Berle, Jr., and Gardiner C. Means, climaxed several decades of growing interest in the evolution of the business corporation. It was an interest which academicians shared with political reformers and with the leaders of business itself. Berle and Means offered convincing evidence to document what was already a widely recognized trend in business organization, the diffusion of stock ownership in large national corporations, on the one hand, and the emergence of a distinct, largely autonomous managerial group on the other. (55)

Materials for the assault upon the Classical view, as well as those for the construction of an alternative model, come largely from the theses advanced in *The Modern Corporation and Private Property*.[51] Berle and Means themselves disclaim originality, recognizing the anticipation of their major theses in the previous decade, but their work is one of the most influential of the century, and the theses defended there continue to be debated and to serve as subjects for research programs. According to John Kenneth Galbraith, of the many important texts published in the 1930s, it ranks second only to John M. Keynes, *The General Theory*. A conference at the Hoover Institution in 1982 to commemorate the publication of the book and to provide fresh insight and evidence on its theses included an impressive list of scholars whose own work had been shaped by the confrontation with the arguments of Berle and Means.[52] The list includes George Stigler, Harold Demsetz, Gene Fama, Michael Jensen, Oliver Williamson,

Henry Manne, and so forth—a Who's Who in American economic thought. Fifty years following its publication, only a handful of the classic texts of economics were cited more frequently in the *Social Science Citation Index*. The theses of the 1932 work constitute the kernel of the Managerial ideology.

Among the great transformations of capitalism, according to Berle and Means, is the Managerial revolution.[53] According to this theory, the role of the stockholder/owner has evolved from that in the entrepreneurial firm where the owner(s) is (are) in control of day-to-day operations and strategic decisions. With growth and specialization, owners in the entrepreneurial firms hire managers, but the owners maintain real control. As large corporations developed in the late nineteenth century, however, owner control was replaced by management control in the so-called modern corporation. The specifics of this Managerial revolution are complex, involving a number of different factors. Most of those factors were already intact at the writing of *The Modern Corporation*, and subsequent developments have reinforced those tendencies.

One of the most frequently cited trends in the Managerial revolution is the diffusion of stock ownership. The quest for capital makes it necessary to expand the equity base of corporations, thereby diluting the power of the original owner. At the same time, large firms require teams of specialists often geographically dispersed, which necessitates professionalization of management. Another significant factor concerns the ability to retain earnings. The legal authority to determine the flow of revenue which will be returned to stockholders and which will be diverted to finance expansion or to other purposes enormously enhances management control and power. Moreover, the general influence of stockholders is further reduced through alternative financial arrangements. Bonds, for instance, issued in cooperation with large investment houses, provide an alternative to seeking funds for expansion through stock offerings.[54] The interest and principal can then be paid from future retained earnings. Tax law changes allowing interest on loans to be deducted offers another enticement to avoid stock issues. At the same time, the development of increasingly flexible general incorporation creates a situation in which a corporation is free to move into any lawful areas of business, in virtually any geographical location, with little restraint on capitalization or debt structure, and with few structural requirements. The courts generally support management in stockholder suits. Following the "business necessity rule," the judgment of the courts will rarely be substituted for the judgment of management except in those cases in which management is clearly abusing the rights of stockholders. And the boards of directors become irrelevant. Orthodox wisdom reinforces the notion by characterizing management as in control of the board of directors as well, through control of the proxy machinery, withholding or selective release of information, and informal and unspoken arrangements with board members concerning their role. If this scenario is reasonably accurate, then management performs the functions traditionally residing in the board.

The sheer size of the modern corporation ensured the power of management. Even with a good deal of information it would be impossible for most stockholders (even owners) to understand complex corporate operations and maneuvers, and management is required to provide little. Communication among widely dispersed stockholders is difficult and expensive. Often, it is impossible to acquire a list of the names of other stockholders. For these and other reasons, a strong case could be made for the divorce between management and stockholders.

The thesis of the Managerial revolution must not be confused with two other, entirely distinct theses. Following the lead of Berle and Means, Micro-Managerialists have taken the divorce of control and ownership to support a much more controversial idea, that of the thesis of "managerial discretion." Micro-Managerialists assert, often only implicitly, that managers, no longer controlled by stockholders, are now free to make decisions with few constraints. The claim is that there is a wide area of discretion within which managers may exercise judgment. Whether there are other constraints which significantly restrict the latitude of managerial decision making is an extremely important question and one to which we must return later. For the most part, however, Micro-Managerialists merely *assume* the truth of the discretionary thesis without argument and focus instead upon the issue of how the discretionary power should be wielded. The ominous questions which this thesis raises are generally ignored. If management is insulated from the traditional control by stockholders, for example, and if there are few, if any, new constraints on managerial discretion, toward what end will the new power be directed? How will the enormous resources of the corporation be employed?

Berle and Means do address the question, at least briefly, and sketch three possible answers.[55] Managers could continue to function as something like trustees for stockholders, regarding the interests of shareholders as primary, even though stockholders are relatively powerless to directly discipline untoward management behavior. Call this the thesis of "managerial trusteeship."[56] Or, managers might take the opportunity to plunder the resources of the firm, utilizing the corporate form to exploit other constituencies. Many, especially those inclined to favor corporate takeovers, assume that this has taken place. Some have referred to this thesis as the "managerial entrenchment" thesis, suggesting that management is entrenched behind layers of protective devices which serve to consolidate power further and to ward off endeavors at discipline or restructuring. Finally, management could choose to use the freedom, not narrowly for their own or for stockholder's interests, but for the interest of society as a whole. This third alternative can be referred to as the thesis of "social responsibility" or the thesis of "managerial professionalism."

Berle and Means reject the first two alternatives, virtually without argument, and claim that as the modern corporation becomes the dominant organizational form, management will increasingly act in light of the best interests of society. Managerial decisions were, they claim, "increasingly assuming the aspect of economic statesmanship." Here, then, lies the incipient notion of social responsibility. Managers are viewed as statesmen or stateswomen, new professionals. Like other professionals they are believed to have a social responsibility. The notion that a component of professionalism is a duty to society has become a commonplace. Labor law makes it one of the criteria of a profession.

In this way, *The Modern Corporation* sets the stage for subsequent Managerial analyses. Micro-Managerialists rarely venture beyond the theses developed there. The truth of the thesis of managerial discretion is quietly assumed and the thesis of social responsibility highlighted.

It is important, however, to recognize that there are two very different theses being asserted as the thesis of social responsibility or managerial professionalism. On the one hand, the thesis can be interpreted as a descriptive or predictive thesis. This is the claim that a big change has taken place, is taking place, or will soon take place, that management values have changed, and that the modern corporation is acting in a socially responsible fashion. This is an empirical thesis and as such should be evaluated in light of relevant evidence. On the other hand, the thesis can be interpreted as a prescriptive or normative thesis about the way corporate managers/corporations *ought* to act. Similarly, the theses of managerial trusteeship and managerial entrenchment interpreted descriptively, as claims about what has occurred, is occurring, or will occur, must be carefully distinguished from prescriptive theses about what ought to happen. It is quite possible, for instance, that one might argue that what has in fact happened is captured in the thesis of managerial entrenchment, but that what ought to happen is represented in the social responsibility thesis or in the managerial trusteeship thesis.

Evaluation of these theses, whether interpreted descriptively or prescriptively, is extremely difficult given the vagueness of the notion of social responsibility or professionalism. Until some degree of precision is reached, it is unclear how to test the empirical claim. If one wishes to assert that managers are increasingly acting as professionals, in socially responsible ways, one must have a definition crafted with sufficient care to allow empirical investigation. Moreover, without precision about what counts as social responsibility, no argument can be constructed because it is not clear what conclusion is to be defended. Unfortunately, as the next section illustrates, since Berle and Means there has been little movement to refine further the significance of the thesis.

MANAGERIAL PROFESSIONALISM

If the theses of the Managerial revolution and managerial discretion are true, the modern world is haunted by the specter of a managerial class in possession of awesome economic and social power. Toward what end will the discretionary power be used? In spite of the threatening nature of this scenario, Managerialists portray the revolution as a godsend. Liberated from the narrow-minded constraints of stockholders seeking only profit, management is pictured as free to act in a socially responsible way. In this way, the problem is framed as how to instill in management the correct values. That the real problem might well be the existence of managerial power and discretion is conveniently ignored. The ideology of professionalism, which continues to be quietly invoked, can serve to dissuade these fears. "Professional" managers have the knowledge, skill, and integrity to use their power for the welfare of all.

The problem, however, is that the claims concerning social responsibility and professionalism are largely vacuous. Although the Managerialists apparently reject the single simple principle of profit maximization, nothing substantial is ever proposed as a substitute.[57] No criteria by which to make a decision are ever developed. Appeal to the ideology of professionalism thus apparently functions in an attempt to defuse the obvious lack of precision in stating what it means to act in a socially responsible way, in stating how conflicting interests are to be resolved to bring about what is best. Professionals, it can be claimed, must use independent judgment in each case to determine what is required. The disingenuousness of this response is transparent. Reference to the "professional manager" cannot conceal the absence of any concrete guidance.

The vagueness of the claims can be no better illustrated than by examining the texts used to train professionals. Management courses, especially Business and Society courses, should be crucial as a way of integrating the diverse components of the knowledge base and then applying the knowledge to concrete decisions in order to arrive at a "professional" judgment, prescribing what the corporation ought to do in order to act responsibly. Business and Society texts offer the promise of "tools" for making these difficult and complex decisions. Texts routinely discuss the tools of stakeholder analysis, ethical analysis, and something like a social audit or the social assessment system. However, the relationship between these three analytical tools is never clarified, and none offers specific guidance about how diverse factors should be weighed and integrated to make a decision.

Consider the social assessment system touted as a managerial tool for implementing social responsibility. Until recently these systems were described as "social audits," since they bear some similarity to financial audits.[58] Currently, many believe the disanalogies with a financial audit outweigh the analogies and seek, therefore, to avoid connoting commensurable quantitative measures which can be summed to yield a bottom line in the area of social assessments.[59] Consequently, the preferred language is of "social assessment." A social assessment system offers a structured approach for considering social impacts. The SAS identifies and classifies major social issues which are likely to be of concern to the firm. Those about which the firm can do nothing are ignored—perhaps crime, innercity schools, or trade deficits. From the issues over which the firm can have some control, the firm must identify the ones most likely to arise as significant issues.

General Electric created the Public Issues Committee of the Board in the late 1960s to engage in this kind of forecasting. Other corporations depend upon outside specialists for information gleaned from polls and social trends. These issues are then classified. In *Business And Society: A Managerial Approach*,[60] for example, Frederick D. Sturdivant classifies these into minority group issues (hiring, job training, promotion, etc.), employee-related activities (benefits, equal opportunity in promotion, job safety, etc.), aid to higher education, consumerism issues, political issues, and so forth. According to Sturdivant, all issues can be satisfactorily brought into five categories: human investment; ecology; consumer welfare; openness of the system; and responsiveness to social issues. In the first are the issues of job enrichment, discrimination, job training, benefits, working conditions (including safety), unionization, and so forth. Those issues to be included in the second and third are fairly evident. The "openness of the system" includes questions of communication internally and with outside groups, participation in the decision-making process, due process, etc. The final category, to some extent a miscellaneous one, includes traditional philanthropic items or nontraditional ones.

With this classification system, a spreadsheet can be formulated. A matrix is constructed with the interests of different constituencies (different "stakeholders," in the new jargon), represented in columns, and the different issues, represented in rows. The social assessment system next requires developing some way of *measuring corporate performance* in each box of the matrix. In some areas, actual measurements are not difficult. It is not difficult, for instance, to achieve measures of lost days, injuries, and so forth for employees. In others, measures would be more evasive. Having developed measures, the next step is to *evaluate performance*. Here, standards or norms must be found. One indicator may well be industry standards; in other areas, standards may be legally mandated. Given this array of measures, the professional manager is then instructed to develop a plan. The plan identifies deficiencies or excesses. For instance, health benefits may be far above industry standards but working conditions rated very low. Affirmative action figures may look very poor but the corporation may be expending funds in the area of community development. That expenditures are above or below the standards is not itself reason for change. The one exception is legally mandated norms. Managerialists tend to claim that for socially responsible corporations following the law is not sufficient. In all other areas, however, the manager observes where expenditures are above or below the chosen standards, and then makes a determination concerning how to act responsibly. That is, the professional manager is to reach a *professional judgment* of the socially responsible course of action. This judgment is a plan for action. The gathering of data in the SAS is apparently akin to a physician accumulating data in order to make a diagnosis. The diagnosis for the manager may be that insufficient resources are being expended in the area of affirmative action, or resource conservation, etc. Admittedly, it is virtually impossible to exceed the norms in all categories. Thus, hard decisions of resource allocation must be made. Finally, of course, the hard decisions which constitute a plan must be *implemented*. The plan for social responsibility must be actualized.

Nowhere in the social assessment system is there any guidance provided for diagnosis or prescription. Any analogy with the medical professional is remote. When a physician monitors a patient, there are often very clear norms which are relevant. Blood pressure, pulse, respiration rate, involuntary responses, presence of certain substances in the blood or urine, and so forth, are all judged against fairly well-defined standards based on normal human characteristics. In the social assessment system, the standards amount to little more than what the law requires or what others are doing in the industry. Further, diagnoses and appropriate prescriptions often follow routinely from data collection; heart attack is signaled by a number of symptoms, and the profession establishes a recommended course of treatment. The course of treatment is usually stated in great detail, and physicians deviating from protocols are liable for malpractice. The social assessment system offers no diagnoses or appropriate prescriptions based on data collection. Is obeying environmental law like having a patient's blood pressure within normal limits? No answer is ever provided. Would exceeding legal requirements be socially responsible if it came at the expense of increasing efforts in affirmative action? There are no criteria for diagnosis or prescription.

Sturdivant's text also reflects the broader problems in Business and Society texts, i.e., the unspecified nature of the relationship of the social assessment system with other tools such as stakeholder analysis and ethical analysis. Stakeholder analysis is introduced at the very beginning of the text. The idea here is that stakeholders should be identified in order to understand where the constituencies are "coming from."[61] This identification appears to be nothing more than the kind of identification proposed in the social assessment system. How the manager should use that information is no more clear in the discussion of the stakeholder analysis than in the discussion of the social assessment system. And how are the assessment and the stakeholder analysis related to ethical analysis? In a later chapter on ethics, there is a brief discussion of substantive ethical standards which should be employed, but the discussion runs at such a level of generality as to be entirely unhelpful in making any difficult decision. Further, there is no explicit attempt to integrate any of these three approaches. Is the ethical analysis relevant to the stakeholder analysis? If so, how? Is ethical analysis to be involved in the Social Assessment System? If so, how? Are these three merely different names for the same kind of analysis? Is stakeholder analysis merely ethical analysis? Not everyone would agree. An article in *Academy of Management Executive* titled "Strategies for Assessing and Managing Organizational Stakeholders"[62] proposes an analysis which is tantamount to identifying stakeholders for the purpose of encouraging friends and disarming or harming enemies.

These same difficulties are evident in other texts. In the first chapter of *Business and Society: Corporate Strategy, Public Policy, Ethics*, for example, William Frederick, Keith Davis, and James E. Post identify six challenges which confront modern business: the need to achieve ecological balance; the human element in work; improving economic and social productivity; global pressures, demands, and needs; balancing ethics and economics in business decision making; and helping design social partnerships for resolving society's major problems.[63] But how should the "balancing" of ethics and economic issues be done? Moreover, is ethics relevant to the discussion of the ecological balance? Is it relevant to the task of improving economic and social productivity?

In a chapter on social responsibility, Frederick, Davis, and Post present both sides, then attempt to give the appearance of not taking sides by presenting an "analytical approach" to corporate responsibility. What this amounts to is unclear. They claim that managers should make a "*balanced judgment* about the company's social involvement based on" an understanding of the strengths and weaknesses of each perspective.[64] But what is to be balanced? In the very next chapter, there is a presentation of an "analytical approach to ethical problems." Managers are instructed to consider three questions: First, what is the utility of possible actions, the costs, and benefits for all? Second,

Are human rights being respected? Third, Is there justice, a fair distribution of costs and benefits? The analytical framework suggests that if the answers to all three questions is Yes—that is, if utility is promoted, if rights are respected, and if the distribution of benefits and burdens is just—then a proposed action is morally permissible. If, on the other hand, the answer to each is No, then the proposed action is probably wrong. If there are conflicting answers, careful weighing and balancing is urged.

But how is this "analytical approach to ethical problems" related to the "analytic approach to corporate responsibility"? At least in the former there is the semblance of a decision rule. But is the ethical analysis to be used in deciding whether a firm has a social responsibility? Is a social responsibility some kind of a responsibility distinct from a legal or a moral responsibility?

To complicate matters even further, Frederick, Davis, and Post later turn to discuss strategic management and social assessment systems, to discuss the implementation of social responsibility. None of the issues are further clarified. Nor do the authors address the relationship of the social assessment system to the analytical approach to social responsibility, or the analytical approach to ethical problems.[65]

What of criteria by which to determine whether a corporation has acted responsibly? In medicine an important test in determining whether a physician acted in a professionally responsible manner in applying the general body of knowledge is whether a patient is returned to health, or whether the patient returns to health as quickly as those treated by other suitably trained professionals. What is the test for the professional manager? Will the test for the professional manager be a healthy firm? This is no help because there is no way to measure a healthy firm, unless by a healthy firm one means an economically profitable one.[66] Yet this standard is usually rejected as one by which to guide action, and it would be odd to introduce it as a measure of successful action. Short of some test like that, there is no standard against which to judge the effectiveness of the socially responsible manager.

Although Managerialists never explicitly adopt economic profitability as a standard for measuring the health of a firm, at times their position appears to come close to that. Surfacing again is the optimistic assumption that social responsibility pays. As Sturdivant boldly puts it in the opening paragraph of his text, "It is a fundamental premise of this book that corporate social responsiveness is not at the expense of the firm's profit objective, but rather that responsiveness enhances the company's long-run economic performance."[67] The world is far from a zero-sum game in this view. By doing what is socially responsible, the manager does what is best for all, and that appears to be interpreted as being best for each constituency. Apparently, by doing what is best for all, labor will not profit at the expense of stockholders, nor vice versa. But how is this win-win situation possible? What is the nature of the "system" of which the corporation is a part which makes this possible?

Finally, it should be noted that the vagueness of the Micro-Managerial position is no less apparent in the discussions of personal values of managers. An important component of the professional, according to the ideology of professionalism, is the integrity of the professional. Hence, Managerialists stress the important role played by the personal values of top management in determining corporate decisions directly, and indirectly through the influence of the values and behavior of subordinates, and exhort managers to cultivate values which yield socially beneficial consequences. The emphasis upon the social assessment system presupposes not only the discretionary ability to make the necessary judgments and implement strategies consistent with the decision, but that within this discretionary ability, the key determinant will be managerial values. Moreover, perhaps understating other key factors, the role of top-level management in determining subordinate values is stressed. Citing a couple of studies, Frederick, Davis and Post,[68] for instance, claim that

> research findings show that values and attitudes of managers are a critical factor in an organization's ethical performance. Giving strong ethical leadership and setting a high ethical tone through the example of their own behavior are essential steps for an organization's managers, especially top-level executives whose visibility and influence are the greatest. (57)

Given the critical role which personal values are alleged to play, Managerialists are conspicuously silent on precisely which values should be cultivated. Discussions repeatedly collapse into the stakeholder model, and managers are encouraged to balance wisely the interests involved, to find a "satisfactory," an "optimal," or a "socially responsible" solution. What such a solution would look like is never clear. Merely asserting that the modern corporation is involved with many stakeholders and claiming that responsibilities arise from these relationships does little to specify the content, scope, or force of the responsibilities.

Philosophers interested in the topic of business ethics have attempted to overcome the vacuousness by identifying the alleged grounds of the responsibilities more clearly (e.g., which arguments, if any, support the view that being an employee entails rights beyond those specified in contracts or termination at will) and by fleshing out the alleged content and scope of the responsibilities in more detail. In so doing, such philosophical analyses generally presume with the Managerialists the theses of the managerial revolution and managerial discretion, passing over the ticklish empirical questions of whether the theses are accurate and the tough normative questions of whether managerial discretion is desirable. To these we now turn.

8

Evaluating Micro-Managerialism

Both of the core theses of Micro-Managerialism, the descriptive and prescriptive theses of social responsibility, are associated with the theme of the "big change." According to the first, business, especially the large modern corporation, has entered into a "new era" in which the ethically responsible behavior of contemporary corporations stands in sharp contrast to the earlier days. According to the second, business, especially the large modern corporation, should act in a socially responsible way. This chapter is devoted to an evaluation of these two theses.

Lacking a clear notion of what will count as socially responsible behavior, assessing either thesis presents a formidable challenge. Nonetheless, there is some evidence which bears upon the thesis interpreted descriptively, and in the first section, that evidence will be considered. The remainder of the chapter will address the prescriptive thesis of social responsibility.

DESCRIPTIVE THESIS OF SOCIAL RESPONSIBILITY

Edward S. Herman's *Corporate Control, Corporate Power*[1] is devoted largely to an analysis and empirical investigation of the theses expounded by Berle and Means, including the descriptive thesis of social responsibility. A critical issue is the thesis of managerial discretion. As we have seen, Berle and Means suggest that because of the Managerial revolution, management is relatively free to act, but their analysis tends to ignore other strong incentives which may narrow the scope of discretion. Hence, in separate chapters, Herman tests

179

various hypotheses relating to the extent to which corporate behavior can be explained as the consequence of control by the boards of directors, interlocking directorates, financial institutions, or managers with increasingly strong incentives to profit maximize because of stock option plans, or stock ownership, and so forth.

In a final chapter, Herman turns more directly to the corporate responsibility debate and examines the "record." If the idea of the Managerial revolution is correct, if managers of the large, modern, managerial corporations have wide discretionary ability, and if the professionalization of management is producing socially responsible behavior, then one would expect to find significant behavioral differences between the large modern managerial corporations and "entrepreneurial" firms in which managers are owners. The large modern corporations should be expected to reflect the public spiritedness predicted by Berle and Means and applauded by the Managerialists. One might also expect very large modern firms to behave more responsibly than smaller modern firms, given the greater insulation from stockholder control and greater resources with which to "do good." The evidence gathered by Herman, however, speaks against the idea that we have entered into the new age of social responsibility.

Although it is impossible to get information on corporate charitable contributions broken down by firm type (i.e., owner or nonowner controlled), Herman notes that contributions decline as a percentage of profits as company size increases.[2] Further, tax laws allow a deduction for charitable contributions of up to 5 percent of taxable income. Since 1944, however, contributions have remained dramatically below 5 percent, hovering around 1 percent.[3] Corporations are not acting increasingly to meet social needs through charitable giving, as one would have expected. Larger corporations do not seem to demonstrate greater conscience measured in this way than smaller ones.

Corporate contributions account for only a small fraction of total charitable monetary contributions in this country. Measured in constant 1990 dollars, in 1960, corporations and foundation contributions accounted for only $6 billion of the total $54 billion in monetary donations. By 1990, of the $123 billion total monetary donations, all but $13 billion came from individuals.[4] Real monetary donations per capita increased from $298 billion in 1960 to $493 billion in 1990, an increase of over 65 percent, although, as a percentage of GNP, this is a decline from 2.2 percent in 1960 to 2.0 percent in 1990.[5] During the same period of time, corporate and foundation giving increased only

46 percent, nearly 20 percent less than individual giving. Somewhere between 54 percent and 65 percent of the total giving is to religious institutions, suggesting that individuals are not inclined to give to the needy either, except that some of the money given to religious institutions will make its way to programs for the needy.

In *The Work of Nations: Preparing Ourselves for 21st Century Capitalism*,[6] Robert B. Reich makes an important point about giving. By far the great bulk of the contributions of the very wealthy does not go toward providing for what most would consider to be great social needs, but to those educational and cultural institutions which support the better-off members of society.[7] Contributions are primarily to symphony orchestras, art museums, and private universities and colleges which are already well endowed. At the same time, large corporations are often among the most vociferous proponents of reducing taxes, individual income taxes, corporate taxes, and sales taxes, at every level. These cutbacks have resulted in increasingly tight budgets for both higher education and education at the K–12 levels. Reich notes that the corporate share of local property tax revenues, a key revenue source for K–12 in most states, dropped from 45 percent in 1957 to around 16 percent in 1987. Public universities have also felt the squeeze from state revenues. In public, four-year institutions, for example, tuition rates have been skyrocketing since 1975. This increase is not the result of increasingly higher wages to faculty, energy costs, or capital expenditures. Instructional costs per student have remained relatively stable in constant dollars, while the increase has gone to make up for the revenues which are no longer being provided for by the state. In short, the cost of public higher education has remained relatively constant, but the proportion of the cost paid by the students has increased dramatically.

What about concerns with externalities such as plant relocation and the impact on local communities? Are large managerial firms more sensitive than others? Herman indicates that while "solid evidence on shutdown rates by firm size and ownership characteristics is scarce," one of the few studies, by Barry Bluestone and Bennett Harrison, shows a higher rate of shutdowns by conglomerates than either independent or other corporate owners in New England.[8] Blueston and Harrison also have evidence showing that the rate of shutdown in the South was higher than in any other part of the country.[9] Herman concludes that while this evidence is far from conclusive, it "suggests that large managerial corporations may be taking advantage of their greater flexibility to abandon local communities and workers more readily than small, local enterprises."[10]

In the area of pollution control the story is dismal. To quote Herman, writing in the beginning of the 1980s:

> The responses of large managerial firms in the last decade to appeals and pressures in the area of pollution control have been profit-protective and have not displayed greater than average concern with non-industry (larger community) values. U.S. Steel was described by the deputy administrator of the Environmental Protection Agency (EPA) in 1976 as having "compiled a record of environmental recalcitrance second to none," and other major managerial firms in the steel business also have struggled furiously against environmental controls. General Motors and Union Carbide, leading managerial firms in the automobile and chemical industries, have both been singled out for criticism of their undistinguished performance on environmental issues, and another sizable managerial firm, Hooker Chemical Company, a subsidiary of Occidental Petroleum, has been the subject of exceptional publicity for its role in the contamination of Love Canal and its extensive and sometimes illegal dumping of toxic chemical wastes elsewhere. In the paper and pulp industry a Council on Economic Priorities study of 1970–71 showed the two leading firms in the industry, International Paper and Crown Zellerbach, both managerial, as being uncooperative in providing data and having undistinguished performance records in pollution control. The two companies that were praised for leadership and innovation in pollution control were Weyerhaeuser and Owens-Illinois, the former still owner-controlled, the latter long dominated by the Levis family and probably owner controlled well into the 1960s, when the basic plant designs and control policies were established. The poorest performers, as rated by the council, were St. Regis, Potlatch, and Diamond International, three managerial firms. (261–262)

Much the same can be said in the areas of occupational health and safety, where the scandals of recent times seem to be evenly distributed between owner-dominated and managerial firms. There also seems to be little difference between owner-dominated and managerial firms in a willingness to sacrifice sales and profits for the sake of consumer health and safety.[11]

Whatever else one means by corporate responsibility, it probably means acting within the law. What then of corporate illegality? Dan R. Dalton and Idalene F. Kesner recently examined the relationship between illegal activity and firm size (total sales) among the corporations which appeared on the *Fortune 500* list continuously from 1980–1984 (384 firms).[12] To determine illegality, Dalton and Idalene reviewed *Trade Cases*, a source for consent and litigation decrees relating to violations which were entered in United States federal and state courts, from 1980–1984, of antitrust laws and of the Federal Trade Commission Act. The authors chose as the dependent variable the total number of instances in which firms were "found guilty in litigated cases, were parties to consent decrees, or involved in cases in which the court found substantial merit to the charges against the cited firms."[13] Litigation included price discrimination, tying arrangements, refusal to deal, exclusive dealing, franchise violation, price fixing, foreclosure of entry, reciprocity, allocation of markets, monopoly, conspiracy, and illegal mergers and acquisitions. In this period, 334 violations were reported. This source is by no means exhaustive; it is estimated that the corporate violations recorded in *Trade Cases* constitute only 40 percent of the violations of criminal statutes in the federal courts. There is no estimate of percentage of violations included from state courts. Thus, while the violations used in the study are a substantial proportion of the total, they likely represent less than half. Over 25 percent of the firms were cited at least once.

Two hypotheses were tested in an attempt to determine the relationship, if any, between firm size and illegality. When the corporations were divided into two groups, larger and smaller, the incidence of illegal acts among the larger corporations was twice that of the smaller. When the corporations were trichotomized into small, medium, and large (there were equal numbers in each), a robust relationship was suggested. The larger corporations (top one-third) were three times as likely to engage in illegal behavior as the smaller (bottom one-third). The authors were also interested in the possible relationship between size and recidivism. Of the 25 percent of the firms which were cited for illegal acts over the five-year period, 11.5 percent committed a single illegal act, but 13.9 percent committed multiple acts. Large firms were three times more likely to commit multiple violations than the smaller firms on the list.

As the authors suggest, the significance of the study is far from clear. There are those who argue that one should expect larger corporations to be subject to more legal actions, because of greater productive activity and resultant increase in legal exposure. Moreover, larger corporations tend to have more stockholders and are thus more likely to get involved in more stockholder suits. On the other hand, there are those who suggest that large size may well provide some immunity from legal sanctions. One factor may be the favorable treatment large corporations may receive from regulators, upon whom the regulators rely for much critical information. Theories of agencies being entrapped by the industries they are supposed to regulate also suggest favorable treatment.

In any case, the study does constitute some evidence which speaks against the notion that large, modern firms act more responsibly than smaller firms, even though the study is restricted to *Fortune 500* firms. Given the resources available, the insulation from stockholder pressures (which is alleged by the thesis of the Managerial revolution), and the assumption that the large firms are run by enlightened professional managers, one would expect the largest of the large firms to embody best the new commitment to corporate responsibility. There is little evidence that this is occurring.

As Herman indicates, Berle and Means believed the creation of a corporate conscience in the modern, managerial firm was to arise, not merely from the enlightened professionals, but also from external pressures from government, especially threat of governmental interference, and from public opinion. Herman notes three major paths through which these kinds of external pressures can be exerted on the corporation. One path involves the "machinery of corporate democracy," attempting to get candidates elected to the boards, organizing other stockholders to vote for items. Another involves organizing outsiders through publicity campaigns, boycotts, and withdrawals of business. Finally, there is the use of lawsuits of different varieties, either against the corporation itself, or against regulatory bodies in an attempt to move government to take a more active stand.[14] These means are often used together and may be combined with campaigns in the political arena, seeking legislative and regulatory changes. In this connection, Herman reviews a number of specific instances of each. The Nader-affiliated Project on Corporate Responsibility's "Campaign GM" provides an example of an attempt to use the corporate proxy machinery to affect policy and selection of members of the board of directors. The number of public interest groups has risen dramatically, but each remains rather small, poorly staffed, and poorly funded. There is the attempt to reform corporate policies through investor activism, especially with respect to investments in South Africa. The conclusion which suggests itself, however, is that the pressures which can be exerted on any particular large corporation (e.g., Nestlé) or group of corporations is quite minimal, generally sporadic, poorly organized, poorly funded, and short lived. It is difficult to find in these means evidence that pressures are working to generate a corporate conscience in a large number of corporations. Threat of enforcement motivates, little else.

There is also evidence that other factors which might be presumed to shape the corporate conscience are not working, either. What of the influence of the business school curriculum? In *The Social Responsibilities of Business*, Morrell Heald traces the tension, evident from its inception before the turn of the century, in the business curriculum between the narrower practitioner orientation and the broader academic perspective.[15] And courses dealing with "the social setting of business life" were popular and readily available through the 1920s. There was an uneasiness among many, however, that these were having little impact. Four generations later there are lingering doubts. Research methodology in this area is also problematic. How is one to measure "ethical" or "socially responsible" attitudes, judgments, or practices? Nonetheless, some have ventured into this area. Many of the earlier studies attempted to measure the difference in *ethical attitudes*, if any, between students and individuals already at work as business people. For the most part, no difference was detected. Charles S. Goodman and C. Merle Crawford, for example, surveyed fifteen hundred students at twelve colleges and universities in 1974.[16] Responses to a set of questionable marketing practices were compared with the responses of marketing executives. The students were no more critical of "unethical" practices than the executives. Such studies do not in themselves indicate whether the attitudes of students/business people is high or low. There was, and continues to be, a general perception, however, that those attitudes need improvement.

Under the impulse of the Managerial ideology, the accrediting body for business schools (the American Association of Collegiate Schools of Business) has for many years strongly urged a required course in Business and Society. At least a part of the motivation appears to have been a concern with the ethical standards of business, to produce students with a commitment to social responsibility. One recent study by Bette Ann Stead and Janice J. Miller suggests (at best) that students taking Business and Society courses were made more "aware" of social issues.[17] Students were asked to rank (on a scale of 1–5) the importance of ten social issues (e.g., ecology, consumerism, health and safety, international business, South Africa, etc.). The data suggest that students did not reorder their priorities as a result of a Business and Society course. Students did tend to rate some of the issues as more important than they had before taking the course. Unfortunately, the study did not include any items which might have offered an insight into how addressing the social issues might be weighed against profit maximizing or their own career goals.

In another recent study, William R. Wynd and John Mager attempt to determine whether the Business and Society course changes student attitudes.[18] Wynd and Mager employ a technique first developed by John Clark in 1966. Clark was interested in measuring executives' commitment to personal business ethics and the willingness to accept ethical responsibility for the social effects of business decisions. Clark developed eighteen different situations, eleven dealing with personal ethics and seven with commitment to social responsibility. For each situation, the respondent is asked to indicate whether she or he approves, somewhat approves, somewhat disapproves, or disapproves. The instrument was tested for internal consistency and reliability using executives in a training program at UCLA. Wynd and Mager gave the questionnaire to 345 students on the first day of a Business and Society course, and to 205 different students on the final day of class. They conclude that there "is no difference between student's attitudes on ethical/social responsibility issues before and after taking a course in Business and Society"(489). This should hardly come as a surprise. Much of the business school curriculum, at both the undergraduate and graduate level, focuses on the development of relatively narrow technical skills, using techniques designed to demonstrate strategies and tactics for profit maximizing and efficiency.

In sum, the evidence does not suggest that the modern managerial corporation has developed a corp of professional managers committed to social responsibility. While the evidence assembled here may not be taken to have refuted the descriptive thesis of social responsibility, that is not necessary. The burden of proof is upon anyone who wishes to assert the truth of the thesis. The evidence here merely serves as a reminder that there is insufficient evidence to support that claim. Hence, the claim is unwarranted.

MORAL ARGUMENTS FOR SOCIAL RESPONSIBILITY

Whether or not we have entered into the new era of corporate social responsibility is largely, although not entirely, irrelevant to the question of whether management has a responsibility to act in a socially responsible manner. As I have repeatedly stressed, whether a particular set of values comes to be accepted, or whether a particular pattern of behavior comes to be familiar, does not, in itself, legitimize the values or behavior. Conversely, that the new age of social responsibility has not yet dawned does not necessarily discredit the prescriptive thesis.

Nonetheless, both the descriptive and prescriptive theses are grounded in beliefs about important and dramatic changes in the corporation. If managerial corporations are not, in fact, acting in socially responsible ways, then perhaps the underlying premises are themselves suspect. The descriptive thesis of social responsibility, for instance, is predicted by the claims concerning the Managerial revolution and managerial discretion. This revolution, it is alleged, creates wide discretionary ability for managers. Further, there are incentives for managers to act for the broader social good. Thus, if the predicted behavior is not apparent, then perhaps the Micro-Managerialists have misconstrued the nature of the Managerial revolution. Perhaps managers of the large modern corporations do not, in fact, have the great degree of flexibility to divert corporate resources from fairly short-sighted profit-seeking purposes toward other ends, even longer-term profitability. Although control by owners may have diminished, perhaps Micro-Managerialists are overlooking other incentives equally as strong as that of an owner seeking profits. Moreover, with the unwillingness to address the larger corporate system, Micro-Managerialists are ignoring external factors which might override any other incentives toward social responsibility.

These considerations are relevant to the prescriptive claim as well. The thesis of managerial discretion is the premise upon which much of the Micro-Managerial literature rests, including the voluntaristic strain of the popular literature. Because managers of the modern corporation are alleged to possess the liberty to allocate resources for the social good which do not come into conflict with either their own interests or the interests of major stakeholders, this responsibility is somehow alleged to arise.

That the descriptive thesis appears false raises a difficulty analogous to that posed by the existence of evil for believers in a God who is omnipotent and benevolent. As Epicurus pointed out, thousands of years ago, if there is evil, then God is either not all powerful or not benevolent. A good God would prevent evil if God could, but does not. Therefore either God is not good or not all powerful. Similarly, if the descriptive thesis is false, then either managers have the capability to do good but do not, or they have the desire to act responsibly but cannot. In the concluding section of this chapter, I shall return to the relevance of the thesis of managerial discretion for the prescriptive thesis of social responsibility, and develop this dilemma in greater detail. First, however, it is worthwhile to examine purported arguments in support of the prescriptive thesis. This review will not only reveal the extent to which they rest upon the thesis of managerial discretion, but that even given that crucial assumption, they are weak and amorphous. The arguments rely upon the theses of *The Modern Corporation* and other assumptions, normative and empirical, about the nature of the system within which the corporation exists, but without defending those claims. The weaknesses are especially evident when one remembers that these are attempts to counter the claims within the Classical framework that the sole responsibility of corporations is profit maximization.

Reconstruction and evaluation of these arguments is hindered, as I have already suggested, by two obstacles. First, it is not at all clear what is being asserted. Aside from the rhetoric about acting responsibly, being corporate good citizens, and so forth, it is not clear what is being defended. Second, few arguments are given. The problem is much deeper than the usual one of having enthymemes offered from which complete arguments must be reconstructed. One aspect of this problem is related to the first obstacle. With no clear conclusion being asserted, it is not at all clear what will serve as a relevant premise, making sympathetic reconstruction hazardous. Another, more troublesome feature, is the general hesitancy to venture forth with even a hint of an argument. This is compounded by an apparent confusion between descriptive and prescriptive claims, what philosophers might describe as the naturalistic fallacy.

In any case, a number of arguments or rationales for corporate responsibility can be identified. Nearly all of the arguments in the Micro-Managerial arsenal rely upon claims about the moral significance of the nature of the large, modern corporation. There are few appeals to claims about the larger system. In their form and content, they differ little from those which began appearing in the *Harvard Business Review*, a major forum for the new Managerial philosophy, in 1922. In 1927, dean of the Harvard Graduate School of Business Administration, Wallace B. Donham, argued that the "developing, strengthening, and multiplying of the socially minded business is the central problem of business," and probably of civilization itself. Donham claimed that the "business group, by accident of its position in control of the mechanisms of production, distribution and finance, is in control of the results of science from which most of the discontent arises." The conclusion of the social responsibility of business leadership was "inescapable," he claimed, although he lamented the lack of leaders adequately equipped for the task. But, granting the major claims, from whence does the conclusion derive? From these alleged facts, how does one deduce a conclusion? From what moral principles would this conclusion follow? Donham's argument suffers not merely from obscurity but from a failure to distinguish properties of a collectivity or a system from those of individuals in that collectivity or system. "Business" may control production and distribution, but it does not follow that individuals within that collectivity or system have much control over the actions of the system.[19]

Of the contemporary arguments, the most familiar and most important is the "multiple constituency argument" or the "stakeholder argument."[20] The argument notes that the large, modern corporation involves complicated relationships with a number of different constituencies (stakeholders)—stockholders, potential investors, employees (present, past), potential employees, consumers, suppliers, and the general public, including relevant governmental agencies as well as communities. Beyond this rather innocuous claim, however, it is difficult to discern an argument. From the fact that different interests are involved one would expect reference to another premise, some kind of moral premise, which would license an inference to the conclusion that social responsibility requires taking into consideration the well-being and interests of each constituency (stakeholder group) and "doing the right thing."

One might claim that explicit provision of such a moral premise is unnecessary because what is required is obvious and uncontroversial. After all, the argument requires only the assumption that morality consists in regarding the interests of other humans which are affected by one's actions, especially when these humans are involved in some kind of on-going relationships. But this is not the case. Granting this premise, the argument does not address the very issue which is in dispute. Within the Classical framework, there is no dispute that multiple constituencies are involved in relationships with the corporation. Indeed, agency theorists would define the corporation as a nexus of contractual relations. Nor need there be a dispute with the general idea that morally relevant interests should be accorded consideration in decisions. Certainly the utilitarianism which could be used to defend the Classical framework would agree with this. Natural rights theorists would also concur. Within the Classical framework, for example, relationships with constituents are viewed contractually, consistent with the legal-economic model and the underlying view of the way the overall competitive system functions. In any of the moral defenses of the Classical view, the idea that the interests of affected individuals should be given consideration is also stressed. Autonomy looms large in those views. Corporations, on this view, negotiate contracts and deal with employees as autonomous, mature individuals. Corporations operate within the economic constraints of the market and seek levels of wages and benefits which are as minimal as possible. Employees seek wages and benefits as high as possible. What is fair is the result of the process of negotiation. Relationships with consumers are viewed analogously. In that view, of course, purchase of a commodity is a contract, an exchange. Consumers seek low prices consistent with desired quality; producers seek to achieve highest prices with quality that will be acceptable to consumers. Provided that parties are mature, competent, and noncoerced, the corporation's responsibility is to engage in exchanges with consumers. In the Classical view, treating relevant constituents in this fashion is not immoral; it is respecting the freedom and autonomy of others.

The nature of the hidden moral premise of the stakeholder argument is not obvious and stands in need of development and defense. The key to this argument seems to lie not in the idea that stakeholder interests must be considered, but in the idea that the various constituency interests are to be weighed and balanced, and that the decision will not always be consistent with profit maximization for stockholders. As the Human Resources Network states it, corporate responsibility is the obligation "to balance" the firm's "impact and contribution to its various constituencies: customers, employees, suppliers, shareholders and the larger society."[21] Of course, "balance" is the critical term. Howard Sohn, in "The Corporate Social Responsibility Debate,"[22] puts it this way:

> How a company evaluates and compares the interests and claims of the different constituencies, what constitutes a balance, where priorities lie

given limited resources and capacities—these are the hard questions raised by the constituency approach to corporate responsibility. (141)

Apparently, then, the stakeholder argument is designed to show that this balance should at least sometimes result in decisions which do not maximize profit for stockholders. Managerialists attempt to provide an alternative, but beyond this the nature of the alternative is uncertain. At times, the important distinction appears to be between long-run and short-run profit maximizing. The Classical ideology is taken as advocating only short-run profitability, as opposed to Managerialists who advocate long-run profitability. There is some truth to this. Ideally, Friedman and others would prefer all profits returned quarterly to stockholders. If the stockholders wish to see capital invested in long-term research and development projects, diversification, or expansion, then the corporation can seek to attract new capital through new equity offerings. In this way the market, rather than managers, decides these issues about strategic directions. Managerialists appear to be on the side of those seeking to legitimize the role of managers, not stockholders, in making these decisions. But there are two points to be made about this kind of interpretation. First, there is the presumption that short-run profit-maximization produces morally undesirably outcomes. The ills of society are portrayed as if they are the result of a short-sighted profit-maximizing behavior. Second, if corporate responsibility is identified with long-run profitability, then the argument reduces itself to a tactical debate over the best way to insure long-term profitability. The claim is that by taking into consideration these other interests, and at times giving priority to these other constituencies over short-run profit maximizing for shareholders, profit will be maximized in the long run.

Still other interpretations are possible. Nearly any intermediate text in microeconomic theory will contain a chapter discussing the subject of the goals of the firm.[23] Among the alternatives to profit maximization are the goals of increasing market share, maximizing or increasing revenues, long-term corporate survival, personal enhancement of corporate managers, growth and diversification, and satisficing. If the stakeholder argument merely seeks to make a distinction between profit maximization (even short run) and other goals (including long-run profitability), then which of these goals should be sought? Merely rejecting profit maximization means numerous other goals could be adopted. Moreover, nearly any of these can serve as a tactical device for achieving reasonable or maximal long-run profit. For example, a firm may seek to increase market share during an economic downturn, as the Japanese automotive manufacturers do, as part of strategy to maximize long-term profitability. Or, revenue maximization might serve as the best means for achieving long-run profitability during some periods of time. But is corporate responsibility to be interpreted as a goal distinct from these goals, one which will serve as a means toward long-run profitability? Or, is corporate responsibility a goal distinct not only from these but also from long-run profitability? If the former is the case, corporate responsibility is merely one tactical maneuver among others. Managers could rely upon corporate responsibility during some periods as a means of achieving long-run profitability, and perhaps upon revenue maximization at other times. Short-term profit maximization might also serve as the most desirable tactic for long-term profitability at other times. But if corporate responsibility is a corporate goal distinct from that of long-term profitability, then these other goals might serve as a means to corporate responsibility. For instance, short-term profitability, revenue maximization, diversification, and so forth might each be means for achieving corporate responsibility in different climates.

On either interpretation, without establishing the empirical and moral linkages to support the claim, the stakeholder argument is empty. Consider the first interpretation. This is a very plausible interpretation of the argument, given the long history of the ideas that ethics is good business. But if corporate responsibility is defended as a strategy to insure long-run profitability, that defense needs to be explained. Slogans are no substitute for analysis. By what mechanism will corporate responsibility provide the conditions to insure long-run profitability? Because the Micro-Managerial argument is developed in absence of any discussion of the system within which the corporation functions, it is impossible to evaluate whether such a claim is credible. To evaluate the claim that by increasing market share a corporation would in the long-run maximize profit would be evaluated in light of the prevailing industry conditions and relative strengths and weaknesses of the corporation. Evaluating this claim would require an analogous, although more complicated, investigation. None is offered. More importantly, even if one could establish that adopting the tactic of corporate responsibility would insure long-run profitability, *what moral reasons can be offered to legitimize this as a corporate goal?* In the Classical framework, the argument is that profit seeking in a competitive market is morally legitimate because it produces what is best for all. What kind of argument will Managerialists substitute for this?

Micro-Managerialists are in a difficult situation. If they rely upon competitive market arguments to establish the mechanism according to which corporate responsibility produces what is best for all, those arguments assume self-interested behavior, not corporate responsibility, and run the risk of collapsing into Friedman's argument. Yet, without relying upon competitive market arguments, Managerialists have no convenient means by which to express the connection.

Consider, on the other hand, the possibility that corporate responsibility is interpreted as a goal distinct, not only from these other goals, but also from long-run profitability as well. One implication is that corporate responsibility might entail that one adopt any of these other goals for tactical purposes, depending upon the conditions. In some circumstances, short-term profit maximization might even produce what is most responsible. The same problems, however, confront this interpretation as the former. What are the empirical and moral linkages involved? Assuming that one could operationalize the notion of corporate responsibility, what is the mechanism by which one determines whether these tactics will produce that goal? To answer that, the argument requires examination of the system within which the claims are made. More importantly, by what means is the goal of corporate responsibility morally justified? Is the argument going to be that corporate responsibility produces what is best for all? How will that happen? Again, in the Classical framework, self-interest regulated by competition allegedly assures the social good. By what means do Managerialists believe this will occur?

Hence, the stakeholder argument is, in reality, no argument at all. The argument assumes what needs to be shown, namely, that corporations have a moral obligation to act according to corporate responsibility (however it is interpreted). One other feature of the alleged argument is noteworthy. The argument also assumes the thesis of managerial discretion. Within the Classical model, decisions which deviate from profit maximization will result in elimination of the firm in the competitive market. The assumption here is that managers have a choice to make, and that the wise, professional manager opts for corporate responsibility, for balancing the interest of stakeholders to "optimize" results.

The comments concerning the stakeholder argument are pertinent to all of the other familiar Micro-Managerial arguments. These arguments fail to explain clearly the meaning of corporate responsibility, but they appear to disagree with profit maximization (or at least with short-run profit maximization). They apparently assume that profit maximizing will not always yield socially desirable/morally acceptable results. They assume a robust degree of managerial discretion, an assumption which also conflicts with the claims of the Classical model.

Consider, for example, another "argument," the "public character of corporations argument" or the "social effects argument." This argument involves the claim that the effects of the decisions of the large modern corporation are so far reaching that one cannot pretend that the effects are merely economic. Neil Chamberlain writes that "the corporation has become, by virtue of its size and scope, more of a public institution than a private one."[24] A similar point is made by James W. Kuhn and Ivar Berg in *Values in a Business Society*:[25]

> Corporate influence spreads far afield; a decision that a board of directors imagines to be of concern only to those in the company may have repercussions in the highest councils of government as well as in the homes of ordinary citizens. (60)

Here, again, the thesis of managerial discretion is assumed, without comment. The assumption is that managers can choose whether to adopt the policy of social responsibility.[26] Further, even if one accepts either or both of these claims as a premise in an argument, the conclusion of which is that corporations ought to act in socially responsible ways, how one would fill in the gap with other premises, moral or empirical, to support that claim remains shrouded in mystery. What is it about the alleged public character of corporations, or about the social effects, which supports a claim about social responsibility? The argument is so vaguely sketched that it might provide ammunition for reaching far different conclusions. If corporations have the character of public institutions, then the conclusion which would seem to follow, as Friedman suggests, is that the public ought to elect the corporate representatives. This point will be developed below. Or, if corporations have serious social impacts, then social control might follow, not corporate responsibility.

Another closely related rationale is the "corporate power argument." This argument posits enormous resources at the disposal of corporations and identifies this with power. Given this power, the argument goes, corporations should act responsibly. This argument, like the earlier one, might be described as the Lilliputian argument: Corporations are giant persons. When giant persons move they have a responsibility to watch out for the little people. This argument is nothing more than a restatement of the public character of corporations argument or the social effects argument. Like those it assumes what should be established. Namely, the assumption is that responsible use of this power involves something other than profit maximization. It does not provide reasons to support this claim. And, like the other arguments, it assumes the thesis of managerial discretion, i.e., that when the corporate giants move, they have a great deal of latitude.

The literature is peppered with other assertions masquerading as arguments. The "corporate citizenship argument" posits an analogy between a natural citizen and the corporation. Just as the natural citizen has certain rights, duties, and responsibilities, so also, the analogy goes, does the corporate citizen. The strength of the argument depends upon what one assumes the rights, duties, and responsibilities of a natural citizen to be. As such, the argument is extremely weak because the least controversial list of rights, duties, and responsibilities would be very short. In fact, the list is probably consistent with the view that citizens may permissibly seek only their own interest provided they follow the law and perform other civic duties. Those other duties might include nothing much more than becoming informed about issues, engaging in debate with others, and voting. If a corporation acted analogously, it would be a good citizen, provided only that it profit maximized within the law. A slightly more stringent version of this argument might suppose that citizens are required to sacrifice something of self-interest in order to contribute to the social good. Perhaps this means nothing more than making some tax-deductible contributions. If so, corporate good citizenship requires little more than some philanthropic efforts. Still, the analogy with the citizen ignores the interesting issue. Is it in the best interests of society if corporations deviate from strategies which would maximize profit for stockholders? What arguments can be offered in support of this claim? A strong version of the thesis of managerial discretion is again assumed.

There is, in addition, a potentially insidious dimension to the analogy. In the eyes of the law, corporations are artificial persons. As artificial persons they neither enjoy all the rights and privileges of natural persons who are citizens, nor are they subject to all the duties and responsibilities. Corporations can hold property, enter into contracts, sue, and be sued in civil cases and in some criminal cases. There are certain punishments which cannot be inflicted upon artificial persons which could be inflicted upon natural persons. Corporations may go bankrupt but they cannot be hung by the neck until dead, electrocuted, or even incarcerated, and to date they are denied the right to vote in local, state, or federal elections. The inclusion of the corporation into a law which had evolved to deal primarily with individuals as natural persons has created numerous problems. To quote again the early English jurist who declared in frustration, "A corporation has no soul to damn, no pants to kick, and by God it ought to have both." Serious constitutional questions concern the extent to which corporate persons enjoy protections under the constitution. Over the past hundred years, corporations have increasingly come to enjoy protection of some constitutional rights. Although corporations have no Fifth Amendment privileges, they do enjoy Fourteenth Amendment protections. Recent decisions also suggest that corporations have First Amendment rights to free speech. But, should corporations enjoy First Amendment protections of freedom of religion? Do corporations have the right not to be discriminated against on the basis of race, sex, creed, or national origin? While this may sound preposterous, some cases have arisen in which corporations have sought damages for discrimination on the basis of race. How these kinds of questions are to be answered is unclear. However, to employ the analogy of the corporate citizen to other citizens is to run the risk of assuming answers to a great number of other issues, none of which is without controversy or without significant political implications for the distribution of political power in our society.

There is one other kind of argument which must be considered. Some philosophers have developed "Moral Personhood Arguments" in an attempt to achieve much the same end. Peter French, for example, has argued that corporations are entities which satisfy the conditions under which it is possible to ascribe moral agency.[27] Quite simply, French believes, corporations can meaningfully be said to act intentionally. A corporation acts intentionally, French claims, when the rules which structure the organization are followed. For instance, if the board of directors votes to empower the CEO to act in a particular way, and the CEO does, then the corporation can be said to have acted intentionally. If corporations are moral agents, then French believes that all the rights, privileges, duties, and responsibilities of full-fledged moral persons should be ascribed to them. In essence, corporations are full-fledged moral persons. French's aim is to demonstrate that corporations have moral responsibilities, and that these responsibilities require that corporations act in a socially responsible way. There are other theorists who claim that although corporations are not moral persons in the same sense as natural persons, there are important relevant similarities between corporate and natural persons, and these similarities are sufficient to establish that the corporation has moral responsibilities.[28]

Whether such arguments succeed in establishing that corporations are in some sense moral agents or moral persons with the attending moral responsibilities is an important theoretical issue. However, even if, for the sake of argument, one were to grant complete moral personhood to a corporation, this does not in itself provide an answer to the question of whether corporations ought to act according to the principle of profit maximization or to act in some way which may require occasional or frequent deviation from profit maximization. For one thing, this argument is completely independent of what morality requires. Classical Liberals who rely upon utilitarianism might accept the argument and then assert that corporations and natural persons should seek to maximize their own good (utility) provided they do no harm to others. And even if one accepted a moral theory in which persons or agents have a number of duties, and maximizing social utility is only a weak one, it might nonetheless be the case that only by profit-maximizing behavior would corporations discharge their responsibility. Even if corporations are moral persons they are a very different kind of moral person and exist in a very different kind of environment. Very likely, the underlying assumption is again that profit-maximizing behavior by corporations will not produce socially desirable outcomes in every case and therefore corporations should deviate from that principle occasionally. Also presumed is the idea that corporate moral agents, like natural moral agents, have the liberty to deviate from that path. Managerial discretion continues to loom large. But is it probable that the system of constraints which describes the milieu in which natural moral agents make decisions is in important respects similar to the milieu in which the large modern corporation operates? What theory of the economic and social system is being assumed?

In short, these arguments are woefully inadequate and generally question begging. However, further refinement would not only disclose the moral assumptions which are presupposed, most of which might likely prove unacceptable, but also demonstrate more clearly the extent of the dependency upon the assumption of managerial descretion and related claims concerning the incentive structure of the corporation and of the larger system. Thus, moral analysis should proceed by examining the underlying descriptive claims involved.

MANAGERIAL DISCRETION

The thesis of managerial discretion is an empirical thesis, a thesis about "the facts," about the world. As such, what is the relationship of this descriptive thesis to moral reasoning about the corporation? Just how important is the truth of the thesis to moral reflection on corporate responsibility?[29]

Philosophers have worried, at least since the time of Hume, about the relationship between the "is" and the "ought," between science and ethics, between the world of facts, as it were, and the world of values. I have been harshly critical of tendencies which appear to confuse reasoning appropriate to the defense of descriptive assertions, and reasoning appropriate to the defense of prescriptive judgments. This is not to suggest, by any stretch of the imagination, that facts, that theories about the world, are irrelevant to our moral judgments, whether practical or theoretical. Consequently, a few words are in order to clarify this relationship.

Amid all the controversy surrounding the thorny issues involved, one consensual principle, an almost Archimedean point, has emerged. This principle, which can be characterized as the "physical possibility principle," asserts that "ought" implies "can." Variously invoked in criticisms or defenses of one or another ethical theory, this principle is widely accepted and should not be exclusively identified as a principle held only by ivory-tower philosophers. Under different guises the principle is reflected in law and our common, folk sense. Application of the principle to the area of the moral responsibilities of corporations suggests the importance of a more serious inquiry into political and economic reality than many involved in the investigation of questions of corporate obligations have hitherto been willing to undertake.

The physical possibility principle was probably utilized by the Epicureans in an attempt to defend the theory of ethical egoism. For the Epicureans, atomism in physics lent support to the theory of psychological hedonism in psychology, the claim that humans seek only pleasure for themselves. The implications for ethical theory were, they believed, obvious and immediate. If humans can do nothing but seek their own pleasure, then by invoking the principle that "ought" implies "can," it should follow that one can have no obligation to do anything other than seek one's own pleasure. One cannot, the physical possibility principle suggests, have an obligation to do what one cannot. Although a defense of ethical egoism, this argument itself does not establish ethical egoism. At best it shows that if humans have any moral obligations at all, these are obligations to seek one's own pleasure; the argument establishes the falsity of alternative theories. To develop an argument for ethical egoism, one further premise is needed, one which many would be willing to grant. Namely, if one grants that humans have obligations, ethical egoism would follow. The beauty of this defense is that it marshals the facts, or at least a theory about the facts of the world, in support of an ethical theory, by appealing to a relatively uncontroversial principle.

Two important responses are possible. One might, with Bishop Butler and others, choose to attack the theory by attacking the description of the facts, attacking psychological hedonism. By demonstrating that an empirical theory, psychological hedonism, is false, a moral defense could be rebutted. The facts are relevant to moral theorizing. An alternative attack involves more risk, relying as it does upon a slightly more controversial principle. One might argue that in order for a human to have an obligation it must not merely be physically possible for an agent to act to discharge the obligation, it must also be possible for the agent not to act. The principle here, call it the "discretionary principle," is that "ought" also implies "cannot," in the sense that an agent has freedom or discretionary power in acting. Thus, one might argue that if psychological hedonism is true, morality as such is impossible, since humans are determined, as it were, to seek their own pleasure—they have no discretionary power, no freedom, to do otherwise. This argument is rhetorically interesting insofar as it attempts to show that the defense of ethical egoism fails even if psychological hedonism is correct.

Much more work is required to distinguish different versions of these two principles. Clearly, there are different senses of "possibility" and "discretion" involved. When we claim that Jones has no obligation to flap her wings and fly because she cannot, for example, we are using a different sense of possibility or impossibility than when we say that Jones cannot have an obligation to help the poor since he is destitute and impoverished himself. Or, suppose Jones, Inc., functions in a competitive industry within which behavior deviating from profit maximization quickly results in the failure of the firm. Does Jones, Inc., have a responsibility to act in any way other than profit maximization? Even in many of these weakened senses, "ought" implies "can."

The physical possibility principle's application to the Classical framework can be illustrated by considering a parallelism with the arguments employed in defense of ethical egoism. If one assumes that the system, as described within that framework (universe of Classical or neo-Classical economics), with the concomitant theory of the firm as a black-box profit maximizing unit, and if one further assumes some version of the physical possibility principle, then it would appear to follow that the *corporation can have no obligations other than to maximize profits.* It cannot have any other obligations because corporations cannot act otherwise (without guaranteeing elimination). Again, this argument does not suffice to establish that a corporation has any obligations whatever; it merely purports to demonstrate that if a corporation has any obligations at all, they would be obligations to maximize profit for itself. The argument would, if successful, show that any claims of the Managerialists are false, since any corporation which sought to do other than to maximize profit would be eliminated by the efficient working of the market. Since it cannot do otherwise, it can have no obligation to do otherwise. If one were willing to grant a further premise, that a corporation does have moral obligations, then it would follow that the sole obligation of the corporation is to maximize profit.

There are a couple of responses open to a Managerial critic here, analogous to those made against ethical egoism. One response actually plays into the hands of those who claim that a corporate behavior is not subject to the canons of morality. Suppose one were to grant the discretionary principle in this case, the idea that ascription of obligations to an agent, say a corporate agent, requires that the agent possess the ability to do otherwise, i.e., that "ought" implies "cannot" as well as "can." If it is impossible for a corporation to exist without maximizing profit, then it has no power of discretion and cannot be said to possess any moral obligations. This is, in my judgment, one of the most interesting arguments of which I am aware that a corporation has no obligations.

There is another response available. One might attack the above defense of corporate egoism as well as the argument for corporate amorality by showing that the corporation can do otherwise. As

Butler attacks psychological hedonism, one might attack the economic models and the associated theory of the firm which support
those conclusions. This, historically, is one of the most important
strategies employed by the Managerialists. Given the intuitive appeal
of the physical possibility principle and the discretionary principle, it
is not surprising to find that Managerialism has fashioned its major
attack along just this line.

At the heart of Micro-Managerialism is the thesis of managerial discretion. In the assault upon the Classical position, Micro-
Managerialists can employ this thesis to undermine the claim that
the corporation can do nothing other than maximize profit for stockholders. Thus, the thesis can serve as a powerful tool against the
Classical view. Alone, however, it does not establish that a corporation has moral obligations. It may establish that the ascription of
moral responsibility is possible.

Aside from simplicity, this analysis of the dispute between the
Classical and Managerial frameworks has the virtue of identifying
the source of one of the major points of contention. At bottom, the
contention is not over moral values or moral principles. Rather, the
dispute rests upon a disagreement over the nature of the firm and
the system within which the firm functions. That dispute, in turn, may
be related to the acceptance or rejection of certain economic models.
Whether the corporation has any moral obligations at all, and, if so,
the extent of those obligations, hinges upon a determination of the
nature of the corporation and the nature of the market of which it
is a part.

It is critical, therefore, that those investigating the question of the
corporate moral obligation do more than blithely accept the thesis of
managerial discretion as a given and begin to assess relevant evidence.
Philosophers in particular cannot plead that such an investigation
is beyond their purview as philosophers. Without some evidence to
support the thesis of managerial discretion, one has no right to build
moral arguments based on that premise.

In this light, I want to develop a line of criticism of Micro-
Managerialism which takes the form of a dilemma. The thesis of
managerial discretion is either true or false. Obviously, there are
degrees of discretion, but the real issue hinges on the assumption
of a very wide range of discretionary ability. Thus, this robust thesis
of managerial discretion is either true or false. I will argue that if the
thesis is true, then this concentration of power is inconsistent with

our deepest shared convictions about a liberal democratic society and is, therefore, illegitimate. On the other hand, if the thesis is false, then management cannot meaningfully be said to have any corporate responsibilities inconsistent with profit maximization.

Consider the first horn of the dilemma. Suppose that corporate managers have great freedom over the dispersal of corporate resources. Would it then follow that we should devote our ethical expertise to the task of determining the responsibilities of the corporate manager? No. By assuming managerial discretion and discussing how managers should use this liberty, Managerialists are also accepting another extraordinary premise. Framing the problem in this fashion assumes the legitimacy of managerial discretion. Yet, if the world is as these Micro-Managerialists assume, that world embodies values which are alien to the mainstream of western liberal democratic thought.

This is the picture of robust managerial discretion as sketched by Berle in *The Twentieth-Century Capitalist Revolution*.[30]

> In practice, . . . corporations are guided by tiny, self-perpetuating oligarchies. These in turn are drawn from and judged by the group opinion of a small fragment of America—its business and financial community. . . . The legal presumption in favor of management, and the unwillingness of the courts to control or reverse management action save in cases of the more elementary types of dishonesty and fraud, leaves management with substantially absolute power. Thus, the only real control which guides or limits their economic and social action is the real, though undefined and tacit, philosophy of the men who compose them. (180)

If this description is an accurate portrayal of reality, as Micro-Managerialists assume, then the solution is not to develop the moral consciousness of the new Mandarins, but to restructure political reality to conform more closely to the representative, democratic, liberal ideals to which the Managerialists claim adherence. Ironically, this description of managerial discretion is not only the one adopted by Micro-Managerialists, but also is the one serving as the major springboard for the most vigorous critics of corporate power and abuse. This is precisely the caricature which generates such works as *Taming the Giant Corporation*, by Ralph Nader, Mark Green, and Joel Seligman.[31] They write that in "nearly every large American business corporation, there exists a management autocracy. One man. . . or a small coterie of men rule the corporation."[32] Or, the "modern corporation is akin to a political state in which all powers are held by a single clique."[33]

The conclusion which these critics draw, namely, that society requires more accountability from these powerful managers, flows much more naturally from the assumption of managerial discretion than claims that the autocrats ought to act in a responsible manner. Framed in this fashion, the solution to having a Czar is not relying upon a moral conversion to insure that the Czar acts responsibly, but in replacing the Czar with a democratic system.

From a much different perspective, but one still resting upon mainstream liberal sentiments, Milton Friedman draws the same conclusion. In "The Social Responsibility of Business Is to Increase Profits,"[34] Friedman argues that if managers have such discretionary power that they are able to raise/lower prices to the customer, for example, in order to act responsibly, or to increase/decrease wages, this is tantamount to taxing various constituencies to promote the common good. His rhetorical excess prompts Friedman to represent this as taxation without representation, a violation of a common shared political principle. Even if one were to deny that this is, strictly speaking, a tax, the point is on the mark. If the Micro-Managerialists are correct, managers of a few hundred enormous companies wield the power to impose substantial benefits and burdens on different sectors of society according to their own fancy. They are unelected. They neither represent nor necessarily reflect the interests of the great majority of individuals or alternative major institutions of the society. In Friedman's words

> We have established elaborate constitutional, parliamentary and judicial provisions to control these [taxing] functions, to assure that taxes are imposed so far as possible in accordance with the preferences and desires of the public. . . . We have a system of checks and balances to separate the legislative function of imposing taxes and enacting expenditures from the executive function of collecting taxes and administering expenditure programs and from the judicial function of mediating disputes and interpreting the law.
>
> Here the [businessperson]—self-selected or appointed directly or indirectly by stockholders—is to be simultaneously legislator, executive and jurist. (123)

Friedman understands that if the sketch of managerial discretion is true, consistent with our political values, we should not be developing "philosopher-kings" as corporate managers whom we can trust to rule over the unenlightened in a socially responsible way, but we should implement radical political changes. If the corporate manager has great discretionary power to "tax" and then spend the proceeds for social purposes, then she becomes

> in effect a public employee, a civil servant, even though [s]he remains in name an employee of a private enterprise. On grounds of political principle, it is intolerable that such civil servants—insofar as their actions in the name of social responsibility are real and not just window dressing—should be selected as they are now. If they are to be civil servants, then they must be selected through a political process. If they are to impose taxes and make expenditures to foster "social objectives," then political machinery must be set up to guide the assessment of taxes and to determine through a political process the objectives to be served. (123)

Neither the criticism from the "left" or the "right" is an attack upon the bigness of the corporate enterprises. The criticism merely demonstrates that the political and moral implications of the thesis of managerial discretion lead in the direction of systemic political and legal reform, not social responsibility.

Consider the other horn of the dilemma. If the thesis is false, corporations cannot be said to have social responsibility in any meaningful sense. There is, I believe, good evidence to support the claim that it is false. Many contemporary theorists continue to speak against the thesis, positing new incentives and control mechanisms which pull managers toward profit-maximizing strategies and which discipline managers who do not conform.[35]

Many would argue that there are incentives for managers to allocate resources efficiently (profit maximize) and disciplines against inefficient behavior which have been overlooked by the Managerialists. Some would even argue that the weak boards of directors provide adequate control. Were the control not adequate, they claim, the market would have replaced them with something stronger. The incentives and disciplines reside in product markets, capital markets, competitive managerial labor markets, or the market for corporate control (the threat of corporate takeover), to name only a few. The idea of a competitive product market providing discipline needs little explanation, and the idea has regained plausibility in light of international competition. With oligopoly, the large, modern U.S. corporations may have been able to blunt competition for many decades, especially with the assistance of the industry-specific regulatory bodies which served purposes other than promoting a strong, competitive environment. As the other major powers of the world have recovered from the destruction of WWII (often with the assistance of the U.S.), international competition has become a reality in many industries. Industry by industry in the U.S., corporations have had to think competitively or face loss of market.

In addition to competitive product markets, there are competitive capital markets which discipline managerial behavior through stock prices. Stockholders may be relatively powerless in influencing managerial behavior through the proxy machinery, board of directors, and so forth, but voting with one's telephone to sell stock may be an effective threat. Most stock transactions today involve huge blocks of shares by major institutional investors. These investors are generally directed by professional managers, assisted by complicated computer programs, seeking the greatest return among a wide variety of investment options. If stocks and corporate bonds do not look attractive, metal, currency, government bonds, mortgage bonds, and so forth are always options. Indirectly, they are seeking to maximize return of the investment of millions of Americans who have contributed hundreds of billions of dollars to pension funds, retirement funds, university trust funds, insurance funds, mutual funds, and so forth. The market, through the investors, judges corporate behavior and discounts inappropriate actions resulting in lower prices. The pressure on corporate mangers is pervasive and substantial.

The reality of this pressure has led many critics of American corporations to claim that managers are so directed toward short-term profits as a way of maintaining stock price that important long-term considerations are neglected. This is not so much a criticism of management as a criticism of the system which punishes those who do not operate to keep the quarterly earnings high. Concentration on short-term return may, obviously, result in neglect of longer-term returns. Research and development may be neglected. Risky technological innovations may be ignored. Costly modernization programs may be delayed or ignored. These kinds of objections have become commonplace. What they all reflect is a recognition that the capital market constitutes a genuine constraint on managerial behavior. Dropping stock prices create, in turn, other pressures upon management to increase earnings. Corporate debt financing becomes more difficult, for example.

Even to the extent that product markets or capital markets may provide incentives for corporations to do other than profit maximize, little solace is provided for the discretionary thesis. Analysts taking exception to the idea of pressures toward profit maximization postulate pressures toward revenue maximization, diversification, etc. That such theories may prove to be a more accurate description of the incentives in particular markets does not, however, mean that managers have more discretion. It means only that managerial competency and firm performance are rewarded according to a slightly different principle. The consequences of failure to adhere to the principle of growth maximization might be equally as dire as the failure to profit maximize in the short run.

Additionally, some postulate a competitive managerial labor market.[36] Theoretically, firms will seek to employ those with promise of maximizing profit (or revenues) for the firm. There is a market for managers with the requisite skills. There is, therefore, an incentive for managers to maximize profit (or revenues) because they are at the same time increasing their own future potential earnings, their own value in the competitive labor market. Operating in ways other than this is self-destructive.

Or, consider the competitive market for corporate control.[37] Whether the recent (tidal) wave of corporate takeovers is on balance a good thing is hotly contested. Some find it a very good thing, as a way for the market to clear inefficiently managed firms. According to this view, managers who fail to maximize earnings for the corporation will lose control of the firm because others will recognize that earnings are lagging and rush in to replace management through corporate takeovers. On this view, corporate takeovers are perceived as something akin to a heaven-sent plague inflicting vengeance upon those who have strayed from the straight and narrow path of profit maximization. If this perception is accurate, it demonstrates another constraint on management—profit maximize or get taken over. On the other side, there are those who find in the wave of takeovers either potential or very real evils. They argue, for example, that to avoid being taken over, many firms take steps to make themselves unattractive, creating debt by buying up their own shares of stock, keeping liquidity low, and so forth.

In this way, critics of takeovers often share the view of those who applaud the activity. Both assume that the threat prompts managers toward profit maximization (at least short term). Critics also complain that takeovers often create enormous debt, and the consequences of the high debt are undesirable. The high debt level, it is claimed, displaces modernization, undermines research and development expenditures, and makes the firms extremely vulnerable in the event of an economic downturn. The long-term effects, they argue, are ominous. Yet, here again, even the critics of takeovers assume that management is strongly influenced by the threat of a takeover or by the resultant debt after a takeover. Behavior of managers to avoid takeovers may not be that of profit maximization, but it is unlikely that fearing takeover, managers will keep aside large sums of money for discharging social responsibility. That would certainly make of a firm a quick target for a raider. Managers of firms after a takeover are often driven to undertake drastic measures to squeeze profit in order to repay the debt incurred.

Moreover, as Herman notes, in *Corporate Control, Corporate Power*,[38] managerial discretion is circumscribed by group decision making, bureaucratization, and divisionalization of large corporations. An individual may have titular control, but decisions reflect the advice, and usually the consent, of a large number of top managers, who in turn reflect numerous pressures from within the corporation. Discretion is also narrowed by the need within large bureaucracies for standardization, necessary in order for complex information to be channeled in an appropriate and timely fashion so that decisions can be made. This requires, as Herman notes, "control processes, rules of behavior, and standards of evaluation that serve to limit discretion and channel behavior in accordance with rational rules of control."[39]

After reviewing the evidence for managerial discretion, not merely that stemming from these internal bureaucratic constraints but that concerning the influence of boards of directors, financial institutions, and so forth, Herman concludes:

> Thus a number of forces, some evolving side by side with the managerial revolution itself (size, decentralization of operation, professionalization of management), have tended to constrain independent managers, limit the size of their discretion, and press them toward a profit orientation at least as unequivocal as that of owner/managers. This leaves room for a certain amount of "expense preference," the periodic emergence and cutting back of organizational "slack," and other modes of sharing in corporate surpluses by active managers, but these are neither new nor demonstrably a special feature of managerial firms. (247)

Thus, there is good reason to believe that managers do not have the wide degree of discretion suggested by the Micro-Managerialists.[40] If there is little possibility for corporations to do other than profit maximize, it makes little sense to argue that corporations have a responsibility to act in that way. Such an activity would be self-destructive. It is imperative to recognize the moral relevance of reality. If the existence of one or another market constrains management, and if corporate behavior yields socially undesirable behavior, the solution is political regulation of the market, or government taking a role in reordering the incentive structures in the market, not moral conversion or social responsibility.

In short, Micro-Managerialism is sorely inadequate, unable to produce a persuasive argument for the thesis of corporate social responsibility. As I have indicated, Micro-Managerialism rests heavily upon the thesis of managerial discretion. If true, the thesis would entail radical political changes aimed at circumscribing managerial latitude and making it accountable, not a call for social responsibility. There is good evidence, however, that it is false.

A more adequate version of Managerialism avoids these difficulties to some extent. That other Managerialism locates the theory of the modern corporation, the theses of the Managerial revolution, managerial professionalism, and managerial discretion within a larger account of the economic, political, and social system. That context also implies much less latitude for managers, making social responsibility largely irrelevant. That is the subject of the next chapter.

9

Macro-Managerialism

Given the inability of Micro-Managerialism to provide a coherent and morally defensible argument in support of the prescriptive thesis of social responsibility, the question is whether the materials for an adequate defense can be garnered from the Macro-Managerial strand of Managerialism. That is the focus of this and the next chapter. The examination revolves primarily around two key theories widely assumed by early Macro-Managerialists: Keynesianism and pluralism. Together these constitute the outlines for a Revisionist Liberal theory of political economy which might be called New Deal Liberalism. The Keynesian framework provides the means by which to discredit the economic theory upon which Classical Liberalism and the Classical ideology rested, while holding out the promise of a solid economic rationale for the more than minimal, active, interventionist state of Revisionist Liberalism. Pluralism provides Managerialists a descriptive model by which to understand how the larger "system" functions, as well as a prescriptive model according to which changes arising from democratic processes can be legitimized. Thus, if the more than minimal state, with regulatory and welfare dimensions, arose from a democratic process in a pluralistic society, prescriptive pluralism would render the developments legitimate. As Keynesian doctrines have fallen from favor lately, it should come as no surprise that Managerialists have either retreated into Micro-Managerialism, or have attempted to rest their Macro-Managerial views solely upon pluralism.

The meaning of corporate responsibility, then, must be interpreted in this light, and arguments reconstructed with those premises. The analysis suggests, however, that in this context the discussions of corporate responsibility become either largely irrelevant or border on the deceptive and exploitive.

Rather than admitting the irrelevance of corporate responsibility, reflective Macro-Managerialists stress the "limits" of social responsibility. This is apparent in one of the finest and most authoritative illustrations of the Macro-Managerial position, *Social Responsibilities of Business Corporations: A Statement on National Policy by the Research and Policy Committee of the Committee for Economic Development.*[1] An analysis of this statement will introduce Macro-Managerialism and the argument which I develop.

SOCIAL RESPONSIBILITY:
THE COMMITTEE ON ECONOMIC DEVELOPMENT

Just as the National Association of Manufacturers (NAM) played an important role in disseminating the views of the Classical ideology, the Council on Economic Development (CED) played an increasingly important role in the development and dissemination of Managerialism after WWII. Gradually, the CED moved from consideration of strictly economic issues toward concern for social problems. In 1971, the CED published *Social Responsibilities of Business Corporations,* which represents the work of the Research and Policy Committee. The list of members of that committee, as well as the assisting Business Structure and Performance Subcommittee, is extremely impressive. Presidents, vice-presidents or chairs of the boards of directors from AT&T, General Motors, Heinz, Newsweek, Inland Steel, United Fruit, Caterpillar, Owens-Illinois, General Electric, Morgan Stanley & Co., and 3M are represented. Revealing the degree to which the Managerial perspective was shaped and informed by academia, one finds among the advisors Alfred D. Chandler, Jr., Richard Eells, Richard M. Cyert, and Fritz Machlup. Others, such as Charles Schultz (then of the Brookings Institute), Walter W. Heller (the University of Michigan), and Carl Kaysen (director, Institute for Advanced Study, Princeton University), served on the research advisory board. Hence, the statement by the CED is authoritative and especially reflective, carrying something akin to canonical status.

While many Micro-Managerial themes and arguments appear in the CED statement, these are placed against a broader background which more directly addresses questions of the appropriate role of government and the large corporation, and which finally illumines the limits of social responsibility. The brief statement, running only slightly longer than sixty pages, contains a short introduction and five chapters:

1. The Changing Social Contract with Business
2. The Evolving Corporate Institution and Managerial Outlook
3. Enlightened Self-Interest: The Corporation's Stake in a Good Society
4. Widening Parameters of Social Performance
5. A Government-Business Partnership for Social Progress

The introduction describes the scope of the statement. The focus is upon "social responsibilities," rather than economic ones, and is restricted to the responsibilities of large, public-owned corporations, although it is suggested that much of what is asserted will apply to a broad range of smaller enterprises and even individual business persons. The statement also notes that it is concerned with questions of corporate structure or the complicated issues of business-government relationships only as these impinge upon the "central concern with social responsibilities." The scope is also restricted to the U.S.

The basic purpose of business, it is alleged, is "to serve constructively the needs of society—to the satisfaction of society"(11). Advocates of the Classical ideology could agree with this statement, but it would be interpreted as indicating that the function of business is to meet needs through profit maximizing by means of the productions of goods and services. In the view of the CED, "American business has been the source of generating substantial economic growth, increasing employment, rising wages and salaries, employee benefit plans and expanding career opportunities."(11). The competitive market is praised as having "served as an effective means of bringing about an efficient allocation of a major part of the country's resources to ever-changing public requirements" (12). However, the CED statement argues, the public now demands more. Corporations are expected to play a part in alleviating social problems. Expectations for creating a good society include the following six goals (13):

a. elimination of poverty and provision of good health care
b. equal opportunity for each person to reach his or her full potential regardless of race, sex, or creed
c. education and training for a fully productive and rewarding participation in modern society

    d. ample jobs and career opportunities in all parts of society

    e. livable communities with decent housing, safe streets, a clean and pleasant environment, efficient transportation, good cultural and educational opportunities, and a prevailing mood of civility among people.

According to the report, these goals represent a consensus of sorts and have for years been "articulated, advocated and worked for by leaders in American politics, business, labor, and education" (13). The report claims that although public opinion trends are "not the only criteria for formulating sound business or public policy," they are a "basic consideration" in a "democratic society" and usually determinative in the long run (16). Hence, in the language of the CED, "the contract" between society and business has been rewritten. Interestingly, insofar as there is an argument here, it is one in which corporations are characterized as responding to clearly articulated demands in society.

This framing of the issue has a tendency to place the corporate response on a par with responses to other standard market pressures. The corporation is characterized as merely reacting to clearly specified requests by a homogeneous society. If the public wants better mousetraps or fast foods, corporations will respond or suffer the consequences. Beyond this, however, the assertions are consistent with a number of different arguments. One could develop an argument which took seriously the idea of a social contract. Or, one could take the idea of the social contract as a rhetorical device and look elsewhere for an argument. Such an argument might rest upon the idea that the role of a corporation is to satisfy the needs of society, and that society has expressed the need for corporations to address social concerns. Or, the argument might actually be that since public opinion strongly supports social responsibilities, if business wants to prevent government regulations which would require certain actions, it should act preemptively to satisfy these demands. An analogous preemptive argument might be that business should respond before government itself moves to address these demands. Or, the argument might be one of self-interest; that is, if corporations desire to maintain their strategically important position, they should address the concerns of the public. Any or all of these arguments could be constructed in support of this claim. The allusion to the role of the corporation within a democratic society is tantalizing, but too cryptic to provide much of a lead.

Actually, the discussion of social responsibility has two foci. On the one hand, social responsibility appears to refer to the ability to contribute to the achievement of these goals. In this sense, social responsibility refers to the obligation to solve the problems of affirmative action, of unemployment, etc. Discharging social responsibility here tends to be considered in terms of corporate philanthropy. On the other hand, social responsibility also appears to refer to the appropriate balancing of the interests of the various constituencies with whom the corporation is involved. This sense does not involve philanthropy but the distribution of resources.

This latter sense is evident in chapter 2, devoted to a short description of the "Evolving Corporate Institution and Managerial Outlook." In the section entitled "Corporate Growth and Responsibilities," the familiar refrains of Managerialism are introduced. There the history of corporate growth in size and power is sketched. "As corporations have grown, they also have developed sizable constituencies of people whose interests and welfare are inexorably linked with the company and whose support is vital to its success" (19). These constituencies include employees, stockholders, customers and consumers, suppliers, and community neighbors. Beyond these, the document mentions numerous other constituencies with which the corporation interacts—competitors, labor unions, interest groups, educational institutions, the press, and government at all different levels. Thus, what is now referred to as the stakeholder model is introduced.

Suddenly, however, the CED statement moves from describing the different constituencies to describing the obligations and responsibilities which arise therein. No argument is offered. In relations with their constituencies and with the larger society, American corporations are said to operate today in an intricate matrix of obligations and responsibilities that far exceed in scope and complexity those of most other institutions and are analogous in many respects to government itself. "*The great growth of corporations in size, market power, and impact on society has naturally brought with it a commensurate growth in responsibilities; in a democratic society, power sooner or later begets equivalent accountability.*"[2] This section echoes many of the arguments of the Micro-Managerial perspective which have already been discussed and discarded: the stakeholder/multiple constituency argument, the social effects argument/the public character of corporations argument, the corporate power argument, and the corporate citizenship argument. None are developed. This passage concludes by noting that a great body of law has evolved which is intended to insure that corporations exercise their power ethically, compete vigorously, and treat employ-ees fairly, etc., but urges that corporations behave in accordance with social customs, high moral standards, and humane values (21).

The first sense of social responsibility might be related to this model by claiming that the social goals which the corporation has a responsibility to help achieve are reflected in the obligations to secondary constituencies, but this is not entirely plausible. Further, it is noteworthy that though there is something like an argument for social responsibility here, the exact nature of the argument is difficult to discern. Moreover, it is not at all clear how or whether these arguments relate to the public opinion argument in the earlier chapter. Here the responsibilities arise either from corporate power, or corporate relationships, or both. There are often references to the pluralistic democratic society, but it is still not clear at this point how that is relevant here. Why, for example, does having power in a democratic society beget "equivalent responsibility"? In sharp contrast to advocates of the Classical framework, however, there is no loud chorus of lamentation over the creeping socialism of the government, and the increasing legislation in some areas is embraced warmly. In other passages there is a measured resistance but no call to storm the barricades and roll back the legislation of the New Deal, New Frontier, and Great Society. The New Deal state is accepted.

The Micro-Managerial themes of the CED statement continue in the next section of chapter 2, "The New Managerial Outlook." Here, the theses from *The Modern Corporation and Private Property*, by Berle and Means, are very near the surface. The changing structure of the corporation is mentioned and with it the rise of professional managers. The large corporation has become a permanent institution.

As a permanent institution, the large corporation is developing long-term goals such as survival, growth, and increasing respect and accep-tance by the public. Current profitability, once regarded as the dominant if not exclusive objective, is now often seen more as the means and powerful motivating force for achieving broader ends, rather than as an end in itself. Thus, modern managers are prepared to trade off short-run profits to achieve qualitative improvements in the institution which can be expected to contribute to the long-run profitable growth of the corporation. (22)

This passage could be ignored as another example of the confused public character of corporation argument except that it reveals a much more precise understanding of social responsibility. According to this interpretation, social responsibility may conflict with short-run profitability, but is not inconsistent with "long-run profitable growth." Profitability, in this view, can serve as a "means" and a "motivating force" for broader social ends. The scenario clearly pre-supposes that the large, modern corporation has a great deal of flex-ibility, of discretion, in choosing whether to seek short- or long-run profitability. The assumption is that the competitive environment allows forsaking short-run profitability. The idea that the professional managers are distinct from owners/stockholders, and are freed from the immediate pressures by stockholders, is also introduced to support the idea that managers are consequently freer to take the longer view. The professional manager is a "trustee balancing the interests of the many diverse participants and constituents in the enterprise" (22). This "interest-balancing involves much the same kind of political leadership and skill as is required in top government posts" (22). Managers must "exercise statesmanship" and obtain something like "the consent of the governed." The section closes with the importance of educating future managers to fulfill these tasks and argues that to be insensitive to the environment of business "could be disastrous." "It becomes necessary for the corporation's own existence that it be highly responsive to the environment in which it lives" (24).

Thus, the argument appears to be that the careful discharge of responsibilities (to achieve social goals and/or to the various con-stituencies) leads to long-term profitability. Problems associated with this kind of claim were considered in detail in the previous chapter. Most importantly, with no careful operational definition of what constitutes a satisfactory balancing of constituent's interest, there is no way to test the claim that this leads to long-term profitability. No description of the kind of system which would allow this di-vine harmony between competing interests is sketched either. With no criteria to determine social responsibility for balancing interests, the claim that discharging one's responsibilities results in long-term profitability tends to collapse into the claim that corporations ought to focus upon long-term profitability, and that the corporation has correctly discharged those duties if the resolution is conducive to long-term profits. Social responsibility is a means toward long-term profit.

This same argument is continued in chapter 3, "Enlightened Self-Interest: The Corporation's Stake in a Good Society," although here the focus has shifted from balancing the interests of constituencies to the responsibility for contributing to the achievement of social goals. The argument, if strong, would serve both purposes. The chapter is designed to offer a clearer rationale of the role "business must play in the national community—a role as a responsible participant determined to resolve any conflict with humane values or the social environment" (25). Four questions are addressed:

a. Why should corporations become substantially involved in the improvement of the social environment?
b. How can they justify this to their stockholders?
c. How can companies reconcile substantial expenditures for social purposes with profitability?
d. What are the limitations on corporate social responsibilities?

Building upon the claims of the previous chapter, the response to the first three questions is that long-term profitability demands that corporations become involved in the improvement of the social environment. The key to the answer, according to the CED statement "lies in a clearer perspective of business as a basic institution in American society with a vital stake in the general welfare as well as in its own public acceptance." In general, the answer appears to be that what is in the "enlightened self-interest" of the corporations is congruent with the general welfare of the nation. The claim, without being trite, is that what is good for General Motors, etc., is good for the country, and vice versa.[3]

The notion of "enlightened self-interest," of course, invokes Adam Smith and laissez-faire ideas, but it is clear that something much different is involved. While continuing to extol the virtues of the market, asserting that the "competitive marketplace remains the principal method of harmonizing business and public interests, because it has proved over a long period of time to be an efficient way of allocating economic resources to society's needs," the CED statement recognizes the need for government to intervene to promote competition, as well as to "guide economic activity toward major public objectives, as determined by the political process, when these cannot be achieved through the normal working of the marketplace." Now, in point of fact, Adam Smith would probably have agreed with this final caveat, but it sharply contrasts with the traditional view of the Classical

Liberals who believe that the function of government is exclusively to prevent harms. The CED statement goes much further. Not only is there an expanded role for government to guide economic activity toward public objectives, but there is the claim that contemporary reality has "diverged" from the laissez-faire model.

At this crucial juncture, however, the line of reasoning becomes fuzzy. There is allegedly a "body of understanding" that is the basis for enlightened self-interest. This understanding recognizes that the "corporation is dependent upon the goodwill of society, which can sustain or impair its existence through public pressures on government," and that corporate self-interest is "inexorably involved in the well-being of society of which business is an integral part" (27). This understanding of the manner in which corporate and social interests are intertwined is supposedly at the root of numerous legal changes. Examples include the 1935 amendment to the IRS code which allow corporations to deduct up to 5 percent of pretax income for charitable contributions.

> Since then it has been substantially refined through corporate practice and sanctioned by the courts. *In various decisions, the courts have established the legality of corporate contributions for social purposes that serve the interests of the firm as broadly defined, even though they provide no direct benefits to it.* In the 1953 landmark A. P. Smith case, the New Jersey Superior Court upheld the right under common law of a manufacturing company to contribute private funds to Princeton University. *The court held that it was not just a right but a duty of corporations to support higher education in the interests of the long-range well-being of their stockholders because the company could not hope to operate effectively in a society which is not functioning well.* (27, italics in the original)

The enlightened self-interest argument, then, appears to be that long-run corporate interests are commingled with those of the community, and the corporation may, or ought to, contribute in ways to provide for the general well-being of the community in order to insure the well-being of both.

> Indeed, the corporate interest broadly defined by management can support involvement in helping solve virtually any social problem, because people who have a good environment, education, and opportunity make better employees, customers and neighbors for business than those who are poor, ignorant and oppressed. (28)

The doctrine of enlightened self-interest is also invoked to claim that it is in the long-term interest of stockholders to have corporate funds expended thus. The argument that it is in the enlightened self-interest of business to accept these responsibilities is also reinforced by the preemptive arguments that if corporations do not accept responsibility, the "interests of the corporation may actually be jeopardized" by increasing governmental regulation.

The extraordinary implausibility of this enlightened self-interest argument for social responsibility becomes apparent the moment one reflects upon the actual incentives functioning. Consider the problems in attempting to deal with any of the six goals of the good society. The idea that the interests of the corporation are intermixed with the local or national community makes sense only on the assumption of something like a hermetically sealed nation state. That is, the idea makes sense only if the nation is the sole or primary market for the goods and services produced, for materials, investment, and labor, and/or the costs of providing the factors of production and healthy demand cannot be externalized to others without significant long-term negative impact on corporate well-being. For example, one goal of a good society was the realization of "ample jobs and career opportunities." Now there is no doubt that the existence of an adequately trained workforce in ample supply is in the interest of the corporation, if for no other reason than the downward pressure which would be exerted on wages and salaries. But, there is no particular interest in finding workers within the particular region within which the corporation currently operates. There is no particular interest in finding workers even within the national boundaries of the home country. Consider a corporation, competing in the global market, faced with a decision to expand capacity by building new production facilities. Global competition can make it economically unfeasible to invest in the U.S. if wage scales in other parts of the world are significantly lower (provided other costs do not negate the labor cost savings). The problem of global competition notwithstanding, the corporation's interest in having an ample pool of well-trained workers does not necessarily translate into an incentive to provide resources for the training. Corporate resources can be freed if the costs of training can be shifted onto others, even onto the public sector. Further, by pooling resources to lobby the government to pick up the costs of training, the costs for the individual corporation are even lower, and the likelihood of success even higher. Thus, the corporation would have an interest in shouldering the costs of training a workforce only if the costs could not be externalized, and only if trained workers could not be found elsewhere.

Similar considerations are present when one reflects upon the corporate interests in the other stated social goals. What interest does the corporation have in livable communities? Less mobile workers have an interest in these, but at best corporate interests would be mingled with the livable communities of workers, not society as a whole. A final set of examples should make the point. Consider a corporation based in the U.S. with the opportunity to sell goods to another country when the U.S. considers this contrary to the national interest. If the company loses the sale, another corporation from another country will provide the goods. If the sale is lost, the corporation will suffer greatly, laying off many U.S workers and cutting dividends to stockholders. By what stretch of the imagination would anyone assume a strong congruence of interests between a corporation and the nation?[4] These problems are not unique to the global setting. Regions and communities within the U.S. continue to play off against one another, forcing corporations to decide where to move plants for low-cost labor, for highly skilled workers, or for tax breaks, etc. These are not win-win situations. Corporate interests may be mixed up with one community's good at the expense of another community.

Hence, although the CED argument for enlightened self-interest is much more sharply drawn than similar Micro-Managerial arguments, that clarity merely discloses more readily its weakness. As if sensing the vulnerability, the CED statement moves immediately to focus upon the limitations of corporate responsibility in the closing paragraphs of chapter 3. None of the kinds of problems mentioned here are specifically noted, but it is quite evident that the limits arise in large part from the fact that market incentives for corporations are often not likely to insure that corporate interests are congruent with social goals. The statement urges some sacrifices for the long-run but recognizes that too many short-run sacrifices will entail no long-run to worry over. Management "must concern itself with realizing a level of profitability which its stockholders and financial market consider to be reasonable under the circumstances" (33).

Chapter 4 continues the discussion and is devoted almost entirely to the question of limits. There are, the statement asserts, at least four questions which arise in light of calls for corporations to assume social responsibilities. First is the question of the appropriate scope of involvement from the position of the individual corporation or manager given the limitations of company resources, and this discussion adds nothing to the criteria already developed in chapter 3. Namely, involvement is confined to efforts consistent with reasonable profits. Second is the question of the appropriate role from the standpoint of society. What kind of mix of business corporations, government, education, labor, private foundations, and volunteer groups is most desirable from the perspective of public policy? Third, to what extent can the corporation or manager take on these responsibilities in light of prevailing market conditions and to what degree will government need to intervene to alter the rules which govern the economic system? Finally, how is the social performance of business to be evaluated?

These are important questions. The answers which are proposed call for initiative from both the corporate sector and government. Corporate voluntarism is not working, according to the report. The statement claims that

> the over-all pattern of voluntary individual and cooperative corporate activities to improve the social environment is quite spotty and not really substantial, either in terms of the magnitude of the nation's problems or of the business resources that could be applied to them. (43)

The statement calls for an expansion and intensification of voluntary efforts and suggests the possibility of a consortium to organize efforts (within constraints of antitrust legislation). Chapter 4 concludes with a few paragraphs on a procedure for evaluating corporate performance. But given the recognition of the market constraints on the individual corporation, it is apparent that voluntarism, even organized voluntarism, will not work to solve the problems. Thus, chapter 5, which concludes the CED statement, calls for a "partnership" between government and business in order to obtain "social progress." In an important sense, chapter 5 constitutes a response to two questions raised in the previous chapter but left largely unaddressed. One question concerned the appropriate scope for corporate involvement in social issues, from the point of view of society, judged by the comparative advantages of getting social problems dealt with by business corporations, government, and other institutions. The other concerned the extent to which government needed to alter market structures.

This chapter provides an extremely revealing insight into the underlying assumptions of the appropriate role for the corporation and government. Given the limitations noted earlier, the authors of the CED statement infer that government must take the lead in providing incentives for corporations to address many of the most pressing social concerns. In contrast to the overall negative view of government in the Classical ideology, the CED statement sees government as a facilitator and as a mechanism, a process, through which the goals of society are established. Through the political process, the goals of society are established. The political process also sets priorities and "develops strategies" for accomplishing these goals most effectively "to the satisfaction of the public" (51). The CED statement recognizes and accepts as legitimate the incentive for profit as "the only practicable way of unleashing the power and dynamism of private enterprise on a scale that will be effective in generating social progress." (51) Corporations are characterized as playing a significant role in actually executing social programs through the incentives provided by the government.

> Social consciousness and good citizenship, while important prerequisites, cannot realistically be expected by themselves to bring business resources to bear on the country's social problems on the massive scale that is needed. To achieve this, government must create market conditions that will induce business enterprises to apply their operational capabilities to those public tasks they can carry out more efficiently than other institutions. (51)

This is a call for "privatizing" some of the functions of government, as well as a call for increasing incentives in new areas. "Government could create major new markets not only in such areas as urban redevelopment and the building of new cities, but also in mass transportation, medical services, education, and many municipal services." Positive inducements would include cash payments to individuals, loans, credit guarantees, insurance, tax benefits, and so forth. The CED statement also accepts, in principle, the necessity for a number of "governmental controls, regulations, and disincentives designed to influence the social performance of business." Specifically mentioned are civil rights/equal employment and environmental regulations.

> These and other regulatory measures are essential in many fields to ensure that *all* businesses, and not only the financially strong and more social

responsible ones, act in accordance with the public interest. While business should develop its capacities for self-regulation and self-policing to the fullest extent possible, there are bound to be areas beyond the effective reach of these self-imposed constraints which can be regulated effectively only by government. This has proved to be the case with various automobile safety features, initiated by individual companies, which had to be prescribed as standard equipment through federal regulations. (58)

Quite obviously, this is a much different framework from that offered by the Classical perspective. Government activities in a number of areas are not only accepted as legitimate, but there is a strong call for government to do more. The appeal is for government to create markets, not for government to create governmental agencies to deal with problems. What government may rightly do, in this view, appears to be circumscribed not by the vision of the minimal state but by some vision of a liberal democratic society in which the majority arrives at consensus goals and government assists in achieving those goals in partnership with business. The market is praised, but the shortcomings of the market are recognized. The market has not, and will not, solve many of the most pressing problems confronting the society. Government must take action by "guiding" the market.

In short, there is very little room for social responsibility, given the constraints of the market.

KENYESIANISM

The CED statement recognizes, from a very practical point of view, the limitations on corporate responsibility arising from market constraints. The extent of the limitations are even more pronounced from a theoretical perspective. The theoretical core, a variety of Revisionist Liberalism, serves Managerialists in a number of ways. A central challenge for all Revisionist Liberals is to demonstrate that a more than minimal state is morally legitimate, and that interference in the market is consistent with the commitment to liberty and human development. Both Keynesianism and pluralism support those conclusions. Keynesianism offers a dramatically different way of conceptualizing the role of government in a free, liberal society. But while this provides Managerialism with an arsenal of arguments to wield against the Classical ideology, I want to argue that the intellectual rationale for social responsibility is at the same time largely undermined.

Keynesianism can be taken to refer to a set of economic beliefs and resultant policies which came to hold the status of orthodoxy through the 1960s.[5] By President Nixon's term, he could quip, "We're all Keynesians now." Although many of the fiscal policies which came to be associated with Keynesianism have been abandoned or refined, many of the basic ideas persist and continue to guide thinking about policy formulation. Within the Classical economic model, of course, governmental intervention is unnecessary, because individuals, whether natural or artificial (corporations), need only act in self-interest, and competition will insure that the outcome is in the interest of society as a whole.

The folly of any intervention or regulation is reflected in a number of tenets of the Classical theory. One doctrine with important political overtones was the idea that the system would reach equilibrium at full employment. According to this idea, if there were some unemployment, the unemployed would bid for work at a wage lower than the current market wage. The oversupply would lower the wage rate, and business could hire more workers. Impediments in the economy, such as monopoly, labor unions, and government interference, could interfere to prevent equilibrium, but in a free market, unemployment would be no problem. The existence of unemployment, in fact, could be taken as proof of impediments. The solution was not government interference, but the elimination of market impediments. If government should take an active role, it would be to restore the competitive market, not to interfere in its natural workings. Within the Classical model there was also the tenet that expenditures equal income in the system. Whatever is earned is either spent on consumption items, invested, or placed in savings. Classical theory presumed that money which was put into savings would flow back into the economy because no one desired money for its own sake. Savings would be made available for loans to others who would either purchase consumer or investment items. Interest rates would fluctuate according to the law of supply and demand, and this would automatically calibrate the amount of investment in society. Nonetheless, all income would flow back into expenditure. Additionally, there was the assumption, popular again today among some of the supply-side economists, that supply creates demand. This assumption was known as Say's Law and is based on the idea that the production of goods provides sufficient income to purchase the goods. Money, having no value in itself, is merely a medium of exchange. Goods are always therefore produced for other goods. There can never be an excess supply. There were other doctrines in the Classical position, such as the notion that government budget should be balanced, warnings that high tax rates reduce incentives to work and invest, and the idea that government is a nonproductive drain on the economy, all of which would lend support to a policy of laissez-faire.

The Keynesians challenged these tenets. With millions unemployed during the Depression, questions of economic theory and political policy, often considered dry, dull subjects for abstract, academic quibbles, became life and death issues. Those grounded in the Classical tradition continued to countenance non-intervention, and patience. In the long run, the system would reach equilibrium at full employment if only the meddling government would leave well enough alone. Reflecting a very different view, Keynes and others argued that government must take vigorous and decisive steps to interfere in the market. One of the most salient and widely emphasized features of Keynes's thought was his claim that an economy can reach equilibrium at points other than full employment. If this claim were true, then the system would not automatically solve the problem of unemployment without exogenous or outside forces coming into play, such as the government.

One reason for the rejection of this axiom was that Keynes believed that total expenditure in the society did always equal income and that supply did not create demand. In the Keynesian system, there are three key determinants of the level of overall economic activity and hence employment: (1) the average propensity to consume; (2) the marginal efficiency of capital; and, (3) the real rate of interest. The first variable concerns the amount of consumption in society, the second and third relate to the level of investment. Since, Keynes believed, the average propensity to consume remains relatively stable over a long period of time, the second and third variables are therefore the most important ones in most cases. In short, investment is the critical factor in determining economic activity and employment. If investment fell, production would fall, and hence employment would decline. In the Classical system, falling investment would trigger lower interest rates, thereby enticing more investment automatically. However, Keynes rejected the idea that the rate of interest is the sole or most important factor in determining levels of investment. According to Keynes, investment decisions are based on the difference between the expected rate of return on an investment (marginal efficiency of capital) and the interest rate. If potential investors expect a sluggish economy, the low interest rates will not invite investment. Hence, expenditures will not equal income, as savings accumulate. Production falls, employment declines, which in turn triggers less income and in turn less production. Keynes also argued that individuals might save money which would not find its way back into circulation because, in contrast to the Classical assumption that money has only extrinsic value, is only a medium for exchange, money itself, Keynes argued, can have some value which induces people to save. In any case, expenditures for some reason or another may not equal income, and production would slow. The three strategic variables might be such that the economy was in equilibrium at a point of low economic activity and high unemployment.

A number of possible remedies are identified by the new economics to alter the variables in such a way as to induce growth and employment. For Keynes, the most important are those which stimulate increased investment, such as reduced taxes, lower interest rates, accelerated depreciation measures, investment tax credits, and so forth. Only if these indirect measures do not result in increased GNP are direct governmental measures recommended. These measures involve direct government spending, the intent of which is to increase the over-all consumption level, thereby inviting increased production in the private sector, stimulating the prospects for investment, and bringing about higher levels of employment. Any of these tools might bring about deficit spending, but Keynes was extremely wary of deficit spending except in extreme emergencies, and then only temporarily.

The moral relevance of this Keynesian attack should not be overlooked. The dominant moral defense of Classical Liberalism is utilitarian, a tradition which has long been closely associated with economic thought. As demonstrated in the earlier chapters, the utilitarian defense rested upon an Economic Premise that claimed that the minimal state with laissez-faire produced what was best for all, i.e., maximized net utility. If correct, Keynesianism destroys the utilitarian defense of Classical Liberalism by undermining the Economic Premise. At the same time, Keynesianism suggests an alternative utilitarian defense of the more than minimal state. If the market is not self-regulating, if the market threatens to render millions unemployed at equilibrium, then the utilitarian argument could support an active, Keynesian, mixed economy. If Keynesian policies, well administered, optimize utility, then utilitarians would morally endorse that new system. Thus, one of the most critical components of the debate between the Classical and Managerial ideologies is the debate over how the market functions; it is not primarily a debate over ethical values and principles. Even if social utility is accepted as only one important moral consideration among others, the Economic Premise remains crucial. The moral issue largely turns upon the economic.

Another key idea in the Classical framework was the stability of the system, a characteristic with obvious social utility. If full employment is reached in the laissez-faire system only after prolonged periods of massive unemployment during which time the system is threatened with revolution, then the utile course of action might well be abandonment of the laissez-faire system. Although the Classical system had prided itself on stability, depressions could be taken as examples of the potential instability of the system. A new system, with government regulating business cycles, might well be more stable and hence more utile in the long run. During the years of the Depression, concerns over stability were not idle concerns of only intellectual interest. Communism was perceived as a real and dangerous threat. To some extent, fascism was also beginning to be feared. Even if the market in the U.S. was a competitive market, and even if competitive markets reach equilibrium at full employment, many believed that unless government took steps immediately to alleviate the suffering among the millions during the Depression, the entire system would be lost in a revolution. In that case, not only would private property and the freedoms of the market be lost, but many of the other values cherished by many Americans would be forfeited. Keynes and others perceived an active role for government as a way of saving capitalism against the evils of communism or fascism.

These arguments can be coupled with others concerning contemporary reality. As explained earlier, utilitarian considerations of the net social utility of laissez-faire rest upon what I have called the Existence Premise. The social good arises from self-interested, profit-seeking behavior only if there is a competitive market in existence. Based upon their understanding of economic history, some Managerialists could adopt the position that in fact the competitive system assumed in the Classical models had never existed or, if it did, had vanished even before the the old west disappeared. This argument can concede that if free, competitive, laissez-faire capitalism existed, this would be optimally utile, but counter with the claim of nonexistence. For instance, if monopolies, oligopolies, and trusts dominate the markets, then government nonintervention will not produce what is optimal unless one believes that these kinds of markets yield maximally utile outcomes. Few believe this. If reality is perceived in this way, the question becomes how best to insure the public good. One method would be antitrust legislation in an attempt to move reality closer to competition. Another means would be regulation, government acting in ways perceived to be more in line with public interest. Either of these could be justified on utilitarian grounds.

Thus, Keynesianism could function in an attempt to legitimize a government which is active in the economy but does not supplant the over-all efficiency. The system involved the establishment of new governmental agencies and functions which are required to gather the information necessary to make economic policy decisions. Government needed to keep its fingers on the pulse of the economy, on the key variables identified by the Keynesians, and to take action occasionally. And, to a much greater degree than the Classical framework, Keynesianism fused the political and the economic. If the economy is not self-regulating, the questions about acceptable or desirable rates of growth, investment, unemployment, and so forth remain open. Economists see themselves as pure technicians. Economic theory is seen as identifying key variables and the relationships among variables. Economic theory does not itself prescribe desirable rates of growth, investment, or unemployment. That is a political decision. In this fashion, Keynesianism opens the door for politicizing the economic. The theory suggests leaving individual economic actors free to do, but manipulating variables through altering incentives and disincentives.

Nothing here poses a threat to the business community. With Keynes, the Managerialists could continue to claim that private enterprise, free market capitalism, is the most efficient and productive system in the world, sounding the same theme as those in the Classical ideology. Modifications were viewed as necessary in order to keep the system from being destroyed during a depression in which great masses of the unemployed would turn toward fascism or communism in order to alleviate suffering. In Keynes's view, occasional government intervention, usually of an indirect nature, was sufficient to keep the system functioning smoothly at nearly fully employment. Such, at least, was the Keynesian dream. Keynesianism, then, could function within the

Managerial ideology to legitimize limited government regulation of the economy, and in ways greatly beneficial to business, especially to corporations with resources to make the sophisticated cases necessary for convincing political bodies that special, favored treatment is healthy for the economy as a whole. Keynsianism could work quite well as a legitimation of reduced taxes and sweetened incentives for businesses, and the Keynesian model allowed the Managerialists to incorporate the rhetoric of free market economics with little alteration. The alterations themselves could be justified on grounds of hard-headed pragmatisim, an attribute for which the American business community has always prided itself.

There would be a threat to those in the economic sphere with great control, but the new system promised greater control of a different nature, if only business could learn to make the new system work. That required skills in the political arena. If government were to enter the economic sphere, there would be competition for control. Nonetheless, the new system offered the potential for greater control over the environment. In the quest for profit and survival, firms must focus upon at least three variables: efficiency, innovation, and control of the external environment (e.g., markets). By the late nineteenth century, control of markets was of central importance to the key economic actors.[6] Efficiency and innovation did not prove adequate for survival in a period of wild economic upswings and downswings or in a situation of fierce competition. In an effort to control the environment, firms experimented with pooling arrangements, cartels, horizontal integration, and trusts as means of stabilizing the market. Pooling arrangements and cartels were notoriously fragile. Monopolies and trusts were realities, but with antitrust legislation, the government had begun to exercise some competition for control. The new system held the potential for providing new means of controlling the economic environment through the mechanism of government, if only business could be guaranteed that the process would yield desirable outcomes. Clearly, the implicit message for business is to become politically involved.

What, then, of the role for the business community in this new system? If one adopts something like the Keynesian framework, what is the role of the large corporation in the free society? At the political level, the role of the business community would be analogous to that of other significant players. As participants in the democratic process, different representatives of the business community would attempt to convince the government about what should be accepted as desirable levels of growth, unemployment, etc., and about specific policies which should be adopted to reach those goals. Representatives of the business community, in fact, would have a number of special advantages in making a case. Corporations have long been better organized and better funded than any other segment of the population. Corporations are involved in industry trade groups, where information can be gathered and resources combined to support lobbying efforts. Corporations also possess resources unavailable to other "citizens" in the political process. Thus, it is no surprise that representatives of the corporate community began to see the wisdom of becoming actively involved in government.

Nothing in this framework entails, or even suggests, that corporations should act in any way other than to maximize profit. On the contrary, the assumption of profit maximization is as equally at home within the Keynesian framework as in the Classical framework. One might argue that the mixed economy maximizes net utility for everyone provided that corporations in the private sector continue to pursue profit-maximizing ends, an assumption ordinarily made. If there is a problem with unemployment, for example, the solution is not for large, managerial firms to deviate from their own attempts at efficient operation by hiring workers unnecessarily, or by keeping wages low (if this were possible) in order to hire more workers. The solution to the problem would rest in economic adjustments at the macro-level. These social responsibilities are the responsibilities which have been assumed by government. What seems to follow is not that corporations ought to do something other than act according to principles of efficiency, but that corporations should not lobby to roll back the policies of the New Deal. Social responsibility from this perspective, then, amounts to nothing more than accepting the legitimacy of the new role of government. There is no compelling argument which can be constructed from within this framework to suggest that corporations ought to act to do anything other than profit maximize within the constraints of the law.

Given this background, the argument in the statement by the Council on Economic Development should come as no surprise. If there are problems which are not being adequately addressed by the market, the government should act to create incentives to prompt private enterprise to take steps in the directions deemed politically desirable.

OLIGOPOLY, MONOPOLY, AND EXTERNALITIES

In the debates over the appropriate role of government in a free society, economic issues often dominate. In particular, two other issues, the existence of oligopoly or monopoly, on the one hand, or externalities, on the other, are often raised by Managerialists as examples of the inadequacy of the Classical ideology and as the bases for arguments for expanding government influence in the economic realm. But the arguments which work to undermine the assumptions of the Classical model do not provide good reasons for doing anything other than profit maximizing within the law either. Social responsibility is irrelevant.

By the turn of the century oligopoly or monopoly characterized virtually every major industry in the U.S.[7] Representatives of the Classical ideology tended to ignore the manner in which the structure of the markets had changed in the U.S., the degree to which large corporations had become the dominant organizational form, and the extent to which oligopoly and monopoly characterized the important industries. There was the general pretense that large corporations differed little in social or economic significance from the "mom-and-pop" corner grocery store. Insofar as oligopolistic or monopolistic tendencies were addressed, they were often cited as the result of governmental interference, not as a reason for interference. Adam Smith believed that monopolies could arise only as a result of governmental interference, and the Classical ideology generally emphasized this line. Hence, the general response to governmental attempts to regulate industries, whether at the federal, state, or local levels, was negative.

Beginning in the late nineteenth century, however, the relationship between government and business was undergoing a profound change. The first big businesses in the U.S. were railroad companies, oil, and steel. In an attempt to regulate the railroad industry, the federal government established the Interstate Commerce Commission (1887) to determine questions of prices, fair return, market entry, routes, and so forth. When trucks and busses began to constitute viable competition, these were regulated by being subsumed under the ICC umbrella. As Congress turned to other industries, the ICC became the model for developing regulatory agencies in very different areas. Congress also took measures to insure a modicum of competition by attempting to regulate trusts through the Sherman and Clayton Acts.

A number of different kinds of responses were theoretically possible. The response to oligopoly or trust might have been socialization or nationalization of the large corporations in major industries. If those who owned and operated the railroads, for example, could not be trusted to act in the public interest, then the government could nationalize the railroads and operate them. This was not politically feasible in the U.S. Another solution might have been stringent enforcement of tough antitrust legislation, breaking up trusts and oligopolistic industries, and attempting to recreate genuinely competitive markets. This was probably not politically feasible either. Nor was this alternative without costs. Markets with real competition are volatile. That volatility is generally unattractive not only to business but also to workers and consumers. In addition to considerations of stability, one could also develop arguments for the economies of scale which could be achieved in less than competitive industries in which large organizations flourished. Consequently, regulation was selected only when "self-regulation" became politically untenable. The government could oversee various industries to insure that the economy in these sectors operated in the "public interest." The agencies, in principle, would weigh the differing interests and arrive at decisions. By controlling market entry, prices, return on investment, routes, etc., the regulators could hope to treat investors, consumers, and the general public fairly.

In contrast to the proponents of the Classical ideology who resisted these developments throughout this century and the last, Managerialists accept not only the reality of oligopoly but also the legitimacy of government regulation. Managerialists call attention to the existence of noncompetitive markets as another means of undermining what they believe to be the obsolete and simplistic view of the system which lies at the heart of the Classical ideology. Beyond this, Managerialists accept in principle that government has a role in this kind of regulation as a way of insuring the public good. Again, the moral reasoning could be utilitarian, optimizing public welfare.

But, again, there is nothing to suggest that corporations should act in any way other than profit maximization within the constraints imposed by the regulators. The assumption is that the regulatory environment is adversarial. Corporations make a case for a rate hike, for example, while those opposing the increases are also asked to testify. The regulatory board serves as the judge of the wisdom of the proposals. Corporations are not asked to determine what is in the public interest, although arguments presented by all parties will take the form of public interest arguments. Profit maximization within these constraints should insure actions consistent with the public interest. The regulatory body has the responsibility to represent the public interest, not corporations.

In the end, regulatory agencies posed no more threat to the interests of the dominant corporation than the adoption by the federal government of macropolicies. By the 1970s, the scholarly debate was not whether agencies primarily reflected the interests and needs of the large corporations in industries which were purportedly to be regulated for the public interest. The debate hinged on whether the regulatory agencies originally acted in the public interest and were then captured, or whether in their very inception they represent the influence of corporations seeking to control markets through the facade of the government.[8] Cross-industry regulation held the promise of making capture more difficult, but the evidence remains mixed. The results of the regulatory reform movement of the 1970s also seems to have produced few tangible results.[9] By the late 1970s, before the Reagan revolution, policy began to shift away from regulation toward deregulation.

Regardless of the contours of the debate, there is, from the public policy perspective, never an inclination to assume or rely upon the idea that a corporation should be a "good citizen" in any sense except to be honest and to seek profit within the regulatory rules established. Neither in the strong regulatory environment nor where there is movement toward deregulation is anything more than profit maximization within the boundaries of the law assumed. The models assume profit-maximizing behavior for efficient production.

Thus, it is still not clear why Managerialists would claim that corporations ought to do something other than profit maximize. The economic and political world may be much different from that posited by the Classical ideology, but as yet there is no good reason to believe that the role of the firm should be other than profit maximization, even with an active government. Government is the entity shouldering many new social responsibilities.

Or, consider the argument from externalities. By the turn of the century, a number of economists had begun to focus upon externalities in the markets of industrial capitalist countries. Economic texts continue to devote some attention to positive and negative externalities. Jones's enjoyment of her neighbor's well-kept flower garden is an often used example of a positive externality. Jones enjoys the benefits of the garden without having to pay for the garden. The price here is free. Negative externalities involve situations in which the total costs of production, social costs, are not reflected in the price of the product. The production of steel, to take another familiar example, may involve the spread of pollutants over a wide area. These pollutants may create not only lowered property values but significant increases in maintenance costs, as well as increase in respiratory diseases and death. These are real costs to society, but society bears the cost of production. The buyers do not. The costs are externalized.

In the ideal market of perfect competition, externalities do not exist. In the real world, however, there is substantial evidence that significant negative externalities persist. Their existence constituted another facet of the attack upon the Classical understanding, not only suggesting that the real world is very different from the ideal market, but also lending credence to the idea that government intervention is necessary to overcome the injustice of negative externalities. That the costs of production are not being paid by individuals enjoying the benefits of the production but by others can be considered unfair, unjust. Government intervention is required, it is often argued, to insure that real costs are reflected in the price, and/or to protect or compensate losers.

Thus, externalities could be taken as the starting point for an argument supporting the necessity of government regulation in certain areas. Here, again, there is little to support the idea that corporations should do something other than maximize profit within the con-straints of the law. Consider the following commonly cited scenario. Suppose a corporation exists in an industry with substantial negative externalities. Suppose the production processes involve serious pollu-tion of the air which contributes to acid rain, property destruction, respiratory disease, and some "extra" deaths. Profit maximization re-quires continuing to employ this process, since no others are available at prices which will allow the firm to be competitive with others utilizing the old technologies. Does a firm have a responsibility to introduce the new technology or to raise prices in an attempt to internalize costs on its own? One's intuitions might suggest that morality requires something like this, but those intuitions may be misleading. A corporation in such a situation cannot single-handedly confront the problem of externalities. The competitive environment would make it suicidal for the firm to deviate from the standards in the industry except where new technology was in fact profitable. Thus, how can a firm have a responsibility to do something which will in short order contribute to its demise? The solution would appear to be that government ought to act to internalize costs on the industry as a whole. There are still problems of equity here, since some firms will be in a better position than others to weather the new requirements. In fact, there is a tremendous incentive to delay new capital expenditures for environmentally superior technology until the government requires it, because this will usually insure maximum depreciation of the old equipment and timely purchase of new equipment. Nonetheless, morality does not seem to require self-sacrifice in situations like this. There may be a responsibility to solve the problem, but that responsibility may not reside primarily on the corporation or corporate managers. At most, corporations may have a responsibility in this kind of situation to support legislation which would remedy the problem of externalities. Even this, however, is not necessarily contrary to long-term profit maximization. Participation in the political process would increase the likelihood that the regulations finally adopted were those most comfortable for the industry.

To conclude, even by accepting the reality and legitimacy of the new role for government in the regulation of the economy, Managerialists have not provided any good reason to suppose that corporations ought to act in ways other than profit maximization. There is, nonetheless, a slightly different tone involved. Government involvement and regulation of the economy is not resisted in principle. But the responsibility for dealing with problems of growth, unemployment, externalities, oligopoly, monopoly, and so forth does not rest upon the corporation. The tone is that profit will be maximized within the constraints imposed by regulation. Corporations will become "good citizens" by making sure that their interests are represented in the political process generating those regulations.

Not surprisingly, then, the discussion shifts to an understanding of the real system, the political process. In the Classical view, the economic system is central, and the political process peripheral. By accepting the role of government in the economy, the political market becomes central. Managerialists understand the political process through the theory of political pluralism. What corporate responsibility means within that framework may well be something other than profit maximization.

10

The Meaning of Corporate
Responsibility in a Pluralist Framework

Pluralism is an even more fundamental component of the Managerial framework than Keynesianism, and not merely because Managerialists have recently sought to disassociate themselves from an economic theory which came under sustained attack during the crises of the 1970s and continues to be viewed with suspicion in some quarters. Managerialists remain committed, after all, to the general "Keynesian" ideas that government has a responsibility to take an active role in the economy to some extent, to soften the business cycle, to encourage growth, productivity, and investment, and to maintain acceptable levels of employment. Pluralism was fundamental even during the heyday of Keynesianism, for, as explained in the last chapter, macroeconomic theory itself introduces noneconomic political considerations. Economic techniques, adequately refined, may recommend strategies for achieving "acceptable" levels of unemployment, growth, investment, etc., but offer little, if any, guidance for what is to count as an acceptable level, which is a political determination. Pluralism provides not only a model with which to understand the process leading to those determinations but also a means by which to legitimize the outcomes of the process. More importantly, the incorporation of Keynesian theses will not explain the Managerial acceptance of the legitimacy of an active and expanded governmental role in areas such as a social security system, legal protections for unionization, or a number of other developments associated with the programs of the New Deal, New Frontier, and Great Society. Again, pluralism purports to be able to explain why and to some extent how

235

these programs arose, and to provide for their moral legitimacy. In the same vein, pluralism can be used to explain and legitimize the dominant Managerial theme of the big change.

Pluralism provides a larger framework within which to view the transformation of the capitalist system in the U.S., including the growth of big government. Thus, Managerialists claim to have not only insights into the working of the new system which has evolved but also a deeper understanding of the nature of forces which drive the society. In a sense, they claim to have grasped the nature of the "real system," in contrast to the mythic market system which stands at the heart of the Classical business ideology. That understanding is premised upon an interpretation of a democratic society as a pluralistic society. Pluralism is so central to the Managerial perspective that the stakeholder model itself is pluralism writ small.

In this chapter the general features of the pluralistic model will be traced, and Managerialists' use of the model to their own ends will be illustrated. The major tasks, however, are to explore the meaning of corporate social responsibility in this context, and to evaluate arguments which can be constructed from the materials of pluralism.

DESCRIPTIVE PLURALISM

In an attempt to explain social change, social science is concerned to identify different kinds of societies and then to formulate and test theories about their properties and tendencies. Both Plato and Aristotle proceeded along these lines, creating political typologies and then attempting to identify the dynamics functioning within each. An understanding of the dynamics, in fact, significantly shapes our normative judgments about a particular kind of system. In large part because of the instability believed to be inherent in democratic societies, for instance, neither Plato nor Aristotle thought highly of the democratic form. Pluralists think otherwise.

Although pluralists themselves often tend to blur the distinction, descriptive pluralism must be distinguished from prescriptive pluralism. As a descriptive theory, pluralism purports to *describe* the features of a pluralistic system, to *explain* political change, and to *identify* the tendencies inherent in this system. As such, descriptive pluralism does not offer judgments about whether a pluralistic society or changes within a pluralistic society are good or bad, morally legitimate or morally illegitimate. Pluralism is usually, however, put to those larger normative tests. Prescriptive pluralism can be characterized as a theory which *advocates* and *prescribes* a particular kind of system, a pluralistic system, and at the same time offers the means by which to *legitimize* changes within the system. Managerialists rely upon both descriptive and prescriptive theories of pluralism.

There are narrower and broader senses of pluralism, and each can function as a descriptive theory or a prescriptive/normative theory. In the narrower sense, descriptive pluralism is a *political theory* which describes the basic features of a pluralistic political system and identifies its important characteristics and tendencies. Roughly, pluralists contend that in a pluralistic political system there are multiple centers of power, and the American system, with the constitutional system of checks and balances, including the different levels of power, federal, state, county, and local, is identified as a pluralistic system. Prescriptive pluralism at this level defends or advocates this kind of pluralistic political structure as legitimate and claims that outcomes of such a legitimate process are themselves legitimate.

In the broader sense, descriptive pluralism is *a theory of political economy* which describes the basic features of a pluralistic society and identifies its important characteristics and tendencies. Pluralism in this sense is closely associated with pluralism in the narrower political sense, because pluralists contend that without a pluralistic distribution of power in society at large, the legal, institutional trappings of a pluralistic political system would hardly provide any guarantees against the abuses of a concentration of power. Prescriptive pluralism in this sense defends as legitimate a society in which there are competing groups of power. The pluralistic political system is defended in part as a means by which to insure that these centers of power remain diffuse.

Political theories and theories of political economy confront an especially troublesome problem in the U.S. The language and rhetoric of the political culture involves the rejection of elitist visions, such as those of Plato and Aristotle, and the adoption of the democratic ideals of popular citizen participation, majority rule, equal opportunity, and so forth. Unfortunately, the democratic rhetoric does not comfortably square with the language of the Constitution or political reality.[1] Pluralists maintain that the system in the U.S. is pluralistic and insist on describing that system as democratic.

In contrast with the Articles of Confederation, the U.S. Constitution does represent a move toward centralization, but according to the document power is largely decentralized. The document by no means embodies majoritarian participatory democratic ideals; on the contrary, it reflects as great a fear of the great unwashed masses as of tyranny in the person of another King George. Originally, the constitutional protection against both forms of tyranny was institutional and electoral, i.e., the guarantee of states' rights, and the restriction of the franchise to white, propertied males. Institutionally, the federal government was to provide an arena within which certain interests (e.g., states) could compete and rule. The outcome of the struggle for power was believed to yield what was in the best interest of the country. Even after the franchise was extended, these basic institutional protections remain. Originally, the sole point of access for the popular will was through elections to the U.S. House of Representatives. Until the late nineteenth century, of course, members of the Senate were elected by the state legislatures, insuring state governments a protection against the popular will of the nation. State legislatures themselves generally took pains to provide protection against too much popular influence at the state level. The executive branch is led by a president elected, not by popular vote, but by the electoral college, with the Senate again playing an important role. The judiciary is led by justices appointed for life terms by the president with the advice and consent of the Senate. The Bill of Rights further secured the power of the states against the federal government. The First Amendment provides that "Congress shall pass no law . . . ," leaving the door open that the state legislature might well choose to pass a law abridging freedoms of various kinds.

Until the revolution surrounding the interpretation of the Fourteenth Amendment, none of the Bill of Rights could be applied to limit the power of state governments. Subsequent movements which have increased the power of the federal government, movements associated with the crises of the Civil War, the Great War, and WWII, the Progressive Era, and the Depression, should not obscure the extent to which this system has remained radically decentralized, and the degree to which the political system remains insulated from the popular will.

This tension between political reality and the rhetoric of popular majoritarian democracy has made for interesting and innovative theories of social science, constitutional interpretation, and political philosophy. Historically and conceptually, these three very different kinds of theories function together, mutually reinforcing one another.[2]

The Classical business ideology attempted to deal with the tension in its own way. The central idea in this ideology is that of "the system," interpreted primarily as a socioeconomic market system in which individuals compete. Relying upon Classical Liberalism and Classical economic theory, the political dimension is and/or should remain peripheral to the system, interfering only to insure that the basic features of the system, free exchange, property rights, contract rights, etc., are protected. Large corporations and combines are assimilated into the model as if they were nothing more than another, ordinary individual, or as if they were not significantly different from the mom-and-pop grocery store on the corner. In spite of obvious evidence to the contrary, the Constitution is interpreted as a document embodying the ideals of the minimal state and the principles of the laissez-faire capitalist market. Not only does this not square with the plain meaning of the Constitution, it does not correspond to political reality. Historically, the powerful interests of the states often worked strenuously (and continue to work) to resist movements toward competitive markets. While ignoring constitutional, institutional factors, the Classical ideology emphasizes instead the electoral dimension of the political system. In this model, political behavior is explained by appeal to individuals, and the general presumption is that just as the consumer is king in the market, in the political arena "the people" are king. Democracy is interpreted as if it were a free market of votes. Not only does this ignore institutional constraints on the electoral process, but the image of the political arena as a free market in votes also poses serious difficulties for the doctrine of laissez-faire and minimal government. While the emphasis upon electoral politics imbues the ideology with a democratic, even a majoritarian, hue, "the people" have demonstrated time and again little patience with minimal government and free markets. If the political market democratically chooses to interfere in the economic market, then on what grounds can advocates of the Classical position complain about the more than minimal state arising?

This illustrates the deep ambivalence in Classical Liberalism toward democratic principles. If the function of government is to be limited to protection against harm, public or private, then there is little for a democratically elected Congress to do. Even if the democratic process yields outcomes which extend the scope of government beyond the range of the minimal state, the outcome is judged illegitimate. Even if the public harm principle is interpreted loosely, and taxation for the construction of infrastructure is considered to be morally legitimate in the minimal state, there is little for a legislature to do. Congress would be limited primarily to public works projects. Given the tendency to rely upon market solutions, the Classical Liberals would likely opt for letting the market meet most of the public's needs for infrastructure.

By adopting the pluralist model, Managerialists have incorporated one of the most powerful and widely accepted contemporary theories, one which avoids many of these pitfalls. In the years after WWII, pluralism has assumed the position of near orthodoxy in political science.[3] In political science, the perspective is represented in the works of V. O. Key,[4] Robert M. McIver,[5] Seymour M. Lipset,[6] Robert A. Dahl,[7] David Truman,[8] and E. E. Schattschnieder.[9]

Pluralism solves the problem of the tension between democratic ideals and reality with a new definition of democracy, captured in Joseph A. Schumpeter's claim that "the democratic method is that institutional arrangement for arriving at political decisions in which individuals acquire the power to decide by means of a competitive struggle for the people's vote."[10] As this definition suggests, pluralists are not concerned primarily with the nuances of electoral politics. That only a small percentage of the American electorate participates, for example, is no reason to suggest that this is a nondemocratic country. The important feature of the political system is the open and free competition for the vote, which provides some check on the power elites. Pluralists recognize that citizens do not directly participate in decision making, leaders do, in the context of bargaining, accommodation, and compromise.

Thus, for pluralists, a pluralistic society in which there is open and free competition for the vote is a democratic society. Accordingly, a democratic society will have many of the liberties associated with liberal, democratic societies, such as freedom of the press, speech, assembly, and so forth, since these are required for open competition for the vote. Aside from the minimal requirements for open competition for the vote and some degree of participation, however, pluralists are little concerned with the Constitution as a legal document, or with particular laws or legal principles.

Pluralists do not identify democracy with a set of legal procedures per se. Two kinds of "law" must be distinguished. In one sense, "law" refers to the fundamental procedural norms according to which substantive law, "law" in the second sense, is enacted. As long as the fundamental procedural norms require open competition for the vote and insure some degree of participation in the political process, pluralists describe a society as democratic.

For pluralists, the important guarantee of freedom and liberty is not the Constitution but the diffusion of economic and political power among competing groups. These groups may agree on nothing more than the common commitment to the fundamental procedural norms and may have dramatically different ideas about what kinds of laws should be passed, about the role of government in regulating the economy, and so forth. Hence, like models derived from assumptions of Classical economic theory, pluralism offers a competitive model of democracy and politics, but one which differs in crucial respects. In those, the basic actors are self-interested, utility-maximizing individuals competing in a market. Given important assumptions about the conditions defining the market, theorems that competition in the political or social market yield optimal outcomes can be proved. If optimality is morally relevant, then the Classical-based models also provide a means of legitimizing outcomes. Pluralism, on the other hand, is much more sensitive to the institutional framework of the political process and identifies the pluralistic nature of the constitutional system of checks and balances, with the electoral system being one important component of the system of checks and balances.

The basic actors in the pluralistic framework are not individual, self-interested utility maximizers but self-interested groups, each of which is attempting to maximize power. Rather than attempting to explain change by beginning with individuals making rational choices in a competitive environment, or by following Marxist explanations attempting to explain change by relying upon a conflict between social classes, pluralism emphasizes the role of groups, institutions, or organizations, in a competitive context.

This pluralistic emphasis is reflected in Frederick D. Sturdivant's *Business and Society: A Managerial Approach*. The author quotes a passage from *The Education of Henry Adams* in the opening paragraphs of his text.[11] As Adams, the great-grandson of John Adams and the grandson of John Quincy Adams, claimed even in 1918, modern "politics is, at bottom, a struggle not of men but of forces. The men become each year more and more creatures of force, massed about central power-houses." In the pluralist model, individuals are not ignored, but they are no longer considered significant variables in explanations of economic or political phenomena. Individuals are members of particular ethnic or religious groups, voluntary organizations, labor unions, trade or professional associations, political parties, and so forth.

Further, pluralists conceive of self-interest rather broadly. Economic interest is an important component of the self-interest which supposedly drives groups, but there is a tendency to assume that the fundamental drive is toward accumulation of power. Since economic resources are useful in the accumulation of power, there is often little practical difference.

Adopting the theoretical stance of the pluralists, the Constitution becomes, for Managerialists, a document incorporating fundamental procedural norms consistent with the pluralist definition of a democracy. Pluralistic democracy, within a pluralistic society, then, is the real system in America. Within this framework, specific laws will come and go, as different political constituencies succeed in the process. Laissez-faire ideas of minimal state government may dominate in one period; welfare-state, liberal ideals will dominate in another period. What remains unchanged is the real system, the pluralistic framework within which different groups compete.

In both the Classical and the pluralistic understanding of society the role of competition as regulator is critical. Pluralists claim that this system of groups, each driven by self-interest, is regulated by competition among groups. Outcomes are the result of the competition. The nature of competition is much different from what is presupposed in formal individualistic economic models, but it is real. And pluralism shares one other important feature with the Classical view. Just as in the Classical model, pluralists contend that competition yields significant benefits.[12] At the political level, competition occurs among leadership groups of ruling elites. At the broader level, there is competition among powerful interests in society. Vigorous competition at both levels allegedly provides security against tyranny. Whenever one group begins to threaten dominance, other groups will form, it is alleged, and coalitions of groups will band together to counterbalance the threat.

In this sense, the system not only offers some protection against tyranny but is supposedly stable. The freedom of the system allows groups to rise to meet challenges of domination, and the watchful eye of self-interest assures vigilance. This suggests that the system has the property of tending toward equilibrium, balancing competing interests. The system is also alleged to be stable in another sense. It is often argued that since all groups are allowed to participate and compete, there is little incentive for any group to seek to overthrow the system. Democracies last, it is claimed, because a broad range of interests are involved. Moreover, like the Classical model, decision making in this system is decentralized. Power is shared. The idea that the system reaches a general equilibrium is one of the major claims of John Kenneth Galbraith's *American Capitalism: The Concept of Countervailing Power*,[13] a favorite of the Managerialists, where recent trends are not only explained in pluralistic terms, but defended. This perspective allows a posture of being in touch with historical and economic reality, of being a tough realist, while also serving to calm any concerns over managerial discretion and corporate power. For Galbraith, the rise of corporate power and economic concentration is no reason for concern because these developments have precipitated the formation of other power centers: Big Labor, Big Agriculture, Big Distribution, and Big Government. These groups constitute an informal system of checks and balances, preventing absolute control in any one sector. Galbraith uses the term "countervailing power" to describe the thesis of self-regulation and the nature of the new competition among groups in this new system of American capitalism. Clearly, oligopolistic markets function quite differently from perfectly competitive markets, but the function of countervailing power is analogous to competition in the ideal system. Oligopolies will not abuse their potential monopoly power for fear that other interests will be aroused. Galbraith argues, for example, that if major tire companies, Big Industry, ever attempted to raise prices above those which are reasonable, and thereby achieve profits as a consequence of monopolistic control, the threat would be met by a representative from Big Distribution, say Sears, which would enter the market and produce tires. Or, if General Foods, from Big Industry, unreasonably raised prices of breakfast food, one of the major chains from Big Distribution, A & P for example, will stand ready to enter the market. Or, in response to unreasonable price increases by Big Industry, Big Government can step in.

This model explains the growth of Big Government, Big Labor, Big Agriculture, and Big Distribution. Big Labor grew as a predictable response to perceived threats to the working person. Government, also perceiving itself threatened, moved to create laws conducive to labor and opposed to Big Business as a way of protecting its own interests and of garnering a constituency among the working class. With this political foundation, Big Government could move to regulate and constrain Big Business. This kind of explanation of historical development sharply opposes the sort of interpretation typical of the Classical ideology. There, events like the growth of Big Government and Big Labor tend to be viewed as deviations from the true system which threaten growth and prosperity, and that kind of event is explained as the result of misinformation, greed, overreaction to the suffering of the Depression, and so forth.

Polemically, the pluralistic model works handily for the Managerialists against the Classical ideology. In the Managerialist scenario, the Classical worldview reflects the character of an earlier stage. What the Classical ideology identifies as the system is, in the pluralist view, nothing more than a description of power relationships which prevailed for a limited period in history. The pluralist model describes the true system which lies behind this transitory stage and explains why the true pluralistic system moves to different stages. That is, groups within the society are fighting for their own perceptions of their needs; self-interest drives change. The pluralistic model also functions to allow Managerialists to co-opt much of the rhetorical vocabulary of democracy, freedom, and free enterprise. Clearly freedom is not only a necessary condition for operation of the system, but the system itself protects freedom through decentralization of power and through the self-regulation of competition.

The American Business Creed notes that the Classical ideology singles out four attributes of the system for special attention.[14] In that view, the system is characterized as unique, natural, stable, and chosen. As the authors of *The American Business Creed* further remark, these attributes do not fit together without some tension. For instance, if capitalism is alleged to be the "natural" system which would develop if unhindered, then how can it also be chosen and unique? If the system is the result of some choice by citizens, then it is difficult to see how it can be considered to arise naturally. Or, if the system is natural, how can it also be unique? A natural system would likely arise nearly everywhere.[15] Further, if the system is chosen, how can it be stable? If the system rests upon the conscious choice of citizens, then at any moment the system would be in jeopardy. The people might choose to abandon laissez-faire capitalism for something else, like a welfare state.

These attributes are incorporated by the Managerialists. Although there is little emphasis upon uniqueness per se, Managerialists were once fond of speaking of the distinctively American character of this system. Galbraith is following this tradition in speaking of "American" capitalism. Moreover, Managerialists can infuse the pluralistic model with nationalism by identifying the creation of the country, the basic documents, with pluralistic principles. The important principles are those which articulate the fundamentals of the political process through which citizens participate and according to which certain freedoms are guaranteed. In this deeper sense, pluralism has remained unchanged through the history of the country, even though capitalism and the political structures themselves have undergone remarkable transformations. Pluralism allows for such change, peacefully and gradually.

The system can also be described as natural, insofar as the ideology assumes that the motivational assumptions are reflective of real humans, and insofar as competition will naturally arise between groups. The pluralistic system is also usually described as stable. Finally, although natural, there is a sense in which Managerialists could claim that the pluralistic system is chosen. If the pluralistic system was in the minds of the founding fathers, and if ratification was required, this system was chosen voluntarily. Furthermore, each generation must choose to perpetuate the system.

The chosen character of the system is nearly as strong within the Managerial ideology as in the Classical, although without taking on the religious overtones. Instead, Managerialists prefer to cast themselves as realistic moderates, fighting for the middle way between extremes. The conservatives, on the right, are perceived as blinded by rigid adherence to the principles of laissez-faire, an adherence which nearly led to the collapse of capitalism during the Depression. The new system was necessary to prevent radical social upheaval. The communists, on the left, are perceived as insensitive to the necessity for freedom in establishing an efficient system which will meet the needs of the people. The mixed system, instituted during the Depression, is the result of the stable and flexible pluralistic system responding to a changing world and unmet needs. Commitment to both the mixed system and the deeper pluralistic values is required. Commitment to the mixed system involves accepting the legitimacy of Big Labor and Big Government. Commitment to the pluralistic values involves accepting the legitimacy of democratic processes through which different political arrangements evolve. The Classical ideology is excoriated for a failure to understand either the mixed system or the underlying values of pluralism.

The fundamental commitment, the sense in which the pluralistic system is chosen, requires a commitment to few principles other than the legitimacy of the political process. Pluralists place little value in any particular constitutional system of checks and balances articulated in a constitution. Only a pluralistic society with competing social-economic groups can provide genuine security against tyranny. What is important in a constitution is that it articulates the ground rules for competition among groups and that groups are committed to abide by the ground rules. Government is primarily perceived as a set of ground rules within which competition among groups will occur. Some ground rules determine how the ground rules will be amended. The Constitution of the United States, for example, contains provisions for amendment. Even fundamental dissatisfaction with the ground rules must be channeled within the ground rules themselves. To alter them, there must be a commitment to the process. For example, a group may respond to the threats of another group in any number of ways, including lowering prices, entering the same manufacturing industry, going to court. These are all permissible. Armed force, revolution, and so forth are not permissible. Once a case has been fought through the courts, the case must not then be fought on the streets with violence. Hence, at this fundamental level, the system is chosen. At the same time, the necessity of choice should not be exaggerated, for in a pluralistic society power is decentralized sufficiently to prevent a group with revolutionary intent from succeeding. Moreover, since the pluralistic system is responding to needs of a good proportion of the population, dissatisfaction with the system should be minimal. The system should be stable.

The various uses of the pluralist model are evident throughout the Managerial literature, including Business and Society texts. In *Social Issues in Business*, by Fred Luthans, Richard Hodgetts, and Kenneth Thompson,[16] for example, a historical perspective is offered which gives a pluralistic explanation of developments. Pluralism functions in another way as well. For Managerialists, it is not enough to provide a historical perspective. Professional managers must be trained to operate in the contemporary arena. Toward that end, Managerialists offer the secret to the workings of the real system, i.e., a pluralistic model. For Luthans, Hodgetts, and Thompson this framework is offered in the second chapter, "Societal and Political Framework for Conducting Business." After having dealt with the "shortcomings" of the laissez-faire notions and the "realities" of the twentieth-century economic sphere, the chapter sketches a pluralistic model. Gailbraith's theory of countervailing power is explicitly employed.

Frederick D. Sturdivant's treatment in *Business and Society: A Managerial Perspective*,[17] parallels that found in *Social Issues in Business*. Sturdivant offers a historical perspective by explaining the origins of big business and the changing structure of business, and then he turns to "The Contemporary Setting and Social Change." Because the emphasis is sociological, the pluralistic foundation is not always apparent, but when Sturdivant turns specifically to political issues, in a chapter on "Corporate Political Behavior," the pluralistic perspective is explicit. Sturdivant, as usual, is hesitant to endorse a position overtly. He pits the Marxist and the pluralist perspectives against one another and at that point turns to consider the question of corporate power. Most of the discussion of corporate power rests upon the work of Edward M. Epstein, *The Corporation in American Politics*.[18] Epstein's view is pluralist, i.e., there are constraints within the system which protect the rest from the potential abuse of corporate excesses. Sturdivant concludes by quoting Epstein. Referring to intercorporate political competition, Epstein claims that the "net result is a degree of political pluralism within the corporate community that has prevented the emergence of a monolithic political force."[19]

Sturdivant devotes sufficient energy to detailing the growth of power in other sectors, such as labor, to complete a standard pluralistic description of the system. In the next edition, this chapter has been moved toward the beginning of the text. This is more logical from the point of view of one who seeks to initiate the future professional manager into the mysteries of how the system works. This understanding should be developed prior to the treatment of specific developments. This suggests that the authors of some of the best-selling texts for MBA courses which deal with social issues have opted for the pluralistic framework of analysis.

There remains a tension, however, between the Managerial claims and this larger pluralistic perspective. As chapters 7 and 8 demonstrated, Micro-Managerial arguments for social responsibility rely upon the thesis of managerial discretion, which assumes that the great resources of the corporation should be brought to bear on social problems as a result of the great power of the corporation. But the pluralistic model suggests that not only economic, but political, competition circumscribes managerial discretion. To argue that corporate power is limited by competition with other corporations and other groups, in accordance with the theory of countervailing power, is to restrict dramatically the power available to any corporation or any group of corporations. On the pluralistic model, there are not only economic market constraints but political constraints. Social responsibility is possible for the corporation only if it functions to consolidate power, or if corporations are competing with one another to act in a socially responsible fashion. These points will be developed below.

PRESCRIPTIVE PLURALISM

As I noted in the introduction and again in the previous chapter, many of the central normative claims of Managerialism appear to be asserted without argument, a bewildering and puzzling state of affairs. In discussions of the new ideology, for instance, the values and principles of the Classical framework are identified and contrasted with those of the Managerial framework, and the latter advocated, but without argument. This lack of explicit defense can be interpreted in a number of ways. Perhaps the most unkind interpretation suggests that this is nothing more than the result of confusion among advocates of the "new" ideology. Historical developments are sketched as if the narrator is merely *describing* trends, but then recent developments are embraced as legitimate, as if telling the story of the development of an event serves to legitimize it. On this interpretation, the shift is the result of confusing "is" with "ought," a confusion of facts with values or principles, a confusion of historical narrative with ethical argumentation. Describing a series of events leading up to the New Deal, to legislation enabling unionization, to shifts in dominant values (e.g., individualism to communalism) is one thing; it is quite another to offer, prescribe, and endorse those developments. The evidence relevant to each task is quite different, and a moral argument is required in the latter instance.

Another, slightly more sympathetic interpretation is possible. Managerialism may rest upon some version of the theory of ethical conventionalism. Ethical conventionalism, a theory with an ancient pedigree and already known to Plato, asserts, roughly, that whatever values and principles a society adopts are the morally correct ones for that society. The theory is often grounded in skepticism, the idea being that since there is no way of judging the correct moral values or principles, there must not be any one set of correct moral values or principles. How such an argument moves from the idea that there is no way of judging which values or principles are correct to the conclusion that therefore the ones which are accepted by one's society are correct always remains somewhat of a mystery. Contemporary versions of ethical conventionalism may not rest upon skepticism but upon theories of language, meaning, or upon related epistemological theories.

Given the centrality of pluralism, however, a much more sympathetic and interesting interpretation is possible. Prescriptive pluralism provides the means by which to provide a defense of the normative positions. Prescriptive pluralism is best understood as a particular instance of a procedural or process argument, a notion explained in chapter 3, where contract arguments were modeled as process arguments. A procedural argument involves the claim that the outcomes of morally legitimate procedures are themselves morally legitimate. Pluralistic arguments would claim that a pluralistic process is morally legitimate and that therefore the outcome of the process, whatever it might be, is morally legitimate. An active role for government in regulating the economy, a welfare role, a role in attempting to eliminate discrimination by sex, race, handicap, or nationality, for example, would be defended quite simply on the grounds that these are the results of a democratic, pluralistic process which is itself morally defensible.

At least three distinct kinds of prescriptive pluralism can be identified. These can best be understood by returning to distinctions drawn by John Rawls in A Theory of Justice.[20] Rawls distinguishes three different kinds of justice: perfect procedural justice, imperfect procedural justice, and pure procedural justice. These notions reflect three different types of process argument, and determining which is involved in prescriptive pluralism is important. Perfect and imperfect procedural justice presuppose that there is an independent standard for determining the justice of a particular distribution, and the problem is developing a procedure for achieving that outcome. In "perfect procedural justice," assuming that there is a standard for determining justice, there is a method or procedure for achieving the just outcome. An example is dividing a pie. If the assumed, independent standard is equal distribution, then there is a fairly simple procedure to yield an outcome which conforms to the standard, i.e., each person receives $1/n$ pieces of the pie where there are n persons. This situation is much different from the situation in which there is (supposedly) an independent standard for determining a just outcome, but there is no perfect procedure for assuring that outcome. Hence, this is dubbed "imperfect procedural justice." This is the case, for instance, in jury trials (at least in some simple jury trials). Here there is an independent criterion for determining the justice of the outcome, i.e., the defendant is really either guilty or innocent of the charge. He either murdered the victim premeditatedly or he did not. The problem is that there is *no procedure which guarantees that the just outcome will result.* A trial by jury, for instance, does not guarantee that all and only the guilty will be found guilty and that all and only the innocent will be found innocent. Thus, imperfect procedural justice is a rough justice which strives to reach just outcomes given a number of hindrances.

"Pure procedural justice" must be contrasted with both perfect and imperfect procedural justice because in these instances there is *no independent standard for determining the justice of an outcome.* In this situation, the justice of an outcome is entirely the result of having been the outcome of a procedure which is determined to have moral worth. As explained earlier, this case is allegedly illustrated by a poker game. Participants freely consent to play, they freely and knowingly agree to the rules of the game, and they bet freely. At the end of the evening, the chips are cashed in, and there is a particular distribution, usually different from what each player had at the beginning of the game. Is the final distribution just or fair? In situations such as this there is *no criterion to judge the justice of the outcome independent of the process itself.* In pure procedural justice, then, the outcome of a procedure, whatever it is, is just, provided that the procedure has been followed, no rules have been violated, and the procedure itself is just or fair. Whether an outcome is legitimate is a purely procedural matter.

Perfect procedural justice is rarely relevant. Hence, our attention can focus upon imperfect procedural justice and pure procedural justice. Tentatively, the structure of the pure procedural argument can be presented in a way analogous to the modeling of hypothetical process arguments (see chapter 3):

1. Any outcome O is legitimate (justified, just) if and only if
    a.   O arose from an initial situation S by process P;
    b.   Process P is a morally legitimate process; and,
    c.   Initial situation S is morally legitimate.
2. O arose from an initial situation S by process P.
3. Process P is a morally legitimate process.
4. Initial situation S is morally legitimate.
5. Therefore, O is morally legitimate.

The idea of imperfect justice can be tentatively sketched in a way almost identical to this:

1. Any outcome O is prima facie legitimate (justified, just) if and only if
   a. O arose from an initial situation S by process P;
   b. Process P is a morally legitimate process; and,
   c. Initial situation S is morally legitimate.
2. O arose from an initial situation S by process P.
3. Process P is a morally legitimate process.
4. Initial situation S is morally legitimate.
5. Therefore, O is prima facie morally legitimate.

The important difference here is that in an argument of imperfect procedural justice, being the outcome of a legitimate process does not in itself guarantee the moral legitimacy of an outcome. In criminal trials, for example, the procedure may occasionally or frequently yield incorrect results. However, being the outcome of the procedure, provided the procedure is morally legitimate, establishes good moral reasons for accepting the moral legitimacy of the outcome. In some cases, the burden of proof is upon someone who would challenge the moral legitimacy of the outcome. In pure procedural justice, this caveat is not necessary. Since pure procedural arguments presuppose that there are no independent criteria by which to judge the outcome, there are no grounds for complaint, provided the procedure which generates that outcome is morally legitimate *and* provided that the procedure has been followed.[21]

Prescriptive pluralistic process arguments can be employed in a wide variety of ways, two of which are most relevant here. First, these arguments can be invoked in the narrow context of the political. In this sense, the procedure involved refers to the primary set of rules in a society to determine law. In the U.S., this refers to the federal constitutional system, with fifty other state constitutions, each establishing procedures for generating law, each containing substantive law which arose from those procedures, and each possessing procedures determining the rules for changing the procedures. An example of the last aspect of the procedure is the article of the Constitution which establish the requirements for amending the Constitution. Pluralists can take the position that legislation concerning unionization, affirmative action, occupational safety and health, environmental protection, and so forth is morally legitimate because it has arisen as the result of a morally legitimate political process. Second, prescriptive pluralism can function in a much broader way. The process invoked may refer, not narrowly to the political process, but, more broadly, to the larger framework of a pluralistic society. Indeed, here is the major locus of pluralist concern. In this sense, prescriptive pluralism might attempt to legitimize values and principles which arise in a democratic, pluralistic society as a result of the competition among groups. The big change which has allegedly transformed our society can be legitimized in this way. The values of the new ideology could be similarly justified. These "outcomes" are not, strictly speaking, the legal or political outcomes of the formal mechanisms of government, but are the outcomes of the competitive interaction of groups within the society quite apart from the political process. This is the kind of argument which Michael Walzer appears to be advancing in *Spheres of Justice: A Defense of Pluralism and Equality*,[22] albeit for very different ends. For Walzer, interactions among groups yields shared meanings. Moral principles are embedded in these shared meanings and can be derived from nowhere else. These meanings and principles are legitimate and binding upon "us" because "we" have constructed them.

But should prescriptive pluralists, Managerialists in particular, be interpreted as adopting an argument embodying pure procedural justice or imperfect procedural justice? Most, following a line of reasoning very similar to Walzer's, appear to opt for the former. Construing prescriptive pluralism as involving pure procedural justice, however, confronts serious difficulties.

The initial attractiveness of interpreting the argument as one of pure procedural justice is that it gives the impression of avoiding appeal to substantive moral considerations. On this interpretation, the claim is that there are no standards independent of the process itself by which to determine the merit of the outcome. Whatever arises is legitimate. The Managerialists can claim that the procedure in a democratic, pluralistic society is morally defensible (fair, just, etc.), and therefore as long as the game is played according to the rules, the outcome, whatever it is, is morally legitimate (fair, just, etc.). More broadly, whatever values and principles arise in a pluralistic society, even if they are not formalized in law, are the morally correct values and principles because they are the outcome of the pluralistic society. This kind of an argument parallels familiar arguments employed in defense of unequal distributions within free market capitalism. Those arguments appeal to the moral defensibility of the game. The free market is interpreted as a game involving free exchange of goods and services. The claim is then that the result of individual free choice in the market is morally legitimate regardless of the equality of the distributions, provided that the rules are followed. Indeed, Managerialists can still evoke this kind of argument in defense of economic inequalities since they can claim that the free market still exists and that government regulation has, in fact, served the function of making the game more fair.

On the surface, this view appears to collapse into ethical conventionalism. Indeed, it confronts many of the same difficulties. For one thing, the theory requires that one clarify the method according to which one determines which values and principles the pluralistic society has created or chosen. Identifying the alleged outcome is extremely difficult regardless of the instrument chosen, and very different theories will be generated depending upon the instrument selected. Should opinion surveys be commissioned, for instance? If so, what will count as acceptance by society? If 51 percent of individuals surveyed respond that they believe that action A is immoral, or principle P is morally legitimate, will that constitute social acceptance? If 51 percent endorse the values of the new ideology, is that sufficient to count as social acceptance? Or, should we require a more substantive majority of 60 percent, 66.6 percent, 75 percent, etc.? A strong case can be made that opinion surveys themselves are an inadequate measure of social norms. What if 90 percent claim that a particular principle P is morally legitimate, but 85 percent of the individuals rarely if ever adhere to the principle? What if 90 percent endorse social responsibility but few act upon it? Perhaps survey research is not the correct instrument for determining society's acceptance, and a more behavior-based instrument should be utilized.

This kind of difficulty afflicts Walzer. Walzer claims that within each sphere of meaning, such as the sphere of education or the sphere of health care, there is an implicit distributional principle according to which the goods within a sphere are to be allocated. Hence, by claiming that the principle in the health care sphere is to distribute health care according to need, not according to the ability to pay, Walzer can attack those who have different ideas about reform of the health care delivery system. But Walzer has little to say about how one identifies this principle as *the* principle in this sphere. Identifying the principle appears as a substitute for providing a defense of the principle.

Even if some values and principles could be identified by a defensible instrument (survey, observation), it is doubtful that there would be very many. In most areas of life, there is likely to be uncertainty, disagreement, unclarity. In these areas, there would be no way of providing moral guidance. Nor does the theory provide resources for dealing with novel situations which arise as society changes. If there are no relevant principles upon which society has agreed to deal with new situations, then any approach would appear to be moral until society makes a clear determination. Conversely, any dissent to clearly accepted principles constitutes an attack on moral principles. Protest is immoral. If certain values and principles have arisen in the pluralistic society, these are moral by virtue of their being an outcome of the pluralistic society. Any attempt to alter these would, by hypothesis, be wrong. There is no ground from which to criticize morally the conventional morality of society.

In addition to these concerns, there are others which arise by virtue of the theory. Two are critical. First, there is no good reason for believing that there is such a thing as a pure procedural argument. Second, although these arguments give the initial impression of not invoking any substantive moral principles, the analysis of the structure of process arguments reveals that an appeal to moral considerations is an essential component of prescriptive pluralism whether interpreted as pure procedure or as imperfect procedural justice. At root, these two points are one. Since the defense of the procedure requires appeal to substantive moral considerations, these considerations will bear upon the type of procedure adopted. And that decision is based in large part upon the outcomes which a process will generate.

The logical structure of process arguments makes the role of moral and empirical claims quite apparent. It should not go unnoticed that Premise 1 requires defense. In the context of the discussion of hypothetical process arguments, an analogous premise was identified as the fundamental assumption of those arguments. Here, this premise is fundamental to these process arguments. The premise cannot merely be assumed; it must be defended. Moral arguments are required to support the claim that this is the morally legitimate way to determine questions of law, social structure, distributions, and so forth. Classical Liberals, for example, would strongly object to the idea that the nature of the state should be determined by a pluralistic process. I have, I hope, persuasively demonstrated the weakness of the Classical Liberal position. That, however, does not provide a defense of this claim.

What reasons can be offered in its support? Managerialists provide few, if any.

Even granting Premise 1, moral considerations are necessary to establish the argument. Premise 1 entails that a moral case be made for the adequacy of the initial situation S and the particular process P invoked. Hence, far from avoiding substantive moral claims, process arguments, even interpreted as embodying pure procedural justice, rest upon them. Pluralists may not merely assume that the procedure is morally defensible. The kinds of considerations to which appeal will be made in an effort to defend Premise 1, Premise 3, or Premise 4 will require appeal to something like natural rights theory, utilitarianism, contractarianism, or Kantianism, for instance. Historically, pluralists began by rejecting the natural rights paradigm for understanding society, for interpreting the Constitution, and for political theory, but there is nothing to prevent natural rights theory being employed at this level. Pluralists often seem to rely upon claims about the stability and/or the utility of the pluralist system, upon claims about the degree to which a pluralistic distribution of power is a guarantor of freedom from tyranny and liberty.

Because prescriptive pluralism as an instance of a process argument requires appeal to moral considerations, there are standards for determining the legitimacy of an outcome which are independent of the outcome. Thus, there is no such thing as pure procedural justice. Consider, as an illustration, struggling with the issue of the distribution of some good in a society. In some specific situations, we are tempted to adopt a process by which to allocate benefits or burdens. But not every process will be appropriate. Procedures which may be appropriate in one context are inappropriate in another. We make that determination in large measure by considering the distribution which would arise by adoption of the procedure. Consider the sphere of medical need. I have a Band-Aid. There are two individuals who come to me. One needs a Band-Aid, another does not. Should we throw the dice to determine who receives the Band-Aid? Of course not. If a procedure is appropriate to a sphere it is because we already understand in some sense how the adoption of a procedure will distribute benefits and burdens. That is, we already possess some independent criteria to determine the legitimacy of the outcome, even though those criteria may not yield very determinate judgments. Given these criteria, we may then search for a procedure to sharpen the judgments. In any case, there would appear to be few important spheres in which there are not some independent standards for judging the outcomes. Rawls's use of reflective equilibrium itself demonstrates the extent to which we judge the adequacy of a procedure by considering the possible outcomes.

There are other reasons for rejecting the idea that what is involved is pure procedural justice. In a pluralistic society, nearly everyone believes that the views of her group, organization, party, association, religious sect has the truth about morality. Thus, nearly everyone will view the pluralistic process as yielding outcomes which only approximate justice. Groups will struggle with others to seek outcomes consistent with their own view of morality and justice. There is wide consensus that the process is morally defensible, and that outcomes carry some strong moral weight. Outcomes possess a certain authority and temporary finality, as it were. Everyone will abide by the outcome of the process without resorting to revolution or rebellion. Disagreements will result in attempting to use the political process or the quasi-political processes to achieve a different outcome in the next go-round. This suggests that in a pluralistic society, while there may exist divergent conceptions of justice and morality, the different visions must share some common features insofar as the overall legitimacy of the pluralistic process is accepted in general. But, the process is accepted in large part because the outcomes it generates approximate those acceptable to the competing groups. In short, it is difficult to imagine a real society in which groups viewed the pluralistic process as something other than imperfect procedural justice.

Pluralists themselves usually appeal to results of the process in an attempt to provide legitimacy. To claim that democratic pluralism is a legitimate process because it protects our interests in liberty against tyranny, that it is stable because it provides for a mechanism for influencing the formation of public policy, that it produces what is best for all, and so forth are all appeals to the consequences or results of adopting the procedure. That is, these reflect appeals to standards independent of the process by which to judge the legitimacy of the process.

MANAGERIALISM AND PRESCRIPTIVE PLURALISM

There is, then, good reason to believe that prescriptive pluralism is best interpreted as involving imperfect procedural justice, not merely pure procedural justice, and, thus, a sympathetic reading of Manageralism requires interpreting that position in this light as well. But, given this understanding, what sense can be made of corporate social responsibility? How adequate are the arguments which can be generated to support the major normative claims?

Appealing to imperfect procedural justice in no way minimizes the need to provide moral argumentation. The same normative tasks confront the defender of pluralism invoking imperfect procedural justice as the defender invoking pure procedural justice. In addition to having to defend Premise 1, the central idea of process arguments, the moral legitimacy of the particular procedure involved must be established, as well as the legitimacy of the initial situation.

Neither pluralists nor Managerialists devote adequate attention to these tasks. However, unless Managerialists can offer a compelling moral defense not only for the basic premise of a process argument, but for the premises which assert that the initial situation and process itself are morally legitimate, then the appeal to the process for legitimation is hollow. Outcomes arising from the pluralistic society or arising from the political process are entirely groundless without this kind of defense. And such a defense is lacking.

Any attempt to suggest that the initial situation and the procedure itself are morally legitimate will confront serious difficulties. These claims have proved to be the Achilles' heel of pluralism. Critics have continually assailed the elitist and conservative biases built into this account. Because pluralism favors the major established players, those with superior organizations and resources, and the individuals associated with those groups, pluralism is vulnerable to objections of being fundamentally unfair. Such objections revolve around Premise 3, Premise 4, or both. For instance, a plausible case can be made that certain organized interests had an obvious and decided advantage when the process began, and, hence, the initial situation is not morally legitimate, not entirely fair. In the U.S., the franchise was so very narrow that significant proportions of the population were unable to participate in the competition for the leadership elites or to organize alternative leadership cliques. Further, the economic distribution already favored certain interests when the game began.

Or, this objection may also be interpreted as directed at the process itself. In the pluralistic process, only strong players will generally have much of an impact on outcomes. There is a built-in bias toward the already strong, mature players. Indeed, there is good evidence that such a system would inherently work to the advantage of well-positioned corporate and industrial interests. The intuitive normative appeal of pluralism rests upon the notion of the fairness of the competition, and the theory of countervailing power assumes the ability of threatened individuals to form groups, and of weak groups to form coalitions to protect their own interests. Mancur Olson's *The Logic of Collective Action: Public Goods and the Theory of Groups* demonstrates the obstacles to the formation of groups to counter the prevailing institutionalized power arrangements.[23] The costs to individuals of organizing groups or coalitions of groups is sufficiently high as to make concerted actions irrational from the perspective of the individual, given the remote probability that such concerted action will be successful and given the small individual gain to be achieved even if the effort is successful. This is especially true where there are individuals of marginal means. The obstacles to organization are extremely high for individuals with significant constraints of education, finance, experience in organization, and experience in the political process itself. Hence, creating an alternative center of power is virtually impossible. Further, given the limited resources, the group has little to offer other groups in exchange for a coalition. Coalition building is thwarted. There is little incentive for established groups to take in these individuals either. The consequence of this kind of a system is that the inequalities persist. Worse, the powerful may exploit the have nots, at least to that point where the marginal costs of organizing begin to outweigh the costs of the status quo. The theory of countervailing power may keep the powerful groups from absorbing one another, but there is little to prevent the powerful groups from mutually taking advantage of the powerless. Robert Paul Wolff puts the criticism this way:[24]

> The application of the theory of pluralism always favors the groups in existence against those in the process of formulation. . . . The theory of pluralism does not espouse the interests of the unionized against the non-unionized, or of the large against small business; but by presenting a picture of the American economy in which those disadvantaged elements do not appear, it tends to perpetuate the inequality by ignoring rather than justifying it. (152–153)

Such a system may continue to be stable, as long as those excluded confront significant individual costs for organizing. The nature of the decentralized process also increases the costs for the immature players. Significant public policy decisions are made in what political scientists now refer to as subgovernments. In the Congress today there are around 250 subcommittees, each of which deals with some rather arcane matter of public concern. Each representative is tied to a set of powerful corporate, labor, and "public interest" groups. Policy formulation and discussion is "public," but only the stronger players really participate. Even knowledge of how the system works is often unavailable to weak and inexperienced players. And even if those players knew how the system worked, there are few financial resources to develop the policy alternatives which may positively affect the well-being of these weak players.

The obvious response to this kind of objection of unfairness is to claim that it is merely carping. To paraphrase Churchill, one might respond that pluralistic democracy is the worst system, except for all the others. Realists suggest that of course the pluralistic system is imperfect, but they will defend it as viable and probably the best in light of human proclivities for mischief. Despite cute turns of phrase, these defenses still rest upon the claim that this is the best system possible, and that claim requires defense. And those defenses confront the same kinds of obstacles associated with attempts to defend free markets as producing what is best for all on the basis of rule utilitarianism/economic theory. They require explaining what best for all means, explaining how one would measure this, and then demonstrating that in reality this system produces what is best for all. But even granting that this could be done, this avoids the issue of whether one might be willing to sacrifice aggregate utility for a system which did take into account the interests of the weakest players in the pluralistic game. Would it be worth settling for the second best, for instance, as a trade-off for a "fairer" procedure?

An even more damaging criticism, potentially, is the claim that contemporary reality is not genuinely pluralistic even with respect to the major actors. This objection is analogous to the objection concerning the Existence Premise used in connection with the utilitarian defense of the free market. If an economic theorem demonstrates that the free market reaches an equilibrium which is Pareto optimal, but the theorem rests upon idealistic assumptions which do not correspond to reality, then there is a serious question of the relevance of the theorem. A similar problem afflicts pluralism. If, for example, a few large corporations dominate, then the legitimacy of the outcomes is in serious doubt because society is not, as pluralism requires, pluralistic. There is no longer even any prima facie case to be made for the morality of outcomes. Thus, the question of corporate power in society is at the heart of the issue. This is an empirical issue with enormous moral consequence.

Pluralists themselves are divided over many of these issues. In *Democratic Theories and the Constitution*, [25] Martin Edelman distinguishes "realists" from "optimalists" in the pluralist camp. Realists accept prescriptive pluralism and argue that the kinds of objections raised here are merely a part of the price of a democratic system which is stable and functional.[26] The optimalists, on the other hand, accept the competitive paradigm of prescriptive pluralism, but do not wholeheartedly endorse the existing political process.[27]

> Rather, they insist upon the need for restructuring the existing political institutions in order to make the American polity *more* democratic. In their eyes, the United States is a democracy whose institutions prevent us from enjoying the full benefits of democratic government. They want to create structures which would make those additional benefits possible. (121)

Although Edelman focuses upon reform proposals for the political process itself, such as restructuring the party system, there is nothing to prevent an optimalist from claiming that the solution is to reform not merely the process but also the power imbalances of society itself.

Thus, just as the moral defense offered within the Classical framework teeters upon the Existence Premise, the claim that contemporary reality resembles the competitive market and produces what is best for all, pluralism rests upon the claim that the procedure which generates outcomes, in both the narrower and broader senses of the procedure, is genuinely competitive. There is another parallel. Keynes and others challenged the theoretical claim that the market would self-correct to overcome problems of unemployment, lack of investment, or growth. An analogous question faces the pluralists. There is some reason to doubt whether the pluralistic society is stable, or whether pluralistic competition produces what is morally desirable. If actors believe that competition for power is healthy and produces what is in the public interest, members of each group begin to think of nothing but the interests of their group. There is no incentive to think about or defend the public interest. It is unnecessary. Moreover, pluralists are wary of moral argumentation, which explains in part their tendency to ignore the kinds of moral arguments which might defend their own theory and to cultivate a cynicism about the moral argumentation of groups which claim to be concerned about the public good. Further, participants in the pluralistic adversarial process will themselves discount moral arguments by competing groups, any arguments pertaining to the public good, as merely thinly veiled attempts to consolidate their own position of power at the expense of others. Relying upon the competitive process to yield optimal outcomes, groups will concern themselves with only their own interests. As a result, no one has an interest in the public interest.

And even if the theory of countervailing power functions, the political process can become so convoluted, with each powerful actor fearing that any change will have a negative impact on the interests of its members, that pluralism may well result in an equilibrium which is nothing more than a policy gridlock. This tendency is exacerbated during economic downturns or economic crises. Lester Thurow's complaint in *The Zero-Sum Society*[28] that because of this kind of gridlock the U.S. cannot formulate a realistic policy to solve the most serious problems is as appropriate today as it was in 1980.

> This is the heart of our fundamental problem. Our economic problems are solvable. For most of our problems there are several solutions. But all these solutions have the characteristic that someone must suffer large economic losses. No one wants to volunteer for this role, and we have a political process that is incapable of forcing anyone to shoulder this burden. Everyone wants someone else to suffer the necessary economic losses, and as a consequence none of the possible solutions can be adopted. (11)

Hence, the Managerial reliance upon descriptive and prescriptive pluralism does not alleviate the necessity of coming to grips with very serious empirical and moral issues which haunt the pluralist model. I am not arguing that prescriptive pluralism is morally flawed. Interpreted as imperfect procedural justice, prescriptive pluralism becomes only a component of a larger normative framework for evaluating outcomes. But without developing such a normative framework, the procedure itself lacks force, and it is impossible to develop judgments about the adequacy of outcomes of the process. That certain outcomes have arisen from the process, for example, may provide prima facie justification, but only at best prima facie justification. This does not answer the question whether the corporation, or corporations within a particular industry, should attempt to defeat legislation once passed, or to support it. Nor does this answer the question whether to work to defeat or to support new legislation.

Throughout, the underlying assumption again appears to be little more than the counterintuitive "enlightened" self-interest argument, that there will be a harmony of corporate interests and public interests. But, within the pluralistic framework, a novel twist is given to this. Corporate responsibility makes little sense given the pluralistic model. Or, one should say, corporate responsibility has meaning, but a very different meaning, from what apologists would like to admit.

Micro-Managerialists want it both ways. On the one hand, Micro-Managerial arguments presume great corporate power and a robust thesis of managerial discretion and claim that this entails great responsibility. I have argued that these assumptions, if true, are morally untenable insofar as they are contrary to our deepest convictions about democratic values. On the other hand, if pressed, Micro-Managerialists are likely to deny that corporate managers have power sufficiently great to constitute a threat. If this is true, however, the thesis of corporate responsibility is undermined, since responsibility requires that one have the ability to discharge the responsibility. The entire discussion is muddled by the failure of Micro-Managerialists to place the corporation in a context. Pluralism provides that context, and Macro-Managerialists use the model to understand the role of the corporation in society. Nonetheless, a similar dilemma arises. If society is genuinely pluralistic, corporate power is checked by other centers of power. This, however, dramatically reduces the extent to which the thesis of managerial discretion can be interpreted robustly and limits the ability to use corporate resources for the public good. If society is not genuinely pluralistic, then the robust interpretation is possible, but prescriptive pluralism collapses.

Consider each of these two possible scenarios in turn, and the implications for determining the appropriate role of the corporation in society, the implications for the meaning of corporate responsibility.[29] First, suppose that society is genuinely pluralistic, that there is vigorous competition among diverse groups, that there is open and free competition for the vote, that the population has some influence (if not control) over the formation of government policy and law. Suppose that the large corporations exist as major actors within the corporate and business sectors, that there is competition with one another on some levels and cooperation at other levels on issues of mutual interest, such as lobbying against legislation viewed as contrary to corporate interests. Suppose also that there is competition from other nonbusiness groups in the society.

Assuming the perspective of the pluralist model, what are the responsibilities of the large managerial corporation in this context? The answer is simple and straightforward: *actors will and should act in such a way as to maximize their own power.* Most would assume that there is little need to add "and should," given the implicit assumption that groups will act in self-interested ways. However, even if groups could rise above their own self-interest, the model relies upon self-interested behavior to produce competition, and competition insures that outcomes will be conducive to the overall good. This is a moral argument akin to the argument for profit maximization within the Classical framework, and, like that argument, this one makes use of the concepts of self-interest, competition as regulator, and a process which yields socially beneficial outcomes.

Conceptually, there is an important difference between power and profit. Although power and wealth are not identical, in our society there is little doubt that they are intimately related, and the pursuit of long-term profit and power will come to very much the same thing. Political influence can insure long-term profitability. Power to shape legislation or to influence regulatory bodies, for example, have an immediate impact on the bottom-line long term. If industries can capture regulatory agencies, for instance, power is a means toward long-term profitability. The result is stability within the industry, an environment in which planning horizons are manageable, growth is relatively secure, returns predictable, and supply continuous. The desire for profits requires control over the external environment, and this control is achieved politically through the regulatory agencies.

These arrangements are "successful" unless the industry stirs the consumers (or at least some of the politically potent consumers) to action through high prices or shoddy products. Such abuses might result in threats of deregulation or even in some cases of movements toward real deregulation. Or, international competition might upset the comfortable regulatory arrangement by offering domestic consumers better-quality goods at lower prices. Deregulation constitutes a loss of power, a loss of control over the environment, and usually a significant threat to profitability. Thus, in spite of rhetoric about "getting government off our backs," there is a strong incentive to retain the comfortable regulatory environment.

Against the pluralistic framework, the stakeholder analysis is given a slightly different hue as well. To gain and retain political power or influence, constituencies must be cultivated to form coalitions of interests. That involves managing perceptions (public relations), as well as actually providing some tangible benefits. The rhetoric about corporate responsibility, viewed through the lens of political pluralism, should be taken as a part of the strategy of maintaining and maximizing power by attempting to co-opt potential adversaries, to convince potential adversaries of a congruence of interests, and to continue to nurture existing coalition members. One of the least useful tactics in this strategy would be to proclaim that the primary interest of the firm is profitability or that relationships are purely contractual and based upon economic considerations. It is much better to speak about "good citizenship." Indeed, corporations are among the best citizens, measured by political participation. They are among the major actors.

Although some would be tempted to castigate this view of corporate responsibility as cynical duplicity, this view follows from the attempt to develop a moral argument from within the pluralistic framework, assuming the scenario that political power is widely dispersed. Morality would tolerate, even require, public relations (not fraud) for the sake of following the principle "Maximize power for your firm or your group." Corporate interests are bound up with thousands whose livelihood depends upon the prosperity of the firm. And this analysis is not reserved for corporate interests alone. The same kind of analysis would hold for government. In the pluralist model, government plays a dual role. On the one hand, it is referee. But its role as referee is extremely minimal. Pluralists do not believe that government can be a good guarantor of liberty and freedom. Only the pluralistic dispersion of political and economic power can do that. On the other hand, then, government, with its own interests and agenda, is merely another actor in the pluralistic drama. The important point, however, is that freedom from tyranny is guaranteed only by groups in vigorous competition for power. Competition regulates the power-maximizing actors. Being a good citizen, being socially responsible, means attempting to maximize power. In practice, that comes to much the same thing as profit maximization.

Suppose, on the other hand, that contemporary society is not genuinely pluralistic. Suppose that there is a single group or a small coalition of groups with such dominance that even if other groups mounted a concerted attempt to organize and prevail, the effort would be in vain. Suppose that this dominant group has sufficient resources to thwart any effective opposition. It hardly matters whether the formal machinery of a pluralistic, democratic society exists. As pluralists stress, a genuine distribution of power among competing groups is most critical. If one assumes, for the sake of argument, that this is the situation in the U.S., then what is the responsibility of the large, managerial corporation? There are, in turn, two cases here.

In one case, assume that the corporation is a member of the non-dominant group. In that case, the pluralist would assume that the corporate sector would work to establish coalitions with others to wrest power away from the dominant group. Thus, corporate responsibility in this case is the same as in the case of a genuinely pluralistic society: one ought to maximize power for one's group. The justification here will vary, however. Prescriptive pluralists believe that the democratic, pluralistic society is morally desirable whether it is an actuality or not. Here, power seeking is a strategy designed to bring about the genuinely pluralistic society. Again, there is hardly any need to preach this. Groups will inevitably act according to the maxim of maximizing power. The point is, however, that power maximization is not amoral or immoral. It is morally required to instantiate pluralism.

Of more interest is the case in which the corporate sector, or a part of it, constitutes the dominant group responsible for the nonpluralistic situation. One would be tempted to claim that corporations within the dominant sector have a responsibility to yield power and influence to others as a means of redistributing power for the sake of restoring the competitive pluralistic situation. This, however, creates a tension within a model assuming self-interested behavior. Moreover, if other-directed behavior is impossible, it cannot be morally required. "Ought" implies "can."

The situation hardly changes even if one relaxes the motivational assumption slightly. If it is possible for particular corporations to yield power and act contrary to their own interests and in the interest of others, it is not clear that they would have a responsibility to act in this way if the action would be ineffective. The situation is analogous to that discussed in the context of negative externalities. Unless the corporations within the dominant group act in concert to disperse power within the society, the actions of a few within that group are likely to be ineffective. The result would not be the wider dispersion of power but the concentration of power in fewer hands. The act of attempting to yield power would likely result in corporate suicide, as the resources of the other dominant corporations moved into the vacuum created by the "public spirited" corporations.

Thus, the notion of corporate responsibility within this scenario at best might mean "act in ways which restore the pluralistic dispersion of power," but the motivational assumptions of the pluralistic model fly in the face of this reading. Even relaxing the requirement, the situation may be such that any move by a particular actor or small group of actors will be ineffective and suicidal. It is an open question whether morality requires suicidal and ineffective actions even when the victim of the suicide is an artificial person, the corporation. Corporate deaths, dissolution, or bankruptcies do have a negative impact upon real persons, employees, managers, stockholders. Would morality require sacrifices on their parts for the sake of some ineffective symbolic act? One would hardly believe that. In short, "corporate responsibility" in this scenario is also without significant sense.

CONCLUSION

Macro-Mangerialism offers a much clearer and more persuasive account of significant structural changes within society than Micro-Managerialism, but precision carries a price. I have argued that Managerialists have incorporated the tenets of Revisionist Liberalism, specifically New Deal Liberalism, but that the most important ramifications are for the formulation of public policy, not corporate policy. The economic doctrines, which I have referred to as broadly Keynesian, are not premised upon any notion that corporations should act to do anything other than seek profit. On the contrary, they require it. The reliance upon descriptive pluralism helps to explain change, but Managerialists fail to develop adequately a defense for prescriptive pluralism. More importantly, corporate responsibility is no more at home within this framework than within the economic one. Power maximization is the operative assumption. While conceptually distinct from profit maximization, there is probably little practical difference. That is not, in itself, a condemnation. The issue is whether that is morally defensible. Managerialists have failed to make the case.

11

Liberalism and the Corporation: The Challenge of the Global Market

What is the appropriate role of the modern corporation in a liberal society? The philosophical analysis of the debate over this fundamental question has focused upon the responses of the Classical and Managerial business ideologies and has unearthed and then evaluated the arguments which can be offered in their support. Reconstructing the arguments required identifying the descriptive and normative models at the heart of each perspective, and because the responses to the fundamental question entail formulating a position concerning the appropriate role of government in the society as well, descriptive and normative theories of political economy were especially central to the investigation. Not surprisingly, the Classical and the Managerial perspectives share a common body of liberal beliefs, values, and principles. That the analysis has emphasized the extent to which each ideology represents a different version of the liberal tradition is not meant to suggest that the nature of the disagreement rests upon disputes over basic, normative theories. Indeed, since normative principles and theories are extremely fact sensitive, much of the disagreement hinges upon disputes over facts, general empirical claims, or descriptive models, rather than basic or fundamental values, normative claims, or ethical theories.

The Classical view that the government should be minimal and that the corporation should be concerned primarily or exclusively with profit rests upon the theory of political morality known as Classical Liberalism. Analysis has revealed the inadequacy of this position. Many traditions of moral theory have been invoked to provide a moral defense of the basic tenets of Classical Liberalism, and three of the most influential and important were examined in detail: natural rights theory, contract theory, and utilitarianism. The obstacles confronting a defense based upon natural rights or contract theory have been shown to be insurmountable. Even if those hurdles could be overcome, we have no good reason to believe that revised theories would not legitimize a much more than minimal state.

As the most familiar, the most complex, and potentially the strongest defense, utilitarianism was examined in detail. While agreeing with critics that morality cannot be reduced merely to the maximization of aggregate utility, the utilitarian defense cannot be ignored, since utilitarianism undoubtedly captures an important component of what is morally relevant. In determining the moral legitimacy of the role of government and the corporation, aggregate social utility is certainly at least one of the relevant considerations. Whether a minimal government with a laissez-faire capitalist market is optimally efficient, whether this arrangement would produce what is best for all, for example, *are* important considerations, even if not the sole or decisive considerations, in determining the moral defensibility of a system of political economy.

However, the actual force of the utilitarian justification of the Classical Liberal position is blunted by several limitations. For one thing, the particular utilitarian defenses which are used rest upon economic theorems demonstrating that ideal markets reach an equilibrium which is Pareto optimal, but these theorems have little relevance to actual situations: the ideal conditions postulated in the proofs cannot be satisfied in the most perfect of actual markets. The fact that actual markets rarely even approach the most perfect approximations further undermines confidence in the relevance of the theorems. Additionally, theoretical limitations of the Paretian notions themselves permit judgments only within a given system, so the normative relevance of the notions is restricted even if they could apply to actual markets. These limitations make it impossible to support judgments concerning the legitimacy of initial distributive states within a system, to compare the efficiency of one system with another, or to judge the legitimacy of situations in which coercive measures (e.g., eminent domain) are used. Given these theoretical contraints, the models are hardly useful guides to making judgments in the actual world.

Another serious shortcoming arises from the theory of utility or value employed in these demonstrations. Economic arguments for efficiency rely upon an understanding of utility which identifies human well-being with the satisfaction of actual preferences, a connection which is tenuous at best. Consequently, even if the economic theorems were relevant and one could establish the claim that a minimal government with laissez-faire markets maximizes utility or efficiency in our actual world, there is little reason to support this political-economic arrangement, since the underlying notion of efficiency bears so little relationship to what we would describe as the real well-being of the society. Surely, there is much more to providing for utility or human welfare than satisfying preferences.

From this, the conclusion is *not* that free markets are not important and that the government should not remain as limited as possible. As liberals of nearly every persuasion have argued, some moral weight is to be attached to markets and to providing individuals with liberty from governmental interference. But the claims invoked to support the position of the Classical Liberals are overly simplistic and largely unwarranted. Without such inflated claims there is little substance to the contention that the minimal state and nothing more extensive is morally legitimate.

Liberalism values freedom and liberty, including a degree of freedom in the market, because of an underlying commitment to provide the conditions within which individuals may flourish and grow. Having served, perhaps, as useful weapons in an attack upon governmental policies aligned with forces obstructing the potentially productive forces of the market, arguments for Classical Liberalism which are cast as arguments for freedom have lost touch with this deeper commitment. Revisionist Liberals recognize that human well-being requires more than merely leaving individuals alone to compete in the market, and that interference in economic freedom for the sake of improving the conditions of general welfare is a trade-off that is sometimes defensible.

The Managerial framework is also firmly grounded in the liberal tradition, but adopts the general tenets of Revisionist Liberalism, thereby accepting the legitimacy of the more than minimal state having responsibility to play an active role in managing the market and providing protection against market failures, externalities, market imperfections, and problems arising from business cycles. The analysis discloses, however, that the relationship between the Managerial ideology and Revisionist Liberalism is unstable. The major components of the theoretical core of Revisionist Liberalism do little to lend support to the Managerial claim that the corporation should act in a socially responsible way, if that is interpreted as meaning that the role of the corporation is to deviate from profit maximization.

Neither of the two strands of Managerialism identified, Micro-Managerialism and Macro-Managerialism, can find support for that claim. Micro-Managerialism focuses almost exclusively upon the organization and emphasizes those transformations in the enterprise which brought forth the large, modern, managerial corporation. Following the line of analysis developed by Berle and Means in *The Modern Corporation and Private Property*, Micro-Managerialism assumes the thesis of the Managerial revolution, the thesis of robust managerial discretion, and the thesis of managerial professionalism/social responsibility. However, the thesis of social responsibility interpreted descriptively, the idea that there has been a big change in the behavior of large corporations because of enlightened management, is probably false. The thesis of social responsibility interpreted prescriptively is defended by arguments which are question begging, vacuous, and without force. These arguments are premised upon the thesis of wide managerial discretion, which, if true, is morally untenable, and, if not true, entails that there is little sense to corporate social responsibility. And there is good reason to believe that wide managerial discretion is false.

By incorporating macroeconomic and pluralistic models, Macro-Managerialism provides a much broader context within which to situate the corporation, but these models also fail to support claims about social responsibility. Although Keynesian macroeconomic arguments, combined with other claims about market failures and externalities, for example, supply reasons for advocating an active role for the government, as Revisionist Liberals have often claimed, none of the arguments suggests or supposes that a corporation should or will act in ways other than profit maximization. Similarly, pluralism provides a powerful descriptive model with which to understand political and social change, but if, within this framework, social responsibility has any meaning at all distinct from profit maximization, it is power maximization. Normative pluralism fails to provide solace for the claim of social responsibility as well.

Throughout this analysis, one critical dimension of the debate over the appropriate role of the corporation has been ignored. For the most part, the controversy surrounding the fundamental question has occurred as if the large, modern corporation and this society existed in a vacuum. Prior to the 1970s that presumption is understandable, even justifiable. Radical changes of the past two decades have rendered that presumption indefensible. Those changes not only highlight the deficiencies of the Classical and Managerial perspectives, but forcefully demonstrate the need for liberalism to reconsider seriously a number of its major tenets. Hence, the fundamental question needs to be recast as we begin to explore the implications of this new context. What is the appropriate role of the transnational corporation in a liberal society *within the context of a global market?*

GLOBAL COMPETITIVE MARKETS AND THE TRANSNATIONAL CORPORATION

We stand, unenviably, in a situation remarkably similar in important respects to that confronted in the early decades of this century by those formulating the Managerial ideology. Aware that their world was being transformed by significant changes in the structure of the corporation, in the nature of markets and capitalism, in the role being played by government, and in the relationship between business and government, convinced that the model of Classical economics served to obscure, rather than to illuminate, these developments, the early Managerialists sought to think through the moral implications of the currents of change as they understood them. In the process, abandoning the basic tenets of Classical liberalism, they reached out to incorporate the ideas of Revisionist liberalism. With the benefit of hindsight, the shortcomings of that enterprise are now, if they were not then, quite apparent.

We too confront the daunting task of formulating a response to the fundamental question in light of an emerging new reality the outlines of which we can perceive only dimly, if at all. We too are convinced that the world is being transformed by significant changes in the structure of the corporation, but the issues today concern not the rise of the modern corporation but the ascendancy of the multinational and transnational corporation. We too are convinced that the world is being transformed by significant changes in the nature of markets and in the nature of capitalism, but the issues today concern not so much oligopoly and monopoly in domestic markets but the globalization and internationalization of markets and capitalism. We too are convinced that the world is being transformed by significant changes in the role national government plays and the rapidly evolving relationship between corporations and national governments, but the issues today concern not whether a strong national government should regulate the economy and the corporation, but whether the nation-state as we know it is any longer economically and politically viable.

In closing this study, I would like to identify the challenges which present themselves to any attempt to formulate a response to the fundamental question in this new context. I propose no easy solutions, only directions for further inquiry. At best, future analysis can be guided by the insights garnered in this investigation.

Within liberalism, as I have contended, the core normative ideals, especially the importance of providing conditions within which humans may flourish are relatively settled. This study has examined the important notion of flourishing or well-being, and, while a complete conceptual analysis has not been offered, progress toward that end has been made. We can safely say how a number of proposals fail. Well-being is not, for instance, merely the satisfaction of actual desires or preferences. In the end, within the constraints identified, each society must struggle with what it understands as human flourishing and well-being in the concreteness of its own experience and circumstances. In the liberal perspective, the goal of the state is to identify and to take some responsibility for providing for those conditions, while being as neutral as possible between competing conceptions of the good. No doubt, freedom, liberty, and diversity remain important among the conditions. Again, the specific conditions which would be most appropriate for any particular situation will depend largely upon the facts and possibilities of that situation and the self-understanding of the members of society. One key issue for most societies will be the role the corporation should play in relationship to those conditions.

The real challenges to developing a liberal response to these questions are not so much normative as descriptive. I am by no means claiming that there are no significant normative disagreements, even within liberalism. Nor am I suggesting that political philosophers should close shop, beat their normative swords into plowshares and seek retraining for work in the departments of international economics and political science, etc.

However, a recurring theme in this study has been the extent to which normative disputes are often at bottom disputes over facts, descriptive models, and theories about the world. As far as possible, as a philosopher, I have avoided any attempt to arbitrate empirical disagreement, although I have suggested, for instance, that there is good reason for believing that actual markets cannot satisfy the ideal conditions assumed in formal economic theorems, that the thesis of social responsibility interpreted descriptively is false, and that the thesis of robust managerial discretion is false. To avoid having to take sides with respect to empirical claims, I have attempted to formulate criticisms, especially criticisms of Managerialism, in the form of dilemmas, showing that regardless of the fact-set presupposed, an unacceptable conclusion followed. The analysis demonstrated the important function of empirical assumptions in the formulation of claims about the responsibilities of individuals, corporations, or governments.

The lesson is not that those in political philosophy, ethics, and Business Ethics should avoid venturing into claims about reality. On the contrary, to say anything of import, it is extremely difficult to avoid making such claims, at least implicitly; one should strive to remain as lucid as possible about the empirical claims and descriptive models which are being presupposed. Thus, the attempt to identify specific concerns for liberalism as we formulate a response to the fundamental question depends largely upon assumptions about what is happening. And what is happening is by no means clear.

A plausible scenario unfolds in this way. The emergence of a global market is not creating a playing field upon which nations and national corporations compete, as if in some kind of an economic Olympic festival, with competitors from the U.S. vying for supremacy with competitors from other nations or with a bloc of nations. Increasingly, the dominant economic competitors are not national corporations. Nor are corporations competing under the banner of a particular nation. This point can be exaggerated, but there seems to be a good deal of truth to this claim. Moreover, the relationship between the corporation and the national government is being radically restructured, just as the nature of the corporation is itself being dramatically altered. There are threats to national sovereignty involved, although there is dispute over the degree to which the erosion has occurred.

Although plausible, this scenario stands in some need of qualification. Unfortunately, as A. G. Kefalas notes, in "The Global Corporation: Its Role in the New World Order,"[1] the literature on the subject of the multinational corporation is "reaching gigantic proportions." In his brief but useful review, Kefalas identifies four major foci of the investigations.

1. various aspects of the decision to invest abroad
2. definition of a multinational corporation
3. growth of the multinational corporation

4. impact of the multinational corporation's activities on the firm itself, on the home and host countries, and on global economic and political welfare.

Clearly, each of these four areas is critical in attempting to formulate a response to the question of the role the corporation *ought* to play in the new world order. The literature is also filled with confusions between attempts to describe the role being played and attempts to prescribe the role which an analyst believes the corporations should play. There is room for a normative analysis at this level.

Given the disagreements over the impact of the activities of the multinational corporations, one would expect disagreements over evaluations of whether these entities are instruments for good or evil, on balance. Definitional disagreements further complicate matters. Conflicting empirical claims can arise from the fact that different researchers employ different definitions of the multinational corporation, and that the transnational is generally described as a particular kind of development of a multinational.

According to the definition used by researchers at the United Nations, in 1992 there were at least 35,000 multinational corporations controlling some 170,000 foreign affiliates.[2] In "A Survey of Multinationals: Everyone's Favorite Monster," *The Economist* attempts to challenge some of the more prevalent misperceptions about the multinational and transnational/global corporations. If one wishes to identify the multinational corporations which have become global, one would probably begin with the largest multinationals. I list, below, the largest 50 multinational corporations, excluding banking and financial corporations.

Arguably, the dominance of these corporations is exaggerated. According to U.N. data, the largest 100 multinationals (excluding banking and financial corporations) accounted for $3.1 trillion of the world's assets in 1992, of which $1.2 trillion was outside the firms' respective home countries. *The Economist* estimates that the total nonresidential assets of the world at around $20 trillion. Thus, the top 100 multinationals would have a 16 percent share of the world's productive assets; the top 300 would have perhaps 25 percent. In *The Economist's* view, "This is not domination."[3]

The number of multinationals has exploded since 1970, but their complexion has changed. In 1970 the U.N. identified 7,000

The 50 Largest Nonfinancial Multinationals, 1990, Ranked by Foreign Assets

Rank	Industry	Country
1. Royal Dutch/Shell	Oil	Britain/Holland
2. Ford Motor	Cars and trucks	United States
3. General Motors	Cars and trucks	United States
4. Exxon	Oil	United States
5. IBM	Computers	United States
6. British Petroleum	Oil	Britain
7. Nestlé	Food	Switzerland
8. Unilever	Food	Britain/Holland
9. Asea Brown Boveri	Electrical	Switzerland/Sweden
10. Philips Electronics	Electronics	Holland
11. Alcatel Alsthom	Telecommunications	France
12. Mobil	Oil	United States
13. Fiat	Cars and trucks	Italy
14. Siemens	Electrical	Germany
15. Hanson	Diversified	Britain
16. Volkswagen	Cars and trucks	Germany
17. Elf Aquitaine	Oil	France
18. Mitsubishi	Trading	Japan
19. General Electric	Diversified	United States
20. Mitsui	Trading	Japan
21. Matsushita Electric Industrial	Electronics	Japan
22. News Corp.	Publishing	Australia
23. Ferruzzi/Montedison	Diversified	Italy
24. Bayer	Chemicals	Germany
25. Roche Holding	Drugs	Switzerland
26. Toyota Motor	Cars and trucks	Japan
27. Daimler-Benz	Cars and trucks	Germany
28. Pechiney	Metals	France
29. Philip Morris	Food	United States
30. Rhône-Poulenc	Chemicals	France
31. E. I. De Pont de Nemours	Chemicals	United States
32. Hoechst	Chemicals	Germany
33. Michelin	Tires	France
34. Dow Chemical	Chemicals	United States

Rank	Industry	Country
35. Total	Oil	France
36. Thomson	Electronics	France
37. Amoco	Oil	United States
38. Saint-Gobain	Construction	France
39. ENI	Chemicals	Italy
40. Electrolux	Electrical	Sweden
41. Petrofina	Oil	Belgium
42. Générale des Eaux	Miscellaneous	France
43. Hitachi	Electronics	Japan
44. Chevron	Oil	United States
45. Sandoz	Chemicals	Switzerland
46. C. Itoh	Trading	Japan
47. Toshiba	Electronics	Japan
48. Xerox	Office machinery	United States
49. Stora	Paper	Sweden
50. Texaco	Oil	United States

Source: United Nations; in "A Survey of Multinations: Everyone's Favorite Monster," The Economist (March 27, 1993): 5.
* Where not available, foreign assets were estimated for ranking.

such corporations, which means that there has been a fivefold increase in two decades. But in 1970 over half of these were from two countries, the United States and Britain. By 1992, fewer than half of the 35,000 firms are from four countries, the United States, Japan, Germany, and Switzerland. Britain ranked seventh.[4]

While the growth of the multinational has long been associated with the loss of sovereignty of the nation-state, it is probably simplistic to identify the multinational corporation (or even the global corporation) as the cause of this. Raymond Vernon's classic book on the relationship of the multinational corporation to the nation state, Sovereignty at Bay,[5] did not suggest that the multinational corporation was the only factor. As The Economist puts it, "the multinational company is merely a part of a much wider force that has eroded sovereignty while integrating the world economy and even, to an extent, world politics. To be sure, international firms do pose all sorts of challenges to national governments."[6] The point is that they are not the only threat. Notably, short-term investment in currencies and securities markets is enormous and is much greater than direct corporate investment. Politically, instantaneous telecommunications may also be weakening political sovereignty. As *The Economist* notes, CNN may matter more than ITT.

From the perspective of our recent past, these developments can be drawn into somewhat sharper focus. Consider, for example, the relationship between corporations and the national government which prevailed through most of the twentieth century. The pattern, in retrospect, is now becoming increasingly clear and is reflected in the title of the recent book by Louis Galambos and Joseph Pratt, *The Corporate Commonwealth: United States Business and Public Policy in the 20th Century.*[7] The idea of the corporate commonwealth emphasizes the extent to which corporate and national interests converged. By the turn of the century, the U.S. economy was dominated by a core of large corporations, and, through the beginning of the 1960s, a few hundred huge corporations continued to occupy a central position in the economy. Within each of the twenty or thirty key industries, two or three giants controlled 70 percent or more of the market. Around the core, thousands of other corporations survived by serving the core corporations as suppliers or distributors, by providing services (legal, accounting, financial, travel, entertainment, hospitality, etc.), or by finding economic niches which large corporations could not serve well.[8]

At the same time, since 1900 the scope of governmental functions has increased, and government has come to play an important role in managing the economy. In the process, corporate interests assumed a very important role in the formulation of governmental policy through regulatory agencies, through the influence of trade and industry associations, and through support for key Congressional elections. Hence the "corporate commonwealth."[9] That the relationship in the U.S. is more adversarial than in other industrialized democratic countries should not obscure the strong mutuality of interests which has evolved.

Following this same kind of analysis in *The Work Of Nations,*[10] Robert Reich makes a strong case that until the 1970s, national interests were well served by this cozy arrangement. Covering much of the same territory as Galambos and Pratt, Reich focuses upon the development of what he calls "economic nationalism," which by the beginning of the twentieth century was established in many places in the world, most notably in the United States, Britain, Germany, France, Italy, and Japan. A major idea of economic nationalism is that national well-being requires consolidated domestic economic power. Following a very traditional line, Reich argues that the major problem in the late nineteenth century was overproduction. As a result of breakthroughs in production, distribution, communication, and economies of scale, overproduction meant low prices and low profit margins. In this situation, developing countries like the U.S. would have found it difficult, if not impossible, to compete with the industrially advanced giants such as Britain. One solution, favored in the U.S. in the nineteenth century, was to establish tariffs and subsidies, "temporary" protections for domestic markets, on the grounds that they would allow industry a chance to incubate and become strong. A second solution was imperialism, finding sources for marketing excess production. This was an outlet for established producers, not developing ones. A third solution, not incompatible with the first, "was to reduce domestic competition by consolidating production within large, nationally based corporations."[11] This could further strengthen domestic industries until they were competitive in the international arena.

While this latter solution was accepted in most countries, there was substantial popular resistance to it in the U.S. The fear of bigness, as noted earlier, aroused intense hostility, resulting in attempts to stem the tide, such as the Sherman Antitrust Act of 1890. These attempts were largely unsuccessful, and may well have contributed to the very development they sought to stunt. Forbidden to explicitly set prices and markets, corporations consolidated, originally through holding companies, which created even larger private combines. By the turn of the century, a set of core corporations was established in the U.S. Reich notes that by then roughly "one-third of the nation's manufacturing assets were consolidated into 318 giant companies." This core endures.

Although, Reich argues, the merger movement at the turn of the century and each of the four subsequent merger movements rekindled, through the coming decades, the debate over the corporate role and revived fears of bigness, economic concentration, and control, the economic well-being of the U.S. came to rest in the hands of this core of large corporations, just as the economic well-being of other countries came increasingly to rest in a small set of core corporations. To claim that what was in the interest of General Motors was in the interest of the U.S., and vice versa, was not an idle slogan. There was a significant congruence of national and corporate interests. The notion that the well-being of citizens was connected to the health of the national economy, "which depended in turn on the success of its giant corporations," constitutes, in Reich's view, the final plank of economic nationalism.[12]

If Reich is correct, the enlightened self-interest argument of the Committee for Economic Development made sense for a period of time.[13] Ironically, however, by the date of the report, those interests were beginning to diverge. The congruence of interests resulted in what Reich characterizes as a "national bargain" being struck, and, by mid-century, the terms of the bargain were clear. The core corporations were allowed to plan and to implement plans for high-volume production without fear of government interference. Economies of scale kept costs low, but prices were coordinated to allow profit margins sufficiently high to support reinvestment, large middle-management staffs, and relatively high working wages with strong unions. The bargain entailed that Big Labor would not upset production with work stoppages on the condition that wages and benefits were maintained. As long as Big Business and Big Labor implicitly agreed not to push wages (and therefore prices) too high, Big Government refrained from serious interference and cooperated by attempting to smooth out the business cycle with macropolicies, by funding education and infrastructure (homes, highways, airports), and by lucrative defense contracts. This account is virtually identical to the pluralistic accounts of capitalism developed in the 1950s and associated with the theory of countervailing power.

Throughout this golden age, Managerialism reigned supreme. No less a figure than Frank Abrams, chair of Standard Oil of New Jersey, recited the standard Managerial litany in an address in 1951:[14]

> The job of management is to maintain an equitable and working balance among the claims of the various directly interested groups . . . stockholders, employees, customers, and the public at large. Business managers are gaining in professional status partly because they see in their work the basic responsibilities that other professional men have long recognized in theirs.

Their "basic responsibilities" referred to the obligations to the public, obligations which "professionals" shared. The professional manager was an "industrial statesman" (99).

The meaning of social responsibility in this context is now clear. According to Reich, there was a fairly extensive range of managerial discretion during those years, and management did exercise it "responsibly," by not violating the conditions of the national bargain. Prices were "administered" by a few giant corporations, and responsibility involved making sure that all stakeholders could get a "fair" share of the increasing revenue. Violation would bring the threat of reprisals, especially from government.

While the corporate commonwealth, the "national bargain" in Reich's terms, was wildly successful in the two decades following WWII, when the other major economies of the world were rebuilding from near-total destruction, the political and economic hegemony of this era was relatively short lived. By the late 1960s, strains appeared, and by the 1970s, these stresses precipitated what Galambos and Pratt refer to as the "second crisis" of the corporate commonwealth. The first crisis had arisen with the Great Depression, and the response to that crisis brought the commonwealth into mature form. The second crisis has arisen with the transformation of the world economy.

Initially, many seemed to believe that the solution was to continue the New Deal policies which had proved effective in the past. The focus upon the domestic political turmoil of the sixties may well have obscured the underlying changes in the American economy. Problems in the economy could be blamed on too much legislation or too much spending on Vietnam without a tax increase. The nature of the change was also obscured to some extent by the phenomenal rise in the price of oil. The corporate commonwealth was, in Daniel Yergin's phrase, the Hydrocarbon Society.[15] But that nearsighted focus upon the escalating price of oil distracted many from the underlying, changing conditions which for the first time made the success of an oil cartel possible. Even the universally disliked seven sisters of the oil industry no longer controlled the price or the supply. And similar changes were engulfing other industrial sectors as well. Only recently has the significance of these changes begun to be understood.

At the same time, corporations themselves have been transformed. Originally, core corporations were nationally based corporations which began extending into other countries for markets, raw materials, and eventually for production. As a means of competing for capital, resources, technology, markets and labor in global markets, however, the large core corporations have become transnationals, identified with nations only by virtue of legal incorporation. The relations with the "home" country have become indistinguishable in many ways from those with "host" countries. As Reich points out, although these mobile and flexible transnational corporations bear names associated with particular nations, like SONY or General Motors, behind the name they are little more than a loosely joined web of profit centers, with parts being continually bought and sold, and production and support services being moved on a regular basis. General Motors now imports as many cars under its own name as the Japanese, and the Japanese automobile manufacturers continue to produce nearly as many of their "imported" cars in this country as they import. SONY owns CBS records and a substantial portion of the Hollywood film-making capacity.

The extent to which the largest and most highly developed multinationals have become, or will ever become, genuinely global or transnational corporations is hotly contested. *The Economist*, for example, argues plausibly that the large multinationals are better described as "multiregionals" and continue to reflect a number of biases toward the home country and region.[16] Traditional patterns of direct investment suggest that multinational corporations from the wealthiest trading partners (especially the Japanese and the U.S.) enjoy investing in one another's country, where markets are mature, conditions relatively stable, and the risk low. Direct investments can be spurred by the reality or fear of tariffs and quotas, and as a hedge against currency fluctuations. Analysis of the direct investment between 1986–1989 demonstrates stronger regional patterns. The U.S multinationals dominated investment in Latin America, and in Asia and the Pacific dominated only in Bangladesh, Pakistan, and the Phillipines. Otherwise, the U.S. dominated only in Saudia Arabia and Papua New Guinea.[17] Direct investment by Japan's multinational's dominated in Asia; that by EC's multinationals tended to be regional neighbors as well, especially Eastern Europe, but also extended to Asia in Vietnam, Sri Lanka, and India. Furthermore, the growth and development of the multinationals has tended to be as multiregionals, as it were. U.S. firms moved to EC, and sales of affiliates there tend to be EC countries. In 1989, for example, 60 percent of the total sales of U.S. affiliates in the EC remain inside the EC countries, even though the historical experience there is rooted in the early 1960s in many instances.[18]

The regional nature of the development reflects the brute reality that there is no such thing as a truly global economy. Discussions of the global economy make sense insofar as they correctly emphasize the extent to which the markets of significant actors in the world have become integrated, in contrast to the past. Still, while capital moves almost instantaneously across borders through electronic transfer, not all borders are equally accessible. Products also continue to face obstacles, many of which are established because of the fiercely nationalistic or particularistic sentiments aroused by large corporations attempting to penetrate new markets.

While all of these factors are important qualifications to oversimplistic perceptions of global corporations and the global market, none blunts the force of analyses such as Reich's. Whether one chooses to refer to these entities as multiregionals or global corporations, the point remains that corporate interests are increasingly becoming decoupled from those of the home country in many important respects, even if a home country bias remains.

The national bargain was never premised upon this reality. Prices for steel and automobiles, for example, can no longer be easily coordinated and passed on to the American public with largesse distributed to labor, investors, and creditors because the corporations with Japanese and West German names have became significant competitors.

As the second crisis of the commonwealth unfolded, the debate over the fundamental question erupted again in the 1970s, this time as the debate over corporate responsibility. The debate proceeded along many of the same lines as it had since the turn of the century. Proponents of the Classical and Managerial frameworks took their customary positions, and philosophers aligned themselves generally with the "progressive" forces of the Managerialists. During this round, philosophers were playing a much more active role in the area of Business Ethics, and management faculty pushed to develop further the Social Issues in Management discipline. Even the solutions were shopworn. Apologists for the Classical ideology preached the gospel of free enterprise, the importance of freedom, the evils of government regulation, the productive virtues of the (capitalist) system, etc. Managerialists proposed instilling values into the future managers, providing ethics courses, or building ethics into the curriculum, pushing corporations into being socially responsive and responsible, etc. Few of us, however, understood the implications of the global competitive forces which had been unleashed.

As the fundamental question of the role of the corporation in a liberal society is internationalized, moving questions which were only occasionally addressed toward center stage will not resolve conflicts about the role of the corporation. The discussions are grounded in obsolescent understandings of the nature of the corporation and outmoded assumptions about effective policies whose parochialism is now apparent. Although proponents of the Classical and Managerial frameworks will attempt to extend their familiar analyses to the new environment, those frameworks are already inadequate as attempts to come to grips with questions of the appropriate corporate role when the focus is primarily national. Those frameworks are even more incapable of providing guidance in the new world.

Most immediately, Reich is close to the target in claiming that Managerialism is dead. It would be nice to believe that transnational corporations have responsibilities to be "good citizens" of the world, but in the context of the fiercely competitive international marketplace, the thesis of managerial discretion, upon which the thesis of social responsibility rests, is even less credible. As Reich puts it, by the last decade of the twentieth century, the "corporate statesman" has "gone the way of the Edsel."[19]

> American capitalism was now organized relentlessly around profits not patriotism. When profitability requires that production be shifted from an American factory to a foreign one, the American executive hesitates not. . . . Nor, in this new global economy, is it clear, in any event, how the top executives of American-owned corporations could be made to take on such national responsibilities. (140–141)

In the global arena, there is no longer necessarily a congruence of interests between the major core corporations and the interests of the nation. There is no longer, if there ever was, much managerial flexibility. There is little room for sentimental attachments to regions or nations, for emotional ties to traditional labor resources or capital, or for cultural scruples against the penetration of new markets with products which are of dubious appropriateness there.

Premised upon economic nationalism, the Classical business ideology will require dramatic retailoring as well. The traditional recommendation that by minimizing government interference in the economy the economic welfare of the American society could be promoted is also less credible. With international competition, real

wages for most Americans have fallen precipitously since the early
1970s, especially in those sectors where the effects of global competition have been most keenly felt. This has also produced even more
staggering inequality in the U.S. From 1977–1988, the average family
income of all families increased by $747 (measured in 1987 dollars),
but the average family income of the bottom 80 percent fell. The
income of the bottom 10 percent of families fell 14.8 percent during
this period, while the income of the top 10 percent increased 16.5
percent.[20] Production and jobs have increasingly been shifted outside
national boundaries. This is not to suggest that the solution is trade
protectionism, quotas, and duties. A return to the good old days of
trigger pricing for steel, for example, which provided direct benefits
to the domestic steel industry and the steel workers at the expense
of the remainder of society, is no longer a realistic possibility. In the
new competitive environment there is little guarantee that among the
new winners and losers, the citizens of the U.S. will not be among
the most significant losers.

     Nor is there much solace in the idea that these sacrifices are produc-
ing what is best for all at the global level. One might have taken the
view that the citizens of the U.S., especially those most advantaged
by the national bargain with the core corporations, had profited at
the expense of most of the rest of the world because of the lack
of real competition during the decades following WWII, and recent
developments are eliminating this injustice. While there my be some
truth to this, there is little guarantee that the ensuing competition
will generate morally legitimate results either. The Classical business
ideology may quietly drop patriotic pretenses, abandon economic
nationalism, and take the higher moral ground by claiming that the
competitive world market produces what is best for all, even though
individuals in particular regions, such as the U.S., might suffer if they
fail to compete effectively. That, we shall be told, is the price for the
benefits of the market. But the very same problems which I have identified as afflicting the economic theorems used to support the claims
for optimal efficiency or maximizing utility are applicable whether the
market in question is national or global. Indeed, although competitive
in a very real sense, the actual world market comes no closer than
U.S. domestic markets to satisfying the ideal conditions assumed in
the theorems; claims about efficiency are therefore up for grabs.

     In these ways, the new era poses serious challenges to liberal-
ism itself. The challenge to the liberal, romantic attachment with

nationalism is extremely strong. Nationalism played a significant role in the liberal struggle against the feudal order and continued to play a leading role throughout the modern period. The ideology of nationalism spread to colonial Third World countries as well, and resurfaced with the dissolution of the former Soviet Union and in eastern Europe and Asia. Throughout, liberal theorists were often, even usually, nationalistic. Marxists were originally deeply suspicious of nationalism and of the idea that national interests were congruent with corporate interests and that these were in accord with the interests of most of the citizens. After the First World War, however, even Marxists had abandoned doctrinal hostility toward nationalism. Workers did not rise up in mass and identify their interests with workers in other countries of the world but instead rallied (often with gentle persuasion) around the national flags. Marxists began siding with national sentiments throughout world against the capitalist colonial powers.

But liberalism's relationship to the nation state and the corporation must be revisited. Revisionist Liberalism has supported the centralization of power of the nation state as the primary instrument for securing the conditions for the well-being of human individuals. Communitarian critics who complain that liberals fail to pay adequate attention to the cultural and ethnic embeddedness of human lives[21] ignore the plain fact that liberalism in the nineteenth century had a strongly nationalistic and patriotic hue. One finds in John Stuart Mill and others the common liberal conviction that there are different peoples in the world, diverse "nations." Upon this nationalistic basis, liberals grounded doctrinal nationalism, the idea that these nations have a right to self-determination. Indeed, doctrinal nationalism has continued to guide liberal thought through the twentieth century, as liberals fought for the self-determination of colonial nations throughout the world and wrote these ideas into the basic documents of the League of Nations and the United Nations.

Domestically, Revisionist Liberals relied upon the nation state to channel safely the productive capabilities of competitive markets toward human well-being, and to buffer the less fortunate from the harsh effects of market competition. Corporations were grudgingly accepted as useful instruments. In this country, New Deal Liberalism is synonymous with arguments offered to support the legitimacy of the corporate commonwealth and is premised, like Managerialism, upon assumptions about the congruence of interests between the corporation and the well-being of the nation.

The standard liberal remedies for market failures, externalities, and the problems associated with the inability of the market to meet many of the needs of citizens are increasingly irrelevant. As markets transcend national boundaries, individual nation states have little ability to deal alone with transnational corporations or international markets. At the world level, there are no mechanisms for coping with market externalities or market failures, or for providing for the needs of the "losers." There are virtually no international safety nets, only the extremely modest resources of agencies such as the Red Cross, and these agencies are more concerned with natural catastrophe, disease, and famine than unemployment insurance or retraining. If a nation state attempts to impose costs for the sake of establishing a safety net, the transnational corporation can threaten to move production facilities and jobs elsewhere. A nation state which seeks to prohibit externalities such as environmental pollution runs the risk of losing production facilities to other countries where standards are less stringent. The transnational corporations can shop the globe for the lowest costs for the factors of production.

Consider, for example, the obvious problem of externalities. Domestic legislation has been drafted in large part to overcome the problems of firms externalizing the costs of production. But this legislation is effective only if the major actors in the industry are unable to move outside the national boundaries where the resistance to externalizing the costs of production is weak or nonexistent. As the markets for products grew in the 1950s and 1960s, there were already incentives to move production facilities abroad. The additional savings to be obtained by avoiding stricter environmental legislation/enforcement provides an even stronger inducement to move outside the country and then import to the U.S. Utility companies will find it difficult to move, of course, but not the petrochemical industry. Domestic attempts to eliminate externalities merely push externalities outside the nation while also exporting jobs and tax bases associated with production facilities and employment.

This is not an indictment of greedy corporate managers. If there were wide latitude for choice, then one might wish to castigate these decisions. The international competitive market, however, leaves little choice in the long run. These pressures cannot easily be resisted, especially not in the for long run. Unless transnational corporations within the international marketplace agree to retain the strictest standards, competition will make "being responsible" self-destructive.

And, because of free-rider problems, there is no way to overcome the inherent instability of these kinds of agreements. Cartels, pooling arrangements, and similar agreements are notoriously unstable whether the arrangements involve setting prices, holding down supply, allocating markets by geographical districts, or "doing the right thing" environmentally.

Thus, the policy instruments of the nation state upon which liberals have come to rely in order to safeguard human welfare are becoming increasingly ineffective. The corporate sector, long assumed to be the engine of production and well-being for the citizens of the nation state, is no longer intimately related to the well-being of any one nation.

In principle, the liberal response to the appropriate role of the corporation in a free society in the global context is unchanged. That is, the appropriate role of the corporation is to provide the conditions within which humans may flourish. Although never actualized fully in the age which is now coming to a close, this principle was dimly recognized, and legislation was imposed to provide a modicum of protection for employees, consumers, and others. How this principle will be implemented in the context of a competitive global economy with transnational corporations remains unclear. Whether it can implemented at all is also uncertain.

Reich and other liberals, clinging to nationalist concerns, pin hopes upon education. The claim is that the transnational corporations need highly trained and versatile employees, and national policy should seek to provide citizens with "world class" education. Transnational corporations may, the argument goes, move production facilities for mass production wherever the labor costs are lowest, because this kind of labor requires little skill or knowledge. The market for the labor elite is smaller, and so a nation has some leverage with which to keep the transnational corporation. This argument is as frail as the hope expressed by Berle and Means that the evolution of the modern corporation would create the socially minded professional manager. Even if a nation devoted enormous resources toward the kind of education necessary to develop the labor talents most sought, the nation is left with little control. The labor elite itself, educated to think globally, may have little incentive to identify with national interests, and little incentive to be willing to make sacrifices for the less well-educated in "their" society, or in any society. Threatened by a nation state with high taxes, the labor elite is probably as willing as the transnationals to move to more hospitable countries. There is no reason to believe the labor elite will not quickly come to recognize its own interests as more closely aligned with the favored transnational corporation than with either the nation state or the less fortunate.

These are the challenges posed for liberalism as we move into the twenty-first century. As we attempt to think through the implications of the new reality, and to examine alternative responses to the fundamental question in the context of the global markets, we must not lose sight of the fact that at bottom the question of the role of the corporation in "the new world order" is normative, and that a defense of any response requires the development of a coherent and defensible theory of political economy. A case by case approach may be necessary as a prolegomenon to understanding the specifics of contemporary developments, but the focus upon cases should not obscure the extent to which discussions of specific cases rests upon assumptions about the larger context and the role the corporation should play.

Notes

1. INTRODUCTION

1. Edward S. Herman, *Corporate Control, Corporate Power* (New York: Cambridge University Press, 1981), 1.

2. Morrell Heald, *The Social Responsibilities of Business: Company and Community, 1900–1960* (Cleveland: The Press of Case Western Reserve University, 1970), provides an outstanding and well-researched historical introduction to one dimension of the question of the corporate role. A thorough study would require an acquaintance with the literature of most of the reform movements of the century and an understanding of the subsequent economic, political, and legal investigations.

3. Framing the question in this fashion was suggested by Frederick D. Sturdivant, *Business and Society: A Managerial Approach*, 1st ed. (Homewood, Ill.: Richard D. Irwin, Inc., 1977), 9.

4. Richard E. Flathman, *Toward a Liberalism* (Ithaca: Cornell University Press, 1989), 3.

5. Francis X. Sutton, Seymour E. Harris, Carl Kaysen, and James Tobin, *The American Business Creed* (Cambridge, Mass.: Harvard University Press, 1956).

6. Within a single ideological orientation there is room for different and even competing theoretical frameworks. For example, the Classical ideology rests upon the framework of Classical Liberalism. That framework, a theory of political economy, advocates minimal government with free market capitalism. Proponents may disagree strongly, however, over what will count as a free market and why a free market is desirable. Some, for example, take a very abstract formal mathematical approach to the understanding of markets, as in the Austrian school. Others, such as Joseph A. Schumpeter, take a much more historical approach, assuming that markets are inherently monopolistic

only to be restructured occasionally through the creative destruction of entrepreneurial innovation. These various perspectives tend to agree on the basic policy prescriptions of the Classical Liberal position.

7. In response to the charge that nothing is more dangerous than a philosopher with a little knowledge of economics, Robert Nozick is alleged to have quipped, "except an economist with a little knowledge of philosophy."

8. See, for example, Betty Bock, Harvey. J. Goldschmid, Ira M. Millstein, and F. M. Scherer, *The Impact of the Modern Corporation* (New York: Columbia University Press, 1984).

9. The distinction between ethical or moral philosophy, on the one hand, and political philosophy, on the other, is no longer viable. When Mary Warnock wrote the preface to the third edition of her *Ethics since 1900* (New York: Oxford University Press, 1978), she noted that the biggest change since the first edition in 1960 was "that it is no longer possible to distinguish moral from political philosophy" (p. vii). As Warnock indicated, all of the influential work since 1960 was in the area of moral psychology or political philosophy.

10. David L. Engel, "An Approach to Corporate Responsibility," *Stanford Law Review* 32 (1979): 1.

11. Milton Friedman, "The Social Responsibility of Business Is to Increase Profits," *New York Times Magazine* (September 13, 1970): 32–33, 122–126. See also his "Monopoly and the Social Responsibility of Business and Labor," in *Capitalism and Freedom* (Chicago: University of Chicago Press, 1962, 1982), 119–136.

12. Sturdivant, op. cit.

13. The same intuitive understanding of the centrality of the debate over corporate role is apparent in other texts. In *Business and Society: Corporate Strategy, Public Policy, Ethics*, 7th ed. (New York: McGraw-Hill, 1988), William C. Frederick, Keith Davis, and James E. Post begin with a chapter on "The Corporation and Its Stakeholders," in which they present an "interactive model" of business and society. After presenting this model they write that "the interactive model of business and society defines clearly the fundamental role of the business corporation in society. It recognizes that corporate decision makers need to take actions that protect and improve the welfare of society as a whole along with their own interests" (13). The first part of the text is devoted to corporate social responsibility in one way or another.

Fred Luthans, Richard M. Hodgetts, and Kenneth R. Thompson, *Social Issues in Business*, 3rd ed. (New York: Macmillan Publishing Co., Inc., 1980), provide a brief historical introduction, discuss the pressing world problems, develop a critique of the Classical ideas, then turn to the question of social responsibilities. At that point, the concern is managing social responsibility in different areas.

14. Richard De George, "The Status of Business Ethics: Past and Future," *Journal of Business Ethics* 6 (1987): 201–212.

15. Warnock's point (see note 9) is relevant here. While moral philosophy has moved toward political philosophy, too much of the work in applied ethics has not. Consequently, the major developments remain largely unattached to work in business ethics.

16. Joseph W. McGuire, *Business and Society* (New York: McGraw-Hill, 1963).

17. Ibid.

18. Ibid.; Sturdivant, op. cit., 1st ed., chapter 3, "Changing Structure and Philosophy of Business"; rev. ed. 1981, chapter 6, "Business Ideology and Ethics."

19. George C. Lodge, *The New American Ideology* (New York: Alfred A. Knopf, 1979).

20. Gerald F. Cavanagh, *American Business Values in Transition* (Englewood Cliffs, N.J.: Prentice-Hall, Inc., 1984), 163.

21. Gerald F. Cavanagh, *Ethical Dilemmas in the Modern Corporation* (Englewood Cliffs, N.J.: Prentice-Hall, Inc., 1988).

22. Keith Davis and William Frederick, *Business and Society: Management, Public Policy, Ethics*, 5th ed. (New York: McGraw-Hill, 1984), cite Sutton (111), Lodge (114), Cavanagh (71, 93, 100, and 121) in an extensive discussion of ideology. This has been largely dropped from more recent editions.

23. George C. Lodge, "The Connection between Ethics and Ideology," *Journal of Business Ethics* 1 (1981): 85–98.

24. Kenneth E. Goodpastor, "Business Ethics, Ideology, and the Naturalistic Fallacy," *Journal of Business Ethics* 4 (1985): 227–232.

25. Tibor R. Machan and Douglas J. Den Uyl, "Recent Work in Business Ethics: A Survey and Critique," *American Philosophical Quarterly* 24 (1987): 107–124.

26. Robert W. Ackerman and Raymond A. Bauer, *Corporate Social Responsiveness: The Modern Dilemma* (Reston, Virginia: Reston Publishing Company, Inc. [Prentice-Hall], 1976).

27. S. Prakash Sethi, ed., *Up Against the Corporate Wall* (Englewood Cliffs, N.J.: Prentice-Hall, Inc., 1971).

28. Richard N. Farmer and W. Dickerson Jogue, *Corporate Social Responsibility* (Chicago: Science Research Associates, Inc., 1973).

29. Ibid., preface, second of two unnumbered pages.

30. Edward S. Mason, "The Apologetics of 'Managerialism,'" *Journal of Business* 31, (January, 1958): 1–11.

31. Ibid. Mason's article itself either rests upon this same confusion or something like ethical conventionalism. Mason may believe that it does

not really matter which ideology, which rationale, or which moral values a society adopts, so long as they are consistent and coherent. After arguing that the Managerial literature provides conflicting and unpersuasive answers to some important questions, he writes that this is unfortunate, "since it seems to be a fact that the institutional stability and opportunity for growth of an economic system are heavily dependent on the existence of a philosophy or ideology justifying the system in a manner generally acceptable to the leaders of thought in the community" (5). The reason that the Classical view fails, according to this view, is that it is no longer acceptable to the "leaders of thought." This is a theory about what is required for economic stability and growth and may also constitute an ethical theory. As such, this theory needs careful examination.

32. Sturdivant, op. cit., 1st ed.

33. Goodpastor, op. cit.

34. In a later chapter, when discussing problems in the Managerial framework, I shall suggest that if the Managerialists are not guilty of confusing descriptive/prescriptive claims, then they may have adopted a theory such as ethical conventionalism. See note 31, above, concerning Mason.

35. John Rawls, *A Theory of Justice* (Cambridge, Mass.: Harvard University Press, 1971).

2. CLASSICAL LIBERALISM

1. Francis X. Sutton, Seymour E. Harris, Carl Kaysen, and James Tobin, *The American Business Creed* (Cambridge, Mass.: Harvard University Press, 1956).

2. I have been unable to identify the citation for this quip. The reference is from Nicholas Lemann in "The Evolution of the Conservative Mind," *Washington Monthly* (May, 1981): 34. Trilling may well have been echoing the theses of Louis Hartz, *The Liberal Tradition in America* (New York: Harcourt Brace Jovanovich, 1955). Hartz argues that America is a liberal society and speaks of the "moral unanimity of a liberal society" which reaches out in many directions (10). Without the fuedal past, Hartz believes that liberalism is often not self-consciously held. Nonetheless, the tenacity with which liberal convictions are held in the U. S., according to Hartz, leads him to speak of "irrational" liberalism: "There has never been a 'liberal movement' or a real 'liberal party' in America: we have only had the American Way of Life, a nationalist articulation of Locke which usually does not know that Locke himself is involved; and we did not even get that until after the Civil War when the Whigs of the nation, deserting the Hamiltonian tradition, saw the capital that could be made out of it. This is why even critics

who have noticed America's moral unity have usually missed its substance. Ironically, 'liberalism' is a stranger in the land of its greatest realization and fulfillment" (11).

3. Richard E. Flatham, *Toward a Liberalism* (Ithaca: Cornell University Press, 1989). The following quotation is from p. 2.

4. John Gray, *Liberalism: Concepts in Social Thought*, (Minneapolis: University of Minnesota Press, 1986).

5. Richard E. Flathman claims in *Toward a Liberalism* that "liberalism has never been a closely integrated or firmly fixed doctrine; its proponents have held to a considerable and frequently changing variety of views and its historians and critics have regularly disagreed concerning its main ideas and tendencies." Flathman also notes that liberalism is characterized by a "suspicion of systematic, programmatic, certainly dogmatic theorizing" (2).

6. William Kymlicka, *Liberalism, Community, and Culture* (New York: Oxford University Press, 1989).

7. Ibid., 10. The next quotation is from p. 10 as well.

8. Flathman, op. cit., discusses the key "liberal principle," which he states as "it is a prima facie good for persons to form, to act on, and to satisfy and achieve desires and interests, objectives and purposes" (6). William A. Galston, *Liberal Purposes: Goods, Virtues, and Diversity in the Liberal State* (New York: Cambridge University Press, 1991), also takes the view that liberalism, properly understood, rests upon a conception of the human good.

9. Smith, Bentham, and Mill are routinely described as Classical Liberals. The reality of each theory, however, is much more nuanced than later doctrinaire advocates of a simplistic laissez-faire philosophy were willing to admit. Smith anticipated a number of "flaws" in the market for which government intervention would be necessary. Bentham's ideas for how the government should meddle in the lives of citizens is notorious. Mill is now most remembered for his idea that individuals should be at liberty in thought and action provided no one would be harmed, but in Mill this is an idea primarily for civil rights. "Free trade" for Mill and other nineteenth-century British liberals was a rallying cry for a limited number of specific evils, such as the Corn Laws. As Gray recognized, Mill's philosophy actually anticipates both Classical and Revisionist philosophies. Irving Kristol, in "A Capitalist Conception of Justice," in *Ethics, Free Enterprise, and Public Policy: Original Essays on Moral Issues in Business* (New York: Oxford University Press, 1978), edited by Richard T. De George and Joseph A. Pichler, 57–69, is a bit wary of anyone after Adam Smith. He writes that "something very peculiar happened after Adam Smith. Something very odd and very bad happened to the idea of capitalism and its reputation after the first generation of capitalism's intellectual fathers" (62). Kristol blames not the socialist critiques but the

Classical economists, Malthus and Ricardo. It is interesting that he mentions neither Mill nor Bentham as an ally.

10. John Stuart Mill, *Principles of Political Economy with Some of Their Applications to Social Philosophy*, books 4 and 5 (1848; modern edition London: Penguin Group, 1988). The following quotation is from the introduction by Donald Winch, 11.

11. Keynes wrote two lengthy articles, one on the doctrine of laissez-faire and the other on communism, for the *New Republic*. The former appeared in *New Republic*, (1926, part 1): 5–73.

12. Generally speaking, "liberty" and "freedom" are synonymous. To the extent that one can make a distinction, "liberty" is a specific kind of freedom, namely, freedom from interference by government (or some other power/authority). In much of this discussion of the value of liberty and the presumptive case for liberty I follow Joel Feinberg in *Social Philosophy* (Englewood Cliffs, N.J.: Prentice-Hall, Inc., 1973), especially chapters 1 and 2. Classical Liberals like Joseph Raz, in *The Morality of Freedom* (New York: Oxford University Press, 1986), deny that there is a presumptive case for freedom but claim, on the other hand, that freedom is intrinsically good. With Feinberg and Mill I find this difficult to accept. Feinberg claims that it is by no means self-evident that freedom is intrinsically good and he is unaware of any demonstrations of this claim. Freedom is a good thing extrinsically because it is useful in achieving other goods, such as happiness. Raz offers no defense of his counterintuitive claim that freedom is intrinsically good except that it is an assumption of his overall theory, and if the theory is adequate, then this assumption must be accepted.

13. John Stuart Mill may have been the first to have identified the harm principle as such in "On Liberty," in *Three Essays* (New York: Oxford University Press, 1975), edited with an introduction by Richard Wollheim.

14. By dramatically gerrymandering either or both of these concepts, a totalitarian or authoritarian government could claim adherence to the harm principle while at the same time judging that nearly all of its citizens were in some way lacking in autonomy or mental competency. Therefore, interference in their sphere of action would not violate the harm principle. While the intension and extension of concepts such as autonomy and mental competency are admittedly vague, within the liberal tradition there is a tendency to accept relatively minimal standards, consistently resisting tendencies to undermine the protections promised by the harm principle. The presumption appears to be that adults are autonomous and mentally competent unless compelling reasons can be given to override the presumption. Criminal law reflects this liberal tendency, and only grudingly accepts as excuses things like mental incompetency or lack of autonomy. One good reason for the reluctance is that aside from a few paradigm cases of mental incompetency

we do not know how to define competency very clearly or how to draw the line in difficult cases. Classical Liberals have tended to settle for extremely minimalist standards, as the history of common law attests.

15. Feinberg's *Social Philosophy* remains one of the best sources for an introduction to the different principles which have been offered as grounds for interfering in liberty, i.e., liberty limiting principles. Also see John D. Hodson's *The Ethics of Legal Coercion* (Boston: D. Reidel, 1983).

16. Whether paternalism is ever morally justified remains, of course, a controversial issue. The principle of paternalism can be characterized as asserting that the autonomy or liberty of an individual can be justifiably limited if intervention would prevent the individual from producing serious harm to himself or herself. The principle of extreme paternalism would allow intervention to prevent an individual from failing greatly to benefit herself. For some defenses of paternalism by liberals see H. L. A. Hart's *Law, Liberty and Morality* (Stanford, Cal.: Stanford University Press, 1983), 31–33, or Gerald Dworkin's "Paternalism," in Richard A. Wasserstrom, ed., *Morality and the Law* (Belmont, Cal.: Wordsworth Publishing Co., Inc., 1971), 107–126.

17. One must be careful about stating this point. Utilitarians, such as Mill, claim that the function of government should be to promote the greatest net social welfare, but then they argue that this is best done by adopting the harm principle.

18. For the concept of harm, see Joel Feinberg's *Harm to Others: The Moral Limits of the Criminal Law* (New York: Oxford University Press, 1984). To my knowledge, Mill never bothered with attempting to define "harm."

19. Neoconservatives like Kristol see little room for even a minimal safety net. In "A Capitalist Conception of Justice," in *Business Ethics: Readings and Cases in Corporate Morality*, edited by W. Michael Hoffman and Jennifer Mills Moore (New York: McGraw-Hill, 1984), 44–50, Kristol suggests that the safety net should be provided for by charity.

20. Some liberals advocate a safety net. It remains unclear, however, how Classical Liberals will justify the safety net without abandoning this construal of the harm/nonbenefit distinction according to the acting/omitting to act distinction. One proposal might be to construe this distinction according to the needs/unneeded goods distinction. That is, harming someone might be understood as not providing them with something they need greatly when one can do so without any great cost or danger to one's self. This construal would solve the problem of the safety net but would also likely lead to a much more extensive state than any Classical Liberal would like to endorse.

21. There is nothing in principle in keeping Classical Liberals from occasionally abandoning free market principles if one could demonstrate a case that these principles would harm the public. Protectionist legislation

in the nineteenth century might have been justified on the grounds that free trade would harm the public interest.

22. Gray, *Liberalism*.

3. NATURAL RIGHTS AND SOCIAL CONTRACTS

1. John Locke, *Two Treatises of Government*, edited by Peter Laslett (New York: Cambridge University Press, 1988). Among the important works on Locke's political philosophy are John Dunn, *Locke* (New York: Oxford University Press, 1984); John Dunn, *The Political Thought of John Locke: An Historical Account of the Argument of the "Two Treatises of Government"* (Cambridge: Cambridge University Press, 1982); C. B. McPherson, *The Political Theory of Possessive Individualism* (Oxford: Oxford University Press, 1962); and James Tully, *A Discourse on Property: John Locke and His Adversaries* (Cambridge: Cambridge University Press, 1980).

2. Louis Hartz, *The Liberal Tradition in America* (New York: Harcourt Brace Jovanich, 1955); Andrew J. Reek, "Natural Law in American Revolutionary Thought," *Review of Metaphysics* 30 (1977): 686–714; Michael Rogin, "Nature as Politics and Nature as Romance in America," *Political Theory* 5 (1977): 5–30; and Roger D. Masters, "The Lockean Tradition in American Foreign Policy," *The Journal of International Affairs* 21 (1967): 253-277.

3. William C. Frederick, Keith Davis, and James E. Post, *Business and Society: Corporate Strategy, Public Policy, Ethics*, 7th ed. (New York: McGraw-Hill, 1988), 86–92.

4. John Rawls, *A Theory of Justice* (Cambridge, Mass.: Harvard University Press, 1971).

5. Robert Nozick, *Anarchy, State, and Utopia* (New York: Basic Books, Inc., 1974).

6. David Gauthier, *Morals by Agreement* (New York: Clarendon Press, Oxford University Press, 1986).

7. Locke rejected the idea that humans had a moral right to commit suicide or sell themselves into slavery. It is not clear, on moral grounds, that Locke can defend this claim.

8. The distinction is basically that reflected in the distinction between civil and criminal wrongs. Some civil wrongs are also crimes. Crimes involve a corrupt mental state of some kind.

9. I have not considered the right of self-defense as a distinct natural right. If I have a right to life and health, and you threaten my life or health, the right of self-defense may be nothing more than my exercising my right to life or health.

10. For a more detailed discussion of harm, see Joel Feinberg, *Harm to Others: The Moral Limits of the Criminal Law* (New York: Oxford University

Press, 1984). I generally follow Feinberg's exposition of harm as an invasion of interest to illustrate how Locke might be interpreted.

11. John Gray, *Liberalism: Concepts in Social Thought* (Minneapolis: University of Minnesota Press, 1986), 46.

12. See H. L. A. Hart, "Are There Any Natural Rights?" *Philosophical Review* 64 (1955): 175–191.

13. Nagel's review originally appeared in *The Yale Law Review* 85: 136 ff. It appears in *Reading Nozick: Essays on Anarchy, State, and Utopia*, edited by Jeffrey Paul (Totowa, N.J.: Rowman and Littlefield, 1981).

14. Since the natural rights are stated vaguely and abstractly, there are many possible interpretations of "property," "contract," and "liberty." The understandings are often associated with the interpretations in English common law. Thus 150 years later, in the United States, where the English common law was in many instances the law of the land through Blackstone's *Commentary*, specific interpretations of those key words could be defended as correct manifestations of natural rights. Attempts to regulate the Union Pacific Railroad, for instance, might be attacked not only as a violation of the constitutionally protected right of property but also as an attack upon the moral natural right of property as well. Moreover, many of the arguments within the Classical ideology concerning judicial restraint and the function of law are similar to the arguments honed by defenders of the common law at least two centuries before.

The common law tradition may also shed light upon Locke's choice of which rights to include on his list of natural rights. The natural rights listed as basic, and the kind of moral laws which can be generated from that list, bear striking resemblance to those of the common law during Locke's time.

Moreover, a defense of common law principles would constitute in his time a defense against the principles of the Courts of Equity. Common law is often described as a body of law developed from judicial decisions based on custom or precedent and unwritten in statute or code. The monarchy in England began an attempt to standardize the law of the realm by sending out jurists to the different districts. The judges would not have complete jurisdiction over all matters (the Church took care of personal property, family law, etc.), but this did represent a centralizing force and usurped the power of manorial courts to some extent. That centralizing force was moderated by other factors. Even before Magna Carta, understandings between the king and representatives of "the people" had been worked out and these understandings became a part of the common law. Common law understandings were often made into statute law, and common law evolved around statute law, as common law courts were called upon to interpret statute law. Equity law evolved partially in response to common law. Quite early in English history, defendants who had lost at common law would appeal to the king during a special time of the year. As appeals multiplied, the chancellor of the exchequer began to handle the cases. Eventually, out of this office an independent court evolved, developing a distinct set of principles for handling the appeals.

As common law developed a reputation for bureaucratic independence from the throne, the Equity Courts developed a reputation for being the political arm of the ruler. Thus, Locke's particular list of rights might well serve as a means of undermining the legitimacy of the Equity Courts which represented for many an example of the abuses of a more than minimal state. By accepting this understanding of natural law, common law could be derived easily from natural law. The law of the land could be defended as a reflection of deeper moral principles which held for all men. See S. F. C. Milsom, *Historical Foundations of the Common Law*, 2nd ed. (Toronto: Butterworth, 1981). For an introduction to common law and equity see D. C. M. Yardley, *Elements of English Law*, 7th ed. (New York: Oxford University Press, 1966); the first edition was by William Geldert. Other important introductions to this area are J. H. Barker, *An Introduction to English Legal History*, 2nd ed. (London: Butterworth, 1979); and F. Pollack and F. W. Maitland, *The History of English Law*, 2 vols. (Cambridge: Cambridge University Press, 1968); and A. W. B. Simpson, *A History of the Common Law of Contract* (Oxford: Clarendon Press, 1975). The idea for the need for equity can be found in Aristotle's *Ethics*, book 5, chapter 10: "An equity essentially is just the rectification of the law, where the law has to be amplified because of the general terms in which it has to be couched. This is in fact why everything is not regulated by law; it is because there are cases which no law can be framed to cover and which can only be met by special regulation."

15. For a history of social contract theory see J. S. Gough, *The Social Contract: A Critical Study of Its Development*, 2nd ed. (Oxford: Clarendon Press, Oxford University Press, 1957).

16. Ibid.

17. Otto Gierke, *Natural Law and the Theory of Society*, translated with an introduction by Ernest Barker (Cambridge: Cambridge University Press, 1934).

18. See my "An Examination of the Fundamental Assumption of Hypothetical Process Arguments,"*Philosophical Studies* 34 (1978): 187–195.

19. Most of the objections I raise against actual, tacit, and dispositional contract arguments are elaborations upon the objections developed in Alan Gewirth, "Political Justice," in *The Concept of Social Justice*, edited by R. B. Brandt (Englewood Cliffs, N.J.: Prentice-Hall, Inc., 1962), 119–169.

20. Stating the conditions for a valid contract is extraordinarily complicated. The history of law is replete with attempts to sort out our conflicting

and shifting intuitions. What information is each party required to provide? In what sense must the contract be voluntary?

21. The exposition here glosses over serious problems in Locke. Strictly speaking, if the contract of government is viewed as the creation of a joint-stock company with property owners as stockholders, how could the nonpropertied citizens be obligated? See Joshua Cohen, "Structure, Choice, and Legitimacy: Locke's Theory of the State," *Philosophy and Public Affairs* 15 (1986): 310–324.

22. There is one objection which is sometimes pressed against contract theories which does no real damage. This is a conceptual objection. If "contract" is a legal notion, a promise enforced by law, then it makes sense to speak of a contractual agreement only in situations in which there is a third party present to enforce the contract. Absent this third party enforcement, it is unintelligible to speak of a contract. Hence, it makes no sense to speak of parties contracting together to create a political or legal order. Morally, this is but a terminological quibble. Even conceding the point about "contract," the theorist could develop a social promise theory of the state, admitting that individuals consent or promise. The binding nature then is not yet legally enforceable but remains morally binding.

23. The Classical Liberal could concede that in general a more than minimal state is possible but claim that in the United States the contract is for a minimal government. This assumes that parties have actually contracted together to form the government of the United States, and that the contract requires nothing more than a minimal government. The constitution will be interpreted as the contracting document. Within this response, constitutional interpretation becomes morally determining. There are serious problems with this attempt to salvage a defense of the minimal state for the U. S. One of the most serious is that of constitutional interpretation. No serious constitutional interpretation would claim that the Constitution is a blueprint for a minimal government. The federal government had very limited powers, indeed, but there was an understanding that those powers involved much more than a protection against harm. There was an apparent understanding, reflected in the preamble, that the new government was to promote the common good. Further, the constitutional framework of the balance of powers appears more like a set of procedures (with built-in checks) to establish how to generate law, not a specific list of natural rights beyond which the federal government could not step. States were allowed great latitude in interfering in liberty which would be inconsistent with the strict minimal government guidelines.

Or the Classical Liberal might admit that the contract reflected in the Constitution is for a more than minimal state, but deny the universality of consent. One can claim that there were or continue to be dissenters to the contract who did not and will not give consent to the more than minimal state. The moral issue then becomes how the more than minimal state can treat those living within its territory (if this language makes moral sense). This is the problem to which Nozick devotes so much attention, the problem of the independents within the protective agency. The argument would be that even a more than minimal government could not interfere with dissidents within its boundaries who objected to the contract unless the interference were to prevent harm. This argument is not that the more than minimal government of the U.S. is morally illegitimate, only that it is illegitimate if it attempts to coerce those not officially giving consent to adhere to the terms of the contract between the citizens. There is solid historical evidence that only a small percentage of individuals participated in the original "ratification," and further evidence that the framers intentionally designed the ratification procedure and the timing of the process to ensure exclusion of large and important numbers of the population. This kind of argument will not establish the illegitimacy in principle of the more than minimal state, however.

24. Rawls, A *Theory of Justice*, 119.

25. See, for example, John Rawls, "Kantian Constructivism in Moral Theory: The Dewey Lectures 1980," *Journal of Philosophy* 77 (1980): 515–572; "Social Utility and Primary Goods," in *Utilitarianism and Beyond*, edited by Amartya Sen and Bernard A. O. Williams (Cambridge: Cambridge University Press, 1982), 159–185; and "Justice as Fairness: Political Not Metaphysical," *Philosophy and Public Affairs* 14, no. 3 (1985): 223–251.

William Galston documents Rawls's shift in the Dewey lectures in "Moral Personality and Liberal Theory: John Rawls's 'Dewey Lectures,'" *Political Theory* 10 (1982): 492–519. The most comprehensive examination can be found in the "Symposium on Rawlsian Theory: Recent Developments," *Ethics* 99 (1989).

26. I am greatly simplifying the nature of Rawls's shift. In the introduction to the "Symposium on Rawlsian Theory of Justice: Recent Developments," Richard J. Arneson notes three general shifts. First, Rawls revises his argument from the original position by relativizing it. That is, Rawls admits that the description of the original position incorporates normatively laden assumptions. As Arneson puts it, the "justification of the principles is relativized to this ideal of the person and thereby to modern democratic culture in which . . . this ideal informs each citizen's ordinary understanding of herself" (696). Second, and in the same vein, Rawls has abandoned the idea that the contract argument can "justify principles of justice for all human societies at all times and to any rational person whatsoever" (696). The "we," it turns out, are those committed to liberal democratic constitutional institutions. The third shift involves an attempt to confront the pluralism

of our society and to achieve an overlapping consensus. The function of political philosophy, Rawls has come to believe, is to articulate a public understanding of fairness in the midst of the pluralism of our political lives which can provide"a morally acceptable basis of social unity, despite stable deep disagreements among citizens" (697). In this sense, Rawls is seeking to demonstrate to political opponents within a pluralistic society that "we" all share some basic understanding. All of these shifts reflect the point I am making.

27. This is the point of what has been identified in the preceding note as the third shift, the attempt to find an overlapping consensus in a pluralistic society.

28. Rawls, A Theory of Justice, 86.

29. Rawls, A Theory of Justice, 120. The first discussion of pure procedural justice is in the context of the exposition of the principle of equality of opportunity. Then, while discussing the problem of choosing the "philosophically favored" description of the original position, he says that the idea of pure procedural justice applies to the original hypothetical choice situation. "Thus justice as fairness is able to use the idea of pure procedural justice from the beginning." In the very next sentence he continues, "It is clear, then, that the original position is a purely hypothetical situation."

30. Ronald Dworkin, "The Original Position," in Reading Rawls: Critical Studies of "A Theory of Justice," edited by Norman Daniels (New York: Basic Books, Inc., n.d.), 18.

31. Robert Paul Wolff, Understanding Rawls: A Reconstruction and Critique of "A Theory of Justice" (Princeton: Princeton University Press, 1977).

32. William W. Lowrance, Of Acceptable Risk: Science and the Determination of Safety (Los Altos, Cal.: William Kaufmann, Inc., 1976).

33. See my discussion in"Ethics and the Organizational Person: Revisiting De George," Journal of Business Ethics 10 (1991): 17–32.

34. Lowrance, 122.

35. Lowrance, 122–123.

36. For another criticism of this and related arguments in professional ethics, see Michael W. Martin and Roland Schinzinger, Ethics in Engineering (New York: McGraw-Hill, 1983), 144.

37. Thomas Donaldson, Corporations and Morality (Englewood Cliffs, N.J.: Prentice-Hall, Inc., 1982), chapter 3, "Constructing a Social Contract for Business," 36–57. For a criticism of Donaldson's theory, see John Kultgen, "Donaldson's Social Contract for Business," Business and Professional Ethics Journal 5, no. 1 (n.d.): 28–39.

38. Donaldson is aware of some of the criticisms of hypothetical contract theory and mentions Paley, Maine, Blackstone, and Marx. Donaldson's response is that hypothetical contract arguments do not claim that there was

an actual state of nature in which some actual contract was constructed. Thus, he believes that these objections miss the mark. Donaldson claims that social contract theories analyze existing institutions and "clarify the *logical* presuppositions, not the historical antecedents, of political power." This follows the response of G. W. Gough in *The Social Contract*. However, this response ignores the problems identified above with hypothetical contracts. Further, if hypothetical contract arguments do nothing more than identify the logical presuppositions of our existing institutions, then they do not provide justification. In this sense, they are merely heuristic devices to unearth our assumptions. Donaldson must apparently either accept that the contract argument collapses into a coherence theory or explain how the contract device will serve to justify arrangements. That will involve overcoming the "So what?" objection.

4. CLASSICAL LIBERALISM AND UTILITARIANISM: FRIEDMAN

1. Milton Friedman, "The Sole Responsibility of Business Is to Increase Profits," *New York Times Magazine* (September 13, 1970): 32–33, 122, 124, and 126.

2. Christopher D. Stone, *Where the Law Ends: The Social Control of Corporate Behavior* (New York: Harper Colophon Books, 1975), chapter 8.

3. Some of the material in this chapter and the next appear in my "Polestar Refined: Business Ethics and Political Economy," *Journal of Business Ethics* 10 (1991): 69–87.

4. Milton Friedman, *Capitalism and Freedom* (Chicago: University of Chicago Press, 1962; 1982).

5. One might wish to distinguish a minimal from a limited state in Classical Liberalism. The minimal state would not have any form of a "safety net."

6. At one point, in *Capitalism and Freedom*, chapter 2, Friedman claims to accept the principle of paternalism, in a limited way. The example he gives, however, suggests that he does not need to adopt the principle. Friedman discusses the problem of children and the mentally deranged. He claims that government responsibilities for these cases may extend much further than they do for normal adults. The debate over paternalism is usually not associated with this issue. Classical Liberals might generally claim that mentally competent adults should be free to do whatever they wish so long as they harm no one else. The scope of freedom may be much less for children and the mentally incompetent without moving to accept paternalistic principles.

7. Friedman, *Capitalism and Freedom*, chapter 10.

8. For a brief description of the Austrian school, see Mark Blaug, *The Methodology of Economics: Or How Economists Explain* (New York: Cambridge University Press, 1980), chapter 3. For a bibliography of the school, see E. G. Dolan, ed., *The Foundation of Modern Austrian Economics* (Kansas City: Sheed and Ward, 1976); and Stephen C. Littlechild, *The Fallacy of the Mixed Economy: An "Austrian" Critique of Economic Thinking and Policy* (London: Institute of Economic Affairs, 1978). Hayek died on March 24, 1992, while this manuscript was being prepared.

9. Utilitarianism can be regarded as a five-step process for reaching a decision: (1) identifying the relevant alternatives to be considered; (2) determining the consequences associated with each alternative; (3) assigning value to the consequences of each alternative; (4) determining the net value associated with each alternative; (5) choosing that alternative which optimizes or maximizes net value. If two alternative equally optimize, then either is permissible. There are problems associated which each of these five steps.

10. One of the best treatments of the different varieties of utilitarianism remains David Lyons, *The Forms and Limits of Utilitarianism* (New York: Clarendon Press, Oxford University Press, 1965). For more contemporary discussion, see Amartya K. Sen and Bernard A. O. Williams, eds., *Utilitarianism and Beyond* (Cambridge: Cambridge University Press, 1982).

11. John Gray, *Liberalism: Concepts in Social Thought* (Minneapolis: University of Minnesota Press, 1986).

12. Herbert Spencer, *Social Statistics: Or, the Conditions Essential to Human Happiness Specified, and the First of Them Developed* (New York: D. Appleton, 1865). See, of course, Richard Hofstadter, *Social Darwinism in American Thought, 1860–1915* (Philadelphia: Beacon Press, 1944).

13. G. E. Moore, *Principia Ethica* (Cambridge: Cambridge University Press, 1903).

14. F. A. Hayek, *The Constitution of Liberty* (Chicago: University of Chicago Press, 1960).

15. Jean-Paul Sarte, "The Wall," in *Introduction to Literature: Stories*, edited by Lynn Altenbernd and Leslie L. Lewis (New York: Macmillan, 1963), 400–412.

16. Quoted from Gray, *Liberalism*, 29.

17. An article in *The Economist* (March 28, 1992): 75, noting the death of Hayek, remarked that this idea reappeared with "new clarity" in his later works, especially his last book, *The Fatal Conceit*: "Hayek was at pains to emphasize that civilisation did not come about by design: rather, it is human actions, with consequences both intended and (more often) unintended, that yield another sort of spontaneous order." *The Economist* suggested that Hayek carried his "distrust of the state to an implausible extreme."

18. F. A. Hayek, *The Road to Serfdom* (Chicago: University of Chicago Press, 1944).

5. EVALUATING THE UTILITARIAN DEFENSE OF CLASSICAL LIBERALISM

1. The following is adapted from Norman Bowie and Robert Simon, *The Individual and the Social Order* (Englewood Cliffs, N.J.: Prentice-Hall, Inc., 1972), chapter 2. Similar counterexamples are standard fare.

2. In economic literature, the debate is cast as one between efficiency and equality, as in Arthur M. Okun, *Equality and Efficiency: The Big Tradeoff* (Washington, D.C.: The Brookings Institution, 1975). In this example (table 1), each person counts for one and no person counts for more than one. The impact of each policy is considered on each individual. Whether an individual happens to be a member of the landed aristocracy, whether he happens to be the duke of such and such a domain, or whether she is terribly poor is irrelevant. Utilitarianism is egalitarian in this sense. It so happens that the utility created for Citizen 1 is far greater than that created for the other citizens under policy A, but this does not mean Citizen 1 counts for more. What counts for the utilitarian is bringing into the world utility.

3. Adam Smith, *An Inquiry into the Nature and Causes of the Wealth of Nations*, edited by Edwin Cannan, with a new preface by George J. Stigler (Chicago, Ill.: University of Chicago Press, 1976), book 1 chapter 8, 74.

4. Mancur Olson, *The Logic of Collective Action: Public Goods and the Theory of Groups* (Cambridge, Mass.: Harvard University Press, 1965); and *The Rise and Decline of Nations: Economic Growth, Stagflation, and Social Rigidities* (New Haven, Conn.: Yale University Press, 1982).

5. In *The Wealth of Nations*, book 5, chapter 1, "The Education of Youth," Smith writes that the "understandings of the greater part of men are necessarily formed by their ordinary employments." He continues: "The man whose life is spent in performing a few simple operations, of which the effects too are, perhaps, always the same, or very nearly the same, has no occasion to exert his understanding, or to exercise his invention in finding out expedients for removing difficulties which never occur. He naturally loses, therefore, the habit of such exertion, and generally becomes as stupid and ignorant as it is possible for a human creature to become. The torpor of his mind renders him, not only incapable of relishing or bearing a part in any rational conversation, but of conceiving any generous, noble or tender sentiment, and consequently of forming any just judgment concerning many even of the ordinary duties of private life." (303). See also Adam Smith,

Lectures on Justice, Police, Revenue and Arms, delivered at the University of Glasgow by Adam Smith, reported by a student in 1763, and edited with an introduction and notes by Edwin Cannan, 1896 (New York: Kelley and Millman, Inc., 1956), 252–258.

6. Harry Braverman, *Labor and Monopoly Capital: The Degradation of Work in the Twentieth Century* (New York: Monthly Review, 1974).

7. Smith's discussion of this occurs in *The Wealth of Nations,* book 1, chapter 8, 76. Smith argues that in a wealthy society, wages will rise, i.e., a rising tide lifts all ships. For a contemporary treatment, see Robert J. Gordon, *Macroeconomics,* 5th ed. (Glenview, Ill.: Scott, Foresman/Little, Brown Higher Education, 1990), chapter 7. With the internationalization of the modern corporation this seems transparently false. See Robert B. Reich, *The Work of Nations: Preparing Ourselves for 21st-Century Capitalism* (New York: Alfred A. Knopf, 1991), especially chapters 1 and 16.

8. David Ricardo, *The Principles of Political Economy and Taxation* (New York: Dutton, Everyman's Library, 1965), 57–61.

9. Amartya Sen, *On Ethics and Economics* (New York: Basil Blackwell Inc., 1987), makes the point that "interpersonal comparisons of utility came under fire in the 1930s, led by Lionel Robbins" (30). See Lionel Robbins, "Interpersonal Comparability and Social Choice Theory," *Economic Journal* 48 (1938): 635–641.

10. For an excellent introductory discussion, see C. Kyke, "Utility as Preference," chapter 3 of *Philosophy of Economics* (Englewood Cliffs, N.J.: Prentice-Hall, Inc., 1981).

11. I am greatly simplifying. Actual preference rankings pose problems. For example, if a mark of rationality is that one does not hold two contradictory statements at the same time, then most individuals are irrational with respect to preference orderings. Many have preference orderings which are circular. We might solicit from Jones that he prefers (1) apple pie to cherry, and (2) cherry pie to lemon, and (3) lemon pie to apple. If one accepts transitivity, then combining 1 and 2 we determine that Jones prefers apple pie to lemon. But 3 indicates a preference for lemon pie to apple. This is irrational. Studies of actual orderings reveal numerous nontrivial examples of such irrationalities. Such irrationalities also pose problems in when combining individual rankings in order to determine a social good. But if we choose to ignore the preferences that real humans have, then are we not imposing a set of values?

12. James Griffin, *Well-Being: Its Meaning, Measurement, and Moral Importance* (New York: Clarendon Press, Oxford University Press, 1986).

13. See the discussion of positivism in Sen, *On Ethics and Economics,* 30–31.

14. Strictly speaking, subjectivistic theories are noncognitive.

15. What follows is a discussion related to welfare economics and collective or social choice functions. As such, I am deviating from a strict reconstruction of the kind of argument which Friedman would probably develop. I cannot do justice to the use of ordinal measures of utility in microeconomic theory per se. This discussion provides a relevant surrogate for the kinds of issues which arise.

16. The rules for determining a collective choice based on individual choices can be viewed as the adoption of either a theory of social value or a theory of obligation.

17. Kenneth J. Arrow, *Social Choice and Individual Values* (New Haven, Conn.: Yale University Press, 1951). For a very good introduction to the problem, see Alfred F. MacKay, *Arrow's Theorem: The Paradox of Social Choice* (New Haven, Conn.: Yale University Press, 1980). For a shorter discussion and one which includes a description of the significance of the dispute over the theorem, see Paul Seabright, "Social Choice and Social Theories," *Philosophy and Public Affairs* 18 (1989): 365–387.

18. The final condition is slightly controversial. This condition rules out procedures which would take into consideration Jones's preferences that he get more than Smith, for example. If Jones prefers a Cadillac to a Mercedes, unless his friend gets a Cadillac, in which case he prefers a Mercedes, his preferences are not independent. Condition I claims that rational procedures will not take into account "irrelevant" alternatives like these. One of the things which makes this controversial, of course, is that many human preferences appear to be dependent upon those of others.

19. The following discussion is based upon Allen Buchanan, *Ethics, Efficiency, and the Market* (Totowa, N.J.: Rowman and Allanheld, 1985), chapters 1 and 2.

20. Vilfredo Pareto, *Cours d'economie politique* (Lausanne: 1897).

21. Allen Buchanan, Op. cit.

22. Allen Buchanan, 14.

23. Kenneth J. Arrow and F. H. Hahn, *General Competitive Analysis* (San Francisco: Holden-Day, 1971). The theorem has two parts. As Sen expresses it in *On Ethics and Economics*, the second part of the theorem states that with "some other conditions (no economies of large scale), every Pareto Optimal social state is also a perfectly competitive equilibrium, with respect to some set of prices (and for some initial distribution of people's endowments)" (34).

24. See the discussion of the First Fundamental Theorem of Welfare Economics in Sen, *On Ethics and Economics*, especially 31–40.

25. Sen, Op. cit.

26. The problem is different from that confronting many explanations in physical science. One might claim that in a perfect vacuum, perfectly spherical round balls with a particular velocity and mass would behave in ways captured by a formula. In the real world, these conditions are not satisfied,

but we nonetheless may find it very helpful to use the formula developed in the context of the ideal model. Among the important differences between this and arguing that one has good reason to believe in the First Fundamental Theorem of Welfare Economics is that the latter is proposed as a theorem derived from these conditions. Moreover, the formula can be tested in the real world and refined. For instance, as a result of testing, coefficients may be introduced into our formula to account for deviations from the ideal which are attributable to the lack of a perfect vacuum, or because the solids are not perfectly spherical, etc.

27. Consequently, some have abandoned the notion of Pareto optimality for an alternative known as Kaldor-Hicks. (Nicholas Kaldor, "Welfare Propositions in Economics and Interpersonal Comparisons of Utility," *Economic Journal* 49 [1939]: 549–552). Roughly, the idea goes beyond Pareto optimality by allowing coercion against "losers" (i.e., those whose preferences have been violated by forcing certain trades) provided that the "winners'" gain is sufficient to compensate the losers. Of all the problems with this idea one is especially pertinent here. The attractiveness of the Pareto notions is that they allow one to make judgments about superior states of systems or optimal states of affairs ("best for all") by apparently avoiding intersubjective or interpersonal comparisons of value. The Kaldor-Hicks principle cannot avoid relying upon interpersonal comparisons. In the U.S., when eminent domain is invoked, residents must be fairly compensated. How are we to determine how much compensation is due? On Pareto principles there is not such a problem. If the homeowner wishes to trade with someone else on an agreed upon price, then the homeowner has determined what the property is worth to him/her at that moment. The exchange satisfies a preference. But, whose preference ranking will determine the compensation due the homeowner if coerced? Those preferences may be wild by our standards, which may explain why the homeowner will not sell in the first place. The homeowner may have such a "skewed" value system that virtually no offer would suffice to entice a trade. Perhaps his ancestors are buried on the sacred property, etc. Market value has nothing to do with the value for this person. Market value discloses only the value which most sellers/buyers might attribute to the property, and even that is an interpersonal value judgment. Thus, Kaldor-Hicks is an attempt to meet this kind of objection, but it does so by abandoning the most attractive feature of the Pareto principles.

6. FREEDOM AND WELL-BEING
IN THE LIBERAL TRADITION

1. In *Liberal Purposes* (New York: Cambridge University Press, 1991), William A. Galston identifies at least three distinct traditions within liberalism of liberal excellence (229-230). In the Lockean tradition, rational

liberty of self-direction is the important end. In the Kantian tradition, the ideal is the capacity to act with the precepts of duty. As Galston puts it, this involves the ability to make duty "the effective principle of personal conduct and to resist the promptings of passion and interest insofar as they are incompatible with this principle." (229) The third tradition is, according to Galston, adapted from Romanticism by John Stuart Mill, Ralph Waldo Emerson, Henry David Thoreau, and Walt Witman. In *On Liberty*, Mill explicitly praises the German Baron Wilhelm von Humbolt, where the Romantic ideal is also apparent.

In my treatment of liberalism, I have emphasized the third tradition.

2. Amartya Sen, *On Ethics and Economics* (New York: Basil Blackwell Inc., 1987), develops this theme in detail, especially in chapter 3, "Freedom and Consequences."

3. This is suggested by Bernard A. O. Williams, *Morality: An Introduction to Ethics* (Hammondsworth, England: Penguin Books, 1973), 101–102.

4. James Griffen, *Well-Being: Its Meaning, Measurement and Moral Importance* (New York: Clarendon Press, Oxford University Press, 1986).

5. The United Nations Development Programme published its first estimate of a Human Development Index in 1990. This combined income level with adult literacy and life expectancy. In 1991, average years of schooling was combined with adult literacy to give a knowledge index. Scaled from 0 to 100 in 1991, the U.S. ranks seventh on the Human Development Index, behind Japan, Canada, Iceland, Sweden, Switzerland, and Norway. See *Pocket World in Figures: 1993 Edition* (London: The Economist Books, 1993), 22.

6. Adam Smith, *An Inquiry into the Nature and Causes of the Wealth of Nations*, edited by Edwin Canan with a new preface by George J. Stigler (Chicago: University of Chicago Press, 1976).

7. The information about piracy and the quotation from Keynes is taken from Clarence H. Cramer, *American Enterprise: Free and Not So Free* (Boston: Little, Brown, and Co., 1972), 36–37.

8. Moreover, mercantilism tended to incite trade wars. It is impossible for all countries to enjoy a favorable trade balance. Trade wars led to more violent conflict as interests clashed across the Old and New Worlds.

9. Joel Feinberg, *Harm To Others: The Moral Limits of the Criminal Law* (New York: Oxford University Press, 1984). The following discussion is based almost entirely upon Feinberg's discussion in chapter 1, "Harm as Setbacks to Interest," especially 37–45 and 55–61.

10. I am sure this example is not original to me, but I cannot remember the source.

11. Nicholas Rescher, *Welfare: The Social Issue in Philosophical Perspective* (Pittsburgh: University of Pittsburgh Press, 1972), 6.

12. Feinberg, *Harm to Others*, 57.

13. John Gray, *Liberalism: Concepts in Social Thought* (Minneapolis: University of Minnesota Press, 1986), 30.

7. MICRO-MANAGERIALISM

1. Robert Jackall, *Moral Mazes: The World of Corporate Managers* (New York: Oxford University Press, 1988).
2. Francis X. Sutton, Seymour E. Harris, Carl Kaysen, and James Tobin, *The American Business Creed* (Cambridge, Mass.: Harvard University Press, 1956).
3. Jackall, op. cit., 168.
4. William H. Whyte, *Is Anybody Listening?* (New York: Simon and Schuster, Inc., 1952).
5. *Fortune* magazine, with the collaboration of Russell W. Davenport, *The Permanent Revolution* (New York: Fortune, 1951).
6. Sutton et al., op. cit., 354–384.
7. Ibid., 358.
8. Loc. cit.
9. Ibid., 354.
10. Loc. cit.
11. Ibid., 359.
12. Edward S. Mason, "The Apologetics of 'Managerialism'" *The Journal of Business* 31 (January 1958): 1–11. For another discussion of the perspective, with a brief bibliography of those in the Managerial tradition, see Robin Marris, "A Model of the 'Managerial' Enterprise," *Quarterly Journal of Economics* 77 (May 1963): 183–209.
13. Adolphe A. Berle, *The Twentieth-Century Capitalist Revolution*, (New York: Harcourt, Brace, 1951). See also, Berle's *Power without Property* (New York: Harcourt, Brace, 1959).
14. Gardiner C. Means, *The Corporate Revolution in America: Economic Reality vs. Economic Theory* (New York: Crowell-Collier Press, 1962).
15. Morris Adelman, "The Measurement of Industrial Concentration," *Review of Economics and Statistics* 33 (November 1951): 269–296.
16. John Kenneth Galbraith, *American Capitalism: The Concept of Countervailing Power* (Boston: Houghton Mifflin Co., 1952).
17. In *The Social Responsibilities of Business: Company and Community* (Cleveland: The Press of Case Western Reserve University, 1970), Morrell Heald makes the convincing case, notably in chapter 1, that the Managerial ideology, at least in nascent form, existed by the turn of the century. I am arguing that this ideology took on mature form by incorporating Managerial ideas, especially those developed in the 1930s.

18. Spencer J. Pack, *Capitalism as a Moral System: Adam Smith's Critique of the Free Market Economy* (Aldershot: Elgar, 1992), perhaps makes Smith out to be too much of a Revisionist Liberal if not a Socialist, but the work provides an antidote to the common view.

19. T. H. Green, *Essays Moral, Political, and Literary* (London: Longmans, Green, and Co., 1875); *Lectures on the Principles of Political Obligation* (London, 1963).

20. Bernard Bosanquet, *The Philosophical Theory of the State* (London: Macmillan, 1930).

21. L. T. Hobhouse, *Liberalism*, with an introduction by Alan P. Grimes (New York: Oxford University Press, 1964; reprinted 1979).

22. Ibid., introduction, 1–2.

23. Ibid., 1.

24. John Gray, *Liberalism: Concepts in Social Thought* (Minneapolis: University of Minnesota Press, 1986.

25. See David Vogel, "Why Businessmen Distrust Their State: The Political Consciousness of American Corporate Executives," *British Journal of Political Science* 8 (1978): 45–78.

26. The distinction does not correspond to that between microeconomics and macroeconomics as Lee E. Preston, "Corporation and Society: The Search for a Paradigm," *Journal of Economic Literature* 13 (1975): 434–453, suggests, but an attempt to develop a more accurate nomenclature is awkward. Preston draws a distinction very similar to the one I am making. He claims that unlike mainstream economic literature, which generally ignores the significance of the corporation, the literature on the corporation and society does not. Preston attempts to identify the "paradigms" functioning in this literature and distinguishes between the "institutionals" and the "organizationals." The former, he claims, "attempt to deal with society and social processes on an aggregative or holistic basis and in terms of major historical and institutional categories, among which the corporate sector is an important, but not the single, object of interest" (438). The legal-political approach is included here, but Galbraith is most prominently displayed as an example. In contrast to the approach of the institutionals, the "organizational analyst and the microeconomist focus on the individual behavior unit, or on an idealized conception of such a unit, and see the progress of events in terms of the action and interaction of separate and distinct behavioral entities" (441). Preston also identifies the "philosophicals," those engaged in philosophical analysis, and claims that such analysis rests upon either the organizational or institutional paradigm.

I agree that the "philosophicals," primarily those working in the area of Business Ethics, presuppose either the institutional or the organizational framework. But I take some exception to a number of other points. First, he claims that the distinction between the organizationals and the institutionals is that between microeconomics and macroeconomics. Although my language suggests this, it can be misleading. What I call Micro-Managerial owes much more to the literature of the organization than to microeconomics. As I will argue, the problem with Micro-Managerialism is that it ignores what is central in microeconomics, demand curves which provide a context for making organizational choices. Second, Preston leaves the impression that these are competing paradigms, and the notion of paradigm, since Kuhn, suggests incommensurability. I believe Managerialism often resorts to both paradigms, and there is no contradiction here.

27. Sutton et al., op. cit., 43.

28. Loc. cit.

29. The authors may also have been unwilling to treat the theoretical core of Managerialism as a part of the ideology because they themselves shared many of these ideas.

30. Frederick Allen, *The Big Change* (New York: Harper, 1952). The same approach is apparent in John N. Brooks, *The Great Leap: The Past Twenty-Five Years in America* (New York: Harper and Row, 1966). This voluntaristic strain should be contrasted with a more structural approach to the "big change." David Lilienthal, *Big Business: A New Era* (New York: Harper, 1953), for example, bases his confidence in the dawning of the new era of competition between big corporations, and competition among business, labor, and government. This pluralistic approach will be treated in my later chapter on Macro-Managerialism.

31. These quotations are taken from Clarence H. Cramer, *American Enterprise: Free and Not So Free* (Boston: Little, Brown, and Co., 1972), 397. Cramer has an extended discussion of the literature of the big change, 395–405, with extensive documentation of the theme. Cramer identifies "two economic statesmen," Adolf Berle and Clarence Randall, as having written on the "challenge and promise" of the big change in twentieth-century capitalism.

32. Cramer, op. cit.

33. Ibid., 396.

34. Frederick Winslow Taylor, *The Principles of Scientific Management* (New York: Harper and Row Brothers, 1929).

35. Abraham Maslow, *Motivation and Personality* (New York: Harper and Row, 1954); and *Eupsychian Management: A Journal* (Homewood, Ill.: Richard D. Irwin, Inc., and the Dorsey Press, 1965).

36. Douglas McGregor, *The Human Side of the Enterprise*, (New York: McGraw-Hill, 1960). For a more critical assessment of these developments, see Michael Maccoby, *The Gamesman* (New York: Simon and Schuster, 1976), especially chapter 8, "The Psychology of Development."

37. William Ouchi, *Theory Z: How American Business Can Meet The Japanese Challenge* (Reading, Mass.: Addison-Wesley, 1981).

38. Sutton et al., in *The American Business Creed*, make the same point with respect to the earlier literature. "In the managerial description of the business role, positive description and moral exhortation are never clearly distinguished. Although American capitalism is said to have undergone, or almost completed, a great moral transformation, the strong element of moral exhortation in the managerial creed suggests that there are still some businessmen who are insufficiently transformed" (359).

39. Gerald F. Cavanagh, *American Business Values in Transition*, (Englewood Cliffs, N.J.: Prentice-Hall, Inc., 1984).

40. Ibid., 176.

41. Ibid., 188.

42. George C. Lodge, *The New American Ideology* (New York: Alfred A. Knopf, 1979).

43. George C. Lodge, "The Ethical Implications of Ideology," in *Business Ethics: Readings and Cases in Corporate Morality*, edited by W. Michael Hoffman and Jennifer Mills Moore (New York: McGraw-Hill, 1984), 116.

44. Ibid., 116.

45. This is quoted from the *SIM Newsletter* of the Social Issues in Management Division of the Academy of Management (Autumn 1990): 2.

46. Richard S. Eells, *The Meaning of Modern Business: An Introduction to the Philosophy of Large Corporate Enterprise* (New York: Columbia University Press, 1960). See also Richard Eells and Clarence Walton, *Conceptual Foundations of Business: An Outline of the Major Ideas Sustaining Business Enterprise in the Western World* (Homewood, Ill.: Richard D. Irwin, Inc., 1961).

47. Morrell Heald, *The Social Responsibilities of Business: Company and Community, 1900–1960* (Cleveland: The Press of Case Western Reserve University, 1970).

48. Ibid., 207.

49. Louis D. Brandeis, *Business—A Profession* (Boston: Small, Maynard, and Co., 1914).

50. Heald, op. cit., 62–63.

51. Adolph A. Berle and Gardiner C. Means, *The Modern Corporation and Private Property* (New York: Macmillan, 1932).

52. The papers of the Conference appear in *The Journal of Law and Economics* 22 (June 1983).

53. Berle and Means denied that the theses advanced were original. They claimed to be expressing what many had by then already accepted as given. They marshaled evidence in support of the claims. The thesis of the Managerial revolution was also incorporated into a technocratic theory

in the context of a class struggle by James Burnham in *The Managerial Revolution* (Bloomington, Ind.: University of Indiana Press, 1960). A favorite source for recent Managerialists is Alfred D. Chandler, *The Visible Hand: The Managerial Revolution in America* (Cambridge, Mass.: The Belknap Press of Harvard University Press, 1977).

54. A major theme of the *The House of Morgan: An American Banking Dynasty and the Rise of Modern Finance* (New York: Atlantic Monthly Press, 1990), by Ron Chernow, is the extent to which large corporations have come to be independent of even large banks in the quest to raise capital. This explains, in part, the necessity on the part of U.S. banks, constrained by Glass-Stegall, to seek profits first in high-risk Third World loans, then in high-risk "junk bonds," and then in high-risk real estate loans.

55. Berle and Means, op. cit., 254-255.

56. Clearly, this idea of "trusteeship" is quite different from the idea of the "trusteeship of management" developed within the business circles. Here, trusteeship is used in the straightforward fiduciary sense of being a trustee for the stockholders. The concept of the trusteeship of management as used in the business community is reflected in the thesis of managerial professionalism or the thesis of social responsibility.

57. The difficulties of applying the simple principle of profit maximization should not be minimized. Even after conceptual clarification (determining, for instance, whether profit should be maximized short-term or long-term) the facts of any situation are likely to be not only complex, but incomplete, unreliable, and sometimes pointing in contrary directions. Moreover, managers are involved in so many decisions that attempting to act on this principle in every situation would likely be counterproductive. Nonetheless, at least there is a criterion, a standard, which serves as a guide for behavior and a benchmark against which performance can be judged. In place of this, Managerialists offer nothing but the professional manager with the role of adjudicating among the many competing interests and determining what is best. The criteria by which to determine "the best," however, is never stated. Hence, no guidance is offered and no method of evaluating the performance of management is possible.

58. See Committee for Economic Development, *Measuring Business's Social Performance: The Corporate Social Audit* (New York: Committee for Economic Development, 1974); S. Prakash Sethi, "Corporate Social Audit: An Emerging Trend in Measuring Corporate Social Performance," in Dow Votaw and S. Prakash Sethi, eds. *The Corporate Dilemma* (Englewood Cliffs, N.J.: Prentice-Hall, Inc., 1973); and, Raymond A. Bauer and Dan H. Fee, Jr., *The Corporate Social Audit* (New York: Russell Sage Foundation, 1972).

59. See, for example, Frederick D. Sturdivant's discussion in *Business and Society: A Managerial Approach*, rev. ed. (Homewood, Ill.: Richard D.

Irwin, Inc., 1981), 166–174. For references, see Lawrence A. Gordon, ed., *Accounting and Corporate Social Responsibility* (Lawrence, Kan.: University of Kansas Press, 1978).

60. Sturdivant, op. cit.

61. Loc. cit.

62. Grant T. Savage, Timothy W. Nix, Carlton J. Whitehead, and John D. Blair, "Strategies for Assessing and Managing Organizational Stakeholders," *Academy of Management Executive* 5, no. 2 (1991): 61–75.

63. William C. Frederick, Keith Davis, and James E. Post, *Business and Society: Corporate Strategy, Public Policy, Ethics*, 6th ed. (New York: McGraw-Hill, 1988), 13–23.

64. Frederick, Davis, and Post, op. cit., 6th ed., 45.

65. In another text, Fred Luthans, Richard M. Hodgetts, and Kenneth R. Thompson, *Social Issues in Business*, 3rd ed. (New York: Macmillan Publishing Co., 1980), write that corporations have five objectives: survival, growth, profit, economic contributions, and social obligations. Here, a rudimentary prioritizing is advanced, one which is likely assumed by other Managerialists. "The five objectives. . . are all interrelated. However, the priorities assigned to them require that attention be given first to survival and growth. Once the corporation is certain of these two objectives, it can then turn to social problems. The major issue is not whether business should or should not assume social responsibility. Rather, the logical issue seems to be to determine at what point business should realize that its survival and growth are assured and social objectives should take top priority" (65).

There is no argument for why survival is important. There may be instances in which it is easy to imagine that the public good calls for the elimination of a particular corporation. And even after assigning first priority to survival and growth, there are problems. Clearly, there is the problem mentioned by the authors of determining the point at which managers make social obligations a top priority. Even if that point could be determined somehow, there is no way of determining the socially responsible way of meeting the social obligations when they come into conflict.

66. For a good discussion of the alleged connection between social responsibility and financial performance, see Jean B. McGuire, Alison Sundgren, and Thomas Schneeweis, "Corporate Social Responsibility and Firm Financial Performance," *Academy of Management Journal* 31, no. 4 (1988): 854–872.

67. Sturdivant, op cit., rev. ed. (1981), 3. Heald, op. cit. 92–93, notes that the idea that ethics is good business was quite popular in the 1920s: "Discussions of business ethics were common in the Twenties and the role of trade associations in promoting this ethical concern was widely hailed. Given the mood of the day, the trade association or chamber of commerce which

did not at some time during the decade produce a code of ethics subscribed to by its membership was derelict in its duty. The idea that "good ethics" were good business, that "He profits most who serves best," helped reconcile those who were less morally minded to a veritable flood of inspirational business literature with a theme of uplift." Heald also quips that this is the spirit of boosterism and service which was satirized by Sinclair in *Babbitt*.

68. Frederick, Davis, and Post, op. cit., 6th ed.

8. EVALUATING MICRO-MANAGERIALISM

1. Edward S. Herman, *Corporate Control, Corporate Power* (New York: Cambridge University Press, 1981).

2. Herman, op. cit., 260. Herman quotes James F. Harris and Anne Klepper, *Corporate Philanthropic Public Service Activities*, Conference Board Report 688 (1977): 5; and William Baumol, "Enlightened Self-Interest and Corporate Philanthropy," in *A New Rational for Corporate Social Policy*, edited by William Baumol et al.(New York: Committee for Economic Development, 1970), 5–11.

3. Loc. cit.

4. *The Public Perspective: A Roper Center Review of Public Opinion and Polling* 2 (September/October 1991): 101. The figures are based on information supplied by the American Association of Fund-Raising Counsel, Inc.

5. Loc. cit.

6. Robert B. Reich, *The Work of Nations: Preparing Ourselves for 21st-Century Capitalism* (New York: Alfred A. Knopf, 1991).

7. Ibid., 279–281.

8. Barry Bluestone and Bennett Harrison, *Capital and Communities: The Causes and Consequences of Private Divestment* (Washington, D.C.: Progressive Alliance, 1980), chapters 2–4. Also Herman, op. cit., 266.

9. Bluestone and Harris, loc. cit.

10. Herman, op. cit., 266.

11. Herman, op. cit., 262.

12. Dan R. Dalton and Idalene F. Kesner, "On the Dynamics of Corporate Size and Illegal Activity: An Empirical Assessment," *Journal of Business Ethics* 7 (1988): 861–870.

13. Ibid., 865.

14. Herman, op. cit., 265.

15. Horrell Heald, *The Social Responsibilities of Business: Company and Community, 1900–1960* (Cleveland: The Press of Case Western Reserve University, 1970), 70–78.

16. Charles S. Goodman and C. Merle Crawford, "Young Executives: A Source of New Ethics?" *Personnel Journal* (March 1974): 180–181.

17. Bette Ann Stead and Janice J. Miller, "Can Social Awareness Be Increased through Business School Curricula?" *Journal of Business Ethics* 7 (1988): 553–560.

18. William R. Wynd and John Mager, "The Business and Society Course: Does It Change Student Attitudes?" *Journal of Business Ethics* 8 (1989): 487–491.

19. The material and quotations in this paragraph are taken from Heald, op. cit., 74–78.

20. Many of the names for these arguments are taken from, or suggested by, Howard F. Sohn's "Prevailing Rationales in the Corporate Responsibility Debate," *The Journal of Business Ethics* 1 (1982): 139–144. Versions of the stakeholder argument appear frequently in the literature. If I am not mistaken, this argument is suggested by Berle and Means and in Richard S. Eell's *The Meaning of Modern Business: An Introduction to the Philosophy of Large Corporate Enterprise* (New York: Columbia University Press, 1960).

21. Quoted from Sohn, op. cit., 141.

22. Ibid.

23. See, for example, Arthur A. Thompson, Jr., *Economics of the Firm: Theory and Practice*, 4th ed. (Englewood Cliffs, N.J.: Prentice-Hall, Inc., 1985), chapter 9, "Goals of the Firm: Profits and Other Considerations."

24. Neil Chamberlain, *The Limits of Corporate Responsibility* (New York: Basic Books, Inc., 1973), 203; quoted from Sohn, op. cit., 141.

25. James W. Kuhn and Ivar Berg, *Values in a Business Society* (New York: Harcourt, Brace, and World, 1968), 60. This book is a text for the Business and Society course developed at Columbia University in the 1960s, known as a Conceptual Foundations course, reminiscent of the title of the book by Richard S. Eells and Clarence Walton, *The Conceptual Foundations of Business: An Outline of the Major Ideas Sustaining Business Enterprise in the Western World* (Homewood, Ill.: Richard D. Irwin, Inc., 1961).

26. Chamberlain's work, as the title suggests, focuses on the limits of corporate responsibility, not on the wide discretionary ability.

27. Peter French, "Corporate Moral Agency," in *Business Ethics: Readings and Cases in Corporate Morality* edited by W. Michael Hoffman and Jennifer Mills Moore (New York: McGraw-Hill, 1981), 163–171. See also my "Corporate Moral Agency: The Case for Anthropological Bigotry," in Hoffman and Moore, op. cit. 172–179.

28. For a general discussion of the issue, see Thomas Donaldson *Corporationsand Morality* (Englewood Cliffs, N.J.: Prentice-Hall, Inc., 1982), chapter 2.

29. This section is based upon my article "'Ought' Implies 'Can': The Moral Relevance of a Theory of the Firm," *Journal of Business Ethics* 7 (1988): 23–28.

30. Adolph A. Berle, *The Twentieth-Century Capitolist Revolution* (New York: Harcourt, Brace, 1951).

31. Ralph Nader, Mark Green, and Joel Seligman, *Taming the Giant Corporation* (New York: W. W. Norton, 1976). I am quoting from excerpts which appear in W. Michael Hoffman and Jennifer M. Moore, *Business Ethics: Readings and Cases in Corporate Morality* (New York: McGraw-Hill, Inc., 1984), 180–199.

32. In Hoffman and Moore, op. cit., 180.

33. In Hoffman and Moore, op. cit., 183.

34. Milton Friedman, "The Social Responsibility of Business Is to Increase Profits," *New York Times*, September 12, 1962, section 6. Reprinted in Hoffman and Moore, op. cit., 126–131.

35. See, for example, Eugene Fama, "Separation of Ownership and Control," *Journal of Law and Economics* 22 (June 1983): 301–326; and "Agency Problems and Residual Claims," *Journal of Law and Economics* 22 (June 1983): 327–350. The general line is that the split between stockholders and management is an efficient response to market pressures and a desirable division of labor. Stockholders supply capital; management makes decisions. One can argue that this arrangement is efficient and desirable because, for one thing, those with available capital are not always good decision makers. Moreover, good corporate decision makers are not always sufficiently well-heeled to be able to supply capital. Stockholders cannot even be legitimately called owners. They are "residual claimants." That is, in return for supply capital they lay claim to some share of the residual earnings. The separation is desirable also because those with available capital may well be risk averse, and the willingness to take risk may be socially desirable.

36. Eugene Fama, "Agency Problems and the Theory of the Firm," *Journal of Political Economy* 88 (1980): 288–307.

37. For a general discussion of the literature, see Kenneth M. Davidson, *Megamergers: Corporate America's Billion Dollar Takeovers* (Cambridge, Mass., Ballinger Publishing Company, 1985), especially chapter 15, "The Merger Market for Corporate Control." Two early proponents of the view that corporate takeovers disciplined inefficient management were Robin Marris, "A Model of the 'Managerial' Enterprise," *Quarterly Journal of Economics* 77 (May 1963): 185–209; and *The Economic Theory of "Managerial" Capitalism* (Cambridge, Mass., The Free Press of Glencoe, 1964), chapter 2; and Henry Manne, "Mergers and the Market for Corporate Control," *Journal of Political Economy* 73 (April 1965): 110–120. More recently, see Michael C. Jensen and Richard Ruback, "The Market for Corporate Control: The Scientific Evidence," *Journal of Financial Economics* 11 (1983): 3–50; this volume is devoted entirely to empirical investigations of the question of corporate control.

I do not adhere to the belief that takeovers represent examples of efficient markets clearing out inefficient management. But the constraints upon management imposed by the threat of takeovers were substantial. Leveraged buyouts began as a way of providing protection against them.

38. Herman, op. cit.

39. Ibid., 246–247.

40. For other constraints, see Ira M. Millstein and Salem M. Katsh, *The Limits of Corporate Power: Existing Constraints on the Exercise of Corporate Discretion* (New York: Macmillan Publishing Co., Inc., 1981).

9. MACRO-MANAGERIALISM

1. Committee for Economic Development, *The Social Responsibilities of Business Corporations* (New York: Committee for Economic Development, 1971).

2. Committee for Economic Development, op. cit., 21, italics are in the original.

3. This argument is repeated in many Business and Society texts.

4. One simple example is that of Dresser Industries which was involved in a dispute between the U.S., the Western allies, and the Soviet Union over equipment for a natural gas pipeline which was to be sold by Dresser France to the Soviet Union. France demanded delivery; the U.S. forbade it. The case appears in William C. Frederick, Keith Davis, and James E. Post, *Business And Society: Corporate Strategy, Public Policy, Ethics*, 7th ed. (New York: McGraw-Hill, 1988), 502–512. Ron Chernow's *The House of Morgan: An American Banking Dynasty and the Rise of Modern Finance* (New York: Atlantic Monthly Press, 1990), contains many illustrations of corporate policy diverging from national policy. The House of Morgan had three centers: London, New York, and Paris. As long as three governments were in accord, conflicts were minimal. When governmental policy diverged, the House of Morgan confronted tremendous pressures. There are also numerous cases of corporations such as Morgan being expected to act in a surrogate capacity for the U.S. government.

5. Dozens of accounts of the Keynesian revolution have been written. In spite of the title, I found Thomas Hailstones's *A Guide to Suppply-Side Economics* (Richmond, Va.: Robert F. Dame, Inc., 1982), chapters 2 and 3 useful at an introductory level. For a more sophisticated treatment I rely upon Robert J. Gordon, *Macroeconomics*, 5th ed. (Glenview, Ill.: Scott, Foresman/Little, Brown Higher Education, 1990), chapter 7. I have not attempted to incorporate an account of either the "New Classical Macroeconomic" perspective or the "New Keynesian" school. Gordon's latest edition includes

chapters on these; chapter 7 includes a discussion of the former, and chapter 8 a discussion of the latter.

6. A concrete example of this is the story of John D. Rockefeller's "plan" to consolidate the oil industry in the 1870s. See Daniel Yergin, *The Prize: The Epic Quest for Oil, Money and Power* (New York: Simon and Schuster, 1991), chapter 2. Yergin notes that between 1859 and 1870, the price of kerosene fell by 50 percent, and by 1870 refining capacity was three times greater than what was needed. The only solution in Rockefeller's mind was "control."

7. This Managerial theme is evident in texts such as Frederick D. Sturdivant, *Business and Society: A Managerial Approach*, 1st ed. (Homewood, Ill.: Richard D. Irwin, 1977), chapter 2. Sturdivant emphasizes the historical background, not only to make the contrast between the robber barons and the new age of enlightened management, but also to emphasize the extent to which the markets were monopolized and the necessity for government action increased.

8. I am referring, of course, to the debate between the "capture-theorists" and those adopting the economic theory of regulatory agencies. For "capture-theory," see Marver H. Bernstein, *Regulating Business by Independent Commission* (Princeton: Princeton University Press, 1955). For a representative of the economic theory of regulation, see George J. Stigler, *The Citizen and the State: Essays on Regulation* (Chicago: University of Chicago Press, 1975); and *Can Regulatory Agencies Protect Consumers?* (Washington, D.C.: American Enterprise Institute for Public Policy Research, 1971).

9. See Leonard W. Weiss and Michael W. Klass, eds., *Regulatory Reform: What Actually Happened* (Boston: Little, Brown, and Company, 1986).

10. THE MEANING OF CORPORATE RESPONSIBILITY IN A PLURALIST FRAMEWORK

1. See, for example, Thomas R. Dye and L. Harmon Zeigler, *The Irony of Democracy: An Uncommon Introduction to American Politics* (North Scituate, Mass.: Duxbury Press, 1978), chapters 1 and 2.

2. Martin Edelman, *Democratic Theories and the Constitution* (Albany, N.Y.: State University of New York Press, 1984), chapter 1.

3. In recent constitutional interpretation, natural rights theory, functional contract theory, and individualistic contract theory remain viable competitors. Liberals (e.g., Justice Douglas) as well as conservatives have invoked natural rights theory (see Edelman, op. cit., parts 3 and 4).

4. V. O. Key, *Politics, Parties, and Pressure Groups*, 4th ed. (New York: Cromwell, 1958); *Public Opinion and American Democracy* (New York: Alfred A. Knopf, 1961); and *The Responsible Electorate* (Cambridge, Mass.: Belknap Press of Harvard University Press, 1966).

5. Robert M. McIver, *The Web of Government* (New York: Macmillan, 1947); and *The Ramparts We Guard* (New York: Macmillan, 1950).

6. Seymour M. Lipset, *The Political Man: The Social Bases of Politics* (Garden City, N.Y.: Doubleday, 1959).

7. Robert A. Dahl, *A Preface to Democratic Theory* (Chicago: University of Chicago Press, 1956); *Who Governs?* (New Haven, Conn.: Yale University Press, 1961); *Modern Political Analysis* (Englewood Cliffs, N.J.: Prentice-Hall, 1963/1984); *Political Oppositions in Western Democracies* (New Haven, Conn.: Yale University Press, 1966); *Pluralist Democracy in the United States* (Chicago: Rand McNally, 1967); and *Dilemmas of Pluralist Democracy: Autonomy v. Control* (New Haven, Conn.: Yale University Press, 1984).

8. David Truman, *The Governmental Process* (New York: Alfred A. Knopf, 1951).

9. E. E. Schattschneider, *The Semisovereign People* (New York: Holt, Rinehart, and Winston, 1960).

10. Joseph A. Schumpeter, *Capitalism, Socialism, and Democracy*, 3rd ed. (New York: Harper and Row, 1962), 269. Quoted from Edelman, op. cit., 57.

11. The quotation is from Frederick D. Sturdivant, *Business and Society: A Managerial Approach* (Homewood, Ill.: Richard D. Irwin, Inc., 1977), 4.

12. This description borrows heavily from Dye and Ziegler, op. cit., 9–10.

13. John Kenneth Galbraith, *American Capitalism: The Concept of Countervailing Power* (Boston: Houghton Mifflin, 1952).

14. Francis X. Sutton, Seymour E. Harris, Carl Kaysen, and James Tobin, *The American Business Creed* (Cambridge: Harvard University Press, 1956), 36–44.

15. Jea Morgenroth has called to my attention the fact that the claims about the tension between the attributes are much more complicated than at first appears. She points out that natural systems may not arise everywhere. Jungles are natural systems, but they are found only under special conditions. When they are found, no two are identical. The rainforests of the Amazon and Congo basin each contain unique species. Even given this interpretation, a problem may persist for the apologist of the Classical ideology who wishes to claim that the system of "natural liberty" is natural yet unique, stable, and chosen. One might interpret the claim that the special (unique) conditions of the new world allow the system to arise naturally, just as those special conditions in the Amazon and the Congo basin allow the rainforests to arise. Admittedly, this hints of a dominant theme in American culture. There remains a tension with the notion of the system being chosen. Furthermore, apologists for the Classical ideology usually believe that the system of free enterprise and democracy (minimal government) should be flourishing in

many other parts of the world, except that this is prevented by either evil leaders or ignorant citizens. It makes little sense to suggest rainforests would be flourishing in many parts of the world.

The tensions to which the authors of *The American Business Creed* point, however, may be much more deeply rooted than the Classical ideology. A dominant and pervasive theme of American culture was the idea that America was an exception to previous history. For many, the new world meant innocence, a new beginning, that things were radically different from the old world of corruption. Once one abandons the theological notions that God has instituted this new world and new nation, and that the miraculous needs no explanation, one confronts the thorny problems of how to explain these developments and how to relate them to previous history. In *The Origins of American Social Science* (New York: Cambridge University Press, 1991), Dorothy Ross argues that American social science itself struggled with these issues. As she puts it, "American social science owes its distinctive character to its involvement with the national ideology of American exceptionalism, the idea that America occupies an exceptional place in history, based on her republican government and economic opportunity" (xiv). Given this traditional commitment to the exceptionalist ideal, the "effort to carry America into Western liberal history was not complete or unequivocal."

The tensions in the Classical ideology may merely reflect the American propensity to believe that somehow the history of this culture is an exception, while at the same time incorporating that history into the rules which describe human activity (social science). The Managerialists confront the same tensions in many ways.

16. Fred Luthans, Richard M. Hodgetts, and Kenneth R. Thompson, *Social Issues in Business*, 3rd ed. (New York: Macmillan, 1980).

17. Sturdivant, op. cit., rev. ed. (Homewood, Ill.: Richard D. Irwin, Inc., 1981).

18. Edward M. Epstein, *The Corporation in American Politics* (Englewood Cliffs, N.J.: Prentice-Hall, Inc., 1969).

19. Ibid., 197, quoted from Sturdivant, op. cit., rev. ed., 61.

20. John Rawls, *A Theory of Justice* (Cambridge, Mass.: Harvard University Press, 1971).

21. I find it difficult to state this simple point logically. For the sake of parallelism, I have employed the biconditional again as a premise in the second argument, but the biconditional is really neutralized by the qualifier "at least prima facie."

22. Michael Walzer, *Spheres of Justice: A Defense of Pluralism and Equality* (New York: Basic Books, Inc., 1983).

23. Mancur Olson, *The Logic of Collective Action: Public Goods and the*

Theory of Groups (Cambridge, Mass.: Harvard University Press, 1965; 1971).

24. Robert Paul Wolff, *The Poverty of Liberalism* (Boston: Beacon Press, 1968).

25. Edelman, op. cit.

26. Edelman claims that Hook, Key, and Dahl are realists.

27. In addition to Schattschneider, Edelman gives as an example Thomas L. Thorson, *The Logic of Democracy* (New York: Holt, Rinehart, and Winston, 1962).

28. Lester Thurow, *The Zero-Sum Society: Distribution and the Possibilities for Economic Change* (New York: Basic Books, Inc., 1980). The quotation is from the Penguin, edition, 1981. Mancur Olson develops the logic of this kind of gridlock in *The Rise and Decline of Nations: Economic Growth, Stagflation, and Social Rigidities* (New Haven, Conn.: Yale University Press, 1982).

29. I have developed these points earlier in "Pluralism and Corporate Responsibility," in *Philosophy in Context*, edited by Joseph P. DeMarco and Richard M. Fox (Cleveland: Cleveland State University Press, 1980), 89–97.

11. LIBERALISM AND THE CORPORATION: THE CHALLENGE OF THE GLOBAL MARKET

1. A. G. Kefelas, "The Global Corporation: Its Role in the New World Order," *Phi Kappa Phi Journal* (Fall 1992): 26.

2. "A Survey of Multinationals: Everyone's Favorite Monster," *The Economist* (March 27, 1993): 5.

3. Ibid., 6.

4. Ibid., 6.

5. Raymond Vernon, *Sovereignty at Bay: The Multinational Spread of U.S. Enterprises* (New York: Basic Books, 1971).

6. "A Survey of Multinationals," 6.

7. Louis Galambos and Joseph Pratt, *The Corporate Commonwealth: United States Business and Public Policy in the 20th Century* (New York: Basic Books, Inc., Publishers, 1988).

8. See, Robert B. Reich, *The Work of Nations: Preparing Ourselves for 21st Century Capitalism* (New York: a Borzoi Book by Alfred Knopf, Inc., 1991), 46 ff.

9. David Vogel's "Why Businessmen Distrust Their State: The Political Consciousness of American Corporate Executives," *British Journal of Political Science* 8 (1978): 45–78, notes, with some irony, that the antigovernment rhetoric of business hardly reflects the extent to which business relies upon government. It is almost as if by joining the populist resentment against

big government, the genuine governmental/business relationships can be obscured. Vogel's argument is much different from the more recent interpretations. Vogel claims that business fails to understand the extent to which it is dependent upon government policies. More recent interpretations suggest that major corporations understood quite well the benefits of big government.

10. Reich, op. cit.

11. Reich, op. cit., 34. Daniel Yergin's *The Prize: The Epic Quest for Oil, Money and Power* (New York: Simon and Schuster, 1991), provides a vivid description of Rockefeller's constant struggle to solve the bane of overproduction in the boom-and-bust oil business. Rockefeller knew quite well that survival depended not on competition but cooperation. If he could not convince a competitor to join, Rockefeller would destroy him. Assuming that the national governments did not wish to reintroduce damaging competition, the issue became one of control. The issue became one of who could control the industries, the national government or the ogolopolies themselves.

12. Reich, op. cit., 34.

13. See the analysis in chapter 9.

14. *Fortune* (October, 1951), 98.

15. Yergin, op. cit., 14.

16. "A Survey of Multinationals," 10–11.

17. "A Survey of Multinationals," 12.

18. Ibid., 13.

19. Reich, op. cit., 140.

20. *Challenge to Leadership*, Urban Institute, quoted from Kevin Phillips, *The Politics of Rich and Poor: Wealth and the American Electorate in the Reagan Aftermath* (New York: Harper Perennial, 1991), 17. See also, Reich, op. cit., chapter 16, "American Incomes."

21. William Kymlicka, *Liberalism, Community, and Culture* (New York: Clarendon Press, 1989), provides an excellent review and analysis of communitarian criticisms of liberalism.

Bibliography

Ackerman, Robert W., and Raymond A. Bauer. *Corporate Social Responsiveness: The Modern Dilemma*. Reston, Va.: Reston Publishing Company, Inc. (Prentice-Hall), 1976.

Adelman, Morris. "The Measurement of Industrial Concentration." *Review of Economics and Statistics* 33 (1951): 269–296.

Allen, Frederick. *The Big Change*. New York: Harper, 1952.

Aristotle, *Ethics*. In *The Basic Works of Aristotle*, edited with an introduction by Richard McKeon. New York: Random House, 1941.

Arneson, Richard J. "Introduction" to "Symposium on Rawlsian Theory of Justice: Recent Developments." *Ethics* 99 (1989): 695–710.

Arrow, Kenneth J. *Social Choice and Individual Values*. New Haven, Conn.: Yale University Press, 1951.

Arrow, Kenneth J., and F. H. Hahn. *General Competitive Analysis*. San Francisco: Holden-Day, 1971.

Barker, J. H. *An Introduction to English Legal History*. 2nd ed. London: Butterworth, 1979.

Baumol, William, et al., eds. *A New Rationale for Corporate Social Policy*. New York: Committee for Economic Development, 1970.

Baur, Raymond A., and Donald H. Fee, Jr. *The Corporate Social Audit*. New York: Russell Sage Foundation, 1972.

Berle, Adolph A. *Power without Property*. New York: Harcourt, Brace, 1959.

———. *The Twentieth-Century Capitalist Revolution*. New York: Harcourt, Brace, 1951.

Berle, Adolph A., and Gardiner C. Means. *The Modern Corporation and Private Property*. New York: Macmillan, 1932.

Bernstein, Marver H. *Regulating Business by Independent Commission*. Princeton: Princeton University Press, 1955.

Blaug, Mark. *The Methodology of Economics: Or How Economists Explain*. New York: Cambridge University Press, 1980.

325

Bock, Betty, Harvey J. Goldschmid, Ira M. Millstein, and F. M. Scherer, eds. *The Impact of the Modern Corporation.* New York: Columbia University Press, 1984.

Bosanquet, Bernard. *The Philosophical Theory of the State.* London: Macmillan, 1930.

Bowie, Norman, and Robert Simon. *The Individual and the Social Order.* Englewood Cliffs, N.J.: Prentice-Hall, Inc., 1972.

Brandeis, Louis D. *Business—A Profession.* Boston: Small, Maynard, and Co., 1914.

Brandt, R. B., ed. *The Concept of Social Justice.* Englewood Cliffs, N.J.: Prentice-Hall, Inc., 1962.

Braverman, Harry. *Labor and Monopoly Capital: The Degradation of Work in the Twentieth Century.* New York: Monthly Review, 1974.

Brooks, John N. *The Great Leap: The Past Twenty-Five Years in America.* New York: Harper and Row, 1966.

Buchanan, Allen. *Ethics, Efficiency, and the Market.* Totowa, N.J.: Rowman and Allanheld, 1985.

Burnham, James. *The Managerial Revolution.* Bloomington, Ind.: University of Indiana Press, 1960.

Cavanagh, Gerald F. *American Business Values in Transition.* Englewood Cliffs, N.J.: Prentice-Hall, Inc., 1984.

———. *Ethical Dilemmas in the Modern Corporation.* Englewood Cliffs, N.J.: Prentice-Hall, Inc., 1988.

Chamberlain, Neil. *The Limits of Corporate Responsibility.* New York: Basic Books, Inc., 1973.

Chandler, Alfred D. *The Visible Hand: The Managerial Revolution in America.* Cambridge, Mass.: Belknap Press of Harvard University Press, 1977.

Chernow, Ron. *The House of Morgan: An American Banking Dynasty and the Rise of Modern Finance.* New York: Atlantic Monthly Press, 1990.

Childs, Marquis W., and Douglas Cater. *Ethics in a Business Society.* New York: Harper and Brothers, 1954.

Cohen, Joshua. "Structure, Choice, and Legitimacy: Locke's Theory of State." *Philosophy and Public Affairs* 15 (1986): 310–324.

Committee for Economic Development. *Measuring Business's Social Performance: The Corporate Social Audit.* New York: Committee for Economic Development, 1974.

———. *The Social Responsibilities of Business Corporations: A Statement on National Policy by the Research and Policy Committee for Economic Development.* New York: Committee for Economic Development, 1971.

Cramer, Clarence H. *American Enterprise: Free and Not so Free.* Boston: Little, Brown, and Co., 1972.

Dahl, Robert A. *Dilemmas of Pluralist Democracy: Autonomy v. Control.* New Haven, Conn.: Yale University Press, 1984.

———. *Modern Political Analysis.* Englewood Cliffs, N.J.: Prentice-Hall, Inc., 1963/1984.

———. *Pluralist Democracy in the United States.* Chicago: Rand McNally, 1967.

———. *A Preface to Democratic Theory.* Chicago: University of Chicago Press, 1956.

———. *Who Governs?* New Haven, Conn.: Yale University Press, 1961.

Dalton, Dan R., and Idalene F. Kesner. "On the Dynamics of Corporate Size and Illegal Activity: An Empirical Assessment." *Journal of Business Ethics* 7 (1988): 861–870.

Danley, John R. "Contracts, Conquests, and Conquerors." *Southwestern Journal of Philosophy* 10 (1979): 171–177.

———. "Corporate Moral Agency: The Case for Anthropological Bigotry." In *Business Ethics: Readings and Cases in Corporate Morality*, edited by W. Michael Hoffman and Jennifer Mills Moore, 172–179. New York: McGraw-Hill, 1984.

———. "Ethics and the Organizational Person: Revisiting De George." *Journal of Business Ethics* 10 (1991): 17–32.

———. "An Examination of the Fundamental Assumption of Hypothetical Process Arguments." *Philosophical Studies* 34 (1978): 187–195.

———. "Liberalism, Aboriginal Rights, and Cultural Minorities." *Philosophy and Public Affairs* 20 (1991): 168–185.

———. "'Ought' Implies 'Can': The Moral Relevance of a Theory of the Firm." *Journal of Business Ethics* 7 (1988): 23–28.

———. "Pluralism and Corporate Responsibility." In *Philosophy in Context*, edited by Joseph P. DeMarco and Richard M. Fox, 89–97. Cleveland: Cleveland State University Press, 1980.

———. "Polestar Refined: Business Ethics and Political Economy." *Journal of Business Ethics* 10 (1991): 69–87.

Davidson, Kenneth M. *Megamergers: Corporate America's Billion Dollar Takeovers.* Cambridge, Mass.: Ballinger Publishing Co., 1985.

Davis, Keith, and William C. Frederick. *Business and Society: Management, Public Policy, Ethics.* 5th ed. New York: McGraw-Hill, 1984.

De George, Richard T. *Business Ethics.* New York: Macmillan, 1982.

———. "The Status of Business Ethics: Past and Future." *Journal of Business Ethics* 6 (1987): 201–212.

De George, Richard T., and Joseph A. Pichler, eds. *Ethics, Free Enterprise, and Public Policy.* New York: Oxford University Press, 1978.

Dolan, E. G., ed. *The Foundation of Modern Austrian Economics.* Kansas City: Sheed and Ward, 1976.

Donaldson, Thomas. *Corporations and Morality*. Englewood Cliffs, N.J.: Prentice-Hall, Inc., 1982.

———. "Fact, Fiction, and the Social Contract: A Reply to Kultgen." *Business and Professional Ethics Journal* 5, no. 1 (n.d.): 40–46.

Donaldson, Thomas, and Patricia Wernhane, eds. *Ethical Issues in Business: A Philosophical Approach*. 2nd ed. Englewood Cliffs, N.J.: Prentice-Hall, Inc., 1983.

Dunn, John. *Locke*. New York: Oxford University Press, 1984.

———. *The Political Thought of John Locke: An Historical Account of the Argument of the "Two Treatises of Government."* Cambridge: Cambridge University Press, 1982.

Dworkin, Gerald. "Paternalism." In *Morality and the Law*, edited by Richard A. Wasserstrom, 107–126. Belmont, Cal.: Wordsworth Publishing Co., 1971.

Dworkin, Ronald. "The Original Position." In *Reading Rawls: Critical Studies of "A Theory of Justice,"* edited by Norman Daniels, 16–52. New York: Basic Books, Inc., n.d.

Dye, Thomas R., and L. Harmon Zeigler. *The Irony of Democracy: An Uncommon Introduction to American Politics*. North Scituate, Mass.: Duxbury Press, 1978.

Edelman, Martin. *Democratic Theories and the Constitution*. Albany, N.Y.: State University of New York Press, 1984.

Eells, Richard, S. *The Meaning of Modern Business: An Introduction to the Philosophy of Large Corporate Enterprise*. New York: Columbia University Press, 1960.

Eells, Richard, and Clarence Walton. *Conceptual Foundations of Business: An Outline of the Major Ideas Sustaining Business Enterprise in the Western World*. Homewood, Ill.: Richard D. Irwin, Inc., 1961.

Engel, David L. "An Approach to Corporate Responsibility." *Stanford Law Review* 32 (1979): 1–98.

Epstein, Edward M. *The Corporation in American Politics*. Englewood Cliffs, N.J.: Prentice-Hall, Inc., 1969.

Fama, Eugene. "Agency Problems and Residual Claims." *Journal of Law and Economics* 22 (June 1983): 327–350.

———. "Agency Problems and the Theory of the Firm." *Journal of Political Economy* 88 (1980): 288–307.

———. "Separation of Ownership and Control." *Journal of Law and Economics* 22 (June 1983): 301–326.

Farmer, Richard N., and W. Dickerson Jogue. *Corporate Social Responsibility*. Chicago: Science Research Associates, Inc., 1973.

Feinberg, Joel. *Harm to Others: The Moral Limits of the Criminal Law*. New York: Oxford University Press, 1984.

————. *Social Philosophy*. Englewood Cliffs, N.J.: Prentice-Hall, Inc., 1973.

Flathman, Richard E. *Toward a Liberalism*. Ithaca: Cornell University Press, 1989.

Fortune magazine, with the collaboration of Russell W. Davenport. *The Permanent Revolution*. New York: Fortune, 1951.

Frederick, William C., Keith Davis, and James E. Post. *Business and Society: Corporate Strategy, Public Policy, Ethics*. 6th ed. New York: McGraw-Hill, 1988.

Frederick, William C., James E. Post, and Keith Davis. *Business and Society: Corporate Strategy, Public Policy, Ethics*. 7th ed. New York: McGraw-Hill, 1990.

French, Peter. "Corporate Moral Agency." In *Business Ethics: Readings and Cases in Corporate Morality*, edited by W. Michael Hoffman and Jennifer Mills Moore, 163–171. New York: McGraw-Hill, 1981.

Friedman, Milton. *Capitalism and Freedom*. With a new preface by the author. Chicago: University of Chicago Press, 1962; 1982.

————. "The Social Responsibility of Business Is to Increase Profit." *New York Times Magazine* (September 13, 1970): 32–33, 122–126.

Galambos, Louis, and Joseph Pratt. *The Corporate Commonwealth: United States Business and Public Policy in the 20th Century*. New York: Basic Books, Inc., 1988.

Galbraith, John Kenneth. *American Capitalism: The Concept of Countervailing Power*. Boston: Houghton Mifflin, 1952.

Galston, William A. *Liberal Purposes: Goods, Virtues, and Diversity in the Liberal State*. New York: Cambridge University Press, 1991.

————. "Moral Personality and Liberal Theory: John Rawls's 'Dewey Lectures.'" *Political Theory* 10 (1982): 492–519.

Gauther, David. *Morals by Agreement*. New York: Clarendon Press, Oxford University Press, 1986.

Gewirth, Alan. "Political Justice." In *The Concept of Social Justice*, edited by R. B Brandt, 119–169. Englewood Cliffs, N.J.: Prentice-Hall, Inc., 1962.

Giercke, Otto. *Natural Law and the Theory of Society*. Translated with an introduction by Ernest Barker. Cambridge: Cambridge University Press, 1934.

Goodman, Charles S., and C. Merle Crawford. "Young Executives: A Source of New Ethics?" *Personnel Journal* (March 1974): 180–181.

Goodpaster, Kenneth E. "Business Ethics, Ideology, and the Naturalistic Fallacy." *Journal of Business Ethics* 4 (1985): 227–232.

Gordon, Lawrence A., ed. *Accounting and Corporate Social Responsibility*. Lawrence, Kan.: The University of Kansas Press, 1978.

Gordon, Robert J. *Macroeconomics*, 5th ed. Glenview, Ill.: Scott, Foresman/Little, Brown Higher Education, 1990.

Gough, J. S. *The Social Contract: A Critical Study of Its Development*. 2nd ed. Oxford: Clarendon Press, Oxford University Press, 1957.

Gray, John. *Liberalism: Concepts in Social Thought*. Minneapolis: University of Minnesota Press, 1986.

Green, T. H. *Essays Moral, Political, and Literary*. London: Longmans, Green, and Co., 1875.

————. *Lectures on the Principles of Political Obligation*. London, 1963.

Griffin, James. *Well-Being: Its Meaning, Measurement and Moral Importance*. New York: Clarenden Press, Oxford University Press, 1986.

Hailstones, Thomas. *A Guide to Supply-Side Economics*. Richmond, Va.: Robert F. Dame, Inc., 1982.

Hart, H. L. A. "Are There Any Natural Rights?" *Philosophical Review* 64 (1955): 175–191.

————. *Law, Liberty and Morality*. Stanford, Cal.: Stanford University Press, 1983.

Hartz, Louis. *The Liberal Tradition in America*. New York: Harcourt Brace Jovanovich, 1955.

Hayek, Friedrich A. von. *The Constitution of Liberty*. Chicago: University of Chicago Press, 1960.

————. *The Road to Serfdom*. Chicago: University of Chicago Press, 1944.

Heald, Morrell. *The Social Responsibilities of Business: Company and Community, 1900–1960*. Cleveland: The Press of Case Western Reserve University, 1970.

Herman, Edward S. *Corporate Control, Corporate Power*. New York: Cambridge University Press, 1981.

Hobhouse, L. T. *Liberalism*. Introduction by Alan P. Grimes. New York: Oxford University Press, 1964; reprinted 1979.

Hodson, John D. *The Ethics of Legal Coercion*. Boston: D. Reidel, 1983.

Hoffman, W. Michael, and Jennifer Mills Moore, eds. *Business Ethics: Readings and Cases in Corporate Morality*. New York: McGraw-Hill, 1984.

Hofstadter, Richard. *Social Darwinism in American Thought, 1860–1915*. Philadelphia: Beacon Press, 1944.

Jackall, Robert. *Moral Mazes: The World of Corporate Managers*. New York: Oxford University Press, 1988.

Jensen, Michael C., and Richard Ruback. "The Market for Corporate Control: The Scientific Evidence." *Journal of Financial Economics* 11 (1983): 3–50.

Kaldor, Nicholas. "Welfare Propositions in Economics and Interpersonal Comparison of Utility." *Economic Journal* 49: 549–552.

Key, V. O. *Politics, Parties, and Pressure Groups*. 4th ed. New York: Cromwell, 1958.

————. *Public Opinion and American Democracy.* New York: Alfred A. Knopf, 1961.

————. *The Responsible Electorate.* Cambridge, Mass.: Belknap Press of Harvard University Press, 1966.

Keynes, John M. "The Doctrine of Laissez-Faire." *New Republic* (1926): 5–73.

————. *The General Theory of Employment, Interest, and Money.* New York: Harcourt Brace Jovanovich, 1935; 1964.

Kristol, Irving. "A Capitalist Conception of Justice." In *Ethics, Free Enterprise, and Public Policy: Original Essays on Moral Issues in Business,* edited by Richard T. De George and Joseph A. Pichler, 57–69. New York: Oxford University Press, 1978.

————. *Two Cheers for Capitalism.* New York: Basic Books, Inc., 1978.

Kuhn, James W., and Ivar Berg. *Values in a Business Society.* New York: Harcourt, Brace, and World, 1968.

Kultgen, John. "Donaldson's Social Contract for Business." *Business and Professional Ethics Journal* 5, no. 1 (n.d.): 28–39.

Kyke, C. *Philosophy of Economics.* Englewood Cliffs, N.J.: Prentice-Hall, Inc., 1981.

Kymlicka, William. *Liberalism, Community, and Culture.* New York: Oxford University Press, 1989.

Lewis, Michael. *Liar's Poker.* New York: Penguin Books, 1989.

Lilienthal, David. *Big Business: A New Era.* New York: Harper, 1953.

Lipset, Seymour M. *The Political Man: The Social Bases of Politics.* Garden City, N.Y.: Doubleday, 1959.

Littlechild, Stephen C. *The Fallacy of the Mixed Economy: An "Austrian" Critique of Economic Thinking and Policy.* London: Institute of Economic Affairs, 1978.

Locke, John. *Two Treatises of Government.* (1689). Edited by Peter Laslett. New York: Cambridge University Press, 1988.

Lodge, George C. "The Connection between Ethics and Ideology." *Journal of Business Ethics* 1 (1981): 85–98.

————. "The Ethical Implications of Ideology." In *Business Ethics: Readings and Cases in Corporate Morality,* edited by W. Michael Hoffman and Jennifer Mills Moore, 115–125. New York: McGraw-Hill, 1984.

————. *The New American Ideology.* New York: Alfred A. Knopf, 1979.

Lowrance, William W. *Of Acceptable Risk: Science and the Determination of Safety.* Los Altos, Cal.: William Kaufman, Inc., 1976.

Luthans, Fred, Richard M. Hodgetts, and Kenneth R. Thompson. *Social Issues in Business.* 3rd ed. New York: Macmillan, 1980.

Lyons, David. *The Forms and Limits of Utilitarianism.* New York: Clarendon Press, Oxford University Press, 1965.

Maccoby, Michael. *The Gamesman.* New York: Simon and Schuster, 1976.

McGregor, Douglas. *The Human Side of Enterprise*. New York: McGraw-Hill, 1960.

McGuire, Jean B., Alison Sundgren, and Thomas Schneeweis. "Corporate Social Responsibility and Firm Financial Performance." *Academy of Management Journal* 31, no. 4 (1988): 854–872.

McGuire, Joseph W. *Business and Society*. New York: McGraw-Hill, 1963.

McIver, Robert M. *The Ramparts We Guard*. New York: Macmillan, 1950.

———. *The Web of Government*. New York: Macmillan, 1947.

Machan, Tibor R., and Douglas J. Den Uyl. "Recent Work in Business Ethics: A Survey and Critique." *American Philosophical Quarterly* 24 (1987): 107–124.

MacKay, Alfred F. *Arrow's Theorem: The Paradox of Social Choice*. New Haven, Conn.: Yale University Press, 1980.

McPherson, C. B. *The Political Theory of Possessive Individualism*. Oxford: Oxford University Press, 1962.

Manne, Henry. "Mergers and the Market for Corporate Control." *Journal of Political Economy* 73 (April 1965): 110–120.

Marris, Robin. *The Economic Theory of "Managerial" Capitalism*. Cambridge, Mass.: The Free Press of Glencoe, 1964.

———. "A Model of the 'Managerial' Enterprise." *Quarterly Journal of Economics* 77 (May 1963): 185–209.

Martin, Michael W., and Ronald Schinzinger. *Ethics in Engineering*. New York: McGraw-Hill, 1983.

Maslow, Abraham. *Eupsychian Management: A Journal*. Homewood, Ill.: Richard D. Irwin, Inc., and the Dorsey Press, 1965.

———. *Motivation and Personality*. New York: Harper and Row, 1954.

Mason, Edward S. "The Apologetics of 'Managerialism.'" *Journal of Business* 31 (1958): 1–11.

Masters, Roger D. "The Lockean Tradition in American Foreign Policy." *Journal of International Affairs* 21 (1967): 253–277.

Means, Gardiner C. *The Corporate Revolution in America: Economic Reality vs. Economic Theory*. New York: Crowell-Collier Press, 1962.

Mill, John Stuart. *Principles of Political Economy with Some of Their Applications to Social Philosophy*. Books 4 and 5 (1848). Edited with an introduction by Donald Winch. London: Penguin Group, 1988.

———. *Three Essays* ["On Liberty" (1859), "Representative Government" (1861), and "The Subjection of Women" (1869)]. Introduction by Richard Wollheim. New York: Oxford University Press, 1975.

Millstein, Ira M., and Salem M. Katsh. *The Limits of Corporate Power: Existing Constraints on the Exercise of Corporate Discretion*. New York: Macmillan, 1981.

Milson, S. F. C. *Historical Foundations of the Common Law.* 2nd ed. Toronto: Butterworth, 1981.

Moore, G. E. *Principia Ethica.* Cambridge: Cambridge University Press, 1903.

Nader, Ralph, Mark Green, and Joel Seligman. *Taming the Giant Corporation.* New York: W. W. Norton, 1976.

Nagel, Thomas. "Libertarianism without Foundations." In *Reading Nozick: Essays on "Anarchy, State, and Utopia,"* edited by Jeffrey Paul. Totowa, N.J.: Rowman and Littlefield, 1981.

Nozick, Robert. *Anarchy, State, and Utopia.* New York: Basic Books, 1974.

Okun, Robert M. *Equality and Efficiency: The Big Tradeoff.* Washington, D.C.: The Brookings Institution, 1975.

Olson, Mancur. *The Logic of Collective Action: Public Goods and the Theory of Groups.* Cambridge, Mass.: Harvard University Press, 1965; 1971.

———. *The Rise and Decline of Nations: Economic Growth, Stagflation, and Social Rigidities.* New Haven, Conn.: Yale University Press, 1982.

Ouchi, William. *Theory Z: How American Business Can Meet the Japanese Challenge.* Reading, Mass.: Addison-Wesley, 1981.

Pack, Spencer J. *Capitalism as a Moral System: Adam Smith's Critique of the Free Market Economy.* Aldershot: Elgar, 1992.

Pareto, Vilfred. *Cours d'economie politique.* Lausanne, 1897.

Paul, Jeffrey, ed. *Reading Nozick: Essays on "Anarchy, State, and Utopia."* Totowa, N.J.: Rowman and Littlefield, 1981.

Phillips, Kevin. *The Politics of Rich and Poor: Wealth and the American Electorate in the Reagan Aftermath.* New York: Harper Perennial, 1991.

Pollack, F., and F. W. Maitland. *The History of English Law.* 2 vols. Cambridge: Cambridge University Press, 1968.

Preston, Lee. E. "Corporation and Society: The Search for a Paradigm." *Journal of Economic Literature* 13 (1975): 434–453.

Progressive Alliance. *Capital and Communities: The Causes and Consequences of Private Divestment.* Washington, D.C.: Progressive Alliance, 1980.

Rawls, John. "Justice as Fairness: Political Not Metaphysical." *Philosophy and Public Affairs* 14, no. 3 (1985): 223–251.

———. "Kantian Constructivism in Moral Theory: The Dewey Lectures 1980." *Journal of Philosophy* 77 (1980): 515–572.

———. "Social Utility and Primary Goods." In *Utilitarianism and Beyond,* edited by Amartya Sen and Bernard A. O. Williams, 159–185. Cambridge: Cambridge University Press, 1982.

———. *A Theory of Justice.* Cambridge, Mass.: Harvard University Press, 1971.

Raz, Joseph. *The Morality of Freedom.* New York: Oxford University Press, 1986.

Reek, Andrew J. "Natural Law in American Revolutionary Thought." *Review of Metaphysics* 30 (1977): 686–714.

Reich, Robert B. *The Work of Nations: Preparing Ourselves for 21st-Century Capitalism.* New York: Alfred A. Knopf, 1991.

Rescher, Nicholas. *Welfare: The Social Issue in Philosophical Perspective.* Pittsburgh: University of Pittsburgh Press, 1972.

Ricardo, David. *The Principles of Political Economy and Taxation.* New York: Dutton, Everyman's Library, 1965.

Robbins, Lionel. "Interpersonal Comparability and Social Choice Theory." *Economic Journal* 48 (1938): 635–641.

Rogin, Michael. "Nature as Politics and Nature as Romance in America." *Political Theory* 5 (1977): 5–30.

Roper Center for Public Opinion Research. *The Public Perspective: A Roper Center Review of Public Opinion and Polling* 2 (September/October 1991). Storrs, Conn.: Roper Center, 1991.

Sartre, Jean-Paul. "The Wall." In *Introduction to Literature: Stories,* edited by Lynn Altenbernd and Leslie L. Lewis, 400–412. New York: Macmillan, 1963.

Savage, Grant T., Timothy W. Nix, Carlton J. Whitehead, and John D. Blair. "Strategies for Assessing and Managing Organizational Stakeholders." *Academy of Management Executive* 5, no. 2 (1991): 61–75.

Schaatschneider, E. E. *The Semisovereign People.* New York: Holt, Rinehart, and Winston, 1960.

Schumpeter, Joseph A. *Capitalism, Socialism and Democracy.* 3rd ed. New York: Harper and Row, 1962.

Seabright, Paul. "Social Choice and Social Theories." *Philosophy and Public Affairs* 18 (1989): 365–387.

Sen, Amartya. *On Ethics and Economics.* New York: Basil Blackwell, Inc., 1987.

Sen, Amartya, and Bernard A. O. Williams, eds. *Utilitarianism and Beyond.* Cambridge: Cambridge University Press, 1982.

Sethi, S. Prakash. "Corporate Social Audit: An Emerging Trend in Measuring Corporate Social Performance." In *The Corporate Dilemma,* edited by Dow Votaw and S. Prakash Sethi. Englewood Cliffs, N.J.: Prentice-Hall, Inc., 1973.

———. ed. *Up Against the Corporate Wall.* Englewood Cliffs, N.J.: Prentice-Hall, Inc., 1971.

Simpson, A. W. *A History of the Common Law of Contract.* Oxford: Clarendon Press, 1975.

Smith, Adam. *An Inquiry into the Nature and Causes of the Wealth of Nations.* Edited by Edwin Cannan with a new preface by George J. Stigler. Chicago: University of Chicago Press, 1976.

———. *Lectures on Justice, Police, Revenue, and Arms*. Delivered at the University of Glasgow and reported by a student in 1763. Edited by Edwin Cannon. New York: Kelley and Millman, Inc., 1956.

Sohn, Howard F. "Prevailing Rationales in the Corporate Social Responsibility Debate." *Journal of Business Ethics* 1 (1982): 139–144.

Spencer, Herbert. *Social Statistics: Or, the Conditions Essential to Human Happiness Specified, and the First of Them Developed*. New York: D. Appleton, 1865.

Stead, Bette A., and Janice J. Miller. "Can Social Awareness Be Increased through Business School Curricula?" *Journal of Business Ethics* 7 (1988): 553–560.

Stigler, George J. *Can Regulatory Agencies Protect Consumers?* Washington, D.C.: American Enterprise Institute for Public Policy Research, 1971.

———. *The Citizen and the State: Essays on Regulation*. Chicago: University of Chicago Press, 1975.

Sturdivant, Frederick D. *Business and Society: A Managerial Approach*. Homewood, Ill.: Richard D. Irwin, Inc., 1977.

———. *Business and Society: A Managerial Approach*. Rev. ed. Homewood, Ill.: Richard D. Irwin, Inc., 1981.

Stone, Christopher D. *Where the Law Ends: The Social Control of Corporate Behavior*. New York: Harper Colophon Books, 1975.

Sutton, Francis X., Seymour E. Harris, Carl Kaysen, and James Tobin. *The American Business Creed*. Cambridge. Mass.: Harvard University Press, 1956; 1962.

Taylor, Frederick Winslow. *The Principles of Scientific Management*. New York: Harper and Row Brothers, 1929.

Thompson, Arthur A., Jr. *Economics of the Firm: Theory and Practice*. 4th ed. Englewood Cliffs, N.J.: Prentice-Hall, Inc., 1985.

Thurow, Lester. *The Zero-Sum Society: Distribution and the Possibilities for Economic Change*. New York: Basic Books, Inc., 1980.

Truman, David. *The Governmental Process*. New York: Alfred A. Knopf, 1951.

Tully, James. *A Discourse on Property: John Locke and His Adversaries*. Cambridge: Cambridge University Press, 1980.

Vogel, David. "Why Businessmen Distrust Their State: The Political Consciousness of American Corporate Executives." *British Journal of Political Science* 8 (1978): 45–78.

Walzer, Michael. *Spheres of Justice: A Defense of Pluralism and Equality*. New York: Basic Books, Inc., 1983.

Warnock, Mary. *Ethics since 1900*. 3rd ed. New York: Oxford University Press, 1978.

Weiss, Leonard W., and Michael W. Klass. *Regulatory Reform: What Actually Happened*. Boston: Little, Brown, and Co., 1986.

Whyte, William H. *Is Anybody Listening?* New York: Simon and Schuster, Inc., 1952.

Williams, Bernard A. O. *Morality: An Introduction to Ethics.* Hammondsworth: Penguin Books, 1973.

Wolff, Robert Paul. *The Poverty of Liberalism.* Boston: Beacon Press, 1968.

———. *Understanding Rawls: A Reconstruction and Critique of "A Theory of Justice."* Princeton: Princeton University Press, 1977.

Wynd, William R., and John Mager. "The Business and Society Course: Does It Change Student Attitudes?" *Journal of Business Ethics* 8 (1989): 487–491.

Yardley, D. C. M. *Elements of English Law.* 7th ed. New York: Oxford University Press, 1966.

Yergin, Daniel. *The Prize: The Epic Quest for Oil, Money, and Power.* New York: Simon and Schuster, 1991.

Index

Actual contract (theory), actual
process argument: *See* Contract
theory
Actual desire, actual preference
accounts of utility, 115–117, 126,
127 ff., 137, 269
Actual rule utilitarianism: *See*
Conventional rule utilitarianism
Act utilitarian(ism), 86–87,
100–101
Agency argument, 76–77
Agency theorists, 204 n. 35
American Business Creed, 13, 14, 27,
142–146, 153, 244
Anarchy(ism, ists), 33, 42, 49, 54,
56, 61, 82, 88
Anti-rationalist argument, 101–104
Anti-utile, 101, 104
Aristotle, 16, 18, 236
Arrow, Kenneth, *Social Choice and
Individual Values*, 117–120
Audit, social, 22, 171–175
Autonomy, autonomous, 33, 33 n.
15, 34, 190

Bentham, Jeremy, 12, 30, 30 n. 9,
84, 89, 102, 114

Berle, Adolf, *The Modern Corporation
and Private Property*, 147, 166–
170, 179, 180, 184, 188, 214,
270
Buchanan, Allan, *Ethics, Efficiency,
and the Market*, 121–126
Business and society, field of, 3, 5,
10–16, 21, 22, 164, 171–175, 185
Business ethics, 3, 5, 10, 11, 18–20,
23, 177. *See also* Ethics

Capitalism: American, 147, 284; big
change in, 154 ff.; democratic,
23; foundations of, 12; Friedman
and, 75–105; industrial and
financial, 8, 150; *laissez-faire*, 24,
25, 30 n. 9, 31 ff., 39, 84, 91,
103, 110, 242, 269; managerial,
142; and market economy, 39,
96, 151, 236; objections to,
111–113; pluralistic constraints
on, 279; problems of, 147–148;
utilitarian defense of, 75–105
Capture-theorists, 232 n. 8, 263
Cardinal measures of utility,
114–116
Cavanagh, Gerald, 15, 16, 17,
159–161, 163

Classical business ideology, 3–6, 9,
    12–14, 19–20, 21, 23–26, 27–28,
    41, 51, 75–105, 125. *See also*
    Ideology
Classical liberal(ism), 6, 9, 14,
    19, 24, 25, 26, 127, 135, 138,
    145; contrast with revisionist
    liberalism, 147–154, 239, 254,
    267–269
Coercion, 29, 33, 38, 52, 123–125,
    136, 148, 268
Coherence theory of morality,
    65–66
Communism, 27, 28, 124, 125, 226,
    245
Communitarianism, 15, 162, 285
Competition, 2, 6, 13, 15, 80,
    85, 92, 96, 104–106, 116, 122,
    142, 145, 150, 151, 161, 166,
    216, 218, 226, 228, 231, 233,
    240–248, 252, 261–265, 271,
    273, 278, 280–286
Conservative, 27, 35, 41, 80,
    102–104, 245, 257
Consequentialist theories of
    obligation, 108, 128
Constraints: on corporate manager,
    see Managerial discretion, esp.
    187–188, 198 ff.; on corporate
    power, 243, 247; formal and
    substantive, on theory of value,
    109, 114, 115, 128–131, 135;
    on forming new groups, 258;
    institutional, on electoral process,
    239
Constructivist fallacy, 102
Contract, contract theory, social
    contract theory, 24, 25, 40;
    actual contract theories, 54–59;
    background and definition,
    51–54; contractarianism, 25, 255;
    contractual relations, 190, 195;

dispositional theories, 59–61;
    hypothetical (nondispositional)
    theories, 61–69; as protected
    interests, 35, 39, 45, 46, 49, 81,
    91, 135–137, 239; Rawls and
    Nozick as hypothetical contract
    theorists, 65–69; social compact
    and the corporation, 69–73,
    211–213; tacit contract theories,
    56–59
Conventional (actual) rule
    utilitarian(ism), 98–104
Corporate, corporation, corporate
    commonwealth, 277–280, 282;
    income tax on, 83, 94, 96; in
    Lockean framework, 45–49;
    as moral persons, 196–198;
    as persons, 46, 49. *See also*
    Managerial discretion; Pluralism
Corporate (social) responsibility,
    2–13, 21–26, 41–43, 49, 50, 52,
    69–73; big change and thesis of,
    154–163; classical ideas and, 75–
    105; corporate power argument,
    194–195; Council on Economic
    Development, statement on,
    210–222; descriptive thesis of,
    169–170, 179–186; enlightened
    self-interest argument for,
    216–220; irrelevance of, in
    Keynesian framework, 222–223,
    228–234; limits of, 219–222; and
    managerial discretion, 198–208;
    managerial ideas and, 141–154;
    managerial professionalism and
    thesis of, 170–177; meaning of,
    in context of global market,
    270–274, 283; meaning of, in
    pluralistic framework, 235–236,
    247, 248, 256–266; moral
    personhood argument and,
    196–197; multiple constituency

(stakeholder argument), 189–194; prescriptive thesis of, 186–198; public character of corporations (social effects argument), 194

Council on Economic Development, *Statement on Social Responsibilities of Business Corporations*, 210–222

Countervailing power, 147, 243–247, 255, 258–261, 279

Davis, Keith, 10 n. 13, 174–176, 219 n. 4

DeGeorge, Richard, 11, 17

Democracy, 44, 81, 90, 118–119, 150, 202, 203, 209, 212, 213, 222, 228, 236–242, 249, 252, 259, 260

Deontological (nonconsequentialist) theories of obligation, 108

Descriptive (v. normative): analysis and language, 4–5, 7–8; classical liberalism not, 31, 78–80; confusion of, with normative, 13–15, 159–163; is/ought confusion and, 21–24; premises, 7–8; role of descriptive claims in moral argument, 92–93, 105, 107–109, 198–204; theories of political economy, 8. *See also* Corporate (social) responsibility, descriptive thesis of; Pluralism

Donaldson, Thomas, 70–73, 197 n. 28

Economic premise, 91–93, 97, 120–122, 225

Eels, Richard, *The Meaning of Modern Business*, 165, 189 n. 20, 210

Efficiency, 25, 31, 79, 85, 93–96, 103, 111–125, 186, 200, 204, 211, 216, 221, 225, 228, 245

Egalitarian(ism), 28, 29, 44

Egoism, 86; ethical, 67, 68, 108; psychological and ethical, 198–201

Enlightened self-interest argument for social responsibility, 211, 216–220, 262, 270, 279

Epicurus (Epicureanism), 28, 187, 198

Equilibrium, economic, 121, 122, 126, 223–226, 268; in pluralism, 243, 261; reflective, 65–67, 256

Ethical conventionalism, 102, 248–249, 253

Ethics, 11–24; instructional courses in, and influence on values, 185–186; and managerial professionalism, 170–177; new age of, in managerial behavior, 154–163; and profit, 144–146; and profit maximization, goals of the firm, 191–192; Adam Smith's understanding of the importance of, in economic theory, 131–135; theory, and the gap from the real world, 18–20; traditions of, and defense of liberalism, 40, 41–43, 78–80. *See also* Contract theory; Deontological/nonconsequentialist theories; Egoism; Ethical conventionalism; Normative; Teleological/consequentialist theories; Theories of value; Utilitarianism

Eschatological, 99

Evaluate (final step in philosophical analysis), 4; philosophical analysis as normative or ethical analysis, 7–8

Evaluative/normative: confusion of evaluative and descriptive,

160–163; contrast with
prescriptive judgments and
function of language, 6–8; role in
utilitarian defense, 107. *See also*
Normative; Prescriptive
Evolutionary argument for
conventional rule utilitarianism,
99, 102–104
Exchange-value, 133–134
Existence premise, 91–93, 104–105,
107, 226, 259
Externalities, 81–83, 122, 151–153,
181, 218, 219, 230, 232–234,
265, 269, 286
Extrinsic (instrumental) good, 32;
freedom as extrinsically good, 84

Fama, Eugene, 166, 204 n. 35, 206
n. 36
Fascism, 27, 28, 152, 226, 227
Feinberg, Joel, 33 n. 15, 35 n. 18, 44
n. 10; discussion of well-being,
happiness in the liberal tradition,
135–137
First fundamental theorem of welfare
economics, 121, 126
Formal constraints: *See* Constraints
Frederick, William C., *Business
and Society: Corporate Strategy,
Public Policy, Ethics,* 10 n. 13, 41,
174–176, 219 n. 4
Freedom, 9; central in liberal theory,
29; central value in liberal
tradition, 127; in classical and
revisionist traditions, 148–150;
corporate freedom of speech, 196;
extrinsic value of, 135; Mill's
argument for, 135; in natural
rights and contract theory, 44–52;
negative and positive accounts
of, 149; in pluralist context,
241–243; presumptive case for,

32; reasons for interference in
(liberty-limiting principles),
32–39, 81–91; and resources, 139;
in utilitarian theory, 79–89, 113,
121, 123; and welfare interests,
136–137
Free-riding, 56, 287
French, Peter, 196–198
Friedman, Milton, 9, 25, 75–105,
117, 123–131, 191–194, 203, 204
Fundamental question: identified,
2; ideologies as a response to,
12–20, 22, 24, 141, 267, 270,
271, 282, 283, 288; nature of,
5–11

Galbraith, John Kenneth, 147, 166,
243
Global markets, global competition,
global economy, 2, 5, 26, 218,
271–288
Good (value, utility): actual and
revealed preference theory,
115–117; cardinal measures of,
114–115; in consequentialist
theories and utilitarianism,
86–93, 108, 109; constraints on
choice of theory and value, 109,
114–117, 127–131; Friedman's
theory of, 80; the good life and
its role in liberal theory, 29, 30,
32; hedonism, 114–115; intrinsic,
32; key concept in evaluative
language, 7; ordinal measures
of, 115 ff.; pluralistic defense of
value changes, 237, 248–249,
256 ff.; role in definition of harm,
35–36; Adam Smith's theory of
value, 131–135; and well-being,
135–139
Goodpastor, Kenneth, 17, 18, 23
Gray, John, *Liberalism: Concepts of*

Social Thought, 28–30, 40, 47, 99, 139, 149–150

Griffen, James, *Well-Being: Its Meaning, Measurement, and Moral Importance*, 116, 128

Happiness, 32, 34, 51, 85–91, 114, 127, 135. *See also* Good; Well-being

Harm: in classical liberalism, 36, 89–91, 135, 138–139, 148, 151, 161, 162, 197, 216, 239; definition of, 35–38; Feinberg and, 135; Friedman's acceptance of harm principle, 82–83; interpreting Lockean bounds of nature, 44–46; in Lockean framework, 47–51, 55, 68; and nonbenefit, 36–38

Harm principle, 36–38

Hart, H. L. A., 34 n. 16, 48 n. 12

Hartz, Louis, *The Liberal Tradition in America*, 28 n. 2, 41 n. 2

Hayek, Frederick von, 84, 100–103

Heald, Morrell, *The Social Responsibilities of Business: Company and Community, 1900–1960*, 2 n. 2, 165, 166, 185, 189 n. 19

Hedonic calculus, 115. *See also* Cardinal measures of utility; Ordinal measures of utility

Hedonism, 114, 115, 198, 199, 201

Hegel, 99, 149

Herman, Edward S., *Corporate Power, Corporate Control*, 1, 179–182, 207

Hodgetts, Richard M., *Social Issues in Business*, 10 n. 13, 175 n. 65, 246

Hume, David, 22, 23, 58

Hypothetical contract (arguments): *See* Contract; Procedural justice

Ideal preferences, 116. *See* Ordinal measures of utility

Ideal rule utilitarian(ism), 104–105

Ideal v. actual markets/state: Friedman's ideal theory, 93–98; ideal markets, 121–123, 126, 268, 284; ideal state, 82, 83, 94, 128–129

Ideology: in context of global market, 267, 271, 282, 283; criticism of the field of business ethics as vehicle for political ideology, 19, 20; definition and normative function of, 15–17; identifying classical and managerial business ideologies and their role in clarifying and reconstructing arguments, 3–6, 11–20, 24, 26; ignored in field of business ethics, 17–20; relationship to theories of political economy, 12, 19, 20, 24–28; treatment of, in field of business and society, 11–24. *See also* Classical business ideology; Macro-managerialism; Managerial business ideology; Managerial revolution; Managerial discretion; Micro-managerialism; Thesis of social responsibility

Impossibility theorem, 117–120

Instrumental good: *See* Extrinsic good; Good

Interest(s), 29, 30, 35, 44, 45, 47, 77, 82, 135; and actual preferences, 128; competition of interest groups, 241, 242, 243, 257–261; of constituency groups, 187, 189, 190, 215, 216, 217; corporate, 217–219, 257, 262, 264, 277, 278; divergence of

corporate and national, 277, 279,
283–286; and objects of desire,
137; ulterior, 135–137; welfare,
135–137. See also Enlightened
self-interest argument; Harm;
Self-interest
Interpersonal comparisons of utility,
120–121
Intrinsic good, 114. See also Good;
Happiness; Utility; Well-being
Is/Ought distinction (naturalistic
fallacy), 21–24, 159–163, 188,
248, 249

Jackall, Robert, Moral Mazes: The
World of Corporate Managers, 142,
143
Justice, 15–17, 124. See also
Procedural justice; Rawls

Kant(ian, ianism), 18, 30, 66 n. 25,
255
Keynes, John Maynard, 12–14, 26,
31, 81, 93, 133, 142, 143, 151,
166, 235, 260, 266, 270; basic
ideas, 222–229; moral relevance,
225–226
Kristol, Irving, 30 n. 9

Laissez-faire capitalism, 31, 32, 39,
84, 88–93, 110, 129, 139, 147,
162, 216, 224–226, 239, 242–246
Legal moralism, 33
Liberal(ism), 27–31. See also
Classical liberalism; Revisionist
liberalism
Libertarianism, 19, 34, 49, 84
Liberty: See Freedom
Life plan, 30, 35, 36
Locke, John, 24, 30, 31, 41, 44–47,
47–56, 148, 161, 162
Lodge, George Cabot, 15–17, 23,
161–163

Luthans, Fred, Social Issues in
Business, 10 n. 13, 175 n. 65, 246

Maccoby, Michael, 23, 156 n. 36
Macro-managerialism, 26, 153–154,
209 ff.; and Keynesianism,
209, 222–229; and pluralism,
235 ff. See also Ideology;
Managerial business ideology;
Micro-managerialism
Managerial business ideology:
attempts to define, 141–147;
contrast with classical business
ideology, 3, 4, 6, 9, 12–14, 19–20,
21, 23–26, 27, 43, 68–74, 93;
and natural rights, 41, 42; senses
of, 147–148; social compact,
69–73; tensions with revisionist
liberalism, 152–154. See also
Classical business ideology;
Ideology; Macro-managerialism;
Micro-managerialism
Managerial discretion, 145, 167–
170, 187, 188, 193, 215, 230–234,
243, 247, 270, 280, 283
Managerial entrenchment, 169–170
Managerial professionalism, 170–
177, 178–186, 193, 205–207,
270, 287
Markets, actual, 93 ff., 121–123,
226, 230, 268. See also Existence
premise
Marx(ism), 27, 99, 112, 147, 149,
152, 159, 285
Means, Gardiner, 147, 166–170,
179, 184, 188, 214, 270
Micro-managerialism, 26, 153 ff.,
179 ff., 209–210, 213, 214, 217,
219. See also Ideology; Macro-
managerialism; Managerial
business ideology
Mill, James, 84

Mill, John Stuart, 30–32, 45, 84, 89, 99, 114, 115, 127, 135, 138, 139, 148, 149, 285
Minimal state, 31–39, 82, 84, 88–90, 93–98, 103, 104, 107, 110, 113–117, 123–125, 139, 147–154
Moral, moral theory. See Ethics
Moral analysis, 4, 5

Nation(al), 28, 41, 132, 133, 150, 158, 216–220, 245, 249; economic nationalism, 277, 278, 283, 284
National Association of Manufacturers, 27, 142
Nation-state, 39, 47, 285–288
Naturalistic fallacy, 21–24, 159–163, 188, 248
Natural rights, theory of, 24, 25, 40, 41–54, 55, 56
Nondispositional contract theory: See Contract theory
Normative, 146, 170, 177, 236–237, 248–257, 260–262, 267, 268, 270; and assumptions in argument for profit maximization, 76–80; decision procedure for managers, 41; Friedman's hesitancy to espouse assumptions, 83, 144, 168, 175, 235, 246–255, 259, 267, 268, 270; and moral analysis, 4, 5, 9; and nature of fundamental question, 5, 7, 24; and nonnormative distinction, 7, 21, 23; and political economy, 7, 12, 19, 20, 31
Novak, Michael, 23
Nozick, Robert, Anarachy, State, and Utopia, 25, 42, 47, 49–52, 61–69, 84

Offense principle, 33
Optimal, optimize, 85, 86, 127–130, 193, 226, 231, 241, 259, 268, 284
Optimalists, 260
Ordinal measures of utility, 113–116

Paretian concepts and arguments, 25, 120–126, 130, 259, 268
Paternalism, principle of, 34–36, 82, 89, 90, 116, 117
Person(s), 46, 52, 195–198
Philosophical analysis, 2–5, 11, 40, 41
Plato, 57, 83
Pleasure: See Good; Hedonism; Theory of the good; Utility
Pluralism, 26, 151, 161, 163, 270, 279; descriptive, 236–248; key idea in macro-managerialism, 209, 214, 222, 234, 235 ff.; prescriptive, 248–266; use in business and society texts, 246–248
Polestar argument, 78–86, 91–93, 95–98, 104–105
Political economy: See Liberalism; Classical liberalism; Revisionist liberalism
Positivism, 78, 84, 117
Post, James E., Business and Society: Corporate Strategy, Public Policy, and Ethics, 10 n. 13, 41, 219 n. 4
Pragmatism, 150
Preference and preference-based utilitarianism, 79, 115-126, 128–139
Prescriptive, 5, 7. See also Corporate (social) responsibility; Normative; Pluralism, prescriptive
Presumptive case for liberty (freedom), 32, 33

Procedural justice, 53–54, 61–69, 249 ff.
Progressives, progressive movement, 1, 238, 282
Promissory argument, 75–76
Psychostructure, 23

Quantification, 114–117, 127–128, 137, 138

Rawls, John, A Theory of Justice, 25, 42, 53, 61–69, 249–251
Realism, 260
Realistic rule utilitarian(ism), 98, 101, 104, 105
Reconstruction of arguments, 3, 4, 9, 12, 16, 24
Reflective equilibrium, 64–67
Regulate, regulation, regulatory agency, 29, 31, 33, 35, 39, 46, 94, 133, 220, 222, 223, 227–234, 242–244, 263, 277, 286
Reich, Robert, 181, 277–283, 287
Revealed preferences, 116
Revisionist Liberal(ism), 27, 28, 32, 35, 40, 80, 84, 93, 139, 146–154, 209, 222, 235, 269, 280, 285. See also Classical liberalism; Liberal(ism)
Risk, 69–70
Rule utilitarian(ism), 86–93

Schumpeter, Joseph A., 4 n. 6, 240
Self-interest, 46, 91, 144, 159, 161, 166, 193, 195, 211, 216–220, 223, 226, 241, 242, 261, 262, 265, 266
Sen, Amartya, 66 n. 25, 86 n. 10, 122, 127 n. 2
Sethi, S. Prakesh, 21, 171 n. 58
Shareholder (stockholder), 3, 5, 10, 22, 75–80, 92, 155, 162–170,

171–176, 180, 184, 189–194, 201, 203, 205, 213, 214–218, 266, 279
Smith, Adam, 12, 30–31, 111, 112, 131–135, 216, 230
Social audit, social assessment system (SAS), 22, 171–175
Social contract theory: See Contract theory
Social Darwinism, 12, 31
Social responsibility: See Corporate (social) responsibility
Social issues in management, 3, 10. See also Business and society; Managerial business ideology
Socialism(ist), 27, 28, 60, 90, 103, 129, 152
Stakeholder, 3, 5, 22, 162–170, 171–176, 189–194, 213, 214, 236, 264, 279
State: See Minimal state; Welfare state
Stockholder: See Shareholder
Stoicism, 28
Stone, Christopher, 23, 75–79, 117
Sturdivant, Frederick, Business and Society: A Managerial Approach, 10, 22, 172–175, 230 n. 7, 241, 247
Substantive constraints: See constraints

Tacit, tacit contract: See Contract
Teleological theory of obligation, 108, 128
Thompson, Kenneth R., Social Issues in Business, 10 n. 13, 175 n. 65, 246
Transnational corporation, 271, 274, 280, 281, 286–288
Two-contract theory, 54. See John Locke

Use-value, 133–135. *See also* Adam Smith; Value

Utile (utility): *See* Good

Utilitarian(ism), 18, 20, 24, 25, 40, 51, 64, 79, 127–129, 138, 148–150, 190, 197, 223–226, 231, 268. *See also* Act utilitarian(ism); Conventional (actual) rule utilitarian(ism); Ideal rule utilitarian(ism); Preference and preference-based utilitarian(ism); Realistic rule utilitarian(ism); Rule utilitarian(ism)

Value: *See* Good

Walton, Clarence, 165 n. 46, 194 n. 25

Welfare, 31, 35, 38, 52, 63, 64, 69, 127–133, 136–139, 209, 213, 216, 231

Welfare principle, 38, 82

Welfare state (more than minimal state), 34, 43, 52, 56, 59, 60, 64, 69, 242, 244, 249

Well-being, 32, 51, 114, 115, 132–139, 217, 269, 285. *See also* Good